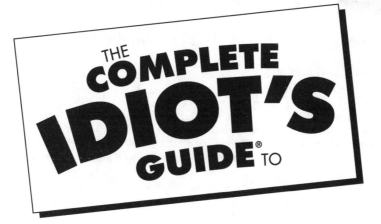

THE
COMPLETE
IDIOT'S
GUIDE® TO

The Gulf War

by Charles Jaco

ALPHA

A Pearson Education Company

To my granddaughter, Elise, whose future inspired me to write this book.

Copyright © 2002 by Charles Jaco

International Standard Book Number: 0-02-864324-0
Library of Congress Catalog Card Number: 2002106348

04   03   8   7   6   5   4   3   2

Interpretation of the printing code: The rightmost number of the first series of numbers is the year of the book's printing; the rightmost number of the second series of numbers is the number of the book's printing. For example, a printing code of 02-1 shows that the first printing occurred in 2002.

Printed in the United States of America

For marketing and publicity, please call: 317-581-3722

The publisher offers discounts on this book when ordered in quantity for bulk purchases and special sales.

For sales within the United States, please contact: Corporate and Government Sales, 1-800-382-3419 or corpsales@pearsontechgroup.com

Outside the United States, please contact: International Sales, 317-581-3793 or international@pearsontechgroup.com

Publisher: *Marie Butler-Knight*
Product Manager: *Phil Kitchel*
Managing Editor: *Jennifer Chisholm*
Acquisitions Editor: *Gary Goldstein*
Development Editor: *Suzanne LeVert*
Production Editor: *Billy Fields*
Copy Editor: *Faren Bachelis*
Illustrator: *Jody P. Schaeffer*
Cover/Book Designer: *Trina Wurst*
Indexer: *Ginny Bess*
Layout/Proofreading: *Angela Calvert, Megan Douglass, Mary Hunt, Sherry Taggart*

Contents at a Glance

Contents

Foreword

Most Americans were still groggily downing their first cup of coffee—or hitting the snooze button for another few z's—when the first of two jetliners roared out of a clear blue sky and exploded into the World Trade Center the morning of September 11, 2001.

That sudden jolt woke America to a world of enemies they never knew they had: a curious terrorist organization called *al Queda*; its leader, the mysterious Osama bin Ladin, who masterminded the strike; and a little-known fundamentalist regime in Afghanistan known as "the Taliban" that made it a crime to recognize any other religion but Islam, barred women from going to school or work, and recruited soldiers from neighboring Pakistan to help fight off Afghan rebels in the north. To each of them, America was the world's greatest manifestation of evil.

Had this been a Steven Spielberg movie, we would have lapped it up, buoyed by the conviction that such boiling hatred is the stuff of Hollywood, not the real world. And we'd have been dead wrong. This was not just another celluloid blockbuster. No, America was under attack and would soon again be at war. Why? Well, if you've picked up this book and continue to read, you're going to find out.

If the September 11 attacks on the World Trade Center and the Pentagon were a ticking time bomb, the Gulf War was the spark that lit the fuse. In this book, globe-trotting war correspondent Charles Jaco skillfully lays out the complex politics and gamesmanship that preceded Saddam Hussein's virtually uncontested invasion of Kuwait on August 2, 1990. Tracing history from Babylonian times and racing forward in lively, sometimes cheeky prose, Jaco explains the rivalries and gangland tactics that brought Saddam to power and the mistakes and miscalculations that almost led to his demise in the winter of 1991.

Almost. American-led tanks and artillery were chasing Iraq's elite Republican Guard up the infamous "Highway of Death," where allied air-to-ground aircraft pounded them from above. U.S. troops were days, maybe even hours, from downtown Baghdad. But just as suddenly as the war itself began, just 100 hours after launching the ground phase of Operation Desert Storm, Pres. George Bush decided to call it off. Saddam Hussein was ready to surrender and America's Arab allies hadn't the stomach for the bloody battle for Baghdad to come.

That fateful decision, whether viewed as practical and prudent, or cautious and compassionate, set the stage for Saddam to maintain his grip on power and for the uneasy peace that followed. The peace required an ongoing commitment of U.S. military jets to patrol two "no-fly" zones, one to the north of Baghdad, the other to the south. The U.S. Air Force would have to enforce the treaty that ended the war, and to do so it would have to take up permanent residence in oil-rich, conservative, Islamic, and Western-phobic Saudi Arabia. The Saudis, who opened their doors to America only because they feared an invasion by Saddam more than they did the presence of Western "infidels" in the land surrounding Islam's holiest sites, never anticipated that their request for help would snow-ball into a decade-long stay on Saudi soil.

Slowly, then, first in a simmer and later in a low boil, the hatred and anger rose. First came the car bomb that destroyed Khobar Towers, a high-rise barracks building occupied by American airmen in Dharan. Then, a few years later came the first attempt to blow up the World Trade Center, when a truck stuffed with explosives was parked in the Twin Towers' subterranean parking garage. Next were the simultaneous bombings of two U.S. embassies in different parts of Africa. Later, the October 2000 attack on the USS *Cole*, in which terrorists pulled up alongside the American warship while it refueled in the port of Aden, Yemen, then ignited themselves and their small boat, killing 18 and wounding dozens more. Each time, Americans reacted with shock and grief, and then, in a day or a week, the world returned to normal. Until September 11.

Like any war, the story of the Gulf War is not in the actual fighting but in the events that led up to the fighting, and in the peace—or lack of peace—that followed. Viewed from a broader, historic perspective, this war was a turning point. And in more ways than one, as you'll see in this gripping account by a veteran journalist.

Tobias Naegele
Editor-in-Chief
Army Times Publishing Co.
Springfield, Virginia

Introduction

The Kuwaiti resistance fighter held me in a bear hug, squeezing as hard as he could while jumping up and down yelling, "We are free! We are free!" Five feet away, three jubilant resistance soldiers emptied their captured AK-47s into the hot blue Gulf sky. Near the seawall where Iraqi troops had lined up and executed Kuwaitis in the first days of their invasion, an Iraqi armored personnel carrier still smoldered, the driver's incinerated hands clutching the steering wheel like a pair of blackened crow's claws.

A U.S. Marine wiped the powdery sand from his face and told me this is what it must have felt like to liberate Paris in 1944. But the jubilation, like the gunfire of the 100-hour ground war, was short-lived.

Operations Desert Shield and Desert Storm involved the movement of more personnel and materiel than any military operation since Vietnam. It required the biggest multinational alliance since World War II. It featured the largest tank battles since Patton, Rommel, and Montgomery squared off in the North African desert 50 years before.

On the surface, the Gulf War had all the elements of classic drama. There was a despicable villain, Saddam Hussein, a man who had tortured, imprisoned, terrorized, and gassed his own people. There was a helpless victim, little Kuwait, a small nation suddenly invaded and brutalized by its larger neighbor. There was a mysterious kingdom, Saudi Arabia, suddenly appealing for help to the outside world. There was the world's oil supply, suddenly threatened by Iraq's invasion. There was the specter of nerve gas and chemical weapons, previously used by Iraq. And there was a diverse international coalition of dozens of nations, united in an effort to drive Iraq from Kuwait.

Those of us who were involved in Desert Shield and Desert Storm as journalists tried to report as accurately as we could about all the events leading up to the war, the action during the fighting, and the aftermath. But we often failed. Why? There are several reasons. The whiz-bang technology used by the Allies resulted in military briefings that looked more like video game parlors. The dictatorship in Iraq, and the authoritarian government of Saudi Arabia both placed serious restrictions on the media. The Pentagon kept journalists on a short leash, often refusing to provide any sort of access to any of the fighting. The politics of the region, from Israel and the Palestinians to the relationship among Jordan, Iraq, and Saudi Arabia, were too complex to be boiled down into a few minutes of videotape or a few column inches of newspaper copy.

Centuries of intrigue preceded the Gulf War. And the attacks against the United States and the current war against terrorism followed it. *The Complete Idiot's Guide to the Gulf War* will take you back in time, to when the biblical prophets strode across the baking Iraqi desert. You'll go inside the Bedouin tents where much of the modern Middle East intrigue was launched. You'll watch as Iraqi tanks rip into Kuwait. You'll burrow into desert foxholes with U.S. commandos hidden only a few miles from Baghdad. You'll fly with the F-117 stealth fighters over the Iraqi capitol. You'll watch from the ground as Allied bombs pulverize the Republican Guard. You'll be there as Allied commanders decide to leave Saddam Hussein alive and in power. And you will know why Operation Desert Storm spawned the blind hatred of terrorists like Osama bin Ladin and led directly to the deaths of thousands of Americans.

How to Use This Book

This book will provide you with a solid summary of what happened, why it happened, and why we continue to live with the consequences of the Gulf War, from Gulf War Syndrome to Middle East unrest to the worldwide war against terrorism. Appendixes provide additional resources on all these subjects.

Part 1, "The Enemy of My Enemy," summarizes the Gulf War, and provides you with background on why Iraq invaded Kuwait, and why the sands of history run deep into the deserts of the entire region. You'll understand how the developed world's unquenchable thirst for oil helped lead to the conflict. You'll also have an appreciation for the inevitable conflict between the Western world and adherents of a fundamentalist, extreme form of Islam.

Part 2, "Desert Shield," takes a look at Iraq's invasion of Kuwait, as well as the almost unprecedented Allied military buildup. We take you back to those uncertain days when Westerners were held hostage at potential Iraqi targets, and when the world wondered whether a military force could be deployed in time to stop Saddam.

Part 3, "Desert Storm—The Air War," provides details on the air campaign against Iraq, including the first few minutes that determined the war's outcome. You'll hear about everything from the experience of a U.S. female POW taken prisoner by Iraqi soldiers to the devastation on the ground caused by massive Allied air strikes.

Part 4, "Desert Storm—The Ground War," offers fresh details about the largely ignored battles of the Gulf War. Far from being a total cakewalk against surrendering Iraqi troops, the ground war featured a number of heated battles, including the biggest tank battle since World War II.

Part 5, "The Storm Doesn't End," will be the most controversial section. It takes you inside decision-making councils when it was decided that Saddam Hussein could remain in power. It looks at how the Gulf War coalition disintegrated, and at how veterans have demanded answers about Gulf War Syndrome. It examines how the high hopes of the Gulf War fell to earth. And it looks at the roots of terror and fanaticism in the Muslim world, and at why the democracies of the West find themselves locked in a life-or-death struggle with the political and religious forces of Islamic extremism.

Extras

These sidebars appear every so often in the text. They'll help you understand the major figures, the terms, and the background of the Gulf War.

Gulf Lingo

Definitions of technical, geographic, or military terms used throughout the book.

Desert Lore

Historical tidbits and "bet you didn't know" segments that help fill in some Gulf War background.

Heads Up!

Quotes from the famous, the infamous, and the obscure in the Gulf War.

Who's Who

Thumbnail biographies of the leading figures in the Middle East before and during the Gulf War.

The Machines

The tanks, guns, planes, missiles, and ships that went to war in the Gulf.

Acknowledgments

First I'd like to thank my granddaughter, Elise, for providing the inspiration for this book. The past is a guide to the future, and it's her future I'm writing about.

My editor, Gary Goldstein, has been professional, funny, and exceptionally patient. My development editor (and future attorney) Suzanne LeVert has been thorough, precise, and a source of good humor. My sources in the diplomatic, intelligence, and military communities have been, as always, invaluable and, at their insistence, anonymous.

And my wife, Melissa, deserves more praise than space allows for being understanding, demanding, loving, critical, and suspicious of bad writing.

Trademarks

All terms mentioned in this book that are known to be or are suspected of being trademarks or service marks have been appropriately capitalized. Alpha Books and Pearson Education, Inc., cannot attest to the accuracy of this information. Use of a term in this book should not be regarded as affecting the validity of any trademark or service mark.

Part 1

The Enemy of
My Enemy

In 2000 B.C.E., the prophet Abraham walked out of the city of Ur. Almost 4,000 years later, American tanks rolled over the same ground. The story of what happened in between is the story of civilization—its gods, its politics, its wars, and its people. In this section, we examine the cauldron of the Middle East and how its turbulent history leads directly from the ancient kings of Babylon and Israel to Osama bin Ladin and Saddam Hussein.

Saddam, the Shield, and the Storm

In This Chapter

- ◆ Talking before fighting
- ◆ Iraq seizes Kuwait
- ◆ The Allies react
- ◆ More than a video game war
- ◆ Prelude to September 11

The Gulf War was the first war broadcast live around the world. Those of us working in broadcast news during Desert Shield and Desert Storm know there's a big difference between pictures on a TV set and real information. Dictatorships in Iraq and Saudi Arabia tried, with varying degrees of success, to control information. The U.S. and Allied militaries kept journalists miles away from most of the fighting. The behind-the-scenes diplomatic moves were often cloaked in secrecy.

Because of all that, much of the information available to the public about the Gulf War has been incomplete, including the information we broadcast live to the world in 1990 and 1991. This chapter tries to fill in some of those blanks with an overview of Operation Desert Shield, Operation Desert Storm, and what followed, including the September 11 attack and the war on terrorism.

All the events mentioned in this chapter will be covered in far greater detail later in this book. As Pres. Harry S Truman once said, "The only thing new is the history you don't know yet."

Where's Kuwait?

After August 2, 1990, many Americans were asking, "Where's Kuwait?" I was in Trinidad with other international journalists covering an abortive coup. As soon as word came down that, half a world away, Iraq had invaded Kuwait, we began scrambling for encyclopedias and atlases.

The rumbling of Iraq's tanks across the border was merely the latest move in a region marked by centuries of intrigue and violence. As well as political tumult, however, this region is also known for its contributions to the world's literature, science, and religion. Indeed, much of our civilization came from the areas we now call Iraq and Kuwait. The area was first settled around 4500 B.C.E. The world's earliest known civilization, the Sumerian, began thriving around 3500 B.C.E., intermingling with nomadic Semitic tribes that originated in what is now Saudi Arabia. The area at the northern end of the Persian Gulf (known in this part of the world as the Arabian Gulf) later spawned the Babylonian and Assyrian civilizations.

From this region came the first writing, the first known wheel, and the first plow. Abraham and Isaac, central figures of Islam, Judaism, and Christianity, came from here. The region became Islamic around 750 C.E. After centuries of decline, the areas occupied by modern Iraq and Kuwait became part of the Ottoman Empire starting around 1481 C.E.

Desert Lore

The Ottoman Empire started in what is now Turkey about 1360 C.E. At its height, it included modern Iraq, Kuwait, Syria, Lebanon, Israel, Turkey, Albania, Serbia, Bosnia, Croatia, Romania, and Bulgaria, as well as parts of Libya, Tunisia, and Russia. After 1918, it was broken up into independent countries by the British.

For a time, what is now modern Kuwait was part of an Ottoman *vilayet* (an administrative district within the empire) that included southern Iraq. In 1899, though, a sheik appointed by the Ottomans to help oversee Kuwait double-crossed them. He signed a deal with Great Britain, trading British protection for his claim as ruler of Kuwait. The British agreed. In 1914, the year World War I broke out, the British recognized Kuwait as an independent country.

The Ottoman Empire jumped into World War I on the side of Germany. They lost, and the British soon controlled much of what used to be the empire. By the early 1920s, both Iraq and Kuwait were more or less independent countries under British administration. But oil had been discovered in the region, and the British tried to make sure they would have a monopoly on any oil produced there.

But tiny Kuwait had to deal with a number of claims against its borders. In 1922, it agreed to creation of a neutral zone between it and Saudi Arabia. In 1932, Kuwait gained independence and agreed to formalize its border with Iraq in a series of letters between the two country's rulers. But in the late 1930s, Iraq's King Ghazi began to claim that Kuwait belonged to Iraq. While all this was going on, oil exploration concessions were granted exclusively to the Kuwait Oil Company, owned by British and American oil interests.

Iraq's monarchy fell in a violent coup in 1958. The new military rulers of Iraq almost immediately began making the old claims on Kuwait. Kuwait became independent from Britain in 1961. Within a week, Iraq again claimed that Kuwait belonged to it. The British, under the terms of their defense treaty with Kuwait, sent troops to Kuwait to prevent any Iraqi invasion.

> **Gulf Lingo**
>
> A **vilayet** was a province or district inside the old Ottoman Empire. The concept served as part of the basis for Iraq's claim on Kuwait, since the Iraqis claimed that Kuwait was originally part of a district governed from Iraq.

The British eventually withdrew, but Iraq's claims to Kuwait kept simmering on the back burner, despite having been rejected by the Arab League and the United Nations. In 1973—the same year as the Arab-Israeli Yom Kippur War—Iraq and Kuwait engaged in several armed skirmishes across their borders. This was also the year of the first OPEC oil embargo against the United States. By now, the issue was one of more than just national pride. The issue was who would control much of the world's oil supply.

By the 1980s, Kuwait had taken control of its own oil reserves and had become one of the world's richest countries. At the same time, Iraqi dictator Saddam Hussein had started a bloody war against his neighbor, Iran. Fearful of their much bigger next-door neighbor, Kuwait sided with Iraq.

The so-called eight-year tanker war between Iran and Iraq soon became a World War I–style bloodbath. Iraq used poison gas against Iranian troops. The Iranians killed thousands of young men in suicide human wave attacks against Iraqi positions. And tankers in the Arabian Gulf carrying oil vital to the Western world became targets of attacks. It began in 1980 and ended in 1988.

In 1988, a cease-fire in the tanker war ended the threat to Kuwait, but not for long. The flash point became the Rumailia oil field, which straddles the Iraq-Kuwait border. Both countries had been pumping oil from this field for years.

Desert Lore

The Tanker War (also called the Iran-Iraq War) started September 22, 1980, when Iraqi troops invaded Iran. It ended in August 1988. An estimated 375,000 Iraqis were killed or wounded. Iran saw an estimated million people killed or wounded. The war featured attacks on neutral oil tankers, which is why the United States reflagged Kuwaiti tankers in 1987, offering them American protection. An Iraqi missile attack on the USS *Stark* (later claimed to be due to "pilot error") killed 37 sailors and wounded 21 others in May 1987. In July 1988, the USS *Vincennes* accidentally shot down Iran Air Flight 655 after mistaking it for an Iraqi fighter. All 290 Iranian men, women, and children on board died.

In July 1990, Iraq wanted to drive up the world price of oil to shore up the country's battered cash reserves. It also wanted Kuwait to forgive $10 billion in debts, money Iraq had borrowed to beef up its military and fight Iran. Kuwait refused to cut back its production or forgive the debt. On July 17, Iraqi dictator Saddam Hussein demanded that Kuwait stop "overproducing." Iraq also accused the Kuwaitis of slant drilling, or angling their drilling equipment so that wellheads inside Kuwait were actually pumping out oil from underneath Iraq. Kuwait denied the charge.

Heads Up!

"We have no opinion on the Arab-Arab conflicts, like your border disagreement with Kuwait .... James Baker has directed our official spokesmen to emphasize this instruction. We hope you can solve this problem using any suitable methods."

—U.S. ambassador to Iraq April Glaspie speaking to Saddam Hussein in Baghdad, July 25, 1990

At this point, Saddam was waiting to see what response might come from the Western powers. He got one on July 25, 1990, in a face-to-face meeting with the U.S. ambassador to Iraq, April Glaspie. Acting on instructions from Secretary of State James Baker, Glaspie told Saddam that the United States had no interest in intervening in an inter-Arab conflict.

That pleased the Iraqi dictator in more ways than one. Satisfied that any action against Kuwait would be seen as a strictly Arab-on-Arab affair, Saddam decided to strike.

Invasion!

The meeting with Saddam may have satisfied the State Department, but the intelligence community in Washington was worried. In mid July, American spy satellites photographed two armored divisions of Iraq's elite Republican Guard moving out of their barracks near Baghdad and heading south toward Kuwait.

By July 21, the Defense Intelligence Agency (DIA)—the Pentagon's intelligence-gathering apparatus—was convinced that Iraq was poised to invade. The DIA told officials in the

Bush administration and at the Pentagon that Iraq had enough men and tanks near the border to launch an attack against Kuwait at any moment.

Who's Who

April Glaspie was the U.S. ambassador to Iraq just before the invasion. At the direction of Secretary of State James Baker, she told Saddam Hussein that the United States viewed Iraq's dispute with Kuwait as an "Arab-Arab" matter. Glaspie was widely criticized for the meeting, criticism that later abated when it became clear she was merely passing on instructions from her boss. A career diplomat, Glaspie was first posted to the Middle East in 1967, in Jordan. After the war, she was reassigned to the United Nations, and later served as U.S. consul general in Capetown, South Africa.

On July 25, the same day Ambassador Glaspie was having her fateful conversation with Saddam Hussein, Central Intelligence Agency Director William Webster came to the White House to brief Pres. George Bush. It was the CIA's assessment, Webster told the president, that Iraq could—and very likely would—invade Kuwait.

By July 27, the DIA briefed Kuwait's ambassador to the United States, telling him they thought an Iraqi invasion was "imminent." Yet, despite warning from two top intelligence agencies, and despite clear spy satellite evidence showing eight Republican Guard divisions massed just north of Kuwait, the Bush administration refused to act.

The president, apparently, was pinning his hopes on an OPEC meeting in Saudi Arabia to defuse the crisis. It failed, and by August 1, both the DIA and the U.S. Central Command (CENTCOM) issued warnings to the White House and State Department that an invasion was probable within hours. Yet there were no warnings from Washington to Baghdad.

It was 6 P.M. in Washington the evening of August 1. In Kuwait, it was 1 A.M., August 2, 1990.

Three divisions of the Iraqi *Republican Guard* that had been stationed just north of the Kuwaiti border began to move south. One intelligence analyst who saw the satellite photos described them as "... three coils of rope uncoiling, or three coiled snakes suddenly straightening out."

Two of the divisions pushed straight south, overrunning token resistance along the four-lane

Gulf Lingo

The **Republican Guard** comprises the most loyal and best trained troops in the Iraqi army. There are seven Republican Guard divisions, each consisting of two tank brigades, a mechanized infantry brigade, an artillery brigade, as well as special forces, reconnaissance, and engineer battalions. These elite troops performed superbly during the Iran-Iraq war of the 1980s. Members are chosen for their military skills and their loyalty to Saddam Hussein.

highway linking the Kuwait-Iraq border with the gleaming spires of Kuwait City. The third heavy armored division swung west, bypassing the Kuwaiti capitol and pushing toward the border with Saudi Arabia. At the same time, Iraqi Special Forces troops, ferried by helicopter, swung out over the Arabian Sea, preparing the drop into Kuwait City from the east.

The Bush administration would later claim that the intelligence warnings were strictly "midlevel," and never percolated their way to the White House. The United States, like Kuwait, was caught flat-footed by the Iraqi blitzkrieg. One problem was that American intelligence in the area was focused on the threat from the fundamentalist government of Iran, and not on any possible moves by Iraq.

Another problem was that Kuwait refused to ask for assistance from the United States. Policy makers at *CENTCOM* had decided that if the Kuwaitis wanted any aid in strengthening defenses, they would have to request it. No request ever came.

The Iraqi armor began moving into Kuwait around 1 A.M. local time. By 5 A.M., they had driven through the Kuwaiti northern oil fields. By 8 A.M., they were in Kuwait City. By 10 P.M., all organized Kuwaiti resistance had ceased. Kuwait had fallen. Saddam Hussein now controlled the oil in Iraq and Kuwait, almost 10 percent of the world's total oil reserves. His crack troops were poised to drive into the heart of Saudi Arabia.

The Shield

On August 2, 1990, the United States had a token complement of six navy warships in the Arabian Gulf, a few dozen military advisors in Kuwait and Saudi Arabia, and two aircraft carrier *battle groups* within the general vicinity—the USS *Dwight D. Eisenhower* battle group in the Mediterranean, and the USS *Independence* battle group in the Indian Ocean.

Gulf Lingo

CENTCOM (the U.S. Central Command) is the American military command responsible for U.S military operations in 19 countries in the Middle East, the Horn of Africa, and South Asia. The region covered by CENTCOM contains 70 percent of the world's oil reserves. CENTCOM contains components from the army, navy, marines, air force, and special forces. Its headquarters is located at MacDill Air Force Base near Tampa, Florida.

The Machines

An aircraft carrier **battle group** is the general term used to describe the minifleet that sails with each U.S. aircraft carrier. Each battle group can contain different ships, depending on the mission. But generally, a battle group consists of the aircraft carrier, one or two cruisers, a destroyer, an antisubmarine frigate, one or two attack submarines, and a supply ship or ships containing ammunition, fuel, and supplies.

The signal was sent immediately to the USS *Independence* to sail into the Arabian Gulf. This order reversed a long-standing Pentagon policy to keep the 1,100-foot-long Nimitz-class nuclear carriers and their battle groups out of the relatively shallow and narrow gulf.

The fear had been that the carriers could be sitting ducks for fast attack boats or missiles in the restricted gulf waters.

But to defend Saudi Arabia and its oil fields, the United States would need more than 85 carrier-based jets. CENTCOM commander Gen. Norman Schwartzkopf met with Pres. George Bush and told him a purely defensive force of 40,000 troops could be airlifted to Saudi Arabia within three weeks. To push Saddam out of Kuwait, Schwartzkopf calculated that it would take 250,000 troops, and that it would take four months to get them in place.

The Diplomatic Dance

The problem was that the United States had to convince the insular countries of the Arabian Peninsula that they needed help. Kuwait, fearful of Iraq up until the very end, had refused to ask for assistance. Saudi Arabia, even with its oil riches threatened, also felt reluctant to ask for American assistance.

There were two reasons for that. One was that the ruling Saudi royal family was worried about pressure from fundamentalists inside Saudi Arabia. The so-called *Wahabi* sect, virulently anti-Western, formed the backbone of Islam in Saudi Arabia, and was often critical of the free-spending, high-living ways of the Saudi royal family. An alliance with the United States could undermine the royal family's already shaky credibility with its own clerics.

The second reason was suspicion of the United States itself. The Saudis had seen the Americans fail to support other allies around the world, from the South Vietnamese to the shah of Iran. They were leery of asking for help from a superpower that might abandon them.

After viewing American satellite photos, and after a visit to Saudi by Secretary of Defense Dick Cheney, the Saudis agreed to the deployment of U.S. troops. A rapid-fire series of meetings with the leaders of Egypt, Great Britain, the European Community, and the United Nations followed. The beginnings of a global coalition had been hammered together.

> ### Who's Who
>
> The Wahabi (also known as the Salifi) are a strict sect of Islam founded in the eighteenth century. They consider all other Islamic sects to be impure and heretical. Wahabism is the official religious ideology of Saudi Arabia. There are offshoots of Wahabism in several countries.

The Build Up

U.S. Intelligence had miscalculated Iraqi intentions, but Iraq returned the favor by miscalculating Saudi defenses. By August 3, the Republican Guard had paused for breath at the

Kuwait–Saudi Arabia border. Had they known that the Western Province of Saudi was essentially undefended except by poorly trained elements of the Saudi National Guard, they could have punched through token opposition and been down the 300 miles of modern highway to *Riyadh* within days.

Instead, the Iraqis stopped at the border, giving the United States time to respond. By August 8, President Bush announced that units of the 82nd Airborne were on their way to Saudi Arabia. The next day, the first units of the 82nd Airborne's 2nd Brigade touched down at an airstrip outside the Saudi city of Dhahran. Their M55 Sheridan tanks and AH-64 Apache helicopters would be enough to delay an advancing Iraqi army, but not enough to stop them. More was needed, and fast.

Desert Lore

Riyadh—which means "the gardens"—is the Saudi Arabian capital. It is at the center of the conservative Saudi heartland, known in Arabic as *Najd*. Riyadh began as a collection of villages around 1450 C.E. By 1818, the royal house of Saud established a capital in the city. Fueled by oil money, the city currently has about 1.5 million people.

Moving a quarter of a million personnel, plus tanks, planes, food, and ammunition, almost stretched American capabilities to the breaking point. But by January 16, 1991, ships, planes, and troops from the United States, Great Britain, France, Egypt, and a half-dozen other nations, were finally in place. An understanding with Israel was also a done deal, despite objections from hard-liners in the Israeli government. To hold the fragile Pan-Arab coalition together, Israel was forced to agree not to retaliate against Iraq for any air or missile strikes inside its territory. Self-defense consisting of shooting down planes or SCUDs was one thing, but direct strikes against Iraq in Iraqi territory would be left to the U.S.-led coalition.

U.S. troops dig in along the Saudi Arabian border facing occupied Kuwait.

The Storm

Operation Desert Shield became Operation Desert Storm at 2 A.M. Saudi Arabian time on January 16. Squadrons of American, French, British, and Saudi jets began pounding locations throughout Kuwait and Iraq.

This air war was something new. Vietnam, Korea, and World War II featured fleets of bombers dropping tons of bombs every day. The idea was to destroy targets by saturation bombing. Desert Storm introduced something new: so-called *smart weapons* designed to pulverize a specific target while leaving surrounding buildings and people unharmed.

The Machines

Smart weapons include missiles and bombs that are guided to a precise target by various means. These include heat-sensing, radar-sensing, and laser-targeting weapons. In the laser-guided versions, a pilot or special forces commandos on the ground illuminate a target with a pinpoint laser beam. The bomb then follows the laser track to the target.

Air Power

The air war was designed to have several phases: First, knock out Iraqi military command, control, and communication networks. Second, disable Iraq's air force. Third, destroy infrastructure like bridges, roads, and rail lines. Fourth, pound Iraqi troops, tanks, and artillery.

The air campaign generally went as planned, although not as advertised.

Iraq was able to continue lobbing SCUD missiles into Saudi Arabia and Israel because coalition fighters had a hard time pinpointing mobile SCUD launchers. In some cases, targets the media were told had been destroyed remained intact after multiple strikes.

But overall, the air campaign was devastatingly effective. Thousands of Iraqi troops died from relentless pounding by B-52 bombers. Tens of thousands more surrendered rather than face the constant air strikes. By the time the ground war began, most of Iraq's army was a shattered, demoralized hulk. Most, but not all.

Ground War

On February 22, 1991, President Bush gave Iraq a 24-hour ultimatum: withdraw from Kuwait immediately to avoid the start of a ground war. Saddam refused, not knowing that forces of 10 nations were stretched out along a 300-mile front in western Iraq, ready to punch into Kuwait with a roundhouse left hook.

Heads Up!

"He is neither a strategist nor is he schooled in the operational arts, nor is he a tactician, nor is he a general. Other than that he's a great military man."

—Gen. Norman Schwartzkopf on Saddam Hussein, January 1991

In the east, Saudi and Arab forces headed up the coastline. Just to the west, the U.S. Marines drove into central Kuwait. To their west, American, French, and British forces rushed into Kuwait and southern Iraq to cut off retreating Iraqi forces.

It was over in 100 hours. Later in this book, we'll go into details of battles like the Battles of 73 Easting, Medina Ridge, Norfolk, and Rumaila. A stunning and complete ground victory in such a short space of time had never before been achieved in the annals of modern warfare. But the end of the war was only the beginning of something more terrible and far-reaching.

Media Circus

We journalists in Desert Storm lived the contradiction: On one hand, images of the Gulf War were transmitted worldwide on live TV. On the other hand, information from the military and all the governments involved was controlled and sanitized as much as possible.

CNN's Peter Arnett became a lightning rod for much of the criticism leveled at the media. Arnett reported live from Baghdad as bombs and missiles fell. He was roundly criticized for becoming a "mouthpiece" for Iraq's government in his tightly controlled, heavily censored reports. But he also provided a valuable glimpse of how the Iraqi dictatorship operated in the middle of the war.

It's a point worth remembering and one that we'll look at later: There's a huge difference between real news and analysis and live reporting of information as an event unfolds.

The Aftermath

It's been said that the twenty-first century began on September 11, 2001, when terrorists slammed hijacked jets into the World Trade Center and the Pentagon. The events leading up to September 11 and the ensuing war on terrorism began decades (perhaps centuries) before, but the Gulf War turned out to be the match that lit the final fuse.

Osama bin Ladin and other fundamentalist terrorists had nursed a simmering hatred for the United States, and the West in general, for years. But the presence of "infidel" troops in the Muslim holy land of Saudi Arabia, and continuing U.S. support for Arab regimes the fundamentalists considered corrupt, pushed them over the edge.

Later on, we'll trace the threads of terror that unraveled from Desert Storm, and how all of it—the war on terror, the Israeli-Palestinian conflict, the continuing presence of Saddam Hussein—is still with us today.

The Least You Need to Know

- ◆ Decades of tension led to the Gulf War.
- ◆ Saddam Hussein invaded Kuwait to control its oil and the United States and coalition nations intervened to prevent him from doing so.
- ◆ Desert Storm was a military victory, but far from a complete triumph.
- ◆ The Gulf War led directly to more terrorism, and our continuing struggle against it.

Chapter 2

The Moving Sands

In This Chapter

- ◆ The wheel, writing, and the Garden of Eden
- ◆ Civilization's cradle rocks with wars
- ◆ The twisted turns of Middle East politics
- ◆ Oil's well that ends … well, not quite
- ◆ The deadliest dictator

Parts of modern Baghdad look a lot like Los Angeles—palm trees, town-houses, and heavy traffic. There's an English-language FM rock station and wonderful restaurants along the gurgling, greasy Euphrates River where you can enjoy *irak*—a fiery local liquor—and crucified fish—fish nailed to a plank and roasted.

But this ancient city is also home to one of the planet's most bloodthirsty dictators and to secret police operatives on every street. How did the birthplace of modern religion, culture, and writing become a sweat-soaked prison where torture is as common as a parking ticket?

War and terror have been incubated here for millennia. In this chapter, you'll find out how a region that spawned ancient heroes and prophets also helped create the terror that still threatens to ignite the world.

The Land Between the Rivers

The ancient Greeks named the flat fertile plains between the Tigris and Euphrates Rivers Mesopotamia, meaning "the land between the rivers." But long before the Greeks saw the area, what eventually became modern civilization took its first steps here. Around 9000 B.C.E., warmer winters from a retreating Ice Age expanded land available for farming. The first villages sprang up in what is now Turkey. Over thousands of years, the descendants of those villagers migrated south, finally settling among the fecund topsoil of the fertile crescent between the rivers.

Desert Lore

Sumer flourished from about 3500 B.C.E. until 1760 B.C.E., when it was absorbed by the Babylonian Empire. The Sumerians lived in about a dozen city-states, each controlling surrounding land and villages. Around 2400 B.C.E., the word *freedom* appeared for the first time in human history, in an inscription of the Sumerian king Urukagina.

Heads Up!

"If a son strike his father, his hands shall be hewn off .... If a man put out the eye of another man, his eye shall be put out .... If a man break another man's bone, his bone shall be broken .... If a man knock out the teeth of his equal, his teeth shall be knocked out."

—Sections 195, 196, 197, 200, Code of Hammurabi, circa 1780 B.C.E.

Civilization Starts

Starting around 4000 B.C.E., Sumer became the world's first civilization. At the same time, the first cities, with between 10,000 and 50,000 inhabitants, appeared. The wheel, the plow, the sailboat, writing, irrigation, and arithmetic were developed by the Sumerians as they ruled the lands between the Tigris and Euphrates. Sumerian ideas about the universe, the relationship between humans and the divine, the Flood, Heaven, and hell were all later incorporated by Jews and Christians. In fact, Sumerian literature probably provided the basis for the biblical books of Proverbs, Psalms, and Lamentations.

The Sumerians had laws, but they were mostly based on the family unit. Wives, for example, could own property and businesses, but could be divorced for any reason, including no reason at all. Children could be sold into slavery by their parents.

Semitic tribes migrating into the area around 3000 B.C.E. from what is now Saudi Arabia and Syria formed the Babylonian civilization. And the Babylonians, especially their king Hammurabi (1795–1750 B.C.E.) had a different idea. To them, laws meant government. So for the first time, justice was codified and the state was given enforcement authority. Deeds, contracts, property rights, and crimes were defined in great detail in the Code of Hammurabi. Hammurabi, the legend goes, received the laws from the god Shamash, much the same way Moses received the Ten Commandments from God some 450 years later.

The Rivers of Babylon

After the autumn of Sumer, two empires fought for control of the fertile land, the Babylonians and the Assyrians. Like waves washing a beach, each would reach a high point, and then recede, each controlling the other several times over the centuries. The Babylonians, who were Semites related to today's Jews and Palestinians, are the best remembered, mostly because of their capital city, Babylon.

At its height around 1685 B.C.E., the Babylonian Empire stretched across most of what is now modern Iraq. The empire featured indoor plumbing, writing, codified laws, astronomy, and military might. When Babylon fell for the first time around 1530 B.C.E., the Assyrians to the north gained the upper hand.

Two hundred years later and to the west, Moses led the Jews out of slavery in Egypt. Around 1300 B.C.E., Moses supposedly received the Holy Law on Mount Sinai from God, similar to the way Hammurabi received his Code from his god four centuries earlier. From about 1200 to 922 B.C.E., Israel united under biblical figures such as Joshua, Saul, David, and Solomon. By 721 B.C.E. though, Israel had split into two parts, with the Assyrians conquering the northern half.

At the height of its power in 750 B.C.E., the Assyrian Empire included modern Iraq and Syria, as well as parts of Lebanon, Israel, Turkey, and almost all of what remained of ancient Egypt. But Babylon came back with a vengeance, and wiped out the Assyrians in a bloody Mesopotamian civil war in 648 B.C.E.

About the same time, the Babylonian ruler Nebuchadnezzar gained infamy in the Bible by sacking Jerusalem in 587 B.C.E. and hauling the area's Jews off to Babylon in what became known as the Babylonian Captivity. But to the east, the Persian Empire had its eye on Babylon.

> **Desert Lore**
>
> Babylon was on the banks of the Euphrates, about 55 miles south of modern Baghdad. The city was first settled around 3000 B.C.E., and its walls finally destroyed in 514 B.C.E. by Persian invaders. The biblical Tower of Babel was probably a ziggurat (terraced pyramid) in Babylon. The spectacular Hanging Gardens of Babylon were one of the original Seven Wonders of the World.

Another Man's Persian

"One man's Mede is another man's Persian," or so goes the ancient undergraduate pun. Not quite. Both the Medes and Persians existed in what became modern Iran. But while the Medes were Babylon's allies, the Persians were its enemies. The Persian king Cyrus the Great conquered Babylon in 539 B.C.E. Twenty-five years later, the Babylonians staged a failed revolt against Cyrus's successor, Darius. Darius flattened the city walls.

Two hundred years later, another Darius, Darius III, ruled a Persian Empire that stretched from modern Turkey on the east all the way to India. But Alexander the Great, determined to eliminate Persia as a threat to Greece, conquered Babylon in 330 B.C.E., and set it up as a capital of his empire. Seven years later, exhausted and wounded, he returned to Babylon, where he died.

Rival empires, from the Greek to the Roman, conquered the region. But by the time of Christ's birth, Babylon was abandoned and forgotten, its irrigation canals broken and silt-filled river water covering much of its glory.

Muslims and Mongols

To the south, Arab civilization had developed largely without interference from invaders. It was largely Bedouin, nomadic tribesmen who believed in a variety of gods and recognized no one's authority outside of their clans. But ideas about a single God from Judaism and Christianity infiltrated the region.

In 610 C.E., a young caravan trader from the Arabian village of Mecca claimed to receive a series of revelations from God (whom he called Allah) and used it as the basis of another monotheistic religion. The religion was Islam, and he was *Muhammad*.

Who's Who
Muhammad was born in 571 C.E. in Mecca, now modern Saudi Arabia. After his revelation in 610 C.E., he was acknowledged as a prophet in a line of prophets that included Moses and Jesus. He converted pagans in Saudi Arabia, waged military campaigns against his enemies, and promulgated a religious philosophy that included a single God, rewards on Judgment Day for righteous behavior, and punishment for transgressors. He died in 632 C.E. Ninety years later, Islam had spread from North Africa to India.

The ruling Arab caliphs who succeeded Muhammad, driven by religion and economics, spread Islam and Arab civilization throughout Arabia, and then Syria. Between 637 and 641, old Mesopotamia became Arab and Muslim. The new religion and the Arab culture spread like a desert sandstorm, conquering modern Saudi Arabia, Syria, Lebanon, Israel, Egypt, Kuwait, Iraq, Iran, Spain, Portugal, and parts of Tunisia, Libya, Pakistan, India, Morocco, and Turkey within 100 years.

Arabic became a universal language, and Islam a universal religion in these areas. While Christian Europe wallowed in the Dark Ages following the collapse of the Roman and Byzantine empires, the Islamic world enjoyed flourishing art, literature, science, architecture, and theology. Christians, Jews, and Zoroastrians lived more or less peacefully under Arab rule.

The new city of Baghdad, just upriver from the remains of Babylon, flourished. Magnificent libraries kept the world's learning alive by translating major works of medicine, literature, science, and philosophy from Greek and Latin. Mathematics and astronomy advanced. The seeds of civilization were saved from the collapse of Greece and Rome, and hybridized with new learning from the Arab world.

Old Mesopotamia was largely immune when tensions between Muslims and Christians erupted into the First Crusade. Enraged by the burning of the Church of the Holy Sepulchre in Islamic Jerusalem, the Christian Europeans took the Holy City in 1099. They were driven out less than 100 years later.

In 1258, the Mongols conquered Baghdad. They sacked libraries and burned texts. By the time Columbus sailed for the New World, Iraq and the Middle East had fallen under a new empire when the Ottoman Turks evicted the Mongol remnants.

Wars Without End

If we need to pick one point where the history of modern trouble and terror in the region begins, the rise of the Ottoman Empire is as good a place as any. War, division, and bloodshed in a modern sense came to the area with the Ottomans just as the early Renaissance was launching itself across Europe. It continues to this day.

Resting on an Ottoman

The non-Arab Ottomans brought corruption and violence to an area that had already seen plenty. In four centuries of Ottoman rule, Baghdad became a backwater devastated by tribal wars and battles against Iran. The Ottomans never pushed into Saudi Arabia, but Arab nationalism and its seething resentment of the Turks was brewing on the Arabian Peninsula, as well as in Iraq.

When the Ottomans jumped into World War I on the side of Germany in 1914, the anti-Turk Arab nationalists had their chance.

The Brits Arrive

The main action of World War I was in the muddy trenches of France and Belgium, as the Allies fought Germany. But the Allies' war against the Ottoman Empire spread from Turkey to Iraq, Palestine to Egypt. The British took advantage of both *Zionism* on the part of the Jews and Arab nationalism to form a homegrown coalition against the Turks.

Gulf Lingo

Zionism is a term coined in 1885 to define the movement for a Jewish homeland on the land of ancient Israel. After World War I, Zionists convinced Britain to endorse such a homeland in Palestine.

Nationalists in what became modern Iraq, Syria, Israel, Jordan, and the Palestinian Territories united with the Allies. By 1916, Allied Russian armies had pushed into Turkey, while the British used their control of Egypt to launch an offensive against Palestine, Syria, and Iraq.

Lawrence and All That

The heaviest fighting was often done by Arab nationalists. In 1916, Arabs in Palestine revolted against the Turks. Revolts were also brewing in Saudi Arabia, Iraq, and Syria.

> ### Heads Up!
>
> "All men dream, but not equally. Those who dream by night in the dusty recesses of their minds wake in the day to find that it was vanity: but the dreamers of the day are dangerous men, for they may act out their dream with open eyes, to make it possible."
>
> —T. E. Lawrence, *The Seven Pillars of Wisdom*, 1922

Enter Thomas Edward Lawrence, the illegitimate Welsh son of a British baron and the family's governess. From 1910 until 1914, Lawrence grew to know the Arabs when he worked on a British archaeological expedition along the banks of the Euphrates in Iraq.

During the war, he became the British Army agent responsible for coordinating and leading military operations with the Arab nationalists. He succeeded in Saudi Arabia, Syria, Palestine, and Lebanon, helping lead Arab armies in victories over the Turks. T. E. Lawrence had become Lawrence of Arabia. His book about the war, *The Seven Pillars of Wisdom*, is one of the most comprehensive and sympathetic accounts of the Arab world ever written by an outsider.

Guided by Lawrence, the British tried their best to grant independence to nations in the area. Iraq got its own king in 1920 and became independent in 1932. As we'll see later, though, tribal and family warfare got worse in Saudi Arabia. And Palestine became such a quagmire for the British that they promised both the Jews and the Palestinians an independent country on the same land.

After World War I, neither oil nor Israel existed as part of the harsh landscape where civilization had begun. But add them to Arab nationalism, religion, and blood feuds, and you have an explosive mixture.

Family Affairs

A few pages back, we talked about Sumerian law, and how it was based on the concept of the family as the highest authority. Family and tribal allegiances in the Middle East continue that tradition. The history of the area is written in blood—not just the blood that's been spilled, but the blood that courses through the arteries of everyone linked by family, religion, culture, and tribe in the area.

These bloody blood relations helped set the stage for the Gulf War, and for the war the United States and its allies are fighting today. What follows is a short country-by-country rundown.

Kuwait—Que Sabah, Sabah

Kuwait's ruling al-Sabah family first arrived from central Arabia in the early 1700s. The *utub*—a coalition of families—elected Sabah bin Jabir as the first emir of Kuwait in 1756. Kuwait became an important trading port, valuable for what was, at the time, its only natural resource: pearls.

Kuwait, like Iraq, ended up as part of the Ottoman Empire. Appointed by the Turks to oversee Kuwait, Emir Mubarak al-Sabah pulled a neat diplomatic trick in 1899. He signed a deal with the British, which guaranteed Kuwait status as an independent country under British protection.

Kuwait sank into the Great Depression with the rest of the world in the 1930s. Emir Ahmad al-Sabah drove a hard bargain when he negotiated the first oil concession with the Kuwait Oil Company in 1934. Oil was discovered four years later, and Kuwait flourished, becoming fully independent in 1961.

Desert Lore _____

In 1919, Kuwait agreed it would only grant oil exploration rights to companies approved by the British government. The Kuwait Oil Company was formed by oil giants Anglo-Persian (now British Petroleum) and Gulf Oil (now Chevron) in 1933, splitting oil exploration in Kuwait between the United Kingdom and the United States.

Saudi Arabia—the House of Saud

Oil and water don't mix, unlike oil and religion. After Muhammad established Islam in Mecca, he was forced to make his famous *hegira* (flight) to the city of Medina by his opponents. Since the seventh century, the two cities have been the two holiest sites in the Muslim world. Whoever controls these two spots on the Arabian Peninsula has the religious and political stature as guardian of the holy places.

The al Saud family originated in oasis towns near modern Riyadh around 1500. Around the time of the American Revolution, Muhammad ibn Saud allied with the founder of the fundamentalist *Wahabi sect*, and helped conquer large portions of

Desert Lore _____

The Wahabi sect of Islam is the godfather of all Islamic fundamentalist movements worldwide. It was founded in Saudi Arabia in the 1700s, and preaches that almost anything invented or developed since Muhammad is probably heresy. It also espouses *jihad,* or holy war, against nonbelievers.

central Arabia. Eventually, the al Saud clan took the area around Mecca and Medina, only to be driven out by the Ottoman Turks in 1818.

The Ottomans and their allies slugged it out with the al Sauds through the nineteenth century. In 1902, the founder of Saudi Arabia, Abd al-Aziz ibn Saud (known in the West as Abdul Aziz), captured Riyadh and led a revolt against the Turks. By 1925, he seized Mecca and Medina from the family ruling them (see next item). Abdul Aziz was now guardian of the holy places, and by 1932, became something new: king of Saudi Arabia.

Oil was discovered in 1938, and the mammoth al Saud family became omnipotent in Saudi religious, political, and economic affairs. The dynasty continues to this day, marked by lavish spending on both the country and themselves.

Jordan—Hashemites in Exile

Like the al Saud clan, the Hashemite family had ruled on the Arabian Peninsula for centuries. The Hashemites (or *Beni Hashem* in Arabic) claim to trace their lineage directly from Muhammad through his daughter, Fatima. They had ruled the holy cities of Mecca and Medina since the tenth century, and their leader always bore the title of *sherif*, or guardian of the holy places.

In 1916, Al-Hussein bin Ali, great-great grandfather of the current king of Jordan, led a successful revolt against the Turks. This Sherif Hussein not only founded the modern Arab Nationalist movement, he fathered a family that was to intertwine the histories of Syria (see next section), Jordan, Saudi Arabia, and Iraq.

Britain and France carved up the old Ottoman Empire. The Brits named the land east of the Jordan River Transjordan. One of Sherif Hussein's sons, Abdullah, was made amir of Transjordan by London. In 1923, the al Saud family and their fundamentalist Wahabi allies kicked Hussein out of Mecca and Medina. Hussein joined his son in Transjordan. Their family rules the Hashemite Kingdom of Jordan today.

Syria—The Sons Rise and Set

Ancient Syria included most of modern Syria, Lebanon, Jordan, and Israel as well as part of Turkey. The area was invaded and controlled by the Hittite, Persian, and Roman empires. Its capital, Damascus, was a vibrant center of both Islam and Christianity.

After World War I, Faysal, one of the sons of Sherif Hussein (see section on Jordan) was elected king of Syria by the Syrian National Congress. But King Faysal was forced out in 1920 by the French, who also carved out Lebanon as a separate country. As a consolation prize, the British made Faysal king of Iraq (as we'll see in the next section).

Syria became independent in 1945 and suffered through s succession of inept military and civilian governments. Syria even united with Egypt briefly to form the United Arab Republic in the late 1950s. Staring in 1963, the *Ba'ath Party* became the only legal political party. After Israel seized the Golan Heights from Syria after the 1967 war, Gen. Hafez al-Assad began to make moves to consolidate power under his pro-Soviet rule.

By 1970, Assad became Syria's ruler. He seized Lebanon and sponsored both Christian militias and the Palestine Liberation Organization. He also allowed terror groups like Hamas and Hezbollah to use Syrian territory, and took the hardest line of almost any Arab state toward Israel. He died in June 2000, and was replaced by one of his sons, Dr. Bashar al-Assad.

Desert Lore

The Ba'ath Party was founded by Syrian socialist Michel Aflaq in 1943. An Arab nationalist party linked with the Soviet Union, it became the sole political force in both Syria and Iraq. But the two branches of Ba'athism split, and each became a vehicle for dictators, the al-Assad clan in Syria, and Saddam Hussein in Iraq.

Iraq—Setting the Stage for Saddam

The British controlled Iraq after World War I. As we noted in the previous section, the Hashemite king, Faysal, was driven from Syria in 1920. Faysal, the great-great uncle of Jordan's current king, was made king of Iraq by the British in 1921.

Faysal (which is often spelled Faisal) died in 1933, one year after Iraq became independent. His son and then grandson held the throne in a regime that let British troops return in World War II. King Faysal II and his family were murdered during a 1958 military coup.

The king was replaced by Gen. Abdul Karem Kassem, who became a classic military dictator. In October 1959, the despot faced a Communist-led revolt, spearheaded by the Iraqi Ba'ath Party. A three-man assassination team opened fire on Kassem, who was severely wounded. One of the gunmen who was wounded, but escaped, was 22-year-old Saddam Hussein, who had already developed an intense Arab nationalism and dislike for the United States.

Various military governments were installed through assassination. In 1961, Iraq claimed Kuwait and its oil fields, based on boundaries from the old Ottoman Empire. The British would have none of it, and sent troops to Kuwait. In 1963, the Ba'ath socialists seized power in another coup.

Heads Up!

"You Americans, you treat the Third World in the way an Iraqi peasant treats his new bride. Three days of honeymoon, and then it's off to the fields."

—Saddam Hussein to U.S. State Department envoys, 1985

Factions within the Ba'ath Party overthrew one another in a series of revolving-door coups. In 1979, the head of the Ba'ath Party became ill, and Saddam Hussein—a man steeped in the politics of violence—took power without firing a shot.

Palestine and Israel—Blood and Land

The decades-long struggle between the Israelis and Palestinians is only marginally about the internecine politics of the Middle East. It's mainly about three things: land, clan, and religion.

After World War I, you'll remember, the victorious British suddenly found themselves in possession of Iraq, Jordan, and Palestine. Iraq had long been a country. Jordan, originally called Transjordan, was carved out of old Ottoman holdings. And Palestine wasn't a country at all, but the generic name for an area between the Mediterranean and the River Jordan, and between French-held Syria and Egyptian territory.

After the French claimed Syria and Lebanon, the British were granted a mandate to rule Palestine and Transjordan by the League of Nations. All this was complicated by the *Balfour Declaration* of 1917, which put the British on record as supporting a homeland for the Jews.

> **Desert Lore**
>
> The Balfour Declaration is named for British Foreign Secretary Arthur James Balfour, who wrote to Zionist leaders on November 2, 1917, favoring a "national home for the Jewish people" in Palestine.

So why did the colonial British bother themselves with establishing a Jewish homeland? There are many high-blown philosophical answers, but in the British Empire's world of power politics, there was only one answer—artillery.

Dr. Chaim Weizmann was a chemist who headed the British Admiralty Laboratories during World War I. He developed synthetic acetone, a primary ingredient of modern explosives. An ardent Zionist and adept politician, he convinced the British Foreign Office to endorse the concept of Israel.

The British split Palestine from Transjordan, defining the boundary as the Jordan River in 1923, at about the same time, you'll remember, that the Hashemites were driven from Saudi Arabia and into Jordan. Urged on by Zionists, Jewish settlers from all over the world trickled into Palestine. By 1936, there were around 360,000 Jews in Palestine, almost one third of the total population.

By 1939, the British needed all the help they could get against the Germans as World War II erupted. So London promised the Palestinians a homeland within 10 years if they'd join the fight. The Muslim Arab Legion and Jewish Yishuv both served in the Royal Army. After the war, the British balked at admitting any more Jews to the region, despite pressure to resettle Jewish Holocaust survivors.

The Jews in Palestine opened a guerrilla front, sneaking refugee ships into Haifa and Tel Aviv, bombing British installations (including officer's quarters at the King David Hotel in Jerusalem), and killing Britain's soldiers. The British responded by hanging, deporting, and imprisoning as many Jewish militants as possible.

Downing Street finally gave up and dumped the entire mess in the lap of the United Nations. The UN came up with two plans, one for partition of Palestine between Arabs and Jews and another for a federal state containing both. The Palestinians and Arab states rejected both; the Jews accepted the partition deal.

As soon as the British withdrew in May 1947, all hell broke loose. Palestinian guerrillas attacked Jewish settlements, while Jewish Haganah (trained militia) forces began driving Palestinians from towns and cities. The civil war became an international one on May 14, 1948, when the State of Israel was formally declared.

Arab League troops (from Jordan, Egypt, and Syria) attacked. Israel tried to seize Jerusalem—which had guaranteed status as an international city—and failed. But the Israelis outfought the Arabs, forcing a 1949 peace deal that gave them 50 percent more territory than the original arrangement. Some 600,000 Palestinians were forced from their homes, ending up in refugee camps.

And so the cycle of terror and counterterror began. Supported by Arab nations from Egypt to Saudi Arabia, various pro-Palestinian groups—most notably the *Palestine Liberation Organization*—began a campaign of terror against Israelis both inside the nation and abroad.

Israel managed to thrive, despite repeated terror attacks. Palestinian rage simmered. In late 1966, Syria began a program of guerilla raids and strikes against civilian targets inside northern Israel. Israel responded by bombing Syria. Egypt, in turn, tried to close the Gulf of Aqaba, which leads to the Red Sea, to all Israeli ships.

On June 5, 1967, Israel struck back, seizing the entire Sinai Peninsula from Egypt and all of the land west of the Jordan River (the West Bank) from Jordan. In six days, the Arabs had suffered another humiliating defeat. Israel kept much of the conquered lands for "security reasons."

In 1972, Palestinian terrorists massacred Israeli athletes at the Munich Olympics. Israel followed with a years-long campaign of worldwide assassinations of militant Palestinian leaders. On October 6, 1973, Egypt and Syria launched a surprise attack against Israel on Yom Kippur, the holiest day of the Jewish year. Israel reeled, but finally prevailed, gaining even more land.

Gulf Lingo

The **Palestine Liberation Organization (PLO)** was formally founded in 1964. Its goal was originally to drive all Jews from Palestine, eliminate Israel, and establish a Palestinian state. The PLO has had a hand, directly or indirectly, in thousands of military and terror attacks against Israelis.

In 1978, Israel signed a U.S.-brokered peace with Egypt. Israel gave up much of its conquered lands, but kept a firm grip on the West Bank and Jerusalem. Deals in the late 1990s with the PLO let the Palestinians have some autonomy over some territory. But Israel said continued bloody terror attacks made a real nation of Palestine impossible.

Sooner or later, the Palestinian-Israeli bloodshed comes up in every Arab, Middle East, or Islamic crisis. The spit of land barely 50 miles across and 200 miles long looms like a giant over wars ranging from the Gulf War to the war on terrorism. As we'll see, it became a convenient tool for Iraq to use to try to unite other Arabs.

The Least You Need to Know

- ◆ Much of civilization began in what's now Iraq.
- ◆ Various empires carved the area up over the centuries.
- ◆ The stage was set for Arab nationalism and modern bloodshed at the end of World War I.
- ◆ Countries in the region are related—and divided—by twisted strings of family, clan, and religion.

Chapter 3

Years of Terror

In This Chapter

- ◆ Saddam takes control of Iraq
- ◆ World War I, Persian Gulf style
- ◆ Iraq uses its chemical weapons
- ◆ The world's most fearful place

In 1988, an exiled Iraqi architect named Kanan Makiya (writing under the pseudonym Samir al-Khalil) produced a profound book that summed up Iraq in its chilling title, *Republic of Fear*. I've spent a good part of my journalism career working in dictatorships, from Castro's Cuba and the mullah's Iran to Duvalier's Haiti and the Islamic military's Sudan. But I've never worked in a place as fearful or as repressed as Saddam Hussein's Iraq.

In the last chapter, we briefly mentioned the Ba'ath Party, and how it came to power in Syria and Iraq. The party still holds a monopoly on power in Iraq. And its absolute goals need a ruthless man to carry them out. In this chapter, we trace the life and career of the most ruthless of the ruthless, Saddam Hussein.

A Village Called Tikrit

Tikrit is a town of 27,000 that squats next to the Tigris River and the old Istanbul-Baghdad railroad tracks. It's about 90 miles north of Baghdad, and there's almost nothing to distinguish it from thousands of other hardscrabble towns scattered among the Middle East's bluffs, canyons, and deserts. Nothing except who was born there.

It was 799 years between the birth of *Saladin*, a brave leader of the twelfth century, and Saddam Hussein. And both came from Tikrit. You'll remember how we've talked about how important family, tribe, and clan are in the Middle East. Tikrit is a perfect example of how that tightly woven web of relationships can affect history.

> **Who's Who**
>
> Saladin (or Salah al Din) was born in Tikrit, in what's now Iraq, in 1138. He's revered throughout the Islamic world as the warrior who drove the Christian Crusaders from Jerusalem in 1187. He was sultan of Syria, Egypt, and Mesopotamia, and was praised by both Islamic and Western chroniclers for his bravery and mercy. He died in 1193.

Thus, it became easy during the Gulf War for Saddam to proclaim that he was "the new Saladin," unifier of Arabs against invaders. But Saddam also created "the Tikrit mafia," an alliance of kinsmen and immediate family members. Saddam's full legal name is Saddam Hussein Abd al-Magid al-Tikriti, meaning "Saddam Hussein of Tikrit." His other clansmen share the same last name, which is probably why an Iraqi government decree in the 1980s forbade the use of full names on government documents. The idea, apparently, was to hide the vast number of al-Tikritis running the government.

Saddam Hussein was born in Tikrit on April 28, 1937. From what little we know, Saddam had a hellish childhood. His father deserted his mother when Saddam was an infant. His mother, clinically depressed, reportedly tried to commit suicide before Saddam was born. She remarried a man who didn't like the boy any more than she did. Saddam was not allowed to attend school, and was shuttled back and forth among various relatives until he was 10, when he ran away from home.

Saddam ended up in Baghdad at the home of his uncle, Khairallah Tulfah. The transformation from faceless urchin to bloody dictator had begun.

Saddam Also Rises

The illiterate 10-year-old went from dusty village streets to a city full of streetcars, cinemas, prostitutes, and intrigue. The king of Iraq, Faysal II, was only two years younger than Saddam, and the government was run, barely, by the king's older cousin. Riots two years earlier had resulted in British troops briefly taking control of wartime Iraq. Soon after Saddam arrived, new rioting erupted over the issue of remaining British control.

Five hundred miles away, Israel was being established, ripped by bloody fighting between Jews and Arabs. Arab nationalism was awakening following World War II and the decline of the British Empire. The loudest voice in Iraq for socialist Arab self-determination belonged to the Ba'ath Party. And Saddam's Uncle Khairallah was a card-carrying member. Khairallah had been court-martialed out of the pro-British Iraqi Army in World War II for allegedly taking part in a "pro-Nazi" coup attempt. His hatred for the West grew.

The teenage Saddam tried, and failed, to enter a military academy, which was the usual route out of poverty for rural youth. Instead, steered by Khairallah, Saddam gravitated toward radical politics. He was focused, organized, disciplined, and almost messianic in his drive for power.

The Young Assassin

Inspired by the Pan-Arabism of Egypt's *Gamal Abdel Nasser*, Saddam became more and more active in politics. He played a minor role in an unsuccessful 1956 coup attempt against King Faysal II. A year later, he joined the Ba'ath Party and, according to some stories, murdered a communist opponent who happened to be his brother-in-law.

King Faysal was overthrown and killed in 1958, but not by the Ba'ath Party. Instead, it was just an old-fashioned military coup led by Gen. Abdul Kassem. In 1959, Saddam and two other Ba'athists attempted to machine-gun Kassem in broad daylight. The plot was bungled, but Kassem was severely wounded. Saddam was shot in the hand while escaping, was sentenced to death in absentia, and fled to Egypt, a hero on the streets of Baghdad.

> **Heads Up!**
>
> "Saddam Hussein thinks he talks to God. He has a message: he has to lead Iraq, make it a model for the Arab countries and then attract the rest of the Arab countries and become the sole Arab leader of modern times."
>
> —former Iraqi government official Said Aburish in PBS interview, 2000

> **Who's Who**
>
> Gamal Abdel Nasser overthrew Egypt's King Farouk in 1952, and became the world's leading spokesman for Arab nationalism. The British invaded Egypt in 1956 because Nasser nationalized the Suez Canal, but withdrew under international pressure. Nasser led Egypt's disastrous participation in the 1967 war with Israel. A close ally of the Soviets, he died in 1970.

Consolidating Power

Saddam finished high school in Cairo at age 24. He enrolled in law school, but never graduated. He was arrested twice for political scuffles, once for waving a knife while chasing another student who disagreed with his views down an alley.

Consider the world presented to a cunning and ambitious Arab revolutionary like Saddam in late 1962: The Bay of Pigs fiasco and the Cuban Missile Crisis had confirmed Cuba as a major international player. Raul Castro and Che Guevara were dispatched to Egypt and Palestine to build support for socialist Arab and African movements. Nikita Khrushchev was funneling billions of Soviet rubles into nationalist uprisings from Vietnam to the Congo. There was instability across the former colonial world. And anyone set to overthrow a pro-Western government could count on plenty of money and advice.

In February 1963, Ba'ath Party generals finished the job Saddam had started, and assassinated General Kassem in Baghdad. Saddam returned immediately from Cairo, and reportedly impressed his revolutionary Ba'ath superiors with his work as a torturer in the basement of King Faysal's old palace.

Saddam ended up being tortured in one of his own jails for two years when conservative generals staged a countercoup. His fierce will kept him from breaking, and he escaped in 1966. By this time, he was one of the top men in the party, and he guaranteed his position by forming the basis for the world's most oppressive security apparatus, the *Jihaz Haneen*, which means, in an Orwellian twist, "Instrument of Yearning."

In 1968, the Ba'athist Gen. Ahman Hassan al-Bakr took over Iraq and made a wolf his top shepherd; he put one of his young cousins, Saddam Hussein, in charge of all internal security in Iraq.

Saddam Hussein salutes his supporters in Baghdad.

Anatomy of a Nightmare

We've talked a lot about the terror of living in Iraq. But how can one party, or one person, keep millions of people fearful and oppressed? Easily, if you're willing to be completely ruthless, and if the average person never knows whether their barber or baker or best friend is a government spy.

Between 1968 and 1978, Saddam was Iraq's deputy in charge of internal security. He used the time to become very rich, skimming profits off of government contracts and "convincing" owners of dozens of legitimate businesses to take him on as a silent partner. He became very powerful, installing al-Tikritis and close friends in hundreds of positions throughout the government. And he became very deadly, using the blueprint from the Jihaz Haneen to set up a security operation with stooges and enforcers on almost every block.

Iraqi security remains sort of like a parfait, with each layer of security operatives and spies pressing down on the layer beneath it:

- *The Special Security Service* is the most feared of all, since it's primarily composed of all men from Tikrit and the nearby region. Started as an elite presidential security force, it's responsible for the safety of the entire Ba'ath Party organization. It's also behind a series of dummy corporations set up to acquire biological, chemical, and nuclear material. Most frightening of all to Iraqis, it's also the spy agency that spies on all other spy agencies, including internal security and military intelligence.

- *The Iraqi Intelligence Service* (also called the *Mukhabarat*) is in charge of civilian internal security, meaning the spies who inform on normal Iraqis suspected of being insufficiently loyal. It's responsible for everything from electronic eavesdropping and propaganda to torture and infiltration of every aspect of Iraqi life.

- *The Military Intelligence Service* (also known as the *Istihbarat*) is the service that keeps tabs on Iraqi troops and officers. Since military service is compulsory in Iraq, this means the agency, effectively, can spy on any Iraqi at any time. It also conducts overseas operations.

- *The Special Republican Guard* consists of about 26,000 troops whose job is to put down any attempted rebellion or coup. The terms "attempted rebellion or coup" are very loosely defined in Iraq.

- *The Republican Guard* is made up of seven armored divisions, stocked with the most loyal soldiers in the regular Iraqi army.

- *The General Security Service* started out in the 1970s as your garden-variety secret police organization. It now runs the day-to-day prosecution of political or economic "crimes" against the regime. It has about 8,000 agents.

With all this violence at his disposal, Saddam was ready to take over. Peacefully.

Total Power at Last

The official word was that old General Bakr was stepping down for reasons of health. The truth was that his cousin Saddam had been the country's de facto ruler for years. So there wasn't much of a transition on July 16, 1979, when it was announced that Bakr was retiring and Saddam Hussein was Iraq's new president.

Similarly, no one was very surprised six days later when Saddam condemned more than 20 party and army leaders to death. After all, Saddam had been intimately involved in a genocidal war against Iraq's *Kurds* and in mass murders and deportations of Iraq's *Shiite* Muslim population.

Gulf Lingo

The **Kurds** are not Arabs. They may have originated in the Caucasus region of modern Russia, or may have come from near the Mediterranean. For centuries, they have claimed an area they call Kurdistan, which sprawls across modern Syria, Iraq, Turkey, and Iran. All of those countries have fought with Kurdish nationalists. Starting with his appointment as internal security chief in 1968, Saddam has been in charge of the killing of tens of thousands of Kurds, often using chemical weapons.

In his own version of ethnic cleansing, the secular Saddam has used religion to his advantage by deporting more than 250,000 Shiites, and overseeing the executions of thousands more. But changes were shaking the Islamic and Arab worlds, changes that would put Saddam and his bloody lust for power at center stage.

Gulf Lingo

Shiite Muslims make up 15 percent of the Islamic world, or about 120 million people. The Shi'a (the word means partisans) split from other Muslims because Shiites believe that Ali, Muhammad's son-in-law, was the prophet's rightful heir. They also believe world leaders should be spiritual and religious as well as political. The religious nature of many Shiite political figures has always created tension in the Islamic world.

War with Iran

In the West, the Iran-Iraq War of 1980–1988 engendered mixed feelings. As one U.S. State Department official once joked with me, "It's like watching your mother-in-law drive over a cliff in your new car. You don't know how to feel." To the average Westerner, it was a fight between Iraq—an anti-Western socialist regime—and Iran—an anti-Western theocracy run by fundamentalist mullahs.

So hardly anyone in the West would have cared if the two countries beat each other bloody (which they did), if it weren't for the oil. Iraq produced about three million barrels of oil a day, while Iran pumped out about five million barrels per day, at least at the start of the war. Moreover, a war could threaten to choke off tanker exports from the entire Persian Gulf, from Kuwait, Iraq, Iran, Saudi Arabia, Qatar, and the United Arab Emirates, which amounted to about 20 percent of the world's production.

> **Heads Up!**
>
> "... foreign experts question how long the populations of these two countries will tolerate the squandering of nonrenewable oil resources on a costly war that does not involve any serious national interest on either side."
>
> —former U.S. foreign service officer John Haldane, 1986

By the time the war ended in 1988, a total of anywhere from 600,000 to one million Iraqis and Iranians were dead. Twice that many may have been injured or maimed.

Beginnings

In October 1978, only 10 months before he took power, Saddam supervised the eviction of a radical Shiite cleric living in exile in the Iraqi city of Najaf. He was the *Ayatollah Ruhoallah Kohmeini,* and he would remember his eviction the next year, when forces loyal to him overthrew the shah of Iran, seized the U.S. Embassy and its hostages, and made Iran a fundamentalist state.

The Ayatollah Ruhoallah Kohmeini was born in 1902. Descended from religious scholars, he became one himself. In 1944, he melded religion and politics in the Shiite tradition by calling for all foreign powers and dictators to be expelled from the Islamic world. He was deported in 1964 by the shah of Iran, but his influence over Iranian political life became tremendous. The shah was overthrown in 1979 and Kohmeini ruled Iran until his death in 1989.

Saddam arranged the ayatollah's eviction from Iraq only two weeks after Pres. Jimmy Carter, Egyptian Pres. Anwar Sadat, and Israeli Prime Minister Menachem Begin reached the Camp David accords, designed to bring peace between Israel and Egypt. But waves of Islamic fundamentalism were washing over the Arab world. Fundamentalists seized power in Iran in 1979. Fundamentalists assassinated Sadat in 1981. Now that he had taken total power in Iraq, Saddam had to ride the fundamentalist tiger without being eaten.

Most of Iraq's population is Shiite. After years of being repressed, would they join with their Shi'a brothers in Iran in a fundamentalist uprising inside Iraq? That was Saddam's biggest fear. In addition, the Ayatollah Kohmeini had vowed revenge for Saddam's campaigns against Iraqi Shiites.

In April 1980, an anti-Saddam group called Ad Dawah tried to assassinate Iraqi Foreign Minister Tariq Aziz with a hand grenade attack. A week later, another attempt was made on Iraq's information minister. Saddam had had enough; he rounded up suspected leaders, tortured them, and deported thousands of Iraqi Shiites into Iran.

Saddam still saw himself as the new Saladin, and the fundamentalist takeover of non-Arab Iran endangered his vision of a Pan-Arab state with Saddam at the helm. So he came up with a plan. The border between Iran and Iraq is mostly rugged mountain ranges. But in the south, where the Tigris, Euphrates, and other rivers dump into the Persian Gulf, the land is marshy and flat, perfect for Saddam's twelve mechanized divisions.

In addition, that region of Iran is largely Arab, not Iranian. It also contains some of Iran's most productive oil fields. Saddam planned to punch into the flatlands, incite an Arab uprising against the Iranian government, and seize the oil facilities. On September 22, 1980, Iraqi jets pounded 10 Iranian air force bases with Soviet-supplied MiGs. But they didn't penetrate the strengthened Iranian hangars, and didn't crater the Iranian runways. Within hours, F-4 Phantoms that the United States had supplied to the shah pounded Iraq.

Iraqi armor slammed into Iran. After a series of bloody engagements, Iraq managed to seize a 30-mile-wide strip of Iran within six weeks.

Israel Attacks

The French had helped Saddam build the 75-megawatt Osirak reactor near Baghdad. He told them Iraq needed the power. Saddam needed nuclear power, but not solely for electricity. Western, Israeli, and Iranian intelligence all presumed the facility was to make fissionable material suitable for constructing nuclear weapons. An Iranian air raid in September 1980 did minimal damage.

> **Heads Up!**
>
> "Under no circumstances will we allow an enemy to develop weapons of mass destruction against our people."
>
> —Israeli government statement, June 7, 1981

If Saddam were building "The Bomb," two targets presented themselves: Iran and Israel. Using nuclear weapons against a fellow Islamic state would have destroyed Saddam's chances of uniting Arabs. Striking at Israel, 680 miles away, would, conversely, have been a no-brainer.

On June 7, 1981, nine Israeli jets streaked into the predawn Sunday sky. Raining bombs and rockets on the facility 12 miles east of Baghdad, they destroyed Osirak completely. One French technician was killed. Iraq protested. Israel ignored it.

Human Waves

Outgunned and outmanned, the Iranian mullahs called on volunteers for their People's Army. Many of these "soldiers," some as young as nine, carried their funeral shrouds into battle, convinced that they would achieve martyrdom and paradise. Iran launched its first human-wave attacks in late 1981.

By 1982, these suicide regiments had enabled Iran to push toward the Iraqi city of Basra, in the Shiite south. In July, 1982, Iran launched Operation Ramadan, sending wave after wave of men and boys into minefields to clear the way for tanks. It was the world's largest land battle since 1945. It was an incredibly bloody stalemate.

In February 1983, 200,000 men and boys, each a religious zealot, launched their kamikaze attacks against the Iraqi city of al-Amarah. Six thousand of them died in one day. In early 1984, one journalist reported that thousands of Iranian children launched a human-wave assault in small units of two dozen each, the children tied together with ropes to keep them from retreating. Saddam knew he had to resort to something more effective than bullets or bombs.

Poison Gas

Under Saddam, Iraq had launched an ambitious program to develop so-called "NBC" weapons—nuclear, biological, and chemical. The Israeli strike of 1981 had destroyed Iraq's nuclear program, but its chemical and bioweapons facilities were still very much operational. Many of the biological and chemical agents used to make the weapons were obtained legally from corporations in the United States, under U.S. Commerce Department export licenses, and funneled through dummy companies controlled by the Iraqi government.

Iraq first launched chemical strikes against Iranian positions in late 1980. Baghdad denied it, but in 1984, a team of United Nations inspectors confirmed that Iraq had used *mustard gas* and a nerve agent called *tabun* against Iranian positions. The Iraqi order of battle was remarkably

The Machines

Mustard gas is a garlic-smelling liquid that produces fumes that burn body tissue. Widely used in World War I, it causes death, blindness, blistering, and severe lung damage. Tabun is a nerve agent that produces uncontrolled spasms, convulsions, paralysis, and death. Iraq's use of tabun against Iran was the first confirmed use of a nerve agent in the history of warfare.

consistent—Iraq's artillery would open up on massed Iranian suicide soldiers with chemical and nerve gas shells. As the Iranian troops struggled to breathe and put on their gas masks, the Iraqis would hit them with antipersonnel shells, scattering spinning shrapnel among the choking troops. Then, more nerve and chemical weapons, followed by more antipersonnel rounds. It was bloody, hellish, and effective.

From 1984 through 1987, Iraq and Iran attacked each other's cities, oil fields, and troop concentrations. Carnage on this level hadn't been seen since World War I. But the war of attrition began swinging in Iraq's favor by late 1987. Iranian equipment, mostly American, was breaking down from overuse and lack of spare parts. But the Iraqis were flooded with fresh tanks, artillery, helicopters, jets, and ammunition from the Soviet Union.

Oil, Hostages, and Uncle Sam

As we'll cover more thoroughly in the next chapter, the United States became involved in the Iran-Iraq war for three reasons:

- Iraq began attacking oil tankers leaving Iran's Kharg Island oil terminal. When the war started, world oil prices were around $11 a barrel. They peaked at over $53 a barrel. Iraqi attacks on oil tankers could drive prices even higher, since most oil used by Japan and about half used by Europe came from the Persian Gulf. So it made sense for the United States to try and protect shipping.

- The United States was afraid that if Iraq lost, the Shiite majority in Iraq would overthrow Saddam and set up a Shi'a government friendly to Iran. Any union of Iraq and Iran, however informal, was America's ultimate Persian Gulf nightmare.

- This was a period of civil war and fundamentalist violence in Lebanon. Several Americans were being held hostage. One, a CIA station chief, had been tortured and killed. Despite its support for Iraq overall, the United States knew the ayatollah's Iran had a good deal of influence with the Lebanese hostage-takers. So around 1985, the United States quietly began swapping weapons with Iran for hostages.

Gulf Lingo

Reflagging was the U.S. policy of placing American crews and the U.S. flag on oil tankers to prevent attacks on Kuwaiti oil vessels. Iran fired missiles at Kuwait. It also hit one of the reflagged tankers in October 1987. The United States responded by destroying two Iranian oil drilling platforms in the Persian Gulf.

The *Stark* incident pulled the United States into more direct involvement. On May 17, 1987, an Iraqi missile hit the USS *Stark*, killing 37 American sailors. Iraq apologized and the United States blamed Iran for the whole affair, saying the Iranians had escalated tensions.

The United States then *reflagged* 11 Kuwaiti tankers to try and discourage any more shipping attacks.

On July 3, 1988, America's involvement took a disastrous turn. The cruiser USS *Vincennes* shot down an Iran Air civilian jetliner, killing 290 men, women, and children. The U.S. Navy claimed the ship had mistaken the Airbus A300 for a hostile Iranian fighter jet.

Finally a cease-fire was signed in August 1988. Millions were dead or wounded. Both economies were devastated. Iraq "won" only in that it emerged with a much stronger army and air force thanks to Soviet resupplies, while Iran's armed forces were a mere shadow of what they had been in 1980.

Heads Up!

"Of the 290 people on Iran Air 655, 170 corpses had been retrieved, 40 were unidentified. A few seemed oddly at peace. Leila Behbahani, 3 years old, was still dressed in her tidy blue dress, black shoes, white socks, and little gold bangles on her wrists."

—Christopher Dickey in *Expats: Travels in Arabia*, Fourth Estate Books, 1991

War with the Kurds

During the war with Iran, Iraq's oppressed Kurdish minority sided with Iran. Although Saddam had been at war with the Kurds since his early days as minister of internal security in 1968, he took his brutality to new heights as the war with the Iranians was winding down in 1988.

There had been scattered attacks against Kurds using a variety of chemical and nerve weapons before, but nothing on the scale of what happened in Halabja. It was March 17, 1988, a Friday. The late winter chill in the foothills near Iran occasionally gave way to hints of spring. But in the hours before the dawn of the Islamic Sabbath, frost covered the ground and most of the 50,000 people in Halabja, almost all Kurds, were asleep. The first calls to prayer hadn't yet sounded from the minarets of the towns numerous mosques.

The first waves of MiG fighters approached from the southwest. They dropped a combination of antipersonnel cluster bombs and nerve gas projectiles. Various agents from mustard gas and tabun to *sarin* and *VX* were in the warheads. The jets made 20 runs over the town, coming in continuing waves as the sun rose.

The Machines

Sarin is a nerve agent that acts much like tabun, producing fumes that blister skin and produce involuntary muscle spasms, loss of sphincter and urinary control, and death. VX is a nerve gas that looks like motor oil and can cause death within 15 minutes of exposure to its fumes.

Men, women, and children fell in the streets, twitching and convulsing. Mothers fell dead in doorways, clutching their choking children. Bodies piled up against houses and walls, death's skull grins welded onto their faces by involuntary muscle constrictions. By the end of the day, 5,000 of Halabja's 50,000 citizens were dead. Another 20,000 had giant oozing blisters spread across their bodies. Many of the wounded were blind. Others had permanent lung damage.

By the end of 1988, Saddam's forces had killed an estimated 200,000 Iraqi Kurds. The illiterate peasant boy from Tikrit had proven himself capable of using poison gas against his own people as well as his enemies.

Streets of Fear

By the end of the war with Iran, Saddam had emerged as the preeminent leader of the region. The United States had supplied him with intelligence information about Iranian ship and troop movements. The Soviet Union had supplied him with their newest weapons, including the T-72 tank. Saudi Arabia had allowed him to use their air base at Dhahran to refuel his jets for strikes against Iran. Kuwait cowered at the sight of Iraq's military muscle.

Heads Up!

"If the general American public were aware of Iraq's human rights violations, as it is aware of human rights violations in countries covered more fully by the media, there would indeed be a great public outcry against U.S. assistance to that country."

—Richard Schifter, Bureau of Human Rights, U.S. State Department, 1988

Saddam continued to develop a chemical and biological arsenal. Reports in the British media even suggested that Iraq staged an underground test of a 10-kiloton nuclear device in 1989. All the while, the United States warmed up to Iraq as its relations with Iran remained hostile. The Reagan administration had removed Iraq from its list of terrorist states. The United States even pushed for more credit for Iraq from the Export Import Bank.

The new George Bush administration was committed to the same policy as the previous administration. President Bush even signed a National Security Directive in October 1989, calling for a policy of more U.S. aid to help influence Iraq. The invasion of Kuwait was 10 months away.

The Least You Need to Know

- Saddam was ruthless in his drive for power.
- The war with Iran solidified his position.
- Saddam developed and used chemical weapons.
- The United States was more worried about a threat from Iran than Iraq.

Chapter **4**

America and the Gulf

In This Chapter

◆ Why we care about the Arabian Gulf

◆ Oil becomes the main issue

◆ The world changes in the blink of an eye

◆ U.S. diplomacy buddies up to Iraq

At the end of the last chapter, we gave the broad outline of U.S. policy that tried to placate Iraq. In the next few pages, we'll supply you with more detail about how the United States became involved in the Middle East generally and in the Persian Gulf region specifically. All of this leads in a direct line to Operation Desert Storm, Osama bin Ladin, and the events that surround us today.

Former U.S. Secretary of State Henry Kissinger once wrote that "People have friends; nations have interests." The Middle East is the working definition of what that maxim means. America's thirst for oil, the Arabs' thirst for power on the world stage, and Israel's thirst for survival have all, at one time or another, been slaked by the same desert wells.

Fill 'Er Up

Around two-thirds of the world's oil and one-third of its natural gas supplies lie beneath the deserts and scarred moonscapes of the Middle East. Those reserves have been there since the days of the Jurassic, but no one cared until August 27, 1859, when the world's first functioning oil well began spewing crude from a hole bored near Titusville, Pennsylvania.

Desert Lore

Muckraking journalist Ida Tarbell's classic 1904 exposé, *The History of the Standard Oil Company*, (New York: McClure, Phillips, and Co.) resulted in the government-ordered breakup of Standard in 1911. Founded by John D. Rockefeller, Standard was the world's largest corporation. The Standard cartel was spun off into companies that formed the modern oil industry, including Exxon, Chevron, Mobil, Amoco, Marathon, Conoco, and Pennzoil, among others.

Heads Up!

"The intimate ties [between the United States and Saudi Arabia] … spring from an overlapping interest in continued Western access to the monumental Saudi oil reserves and thus also in a sound response of a rapidly changing, thinly populated, largely desert kingdom to the challenge and opportunity of sudden massive riches."

—Prof. J. C. Hurewitz, Columbia University, 1990

By 1870, the first U.S. oil company, Standard Oil, was incorporated in Ohio. Three years later, oil was discovered in Russia. The main use for petroleum at this point was for kerosene in lamps, and Thomas Edison's invention of the electric lightbulb in 1882 seemed to doom the oil industry. But in 1896, Germany's Daimler and Benz Company developed an internal combustion engine to power automobiles, and since then the world's need for oil has never looked in the rear view mirror.

By 1901, oil had been discovered in Iran, and by 1908 British Petroleum was busily pumping there. Just before World War I started, the British and Dutch formed the Iraq Petroleum Company (IPC) to divide any oil exploration in the Middle East. After the war, with the British in control of much of the area, the United States was finally allowed to enter the market. In 1922, Exxon was given 24 percent of the IPC.

At the time, it was purely a speculative venture, as companies searched the globe for petroleum to satisfy the planes and trains and automobiles and tractors and factories of North America and Europe. The United States was a minor player because France and Britain controlled the post–World War I Middle East. America, for example, was interested in Saudi Arabia and Kuwait only because they imported U.S. kerosene to use in their lamps.

But everything changed in 1927, when oil was discovered in Iraq. That same year, a financially strapped British oil company sold its rights in Saudi Arabia, Bahrain, and Kuwait to an American conglomerate named in honor of the region, Gulf Oil. The British government would have none if it, though, and drew a red line around all of Turkey, Saudi Arabia, Syria, Iraq, and Palestine. Inside the *red line*, only British companies could explore. That left Gulf Oil with just Kuwait, the tiny island of Bahrain, and a coastal slice of Saudi Arabia near the Hasa oasis. Gulf unloaded the Bahrain and Hasa concessions to another American firm, Standard Oil of California (SOCAL), which eventually became Chevron.

In 1931, Gulf struck oil in Bahrain. In 1933, SOCAL/Chevron brought in Texaco to help explore in Saudi Arabia, and formed Aramco—The Arabian American Oil Company. In 1938, Aramco found oil in Kuwait and Saudi Arabia. In fact, their Saudi oil strike in the Hasa region turned out to contain almost all of Saudi Arabia's oil. Exxon and Mobil eventually joined Aramco, which became wholly owned by the Saudi royal family with the four U.S. oil giants as senior partners. Suddenly, the United States became very interested in the entire region.

> **Gulf Lingo**
>
> The **Red Line Zone** of 1928 gave the British all the oil rights to most of Saudi Arabia, as well as that of all of Turkey, Iraq, and most other countries on the Arabian Peninsula. The Americans, ironically, were left with Kuwait, Bahrain, and a tiny sliver of Saudi Arabia, all of which became giant oil producers.

Israel and Islam

The United States, never a colonial power in the region, became interested primarily because of natural resources and business interests. But there was more than that at work when it came to American support for Israel. American presidents starting with John Adams had written in support of the idea of a Jewish homeland. In 1919, Woodrow Wilson endorsed the Balfour Declaration, calling for the establishment of a Zionist homeland.

As U.S. troops in Europe liberated Nazi concentration camps, the horrors of the Holocaust became apparent to the average American. In 1947, Ralphe Bunche, an African American who would soon become America's ambassador to the United Nations, met with leaders of the Jewish resistance in Palestine, assuring them the United States fully supported U.N. moves to create Israel.

In 1948, the United States became the first nation to recognize the state of Israel, cabling the recognition to Tel Aviv 11 minutes after the independence proclamation. Driven by philosophical sympathy and admiration for Israel's principles, and by an active Jewish voting bloc in the United States, the United States found itself with a staunch ally in Israel. Surprisingly enough, the move didn't earn the United States the hatred of many Arabs and Muslims. That would come later.

> **Heads Up!**
>
> "I can understand you. I am also a member of a persecuted minority."
>
> —African-American official Ralph Bunche to future Israeli Prime Minister Menachem Begin, 1947

In the beginning, Arabs saw the United States as an ally against imperialism from the Soviets and from Britain. In 1956, when British and French troops tried to invade Egypt because the Egyptians had nationalized the Suez Canal, Dwight Eisenhower threatened them with oil sanctions unless they backed off. They did, and America became a hero in the Arab world.

The president went even further and issued what became known as the *Eisenhower Doctrine*. The Eisenhower Doctrine was issued in 1956, and promised American weapons and financial assistance to any Middle East nation threatened by Communism. In the minds of many at the State Department and CIA, Arab nationalism and Communism were synonymous, since the Arab nationalist states—like Nasser's Egypt—began condemning the evils of colonialism at the same time they started nationalizing some basic industries and expropriating private property. That approximate situation lasted until 1967. Syria began a series of guerilla raids and terror strikes inside northern Israel. The Israelis responded with air strikes. The Soviets, wanting to stop the strikes against their ally Syria, asked Egypt to mobilize its troops. Egypt did, and demanded that all U.N. peacekeepers between Egypt and Israel be removed. The U.N. complied, and Egypt immediately closed the Suez Canal to all Israeli shipping. Israel, fearing a sudden strike from its Arab neighbors, struck first, attacking Egyptian, Syrian, and Jordanian forces.

Israel, as we've seen previously, gained huge amounts of territory in what became known as the Six Day War. Pres. Lyndon Johnson began to see Israel as a bulwark against the Soviets, and American aid to the Jewish state increased dramatically.

Arab states noticed the new tilt in U.S. policy. In August 1973, Egyptian Pres. Anwar Sadat traveled to Saudi Arabia to tell King Faysal about an upcoming surprise attack on Israel. The Saudis approved, and agreed to use their oil muscle to help. On October 5, 1973, Soviet-equipped Egyptian and Syrian troops suddenly struck on the Jewish high holy day of Yom Kippur.

> ### Heads Up!
>
> "There's no question that the U.S. was supporting Israel from the beginning, but the big bucks didn't come until after 1967."
>
> —Former U.S. ambassador to Saudi Arabia Richard Murphy, 2001

The sudden attack left Israel reeling. On October 14, Pres. Richard Nixon ordered emergency military supplies sent to Israel. Israel fought back, using American weapons, and retook most of the ground that had been lost. On October 17, 1973, Arab oil ministers with the Organization of Petroleum Exporting Countries imposed a total oil embargo on the United States. A fearful new acronym entered the American dictionary—*OPEC*. OPEC, the Organization of Petroleum Exporting Countries, was formed in Baghdad in 1960. There are 11 members, including Algeria, Indonesia, Iran, Iraq, Kuwait, Libya, Nigeria, Qatar, Saudi Arabia, the United Arab Emirates, and Venezuela. Among them, they produce 40 percent of the world's oil.

Oil Shocks, Terror Attacks

Until 1973, terrorism was something that happened to other nations, especially to Israel, and the TV images of the 1972 massacre of Israeli Olympic athletes in Munich were still burned into everyone's memory. Although a TWA and a Pan Am airliner had been hijacked in 1970, those were seen by the United States as strikes directed at Israel. But on March 1, 1973, Americans became targets. As a reception at the Saudi embassy in Khartoum, Sudan, was ending, gunmen from the Palestinian group *Black September* burst in and took diplomats hostage, including two Americans. One day later, U.S. Ambassador Cleo Noel Jr. and U.S. Charge d'Affaires George Moore were executed.

Gulf Lingo

Black September is the name given by Palestinian militants to September 1970, when Jordanian troops pushed Palestinian armies out of Jordan. The Jordanians were upset at the increasing use of Jordan as a staging area for Palestinian attacks. The Palestinian forces were shoved into Lebanon, setting the stage for years of bloodshed there. The Black September Organization became known to the international community in late 1971, when they gunned down Jordan's prime minister. Black September's operations effectively ended with the 1973 murder of the American diplomats.

The 1973 movie *American Graffiti* was a hymn to U.S. car culture. From '55 Chevys to '32 Ford coupes, the film synthesized teen love, octane, and horsepower. On the Fourth of July 1973, you could cruise to the drive-in on 30-cent-a-gallon gasoline. By Thanksgiving, gas in some places was an unspeakable dollar a gallon. Long lines wound around gas station pumps as panicked Americans felt the squeeze of the OPEC oil embargo.

The American economy was kicked into a two-year recession as energy-fueled inflation ignited. For the first time, the connections among Islamic rage, Israel, and oil were starting to become clearer to Americans. In 1974, though, the terror group most Americans knew best was the screwball Symbionese Liberation Army and its kidnapped heiress, Patty Hearst.

On September 8, 1974, Pres. Gerald Ford doomed his political career by pardoning former Pres. Richard Nixon. That same day, half a world away, a bomb went off in the cargo hold of a TWA 707 over the Aegean Sea, near Greece. Nine crew members and 79 passengers died. The radical Palestinian Abu Nidal Organization claimed responsibility. Its founder, Abu Nidal (Sabry Khalil al-Banna), is a Palestinian militant born in 1938.

Closely linked to Iraq, he split from the PLO because it was insufficiently radical. His organization has committed dozens of terror acts, and has been used by Iraq for overseas assassinations. He was last known to be ill, living in Baghdad.

Throughout the 1970s, intermittent terror attacks around the Islamic world would briefly get U.S. attention, and then fade. But that inattention faded for good in 1979.

The Hostage Crisis

Muhammad Reza Shah Pahlevi—the shah of Iran in 1979—had been on his Tehran throne since 1941. But Islamic fundamentalists criticized the shah for his human rights abuses, his unequally distributed oil wealth, and his pro-U.S. policies. As the shah's secret police cracked down, resistance increased. On January 16, 1979, he fled the country. The fundamentalist ascetic Ayatollah Kohmeini returned from exile, took over Iran, and proclaimed an Islamic republic.

In September, the desperately ill shah was admitted to the United States for medical treatment. Militant crowds stormed the U.S. embassy in Tehran, seized 52 American hostages, and demanded that the shah be returned to stand trial. Pres. Jimmy Carter's repeated diplomatic efforts to free the hostages failed. On April 24, 1980, a U.S. rescue mission failed, with three helicopters crashing and eight American servicemen dead.

The crisis also produced another oil shock, with crude prices tripling and inflation in the United States roaring out of control. America seemed impotent. The hostage crisis and the failing economy cost Jimmy Carter the presidency. On January 20, 1981, the day Ronald Reagan was inaugurated, the hostages were set free after 444 days in captivity.

Heads Up!

"… still there is absolutely nothing doing that makes me feel we will get out of here soon. I just can't understand what our Gov't. is doing to obtain our release. It is very, very discouraging!"

—U.S. hostage Robert Ode, diary entry, August 4, 1980

The Iranian hostage crisis fundamentally changed the outlook of both the American people and the American government. There was now an ongoing realization that Islamic fundamentalism and the politics of Arabian Gulf oil were intertwined, and that much of the Islamic world saw the United States as the enemy.

As we saw in the previous chapter, this situation led to the United States siding with Iraq during the Iran-Iraq War of 1980 to 1988. From the U.S. point of view, Iran had to be stifled and Israel supported. The free flow of oil had to be guaranteed. America became more closely drawn into the region, with increasingly bloody results.

The Terrorist Decade

When all hell broke loose for the United States in the Middle East, it came in a most unlikely place, Lebanon. Lebanon was known as Phoenicia in biblical times, and the Phoenicians became famed as sailors and traders. Part of the Ottoman Empire, it was split off from Syria by the French and granted independence during World War II.

Independent since 1943, Lebanon had an unusual population for the Mideast: half of the population was Christian, the other half Muslim. The Muslims had always complained that the power-sharing agreement that governed the country didn't give them enough power, but the two sides managed to live in relative peace until the mid-1970s.

The U.S. Marines landed in Beirut briefly in 1958 to help put down a Muslim uprising. But otherwise, Lebanon was an oasis of calm, with its casinos, seafront boulevards, and sophisticated life of Beirut earning it the title "The Paris of the Mediterranean."

Problems began as more and more Palestinian refugees fled into Lebanon from Israel, the occupied territories—the land Israel seized in the 1967 war, including the West Bank of the Jordan River—and Jordan. Groups allied with the PLO used southern Lebanon as a base for attacking Israel. Meanwhile, Christian militias, some allied with Israel, started fighting with the Palestinians and their Lebanese Muslim allies. Syria finally stepped in in 1976, with its army occupying much of the country.

Israel punched into Lebanon in 1978 to clear out Palestinian bases. They withdrew in favor of United Nations peacekeepers, but reinvaded in 1982 after a series of bloody Palestinian attacks. The Israelis laid siege to Beirut, shelling it mercilessly. Finally, a multinational force, including U.S. Marines, came to Lebanon to try to restore order.

On September 14, 1982, the Christian Lebanese president, Bashir Gemayal, was assassinated. Two days later, pro-Israeli militiamen invaded a pair of Palestinian refugee camps near Beirut seeking revenge. They beat, murdered, and raped thousands of refugees. A day and a half later, the dusty alleys of the camps were soaked in blood. Corpses, some so mangled they were unrecognizable, were scattered like dead leaves. The *Sabra and Shatila* Massacre left 2,000 civilians dead.

The United States tried to broker a peace and pressure Israel to withdraw from Lebanon. At the same time, the United States agreed to provide more than $2.5 billion in economic and military aid to Israel. The stage was set for the first suicide attack on American interests.

> **Desert Lore**
>
> Sabra and Shatila were two of the dozens of camps set up in Lebanon to handle the flood of Palestinian refugees. Arabs have always claimed that the Israeli army stood guard outside the camps while its Christian militia allies committed one of the worst atrocities of modern times. The Israelis deny it.

On April 18, 1983, U.S. Marines at the U.S. Embassy were under orders not to fire at any intruder unless it was on direct orders of their peacekeeping commander. So no one noticed when the battered car pulled up next to the embassy annex. Within seconds, the suicide driver had set off the explosives packed into the trunk and back seat. Sixty-three people died, including 17 Americans. The United States evacuated its embassy and moved operations to the edge of the city.

Heads Up!

"This criminal attack on a diplomatic establishment will not deter us from our goals of peace in the region. We will do what we know to be right."

—Pres. Ronald Reagan, April 18, 1983

The worst was still to come. The multinational forces doing the peacekeeping work were housed in barracks near the Beirut airport. On October 23, a five-ton Mercedes truck roared toward the compound, picking up speed as guards shouted for it to stop. Under the rules of engagement, they were not allowed to open fire. Two miles away, another truck was slamming into a barracks occupied by French paratroopers.

When the smoke cleared and the pulverized rubble stopped falling, 241 American soldiers, sailors, and marines were dead, the biggest one-day death toll of U.S. forces since Vietnam. Across town, 58 French soldiers lay dead.

On December 12, 1983, the Shiite extremist group *Al Dawa* was suspected in the bombings of the U.S. and French embassies in Kuwait, which killed six people. Al Dawa is a Shiite radical group, supported by Iran, that carried out several attacks inside Iraq during the Iran-Iraq War.

By early 1984, Beirut was a shell-ripped hellhole, as various militias battled each other for control of the once-cosmopolitan streets. The United States decided to pull out its peacekeeping troops. On February 11, Islamic militants kidnapped 50-year old Frank Regier, a professor at the American University.

Desert Lore

The Lebanese Civil War started in 1975 and lasted until 1992 when the Syrian army moved in and the last of the Western hostages were released. Israel sided with the Christians, and Syria with the Muslims. An uneasy power-sharing agreement still continues, under the watchful eye of Syria's military.

The *Lebanese Civil War* was in full swing, and Beirut became a synonym for urban destruction. The so-called Green Line divided Christian and Muslim sections of the city, but the violence was carried out by a smorgasbord of various militias and armed gangs.

On March 7, Jeremy Levin, the CNN Bureau Chief in Lebanon, was snatched off the street. Eight days later, a massive blow was struck to U.S. intelligence efforts when, on March 16, an American named William Buckley, described as a "diplomat," was kidnapped by Muslim militia. It turned out Buckley was the CIA Station Chief in Beirut. He was tortured, taken to Syria, tortured some more, flown to Tehran for more torture, then taken back to Lebanon where he was hanged. A grisly videotape of the execution was handed out by the militants.

On May 8, American clergyman Benjamin Weir was kidnapped. On September 20, 1984, a van loaded with explosives got to within 30 feet of the annex and detonated. Twenty Americans were injured, including Ambassador Reginald Bartholomew. The British ambassador, David Miers, was also hurt and seven people died. Islamic Jihad claimed responsibility. Among the most shadowy of all Islamic radical groups, Islamic Jihad formed in the Gaza Strip in the 1970s. With branches in several countries, headquartered in Syria, supported by Iran, Islamic Jihad has taken part in hundreds of attacks against Israeli targets, civilian and military, including this bombing.

Anti-American attacks escalated for the rest of the decade, as Israel suffered through more terror strikes and the Iran-Iraq War raged. Associated Press Beirut bureau chief Terry Anderson was kidnapped in March 1985. Beirut had fallen apart, and just about all that was left from the old days were the stories told and drinks consumed by swashbuckling journalists holed up at the Commodore Hotel. The American hostages weren't freed until the late 1980's, when the violence began to die down.

> **Heads Up!**
>
> "Beirut night life is not elaborate, but it is amusing. When danger waits the tables and death is the busboy, it adds zest to the simple pleasures of life."
>
> —P. J. O'Rourte, *Holidays in Hell*, Vintage Books, 1989

October 1984 brought one of the most horrifying incidents yet. The Greek cruise liner *Achille Lauro* was on a pleasure sail around the Aegean Sea when it was hijacked. Sixty-nine-year old Leon Klinghoffer, a Jewish American tourist confined to a wheelchair, was murdered, and his body, still in the wheelchair, dumped into the sea. The Palestine Liberation Front (PLO) claimed responsibility. This group formed by breaking off from the Popular Front for the Liberation of Palestine in 1975 and has since split into three factions: pro-PLO, pro-Syrian, and pro-Libyan. The same faction that killed Leon Klinghoffer is responsible for a series of hang glider attacks against civilians in Israel.

In December 1985, 20 people were killed in airport attacks in Rome and Vienna, including the 11-year-old daughter of an Associated Press photographer. The Abu Nidal group, whom we've already mentioned, was responsible.

On April 2, 1986, a small bomb in an Athens-bound TWA 727 killed two Americans. Three days later, a bomb went off at a West Berlin disco frequented by American GIs. Three people died. The Reagan administration held Libya responsible, and launched air strikes against Tripoli, Libya's capitol.

In November 1987, a box of chocolates was delivered to the American University in Beirut. Packed with explosives, it killed seven people and wounded 37 more. Four days before Christmas in 1988, a Pan Am 747 named *Maid of the Seas* was on route from Germany to the United States when it exploded over the Scottish village of Lockerbie. The blast killed all 259 passengers and crew, and 11 people on the ground. The list of dead included 159 American men, women, and children.

The geopolitical world was about to undergo a seismic shift that hadn't been seen since the collapse of fascism at the end of World War II.

The New World Orders Oil

Communism had been a fact of life since the Soviet Revolution of 1917. The Reagan administration came into office in 1980 with a hidden but grandiose plan: spend the Soviet Union and the Communist Bloc into extinction. Soviet Prime Minister Mikael Gorbachev came to power in 1985 pushing *perestroika* (change) and *glasnost* (openness). He had no idea how fast the Soviet system and its satellite states would crumble.

> **Heads Up!**
>
> "General Secretary Gorbachev, if you seek peace, if you seek prosperity for the Soviet Union and Eastern Europe, if you seek liberalization, come here to this gate. Mr. Gorbachev, open this gate. Mr. Gorbachev, tear down this wall."
>
> —Pres. Ronald Reagan in Berlin, June 12, 1987

In November 1989, the Berlin Wall fell. Soviet-allied regimes throughout Eastern Europe fell. The Soviets withdrew from their disastrous 10-year war against Islamic fundamentalists in Afghanistan. The George Bush administration that followed Reagan coined a term: The New World Order.

The United States was now the sole superpower. As it pushed for open borders and free trade among nations to mark the new order of things, the United States plugged itself into an increasingly globalized economy, one that ran on oil.

As we noted in the last chapter, with an eye on the oil that flowed through the Persian Gulf, the United States "reflagged" Kuwaiti tankers to try and keep Iran from attacking them. But behind the scenes, the United States continued to funnel aid to Saddam Hussein as a counterbalance to Iran.

In August 1989, it was revealed that the Atlanta branch of an Italian government-owned bank, *Banca Nazionale de Lavoro*, had funneled $5 billion in unauthorized loans to Saddam, including $900 million underwritten by U.S. government guarantees.

Why would the United States help secretly underwrite one of the world's bloodiest dictators? U.S. policy at the time was to make sure Iran was hurt as much as possible, given the 1979–80 hostage crisis in Tehran and Iran's suspected complicity in Islamic terror strikes against American targets.

As the only superpower left, the United States also wanted to secure the flow of Arabian Gulf oil, not as much for U.S. domestic needs as for the needs of America's allies. In fact, only 7 percent of U.S. oil was shipped through the Straits of Hormuz. But over half of Western Europe's petroleum and a quarter of Japan's came through the choke point.

A cutoff of that oil would mean economic disaster for Europe and Japan. In the newly globalized economy, that would mean disaster for the United States, too. At the end of 1990, the quickest way to keep that from happening at the hands of Iran seemed to be to keep Saddam happy.

The Least You Need to Know

- ◆ The United States was drawn into the Middle East because of oil and Israel.
- ◆ Arab support for America turned to opposition after 1967.
- ◆ Terror attacks against U.S. targets increased in the 1980s.
- ◆ The United States supported Saddam as a counterweight to Iran.

Chapter 5

The Nineteenth Province

In This Chapter

- ◆ Why Saddam decided to seize Kuwait
- ◆ Why relations between Kuwait and Iraq were sour
- ◆ U.S. diplomacy tries to butter up Iraq
- ◆ Saddam prepares to make his move

We've all known someone who lived beyond his means. You know how it goes—big house, three cars, flashy clothes, expensive tastes, mammoth debt, and not a penny in the bank. If you took the suburban cul-de-sac neighbor who maxed out his credit cards to keep up appearances, moved him to a Baghdad palace, and gave him a bloodthirsty streak, you'd have Saddam Hussein at the start of 1990.

To all appearances, Saddam began the new decade in fine shape. He had finally driven off the Iranians. He had slaughtered his Kurdish enemies with calculated ruthlessness. He was freshly stocked with updated Soviet military hardware on the ground and in the air. He had a couple of billion dollars' worth of under-the-table American loans. He had an active chemical and biological weapons program. The Saudis has given him military cooperation and the Gulf countries, including Kuwait, had fronted him billions more in loans and credits for the war with Iran.

But Saddam was flat broke. He owed the Russians for their weapons. He owed $35 billion to richer Gulf oil-producing countries. He owed $50 billion more on world markets. He needed more cash. He needed more oil. He needed Kuwait.

Saddam Eyes Kuwait

Saddam was not pleased in 1989. Total losses in Iraq from the war with Iran and from overdue loans amounted to $100 billion or more. His oil industry, crippled by years of Iranian bombings, accounted for 61 percent of Iraq's gross domestic product. Iraq had to import two-thirds of its food.

Kuwait, right across the border, could provide an antidote to all that. Kuwait had a budget surplus equal to almost a third of its total gross domestic product. It had a balance of payments surplus of $1.5 billion. The average Kuwaiti had an income of more than $27,000 a year. The average Iraqi's was less than $1,000.

What galled Saddam most of all was Kuwait's attitude. Kuwait, along with Saudi Arabia and the United Arab Emirates, had loaned Iraq more than $100 billion for the Iran war. Kuwait was demanding that it be repaid. Iraq's lifeblood was its oil sales. But the price of oil was dropping on world markets because, apparently, Kuwait was overproducing. Saddam claimed it was a tactic aimed at trying to put pressure on Iraq to pay up.

It was actually part of Kuwait's strategy to help end a global recession. After a recession ended, the emir of Kuwait figured, oil prices would jump again.

Strange Bedfellows

The Defense Intelligence Agency (DIA) is the Pentagon's own Central Intelligence Agency (CIA). The DIA's job is to assess possible military threats against the United States and oversee U.S. military intelligence.

The U.S. Central Command (CENTCOM) is the American military group assigned to oversee U.S. military operations in parts of the Middle East, Africa, and South Asia. As we noted back in Chapter 1, CENTCOM is responsible for 19 countries, including Iran, Iraq, and Kuwait.

At the height of the Iran-Iraq War in 1985, the DIA set up a liaison office inside CENTCOM to help coordinate intelligence on the war. At the same time, U.S. policy was tilted strongly toward Iraq. In 1987, the DIA set up a Defense Attaché Office in Baghdad, an office that had access to top Iraqi military commanders. The idea was to make sure that an incident like the USS *Stark*, when an Iraqi missile hit a U.S. ship (see Chapter 3), never happened again. But the DIA was also funneling U.S. intelligence about Iranian ship, plane, and troop movements straight to Saddam Hussein's high command.

In April 1989, CENTCOM's analysts decided that Iraq was the next big threat to the Persian Gulf, given that Iran had been badly weakened and the Soviet Union was teetering on the brink of collapse. In November, the DIA issued a Defense Intelligence Assessment that concluded Iraq was most likely to strike against Syria, not Kuwait.

But things were changing, rapidly, and the United States began to realize that its unstable ally, Iraq, might do something rash. As 1990 began, it became clear that things might get out of control. In May 1990, CENTCOM staged a war game in which Iraq invaded Kuwait. In July, the Naval War College did the same sort of simulation. By that time, the real thing was only a month away.

> **Heads Up!**
>
> "Iraq is unlikely to launch military operations against any of its Arab neighbors over the next three years with the possible exception of Syria."
>
> "To protect its image of moderation, Iraq is unlikely to take military action against Kuwait."
>
> —Defense Intelligence Assessment, Defense Intelligence Agency, November 1989

Historical Claims

If Saddam were going to invade Kuwait, he would need to dress it up in some sort of legitimacy to appease other Arab states. So his Baghdad brain trust fell back on several leftovers from the colonial era. As we mentioned in Chapter 1, Iraq began to refer to the fact that Kuwait had once been part of an administrative area of the old Ottoman Empire that had the Iraqi city of Basra as its capital.

Second, Iraq began to remind the diplomatic community that the border between Iraq and Kuwait had been in dispute for decades, and that Iraqi troops in 1961 and again in 1973 had briefly occupied the border region before withdrawing.

Third, the Iraqis started to complain that their access to the Persian Gulf was choked off by Bubiyan and Warba, a pair of Kuwaiti islands that left Iraq only a narrow channel through which its oil tankers could travel to get to the Gulf and the world beyond.

Country Cousins, Rich Relatives

Greed is one of humankind's prime motivations. So is jealousy. Saddam had enough of both to keep psychologists busy for years. His desire for Kuwait's riches had everything to do with Iraq's desperate financial situation after the war with Iran. But he also wanted control over Kuwait's oil and financial riches to feather his own fiscal nest.

In large part, though, Saddam just wanted to rub the Kuwaitis' noses in the sand. Kuwaitis were famous throughout the Arab world as arrogant playboys. Kuwaitis on vacation in

Egypt, for example, were famous for renting horses to ride around the Pyramids, riding the animals hard until their hearts burst, and then nonchalantly flipping wads of money at the horrified stable owners.

The Kuwaitis, for their part, looked at the Iraqis the same way that wealthy suburbanites might view distant cousins who lived in house trailers. The Kuwaitis thought Iraqis were rude, poor, uncouth bumpkins. Whatever the average Iraqi thought about Saddam, he thought less of his neighbors across the southern border.

Countdown

By the spring of 1990, things had gone from bad to worse. As tension mounted, Saddam was worried about many things, but negative reaction from the United States was not among them. Saddam had insulted the United States in late 1989, when he rejected offered American loans of $400 million as too small. The United States had rushed to increase the amount. American military intelligence even maintained an office in Baghdad.

The United States had stepped up its purchases of Iraqi oil. The United States had imported about 80,000 barrels of oil every day from Iraq through 1987, but by April 1990 the imports from Saddam's government had increased more than eightfold, to 675,000 barrels a day.

Heads Up!

"The United States continues to provide the government of Iraq with limited information on Iranian military activity."

—U.S. State Department options paper presented at May 29, 1990, meeting of the National Security Council

But in early 1990, Saddam had become more and more bellicose. In February, he demanded that all American warships leave the Arabian Gulf. In that same month, he blistered the United States in a speech to the Arab Cooperation Council. In March, Saddam arrested, convicted, and hanged British journalist Farzad Bazoft as a spy. Bazoft was an Iranian-born reporter for the *London Observer* who had covered Iraq extensively during the Iran-Iraq War. He was arrested while investigating a story on Iraq's chemical weapons industry. Under torture, he "confessed" to being an Israeli spy. Bazoft was hanged March 15, 1990, and his body dumped in front of the British Embassy in Baghdad.

Even the United States' friendly policy toward Iraq could only take so much. As evidence came out about Saddam's genocide against the Kurds and his diversion of American loans into his military programs, the United States became uneasy. In March 1990, the United States seized what it said was a shipment of nuclear components headed to Iraq.

A few days later, the United States discovered that Iraq had positioned permanent missile sites that could launch attacks against Israel. In April, Saddam delivered a speech in which he revealed that Iraq possessed binary chemical weapons and was willing to use them against Israel, which drew a strong response from Pres. George Bush. Finally fed up, the United States terminated its loans to Iraq in May 1990.

At the end of that month, Saddam delivered a speech in which he rattled a saber in the direction of Kuwait for its oil overproduction, which was lowering the price of oil and driving Iraq more deeply into debt.

Oddly enough, Saddam delivered that speech just as CENTCOM and the DIA were wrapping up a preliminary computer war game concerning an Iraqi invasion of Kuwait. It was to be repeated and refined a few weeks later, but the message was clear—to evict Iraq's army from Kuwait (and possibly from Saudi Arabia) would require a lot of heavy armor and at least 375,000 troops.

Diplomatic Debacle

By June 1990, the diplomatic meltdown that would allow Iraq to invade Kuwait was well underway. Kuwait had a defense treaty with the Gulf Cooperation Council (GCC), but it was plain that the oil-rich Gulf sheikdoms had little interest in standing up to Iraq. The Gulf Cooperation Council was formed in 1981 with an agreement among a half dozen Persian Gulf monarchies to cooperate in military and diplomatic matters. Members are Kuwait, Saudi Arabia, the United Arab Emirates, Qatar, Bahrain, and Oman.

The *Arab League* was similarly ineffective. The main topic of its March 1990 summit had been to move League headquarters from Tunis back to Cairo. The headquarters had been removed from Cairo in 1978 to protest Egypt's Camp David accord with Israel. But the League did deal with Iraq at that March meeting. It issued a statement blasting Britain for asking that journalist Farzad Bazoft not be executed, and went on record supporting Saddam's decision to hang Bazoft.

Desert Lore

In March 1990, U.S. Customs seized 27 vacuum diffusion pumps purchased by Iraq in the United States. The suspicion was that they would be used to help enrich uranium for possible use in a nuclear bomb. But that same year, the United States let Iraq purchase direct current power supplies used to accelerate ion beams in a weapons program.

Who's Who

The Arab League—formally known as the League of Arab States—was formed in 1945. Currently, 22 Arab nations are members, including Iraq and Kuwait.

The United States was also at loose ends. On one hand, the signals coming from Baghdad were fairly clear. But, as we'll see, on the other hand the United States was still prisoner of its old pro-Iraq policies formed during the Iran-Iraq War.

On April 12, 1990, five U.S. senators, led by Senate Majority Leader *Robert Dole*, traveled to Baghdad to meet with Saddam. The Iraqi dictator lectured the senators about the evils of U.S. policy and ripped into a Voice of America radio broadcast that had criticized him.

> ### Who's Who
>
> Robert Dole, a wounded and decorated World War II veteran, was a Republican senator from Kansas and senate majority leader in 1990. He bitterly denounced Saddam Hussein later, but after his April 1990 meeting told reporters, "I think we can work with him."

He complained about Senate Foreign Relations Committee hearings into his use of poison gas against the Kurds. He blistered proposals for U.S. sanctions against Iraq because of his human rights record.

The meeting wasn't exactly British Prime Minister Neville Chamberlain appeasing Adolf Hitler in 1939, but it did contain a tone of appeasement according to an Iraqi government transcript of the session. Senator Dole assured Saddam that the Bush administration was opposed to economic sanctions. After the meeting, Dole met with President Bush and urged him to be patient with Iraq.

Intelligence Warnings

By mid June, many in America's intelligence and military communities were concerned about Iraq. CENTCOM, fresh from its preliminary computer analysis of Iraq's threat to Kuwait in May, upgraded its analysis to a "Warning Problem." That meant events had changed enough so that what was previously a war game now had at least a plausible chance of becoming reality.

You'll remember a few pages ago when we talked about the DIA analysis in 1989 that an Iraqi threat to Kuwait was unlikely. A year later, the DIA had shifted its position slightly. The CIA, meanwhile, was monitoring Iraq but hadn't spotted anything that overly worried them.

> ### Heads Up!
>
> "This is an extremely dangerous policy about which we can no longer be silent …. [T]he raising of our voice now against this hatefulness is not the most that we will be able to do …. [I]f words cannot provide Iraq's people with protection, then action will have to be taken …. [T]hey [Kuwait] plunged a poisoned dagger in our back."
>
> —Saddam Hussein, Baghdad speech, July 17, 1990

Everything changed, though, on July 17, 1990. That was the day that Saddam delivered his annual speech commemorating July 17, 1968, when the original Ba'ath Party military coup took power in Iraq. His speech set off alarm bells around the world. Saddam accused the United Arab Emirates and Kuwait of overproducing oil to drive down the price. He charged that Kuwait was actually stealing oil from oil fields inside Iraq. And he threatened to take action.

Six days later, newspapers in Baghdad accused Kuwaiti Foreign Minister Sheik Sabah al-Ahmad al-Sabah of being an agent of the U.S. government. The next day, Iraq's Foreign Ministry fired off a memo to Kuwait, listing its grievances. Iraq was demanding that Kuwait …

- Cut oil production to the point where the world price would rise from $18 to $25 a barrel.
- Pay Iraq $2.4 billion to make up for Iraqi defense of "the Arab nation" during the war with Iran.
- Help convince other Gulf countries to declare a moratorium on the money Iraq owed.

Panicked Kuwaiti officials desperately sent cables to the Arab League and the United Nations, denying Iraq's charges and asking for help. Help from the United States was iffy, since U.S. Secretary of State James Baker had cabled the American Embassy in Amman, Jordan, telling them the United States took no position in what was essentially a spat between Kuwait and Iraq, but that the United States remained committed "… to ensure the free flow of oil from the Gulf."

Meantime, the two *KH-11* spy satellites the United States kept in orbit at all times began to pay more attention to Iraq. Scooting 500 miles above the earth, the satellites could relay photo images back to Washington every seven seconds in real time. By the third week in July 1990, they had located what seemed to be 35,000 Iraqi troops and more than 250 tanks assembling just north of Iraq's border with Kuwait.

Saddam was counting on disagreement, miscalculation, and timidity among the Gulf States and America. Given years of support from the United States, he believed any move into Kuwait would be met passively by Washington, a belief, as we'll see shortly, that was strengthened by a face-to-face meeting with the American ambassador to Iraq. At home, he was moving full speed ahead with research and development of not only chemical weapons, but some biological weapons as well.

The Machines

The KH-11 satellite is 43 feet long, weighs 30,000 pounds, and can photograph objects as small as six inches across in clear weather. The photos are sent back to earth electronically almost the moment they're taken. Since the Gulf War, it has been augmented by the even larger and more sophisticated KH-12.

The arguments began immediately among the Pentagon, White House, State Department, CIA, and emir of Kuwait's palace about what the Iraqi troop movements meant. The Kuwaitis nervously whistled past the graveyard and said that they thought these were only exercises. Pentagon officials tended to agree, although many believed it was, indeed, a prelude to an invasion.

> **Heads Up!**
>
> "Iraq conducted a virus research program on three reported viral agents: Infectious Hemorrhagic Conjunctivitis virus, Rotavirus, and Camel Pox .... Iraq nominally initiated a virus research program in July 1990, if not earlier."
>
> —Milton Leitenberg, Center for International and Security Studies, 2000

The arguments and conflicting analyses within the Bush administration began to swirl like dead leaves in an autumn windstorm. Starting on July 20, 1990, the Naval War College, CENTCOM, and the DIA staged a refined version of the earlier computer war game about Iraq invading Kuwait, called Internal Look 90. Internal Look 90 was a computer-simulated attack on Iraq by Kuwait staged from July 20 through July 28, 1990, by the U.S. Central Command and the Naval War College. It refined what became Operations Plan 90-1002—Defense of the Arabian Peninsula.

Its conclusion was a more detailed version of the earlier computer simulation: that ejecting Iraq from Kuwait would require a lot of armor and a lot of men, and the United States had neither in the area.

July 20 was a busy day. First, Internal Look 90 began. Then, U.S. military intelligence analysts deduced that Iraq was moving more tank and artillery units to within 30 miles of the Kuwait border. Bolstered by all that, the Joint Chiefs of Staff asked the DIA to prepare a list of Iraqi targets for U.S. planes to strike.

At this point, a rational person might wonder what was going on. After all, Iraq was making bellicose statements while at the same time moving more and more troops and heavy equipment perilously close to Kuwait. The highest levels in the U.S. military chain of command were asking for target options inside Iraq. Obviously, something was happening. Why wasn't the United States pressuring Iraq, publicly and privately, not to move on Kuwait?

> **Heads Up!**
>
> "Iraq is unlikely to use significant force against Kuwait, such as the occupation of Warba and Bubiyan islands .... [Some] small-scale incursions are possible."
>
> —article in Defense Intelligence Digest, July 20, 1990

The answer isn't likely to build confidence among those who think that Western intelligence, diplomacy, and intelligence work like a well-oiled machine. As we've mentioned, U.S. diplomatic policy was still frozen in a time warp, dealing with Saddam not as a dangerous cutthroat, but as a valuable counterweight to Iran. As we've also seen, not everyone was unanimous in the belief that an invasion was imminent. The Kuwaitis themselves were skeptical. So was an article in a daily briefing book prepared by the National Security Agency and the DIA called the Defense Intelligence Digest.

By July 22, 1990, U.S. spy satellites easily spotted the traffic jam on the four-lane highway leading from Baghdad to the Kuwaiti border, as thousands of tanks, armored personnel carriers, trucks, and four-wheel-drive vehicles headed south. At the same time, two dozen missile launching platforms were seen being loaded on railroad flatbeds moving toward Kuwait.

The DIA concluded that more than 300 T-72 tanks, 150 armored personnel carriers, and 200 artillery units of various sizes were already in place just north of Kuwait's border, with more rolling into position every hour. But while the military and intelligence communities knew exactly what was happening, the White House, the State Department, and international diplomatic bodies twiddled their thumbs.

The Arab League Yawns

Chadli Kibli of Tunisia was 70 years old, and viewed his position as secretary general of the Arab League as a way to enhance tiny Tunisia's status in the Arab world. As he received complaining cables from Iraq and cables from Kuwait denying the charges, he decided that the Arab League would not issue any warnings, nor would it formally mediate between Kuwait and Iraq.

He figured, correctly, that the Kuwaitis lacked the spine and the military resources to issue any strong ultimatums. As we'll see in the next chapter, he was proven right when Kuwait massed troops to protect its northern border, and then withdrew them one week later out of fear of provoking Iraq.

Instead, back-channel appeasement seemed the best option. So Pres. Hosni Mubarak of Egypt and King Hussein of Jordan were pressed into service to talk to Saddam. Baghdad sanguinely assured both men that a peaceful solution was possible. The Saudis even suggested that Saddam might be successfully paid off. The stage was set for disaster.

The Glaspie Conversation

April Glaspie was a 48-year-old career diplomat, the first female ambassador appointed by the United States to serve in the Middle East.

Ambassador Glaspie's position in Iraq, though, was not as precarious as it might have been in one of the Gulf monarchies, since Saddam ran a secular government in which women held many top positions. Saddam only paid lip service to Islamic ideas about the status of women—or anything else—when it suited his own drive for power.

Glaspie was well aware of the cable we previously mentioned that Secretary of State James Baker sent to the U.S. Embassy in Jordan, characterizing the Kuwait-Iraq dispute as purely an inter-Arab affair, and listing talking points for U.S. diplomats, including "The United States takes no position on the substance of the bilateral issues concerning Iraq and Kuwait." She also sat in on the April, 1990 meeting with Saddam and the U.S. senators, and was fully aware of its conciliatory tone.

Heads Up!

"We do not have any defense treaties with Kuwait, and there are no special defense or security commitments to Kuwait."
—U.S. State Department spokeswoman Margaret Tutwiler, July 24, 1990

So when she was summoned by Saddam to Baghdad's presidential palace on July 25, 1990, she knew the Bush's administration's position—that the free flow of oil was important, that the administration opposed economic sanctions against Iraq, and that there was a hands-off policy in place regarding Kuwait.

So while U.S. military officials prepared for a possible invasion, Glaspie parroted the Bush administration line to Saddam, and told him, "We have no opinion on Arab-Arab conflicts like your border disagreement with Kuwait."

Glaspie was hung out to dry during the war and unfairly blamed for encouraging Saddam to invade. In reality, she was merely repeating instructions from the State Department and the White House. That same day, July 25, CIA analysts forwarded an opinion to the National Security Council that Iraq was ready to invade Kuwait. The analysis was ignored.

U.S. Ambassador to Iraq April Glaspie shortly after her July 25, 1990 conversation with Saddam Hussein.

Gassed and Ready

By July 28, CIA Director William Webster was almost completely convinced that his analysts were correct. When he arrived at the White House for a national security briefing, he told President Bush that Iraq would "probably" move across the border, sooner rather than later.

But Webster fudged slightly, saying that he thought the most likely scenario was that Saddam would seize Bubiyan and Warba Islands and the rich northern Kuwaiti oil fields, but that it was "possible" that Iraqi troops could roll through all of Kuwait and possibly into Saudi Arabia.

President Bush and Secretary of State Baker reportedly were unmoved, continuing to insist that the United States would gently push for a diplomatic solution but would otherwise remain neutral.

While the briefings continued, more and more Iraqi troops and tanks were staged near the Kuwait border. These included hundreds of the Soviets' newest armor, the T-72, as well as medium-range ground-to-ground missiles, artillery, fuel supplies, and infantry. The T-72 tank was developed by the Soviet Union in 1971. Its 125-millimeter cannon can penetrate U.S. tanks' armor at 1,200 yards. It carries a three-man crew and can reach a top speed of 60 miles an hour. Until the Gulf War, it was considered a match for the most sophisticated U.S. tanks.

But before Saddam gave the order to move, he had several more cards he wanted to play. He was fully prepared to take advantage of American indecision, Kuwaiti timidity, and Persian Gulf oil money.

> **Desert Lore**
>
> On July 28, 1990, CIA Director William Webster warned the president that Iraq would probably invade Kuwait. He went to the White House with satellite photos of Iraqi troops massing near Kuwait and a pair of CIA satellite analysts to explain the photos. According to a January, 1991 *Village Voice* article President Bush never asked the analysts anything.

The Least You Need to Know

◆ Iraq was nearly bankrupt after the war with Iran.

◆ Saddam had been supplied with new Soviet-made weapons.

◆ Saddam thought he could solve his financial problems by either extorting or invading Kuwait.

◆ The United States, despite having military and intelligence warnings, refused to tell Saddam to back off.

Part 2

Desert Shield

When Saddam Hussein invaded Kuwait in August 1990, the biggest movement of personnel and equipment since Vietnam began. This section tells the
story of what happened before the shooting started. We examine Saddam's
ambitions, how American policy might have encouraged him, and why it
became difficult to form one of history's most unique coalitions to oppose the
invasion.

Chapter 6

The Tanks Roll South

In This Chapter

- ◆ Everyone guesses wrong
- ◆ Diplomacy falls flat
- ◆ Kuwait falls without much of a fight
- ◆ The Iraqis stop in their tracks

The wheel of history often spins on an axle manufactured from mistakes. By the end of July 1990, the Bush administration mistakenly decided that a conciliatory approach could stop any Iraqi moves on Kuwait. The Kuwaitis mistakenly believed they could appease Iraq. And Saddam mistakenly believed that neither the United States nor the Gulf Arab countries would react to an invasion.

Oil, money, and power were the issues. Oil, because Saddam wanted Kuwait's oil production facilities and the United States vowed to keep Gulf oil flowing; money, because Saddam wanted to extort cash from his richer neighbors; power, because Saddam still saw himself as leader of the Arab nations.

Last-Minute Moves

On July 25, 1990, the CIA warned that Iraq would probably invade. Three days later, CIA Director William Webster delivered that assessment to a skeptical White House. By this time, Saddam had three armored divisions of his elite Republican Guard massed within two dozen miles of Kuwait's border.

The weather in July and August in the Gulf region is brutal. Daytime temperatures can top 120°F. Dank wind from Indian Ocean monsoons blows in, jacking up the humidity to more than 80 percent. Every year in July and August, 500,000 Kuwaitis—more than half the Kuwaiti population—leave for elsewhere until the weather moderates. That leaves about 450,000 Kuwaitis and about 1.5 million Palestinians, Indians, Pakistanis, and Filipinos in the country. The foreigners clean the houses, run the shops, drive the trucks, work the ports, and staff the hospitals. They keep Kuwait running.

On July 26, Kuwait withdrew most of its troops from the border with Iraq. The emir of Kuwait believed that too many men massed at the border would provoke Iraq. Besides, he felt confident last-minute negotiations would forestall any invasion.

Slant Drilling

Saddam had accused Kuwait of trying to bankrupt Iraq by overproducing oil and driving down the price. He also charged the Kuwaitis were stealing Iraqi oil through the use of *slant drilling* in the *Rumaila oil field.*

> ### Gulf Lingo
>
> **Slant drilling** is also known in the oil business as directional drilling. The technique was originally developed to steer drill bits around impenetrable rock formations. Saddam claimed the Kuwaitis sunk a well and then drilled on an angle, sucking oil out of his fields. The **Rumaila oil field** is roughly shaped like a banana and straddles the border between Iraq and Kuwait. The border through the oil field was drawn by the British after World War I.

Baghdad claimed that Kuwait had developed a well within a quarter mile of Iraq's border, and then proceeded to pump out more than $2.5 million worth of oil that belonged to Iraq.

Kuwait denied the charges but didn't seem to be exceptionally worried. That's because they thought a deal was in the works to solve the problem in a typically Gulf fashion—pay it to go away.

The Jeddah Disaster

Jeddah, also spelled Jidda, is a beautiful temperate city of 1.25 million people on Saudi Arabia's Red Sea coast. What better place to escape from the suffocating Gulf summer and sign a deal to avoid war than in the luxury of a palm-shaded seacoast resort?

That, at least, was the idea when Saudi Arabia, prodded by Egypt and Jordan, agreed to host an August 11, 1990, face-to-face meeting between Kuwait and Iraq at Jeddah. The Saudis also needed the good publicity. The month before, the annual *haj* to Mecca had turned bloody, with 1,500 people dying as religious pilgrims stampeded in a panic over water supplies.

The meeting was set for August 1. But as always in the Gulf, there was plenty of behind-the-scenes action. On July 28, according to Jordan's King Hussein, there was a private meeting, moderated by the Jordanians, between members of Saudi Arabia's ruling al-Saud family and the ruling al-Sabahs of Kuwait.

Gulf Lingo

The **haj** (short for *hijira*, meaning "the journey") is a pilgrimage every devout Muslim is expected to make at least once in a lifetime. Millions of Muslims from around the world travel to the holy city of Mecca every year. The Saudi government oversees details ranging from security to housing, and food to sanitation.

According to the king, the Saudis and Kuwaitis decided to buy off Saddam essentially by agreeing to most of his demands. Each country reported to not only be willing to forgive their war loans to Iraq, but also willing to give $10 billion each toward helping Iraq pay its other war debts.

While that back-channel meeting was being held on July 28, more mixed signals were flying in Washington. The DIA issued a report speculating that Kuwait appeared ready to capitulate to Iraq's demands. At almost the same time, DIA officials were meeting with Kuwait's ambassador, telling him in no uncertain terms that Iraq was about to invade.

The Koran, the Torah, and the Bible all have object lessons about pride going before a fall. It was a lesson lost on the Kuwaitis. On July 30, Kuwait Foreign Minister Sheik Sabah Ahmed al-Jaber al-Sabah (the emir of Kuwait's brother) was meeting with diplomats from Jordan.

He launched into a sneering denunciation of Iraq, its culture, its soldiers, and its leadership. When the Jordanians warned him that he needed to watch himself, he airily replied that the United States would bail out Kuwait and he had no intention of following through on the deal of two days earlier.

At the Jeddah summit the next day, the Kuwaiti foreign minister told the Iraqis he would give them, at most, $500 million, nowhere close to the

Heads Up!

"If they [the Iraqis] don't like it, let them occupy our territory. We are going to bring in the Americans."

—Kuwait Foreign Minister Sabeh al-Jaber al-Sabah, July 31, 1990, to Jordanian diplomats

$10 billion figure he'd originally agreed to. Saddam's emissaries had been expecting a pay-off of far greater proportions, and they left after only two hours.

The Hands-Off Policy

By July 30, both the DIA and the CIA finally agreed that Iraq intended to invade Kuwait. That morning, Assistant Secretary of State John Kelly trudged to Capitol Hill to testify before a subcommittee of the House Foreign Affairs Committee.

Iraqi soldiers parade through Baghdad just prior to Iraq's invasion of Kuwait.

In a fascinating exchange with Congressman Lee Hamilton of Indiana, Subcommittee Chairman Kelly echoed both Secretary of State *James Baker's* talking points, and earlier statements made by State Department spokesmen:

> *Kelly:* "Historically, the U.S. has taken no position on border disputes in the area, nor on matters pertaining to internal OPEC deliberations."
>
> *Hamilton:* "Secretary [of Defense Dick] Cheney has said the United States' commitment was to come to Kuwait's defense if attacked. Perhaps you could clarify for me just what our commitment is."
>
> *Kelly:* "I am not familiar with that statement …. We have no defense relationship with any Gulf country. That is clear."
>
> *Hamilton:* "Is it correct to say … that we do not have a treaty commitment which would obligate us to engage U.S. forces there [in Kuwait]?"
>
> *Kelly:* "That is correct."

On August 1, 1990, a deeply divided six-member Joint Chiefs of Staff (chief of staff of the U.S. Army, the chief of naval operations, the commandant of the U.S. Marine Corps, the chief of staff of the U.S. Air Force, a vice chairman, and the chairman) met in Washington on a steamy Wednesday afternoon.

They assembled in what the Pentagon officially calls the Gold Room, but which everyone in the military knows as "The Tank." Combat art from various wars hung, simply framed, on the plain white walls. Pale gold drapes enclosed the windows, which were sealed with polished oak shutters. Guarded on the outside, deep inside the Pentagon, with anti-eavesdropping technology built into the walls, ceiling, and gold-carpeted floor, The Tank was the most secure room in the ultrasecure National Military Command Center.

Gen. Colin Powell, chairman of the Joint Chiefs of Staff, sat at the head of the conference table, with the various chiefs of services facing him, along with the joint chiefs staff. Born in New York City in 1937 to Jamaican immigrants, Powell became a professional soldier upon college graduation, and served in the army for 35 years. Through superior political skills and a thorough knowledge of the military, he became the first black man to become chairman of the Joint Chiefs of Staff. (He later served as secretary of state in the George W. Bush administration.)

Among those facing Powell at the table were Gen. Norman Schwartzkopf, head of CENTCOM, and the joint chiefs director of operations, Gen. Thomas Kelly. Schwartzkopf had been called to Washington from CENTCOM headquarters in Tampa to give his read on developments. Kelly was skeptical about the intelligence reports.

Schwartzkopf told his fellow commanders that a top military official in Kuwait had told him the day before that Kuwait wasn't even putting its own forces in alert. If Kuwait wasn't worried, the implication was the United States shouldn't be, either. However, Schwartzkopf said he was convinced the Iraqis might move against the northern oil fields or offshore islands. He just didn't know when. The members of the joint chiefs thanked Schwartzkopf and told him they'd be sure to attend his retirement functions in Tampa the next year.

Seven times zones away, the invasion of Kuwait had begun.

> ### Who's Who
>
> James Baker was born in Texas in 1930. A former U.S. Marine, he served in Pres. Gerald Ford's administration and was his campaign manager in 1976. He also managed George Bush's unsuccessful bid for the GOP nomination in 1980. He was chief of staff and treasury secretary under Pres. Ronald Reagan, and was secretary of state and again chief of staff under Pres. George Bush.

> ### Heads Up!
>
> "They're not going to invade. This is a shakedown."
>
> —Gen. Thomas Kelly speaking to Gen. Colin Powell, July 30, 1990

What Went Wrong?

Before we look at the invasion itself, let's take five and look at what went wrong. In the full light of history, it can be argued that nothing went wrong. After all, if the United States had stopped Iraq from invading Kuwait, Desert Storm would never have occurred. Without Desert Storm, Saddam's nuclear, chemical, biological, and conventional weapons would have been left intact. With his military capabilities intact, Saddam would have had more time to develop and refine them. With that time, Iraq might have been able to develop weapons far more terrible than anything it used in the war with Iran or Desert Storm. With those weapons, Saddam would have been able to unleash a nuclear, biological, or chemical holocaust on anyone who opposed him.

All that may be true enough. But the weeks leading up to the invasion are a case study in what diplomats call "preventive diplomacy." By looking at them more closely, we can understand how clear signals of impending war can be ignored, and how miscalculation can lead to bloodshed:

- Saddam miscalculated American reaction. He felt assured that since the United States had supported him against Iran, and since the Bush administration had been unambiguously conciliatory, that he would be able to either extort or invade Kuwait without U.S. interference.

- American diplomats were not clear enough with Saddam. True, they told him they considered his feud with Kuwait an "Arab-Arab dispute." But they failed to stress that U.S. insistence on protecting the flow of Persian Gulf oil was more important than anything else.

- American intelligence officials gave out conflicting analyses up until a few days before the invasion. That gave the president and secretary of state the option of believing the alternate "Saddam is bluffing" scenario.

- American military leaders also chose to believe the noninvasion option. Among other things, they chose to rely on Kuwait's analysis of the situation.

- Kuwaiti leaders, softened by decades of oil riches and a U.S. military protection, lacked the foresight or spine to stand up to Iraq or to ask for help. But at the same time, they arrogantly rejected their previously agreed-to deal to pay off Iraq and smugly counted on the Americans to bail them out.

- Saddam also felt that if he merely seized Kuwait and left Saudi Arabia alone, he would be able to treat the Kuwaitis the same way he treated the Iranians and the Kurds without interference.

- The United States encouraged Saddam's illusions by continuing to look at Iraq as a counterbalance to Iran.

So the ingredients were in place for war in the desert. All that was necessary was to add tank fuel and stir.

Kuwait Falls

Eleven P.M. on August 1, 1990, was damp and sweltering north of the Kuwait border. The border post along the four-lane divided Abdaly Highway running into Kuwait City was staffed by sweating Kuwaiti enlisted men and a few officers. In the scorching heat of mid-summer, it was hard to find any Kuwaiti officer above the rank of major in the country.

Several divisions of battle-toughened Iraqi Republican Guard troops had been sitting in the desert for days, along with three regular army corps as backup. The Medina and Hammurabi armored divisions were equipped with hundreds of Soviet-manufactured battle tanks, ranging from the state-of-the-art T-72s, to the older T-62 and T-54 models. They were backed by a variety of equipment, including the massive mobile *155-millimeter howitzer*.

As we noted a few chapters back, the Republican Guard was made up exclusively of volunteers, many of them college graduates from the region around Tikrit, loyal to Saddam through ties of kinship and clan. They had won their battle stripes repeatedly in the war with Iran, used repeatedly to counterattack and push back the ayatollah's suicide units. They received good pay, above average perks, excellent food (by Iraqi army standards), and the latest equipment. The regular army, on the other hand, was comprised of draftees, many of them conscripted from politically "unreliable" areas like the Kurdish north or the Shiite south. In a few chapters, you'll see how they became cannon fodder during Desert Storm.

> ### The Machines
>
> The 155-millimeter GH N-45 Gun Howitzer is a Soviet-made cannon mounted on a tank-treaded chassis. It can fire up to seven shells a minute a maximum distance of 19 miles.

> ### Gulf Lingo
>
> The **Mutla Ridge** (more properly the al-Mutla Ridge) is the only geographic feature in all of Kuwait that juts above the desert. It lies about five miles south of the Iraqi border.

The Iraqis had been massed on the edge of high ground near the border, masked from Kuwait by the *Mutla Ridge*. The relatively narrow Mutla Pass was the only choke point between Iraq and Kuwait City, as the Iraqis would discover, disastrously, toward the end of the war.

Border Breakthrough

Around 11 P.M., Iraq's elite Republican Guard troops began to move. Like a snake uncoiling, the Hammurabi armored division and the Tawakalna mechanized division unwound from their parked formations and began moving en masse down the Abdaly highway.

At the same time their tank treads were digging into the asphalt, the Republican Guard's Medina armored division began churning the sand farther west, pushing into the Rumaila oil field. They drove toward the oil towns of Mutriba in north-central Kuwait and Rugei, which sat in the southwest corner of the country right across the border from Saudi Arabia.

Simultaneously, Iraqi helicopter-borne special forces lifted off and swung out over the Arabian Gulf, heading low over the water for a surprise strike against Kuwait City from the east. It was designed to be a well-oiled operation. And it almost was.

Tethered Communications Incorporated is a division of Westinghouse, and on that silent syrupy night as August 1 faded into August 2, several of their civilian technicians huddled in the coolness of an air-conditioned control van north of the Mutla Ridge, inside Kuwait. Above them, floating like a fat cloud, was an aerostat tethered to the van by several hundred feet of cable. An aerostat is a small blimp, attached to a ground control vehicle or structure by heavy cables. The aerostat usually carries radar, although the blimp can also be used to relay communications signals.

The aerostat was equipped with the Westinghouse APG-66 radar system, which scanned 30 miles in every direction, well into Iraq. The technicians worked for the Kuwaiti government and for the American military's U.S. Liaison Office Kuwait (USLOK), and were paid to keep an eye on anything that might be happening along the border.

Something began to happen. They watched their radar screens with amazement as a formation of tanks, armored personnel carriers, mobile artillery, trucks, and rocket launchers appeared on the screen. The machines were so tightly massed that they "… looked like an iron pipe," a pipe speeding downhill from the highlands of Iraq toward Kuwait.

The technicians telephoned Col. John Mooneyham, the chief of USLOK, and reported what they saw. Were they sure? Mooneyham asked. They answered yes, preceded and followed by a stream of profanity. Mooneyham told them to cut the tether, let the aerostat go, and get back to Kuwait City as soon as possible.

Less than two hours later, on August 2, 1990, Iraqi tanks were across the border, heading toward the sleeping capitol and Kuwait's oil fields.

The Royal Run

USLOK immediately passed along word to Kuwait's ruler, Emir *Sheik Jaber al-Ahmed al-Sabah*. Despite his government's sanguine assurances to General Schwartzkopf that Iraq was not going to invade, the emir of Kuwait was the Gulf equivalent of a belt-and-suspenders kind of guy. So he had an escape plan in place for himself and the royal family, just in case.

Who's Who

The emir of Kuwait, Sheik Jaber al-Ahmed al-Sabah, has ruled the country since 1977, and also holds the title of prime minister. He receives half the profits from all oil pumped from Kuwait. In 1986, he dissolved the National Assembly. In 1992, opposition groups won most of the seats in a new assembly. Only 13 percent of Kuwaiti men—those whose grandparents were born in Kuwait—can vote. Women cannot. On September 20, 2001, nine days after the World Trade Center and Pentagon attacks, the emir suffered a brain hemorrhage. He recovered.

The emir and his extended family, which included most of Kuwait's top officials, were joined by lucky government ministers in a Mercedes convoy heading for the safety of Saudi Arabia to the south. Since most of Kuwait's capital was personally controlled by the emir and was mostly invested outside the country, having the financial resources to set up a government-in-exile wasn't going to be a problem.

The emir, though, did forget one thing. Neither he nor any of the officials heading for safety with him ever notified Kuwait's armed forces that an invasion was underway. The officers and men left behind found out on their own soon enough.

A Short Fight

In the early days of the Gulf War, what was left of the Kuwaiti armed forces claimed that they had managed to inflict some damage on the Republican Guard units. Neither CENTCOM nor the CIA have confirmed or outright denied the Kuwaiti claims, which include destroying 30 Iraqi tanks at the pinch point through the Mutla Pass, and shooting down 52 Iraqi helicopters and fighter jets.

What we do know is that, for the most part, Iraqi armor had no trouble slicing across the border and pushing toward Kuwait City. Abandoned by their emir and his advisors, the Kuwaiti military, charitably, did as well as could be expected.

Kuwait had three operational army units, but only the 35th Armored Brigade put up much of a fight. A battalion of outdated British *Chieftain* tanks took up positions on the road connecting Kuwait City with the city of al-Jahrah just to the west.

The Machines

The Chieftain tank was produced in Great Britain from 1970 until 1978. It is 34 feet long, weighs 55 tons, and has a crew of four. It carries a 120-millimeter cannon and has a top speed of 30 miles per hour.

The 35th Armored Brigade managed to make up for the disgrace of being abandoned by the country's top leaders. Outnumbered, outgunned, and almost surrounded, they kept the Hammurabi Division at bay on the road leading to the capitol until their ammunition ran out.

Meanwhile, Iraqi special forces descended on Kuwait City from the east, as Iraq's navy began pounding the coast. By this time, the lead units of the Republican Guard were grinding into Kuwait City. But instead of using the ring roads that circled the city to bypass the urban center and drive for the southern border, the Iraqi tankers drove straight into town and did what most tourists do—got lost.

Because the Republican Guard got lost among the luxury hotels of Kuwait City, the Kuwaiti 15th Armored Brigade, stationed in the southern part of the country, was able to join the emir in Saudi Arabia. The delay also bought time for what was left of the Kuwaiti Air Force to scramble some American-made A-4 Skyhawks and a few French-manufactured Mirage F1 fighters.

But as dawn broke, Iraqi MiG-23s and Su-25s began to pound both the Kuwaiti Air Force field and Kuwait International Airport. By 6 A.M., Kuwait City was under Iraqi control. But it was a sloppy invasion, made apparent by several Iraqi failures:

♦ Kuwait radio and television stayed on the air all day through August 2, broadcasting appeals for help. The Iraqis apparently had trouble finding the broadcast studios to seize them.

♦ Much of Kuwait's army, along with most of its fighter jets, two of its patrol boats, and the majority of Kuwait Air's jetliners, escaped into Saudi Arabia.

♦ The Iraqi operation to capture the emir and his family failed completely because the Iraqi high command couldn't tell time properly. Kuwait's time was one hour ahead of Baghdad's. Iraqi commanders failed to take that into account when setting the time for special forces and Republican Guard units to coordinate operations.

> **Heads Up!**
>
> "... when Iraqi armor/mechanized forces made it to Kuwait City, they decided to push their tanks and tracked vehicles through the city, only to become bogged down."
>
> —U.S. Lt. Col. Fred Hart, *The Iraqi Invasion of Kuwait: An Eyewitness Account,* Army War College, 1993

> **Desert Lore**
>
> The Kuwaiti National Guard was in charge of traffic, police work, and embassy security in Kuwait City. The Iraqis found no National Guard members upon arriving because most took off their uniforms and fled.

Surrounded

By the end of August 2, Kuwait had effectively fallen, although some opposition contin-ued. Hundreds of Westerners and thousands of foreign nationals found themselves trapped, surrounded by an Iraqi force that seemed bent as much on looting as on military occupation.

Some of the U.S. personnel at the American Embassy, trapped in Kuwait City with their families, wanted to make a run for the still-open border. But U.S. Ambassador Edward Gnehm ordered them all to stay, despite appeals for the safety of wives and children.

Their anxiety wasn't helped by word that some British Army officers had been picked up by the Iraqis, jailed, beaten, and tortured. As we'll see in the next chapter, many Westerners were herded to Baghdad and other Iraqi cities to become "human shields" to prevent Allied air strikes.

Individual initiative soon began to provide CENTCOM back in the States with word of what was happening. The U.S. Embassy was sur-rounded, but some Americans, including Col. Fred Hart and CWO (Chief Warrant Officer) Dave Forties, risked their lives to gather informa-tion on the streets and pass it on to CENTCOM. The American government was finally getting firsthand confirmation of what their previous mis-calculations had meant.

> **Heads Up!**
>
> "[The Iraqis were] a motley force without orders and a total lack of basic tactical tenets and discipline. For the most part, Iraqi soldiers milled around, scav-enged for food and water, and seemed to be generally at a loss for what to do next, often looting and stealing ..."
>
> —U.S. Lt. Col. Fred Hart, *The Iraqi Invasion of Kuwait: An Eyewitness Account*, Army War College, 1993

A Screeching Halt

The Eastern Province of Saudi Arabia was familiar terrain to Saddam. During the war with Iran, his air force had been allowed to refuel at the Saudi air base at Dhahran, the principal city in eastern Saudi Arabia, and home to headquarters of the oil company ARAMCO. It's also home to the Dhahran Air Base, which came under repeated SCUD missile attack during the Gulf War.

> **Heads Up!**
>
> "I don't think there's any question at all he [Saddam] would have eventually attacked Saudi Arabia. Nobody on our side knew his intent. We had to assume that if he was militarily capable of something, he might do it."
>
> —Gen. Norman Schwartzkopf, interview on PBS, 1991

Now the entire province, including its cities, coastal port facilities, and refineries was directly in front of his troops, defended by only a few hundred desultory Saudi National Guard troops.

The United States believed that Saudi Arabia was, indeed, next. But Saddam's commanders had apparently outrun their supply lines. The Iraqis were relatively disorganized, even looting supermarkets in Kuwait City to feed the troops. Instead of punching into Saudi Arabia, the Republican Guard stopped at the border, digging in and consolidating its positions.

Saddam was a specialist at keeping enemies guessing and off balance. The sudden halt of his troops at the Kuwait-Saudi border was no exception.

The Least You Need to Know

♦ Saddam Hussein, the Kuwaitis, and the United States all miscalculated what might happen after Iraq invaded Kuwait.

♦ Saddam was determined to have access to Kuwait's oil money and the Kuwaitis didn't think he was serious.

♦ Iraq conquered Kuwait relatively easily, but ran into problems that indicated its fighting force wasn't extremely professional.

♦ Iraq surprised almost everyone by not invading Saudi Arabia.

Chapter 7

Occupation, Frustration, Preparation

In This Chapter

- ◆ The United States tries to hammer together an international coalition
- ◆ Osama bin Ladin meets the Saudis
- ◆ Life inside occupied Kuwait
- ◆ Iraq uses hostages to prevent retaliation
- ◆ The United States starts moving in forces

Eleven P.M. in Kuwait City is 4 P.M. in Washington, D.C. At almost the precise moment that radar technicians first spotted Iraqi tanks pushing toward Kuwait, the Joint Chiefs of Staff were wrapping up their Washington meeting. It took almost five hours for the first word of the invasion to reach the highest levels of the U.S. government. The first few hours—and days—were a study in confusion, both in Kuwait and in Washington.

In this chapter, we'll take a look at how that confusion evolved into determination, at life inside the occupied city, and at the beginnings of Operation Desert Shield. We'll also examine how a fateful meeting between Saudi officials and a hero of the "Holy War" against the Soviets in Afghanistan had deadly consequences far beyond the Gulf.

Initial Confusion

A few days before the invasion, the DIA had sent one of its CENTCOM liaison officers, Maj. John Feeley, to the U.S. Embassy in Kuwait. Before dawn on August 2, about the time the Kuwaiti 35th Brigade was slugging it out in the dark with Iraqi tanks, Feeley fired up the embassy's secure satellite link with CENTCOM and reported that the country had been invaded. It was just about four in the morning, and 9 P.M. on the east coast of the United States.

CENTCOM relayed the information to the Washington office of Secretary of Defense Dick Cheney, the U.S. Vice President as this book is being written. One of Cheney's deputies, Adm. Bill Owens, telephoned the defense secretary with the news. Word was also passed to joint chiefs chairman Colin Powell and National Security Advisor Brent Scowcroft. Scowcroft informed President Bush. Both men were shocked.

Almost two hours later, at 10:50 P.M. Washington time on August 1, the Associated Press moved the following flash: "BULLETIN—Kuwait Claims Iraqi Invasion." Officials from the joint chiefs, DIA, and CETNCOM monitored the situation as Iraqi special forces and tanks began rolling into Kuwait City and shelling broke out around the U.S. Embassy.

The next morning, President Bush met reporters in the White House to condemn the invasion. But he also said the United States would not send troops, a statement that made his top advisors wince. The mini news conference was followed by a meeting of the top Bush advisors. They heard that Kuwait was being conquered rapidly, that the United States had neither ground troops nor jets in the area, and the most that could be done immediately was to offer a squadron of American fighter planes to Saudi Arabia.

Heads Up! _____

Helen Thomas, United Press International: "Do you contemplate intervention as one of your options?

President Bush: "We're not discussing intervention …. I'm not contemplating such action."

Thomas: "You're not contemplating any intervention or sending troops?"

President Bush: "I'm not contemplating such action."

—White House meeting with reporters, August 2, 1990

Later that day, Bush flew to Colorado for a meeting with British Prime Minister Margaret Thatcher. Born in 1925, Britain's first female prime minister, also known as the "Iron

Lady" for her conservative politics, was in political trouble at home, but she was still fiery enough to prod Bush privately at their meeting.

Almost every country in the world, including Arab nations in the Middle East, had publicly condemned the invasion. Thatcher convinced Bush to use the moment to forge an international alliance against Saddam.

 Heads Up!

"Look George, this is no time to go wobbly. We can't fall at the first fence."

—British Prime Minister Thatcher to President Bush, August 2, 1990

President George Bush meets with British Prime Minister Margaret Thatcher after Iraq's Invasion of Kuwait.

What's in It for Me?

Two hundred years before Saddam invaded Kuwait, Napoléon Bonaparte noted "Men are only moved by two levers—fear and self-interest."

That breathtakingly cynical maxim could sum up the involvement of the players in the Gulf War. Saddam's fear and self-interest are self-evident. The $2 million per day's worth of production from Kuwait's oil industry would go a long way toward lining his own pockets and beefing up his bloodthirsty military and security apparatus. He would get rid of any debts on the books to Kuwait. He would control 20 percent of the world's oil production. With the money, he could obliterate Israel and become the new Saladin. But the coalition that President Bush would try and build against Iraq was also moved by Napoléon's twin levers.

Allied Oil

We've already taken a look at the dependence of Europe and Japan on Arabian Gulf oil, and at America's role in protecting the global economy's free flow of petroleum. The early meetings of the president and his advisors focused almost solely on what the invasion would do to oil supplies and oil prices.

There was good reason to worry. Before Iraq invaded, world oil consumption and production were pretty much in equilibrium, about 67 million barrels a day. High production by Kuwait and other Gulf states was keeping the price per barrel around $15 a barrel. After the invasion, oil would shoot up, briefly, to about $34 a barrel. Fears of Saddam controlling 20 percent of the world's oil (40 percent if he seized Saudi Arabia) and their self-interest in preventing that motivated the United States, Japan, and Europe. But it was a far different set of priorities that motivated Middle Eastern rulers.

Convincing the Saudis

On his plane ride back to Washington from the meeting with Margaret Thatcher on August 2, President Bush telephoned Saudi King Fahd, Egypt's Pres. Hosni Mubarak, and Jordan's King Hussein. Of the three, the Saudis were the most important: The Saudis had oil while Jordan and Egypt didn't. The U.S. military, using satellite photos and intelligence by personnel in Kuwait (notably Col. Fred Hart), was estimating that Iraq could drive into Saudi Arabia and occupy its oil fields within days.

In the first few days, the Saudis didn't believe the threat to them was serious. In fact, Saudi army scouts had scooted across the border with Kuwait briefly and reported no Iraqi troops in sight. The Saudis turned down the anemic American offer of a fighter squadron, and demanded a briefing in person. Cheney and Schwartzkopf, along with their advisors met with King Fahd in Riyadh on August 6, showed him the satellite photos, and convinced him that Iraq might move against Saudi. The king suggested the Americans bring other Arabs into the coalition and agreed to allow U.S. troops onto Saudi soil.

The U.S. delegation didn't know that, before their meeting, Saudi officials had met with a variety of people to get their position on bringing "infidel" troops onto the holy soil of Saudi Arabia. As we'll see shortly, one of those people was Osama bin Ladin.

Egypt

Egypt received more U.S. aid than any other country except Israel. Pres. Hosni Mubarak was grateful, but he also knew that agreeing to a U.S.-brokered peace with Israel had cost Anwar Sadat his life. Egyptian fundamentalists had been kept under control through a program of arrest and torture, but there was no telling when they would erupt again.

Mubarak was right to be worried. Two months after Iraq invaded Kuwait, the speaker of the Egyptian People's Assembly (the parliament) was assassinated in a hail of bullets on a busy Cairo street.

Cheney flew from Saudi Arabia to Cairo and asked Mubarak for permission for the carrier USS *Eisenhower* to transit the Suez Canal. He also hinted that Egyptian troops would be most welcome in a coalition. Mubarak mentioned that Egypt owed the United States almost $6 billion in military debts. It was eventually agreed those debts could be written off. Egypt was on board.

> **The Machines**
>
> The USS *Eisenhower* (CVN-69), a Nimitz-class nuclear aircraft carrier, was launched in 1975. The 95,000-ton vessel carries 75 planes aboard and a crew of around 6,000. The *Eisenhower* was the first U.S. Navy combat ship to have women as part of its crew.

Fence Sitting in Jordan

A few chapters back, we talked about how the family of Jordan's King Hussein had been driven from Saudi Arabia in the 1920s. This exile made the current king none too likely to help the Saudis. King Hussein had been standing beside his grandfather when the old man was assassinated by Palestinian militants in 1951. His own troops had driven the PLO out of Jordan in the bloody Black September of 1970. More than half of Jordan was actually Palestinian because of all the refugees. History and demographics told King Hussein he wouldn't survive if he backed the United States. His country was chock-full of Palestinians, making up most of the population, and they supported Saddam.

But at the same time, Jordan feared and distrusted Iraq. King Hussein's survival meant he had to balance himself among more powerful neighbors—Israel, Syria, Iraq, and Saudi Arabia—as well as the Palestinians who comprised the majority of his own population. Jordan had always been the one Arab nation most likely to make peaceful deals with Israel. So King Hussein engaged in a little political theater; he publicly supported Iraq, knowing full well Iraq would lose and that the United States would have to forgive him eventually.

Syria

On the surface, Syria and its dictator Hafez al-Assad had no reason to cooperate with the United States. Syria harbored several militant terrorist groups both in Damascus and in Lebanon's *Bekka Valley*. Syria was a major player in attacks on Israel.

Gulf Lingo

The **Bekka Valley** runs through southern Lebanon, and is home to several wineries and spectacular Roman ruins. It is also home to several terror groups and their training camps, largely funded and supported by Syria.

In 1983, Syria shot down a U.S. reconnaissance plane, killing one pilot and capturing another. Syria, like Iraq, was ruled by the Ba'ath Party through a combination of terror and torture.

But Syria distrusted Iraq. The Syrian and Iraqi branches of the Ba'ath Party split in the 1970s, and Syria closed its border with Iraq. Assad supported Iran in the Iran-Iraq War. Assad also wanted better relations with the West. He brokered the release of two U.S. hostages in Lebanon in the spring of 1990. So Syria joined the coalition a month after the invasion for purely political reasons; Assad hoped the United States would destroy Saddam and leave the Syrian strongman as the sole leader of the Ba'ath party.

The Gulf States

There are, generally, two kinds of rulers in the Arab Gulf—rich and richer. The tiny nations of Bahrain, Qatar, the United Arab Emirates (Dubai and Abu Dhabi), Oman, and Yemen share the Arabian Peninsula with Saudi Arabia. All are ruled by sheiks, and all are rolling in oil money. All, that is, except Yemen, which reunified in May 1990 after a disastrous civil war between Marxists and monarchists. Through accident of geography, Yemen has no oil, is a financial basket case, and is a hotbed for Islamic fundamentalists.

So it was no surprise that Yemen supported Iraq. The Saudis retaliated by expelling a million Yemeni workers and devastating Yemen's economy. The rich Gulf nations, all fearing Iraq and the overthrow of their monarchies, pledged money, bases, and troops to the United States.

Palestinian Rage

One card the ever-opportunistic Saddam always used was the Palestinian situation. Everyone knew that the chairman of the PLO, *Yasser Arafat*, would support Iraq. The trick to holding the coalition together would be to marginalize Arafat by co-opting his political and financial support in the Arab world.

Who's Who

Yasser Arafat was born Muhammad Abed Ar'ouf Arafat in 1929, either in Egypt or in the Gaza Strip. He became head of the PLO in 1969. His campaign for a Palestinian homeland in the 1970s included direct or indirect underwriting of attacks against Israel. Factional PLO fighting in the 1980s reduced his authority. He was a co-recipient of the Nobel Peace Prize in 1994 along with Israeli prime Minister Yitzhak Rabin. Arafat became president of the Palestinian Authority, a quasi-government for Palestinians, in 1996.

The United States succeeded, since countries that had helped Arafat militarily, such as Syria, and countries that had supported him financially, such as Saudi Arabia and the Gulf States, cut him loose, at least for the duration of the Gulf War.

Cooling Israel

In April 1990, Saddam said he had chemical weapons and would use them against Israel. By August, he had deployed dozens of missiles in western Iraq capable of striking Israel. The United States knew Israeli Prime Minister Yitzhak Shamir wouldn't hesitate to use his air force to pound Iraq. But it was also clear that any action by Israel—any action at all—would play into Saddam's hands, fracture the coalition, and turn the invasion into an Arab-Israeli conflict.

But Shamir was already steaming about Bush administration criticism of Israeli settlements in Arab areas of the Occupied Territories. President Bush relied on his powers of personal persuasion and charm in repeated calls to Shamir, assuring him that if push ever did come to shove, the United States would defend Israel. Shamir, over the objections of his own defense minister, agreed. Israel agreed to restrain itself in the hope Saddam could be crushed and that Arab countries allied with the United States would temper their hostility. The courageous Israeli decision was the key to holding the entire coalition together.

Osama Makes an Offer

Neither Cheney nor Schwartzkopf knew it, but as they were preparing to meet with King Fahd on August 6, 1990, the king was studying a proposal forwarded to him by his brother, Defense Minister Prince Sultan bin Abdul Aziz. It was a proposal for *jihad* against the Iraqis formulated by a man named Osama bin Ladin.

The bin Ladin family was well known in Saudi Arabia. Osama's father, Sheik Muhammad bin Ladin, was a construction magnate and multimillionaire with access to the Saudi royal family. Osama, one of his 20 sons, was attracted to the fundamentalist Wahabi brand of Islam. When the Soviet Union invaded Afghanistan in 1979, Osama traveled there with some of his millions of dollars.

Gulf Lingo

Jihad is defined by extremist fundamentalists as meaning "holy war," specifically, holy war against nonbelievers and secular Muslims. Moderate Muslims define jihad as "struggle," a spiritual struggle against the world's temptations.

Osama built roads, schools, and hospitals, using his money and engineering expertise. He began recruiting, training, and paying Arabs to fight as "holy warriors" in Afghanistan, using both his family's money and gifts from other rich Saudis. After the Soviets left in 1989, he returned to Saudi Arabia and was praised as a hero who had used Islam to drive off the godless Russians. But he kept using his money and contacts to support Muslim extremists across the Middle East. So in August 1990, he came to the Saudi defense minister with an idea.

He told Prince Sultan that he could recruit an army of 100,000 holy warriors and use them to drive the secular Iraqis from Kuwait. Pointing at charts and maps of the region, Osama heatedly told the Saudi officials that allowing American unbelievers onto the holy soil of Saudi Arabia was an insult to all Muslims and had to be prevented at all costs.

Prince Sultan reportedly was friendly, but asked Osama what he proposed to do about the Iraqi's 4,000 tanks, massed artillery, Republican Guard units, and chemical and biological weapons. Osama replied, "We will defeat them with our faith."

Prince Sultan promised to pass on the offer, but indicated that it would probably be declined. Osama was enraged and stalked out. He would remain in Saudi Arabia throughout the Gulf War, growing angrier and angrier at the sight of U.S. Christians and Jews bringing their weapons onto the sacred Saudi soil. He became a human time bomb.

> **Desert Lore**
>
> The Soviet Union invaded Afghanistan in December 1979, a little more than a month after Islamic extremists seized the U.S. hostages in Iran. The Soviets occupied the country and tried to prop up its pro-Communist government. They failed, and after a bloody 10-year war, withdrew in June 1989, paving the way for a fundamentalist takeover in Afghanistan.

> **Heads Up!**
>
> "Totalitarians like bin Ladin treat issues as fodder for their apocalyptic imagination. They want power and call it God."
>
> —Prof. Todd Gitlin, New York University, 2001

Occupation!

Within a week of the invasion, the United Nations Security Council passed three resolutions condemning Iraq, slapping an economic embargo on Iraq and occupied Kuwait, and refusing to recognize the occupation government. To the Iraqis, the resolutions were only so much as paper. Commanders had given their troops free rein to pillage Kuwait. They did it with gusto. As sporadic firing erupted near the U.S. Embassy the first day of the invasion, a 22-year-old Kuwaiti woman who worked at the Justice Ministry was being pistol-whipped by an Iraqi soldier. A Kuwaiti man tried to intervene and was shot dead. The soldier then threw the woman to the ground, ripped off her shoes, and burned the soles of her feet with a cigarette lighter. It was a hint of what was to come.

The Iraqis began to fortify their positions with anything they could steal from homes, offices, businesses, and hospitals. Supermarkets were looted to feed the troops. Iraq announced that Kuwait was no longer an independent country, but the "19th province" of Iraq. Kuwaiti license plates were banned, replaced with Iraqi plates that read "Kuwait: Province of Iraq." Executions and detentions of foreign workers and Kuwaitis began immediately. Houses containing pictures of the emir, Kuwaiti flags, or any "symbol of Kuwait" were burned.

> **Desert Lore**
>
> Amnesty International catalogued 38 separate torture methods used by the Iraqis in Kuwait. They included cutting out tongues; cutting off ears; driving nails into hands and feet; raping or torturing prisoners in the presence of relatives; driving bottle necks into a prisoner's rectum; and using flames or electrical shocks on prisoners' genitals.

Resistance and Retribution

After the fall of France to the Nazis in 1940, the French Resistance fought a guerrilla war against the Germans, huddled in basements listening to the BBC for war news. After the fall of Kuwait, those Kuwaitis who couldn't flee to five-star hotel exile in Egypt or Saudi Arabia fought the Iraqis, unfolding outlawed satellite dishes to watch war news on CNN.

The Kuwaiti Resistance was formed largely along extended family lines, with no central command authority. Town by town, block by block, family by family, many Kuwaitis formed irregular units to stymie the Iraqis and pass intelligence on to the West.

One day after the invasion on August 3, women and children took to the streets, carrying pictures of the emir. On August 4, street signs and house numbers began to disappear across the city, frustrating the Iraqis in their drive to hunt down suspected Kuwaiti military officers and government officials. The next day, August 5, The Iraqis

> **Heads Up!**
>
> "Two houses were destroyed and burned. Two terrorists captured. Search is continuing. Fifteen suspects were arrested. Three houses burned."
>
> —Logbook of Iraq's 106th Infantry Division, August 1990

> **Desert Lore**
>
> After the Gulf War, thousands of Iraqi documents were captured by Allied forces. Document 500-1-1 orders Iraqi troops to control the civilian population "… with a hand on the trigger." Document 520-2 was summed up simply in its title line: "Death Penalty for Absenteeism."

ordered all Kuwaitis to return to work. Instead, thousands stayed off their jobs. Saddam finally had to issue orders to deal with the growing problem.

The Resistance went well beyond civil disobedience. Kuwaiti police and National Guard armories were emptied of weapons. Molotov cocktails were dropped from overpasses into Iraqi trucks and tanks. Rocket-propelled grenades were fired into the Iraqi Embassy. The Kuwaitis even took advantage of a shortage of Iraqi transport to ambush occupation soldiers.

> **Heads Up!**
>
> "There were no Kuwaiti puppets which Iraq could use to form a government. Every Kuwaiti was in the Resistance."
>
> —Kuwaiti Col. Ahmad ar-Rahmani, 1994

The Iraqis didn't have enough vehicles for all the troops, so Iraqi soldiers made it a practice to commandeer rides from passing Kuwaitis. The Kuwaitis would lure them into their homes with offers of tea or a hot meal, then shoot them or slit their throats. The Iraqis began to retaliate with executions. Meanwhile, word of what was going on trickled back to the United States.

The Trip Wire

Immediately after his meeting with King Fahd and his stopover in Cairo, defense secretary Cheney met President Bush at the White House and told him the Saudis had given the green light to American troops. Bush ordered the first forces sent, and the Joint Chiefs of Staff sent out directives. Two squadrons of *F-15 fighters* based on the Pacific island of Guam and the Indian Ocean island of Diego Garcia were ordered to Saudi Arabia.

In addition, the aircraft carriers USS *Independence* and USS *Eisenhower* were ordered into the Gulf region immediately, backed up by the carriers USS *Saratoga* and USS *John F. Kennedy*. In addition, the 2nd Brigade of the legendary 82nd Airborne Division arrived in Dhahran, Saudi Arabia, on August 9. The brigade, which served as the fast-responding "ready brigade" had around 2,000 men, some light antitank weapons, and its M551 Sheridan tanks. The 82nd Airborne Division (nicknamed the "Eight-Deuce," officially the "All American") was formed as an infantry division in 1917. In 1942, it became the first airborne unit in the U.S. Army. Based at Fort Bragg, North Carolina, the 82nd has seen action in World War I, World War II, Vietnam, Grenada, Panama, and Desert Storm.

> **The Machines**
>
> The F-15 Eagle first entered service in 1974. The F-15 models A and C are single-seat fighters, while the F-15/B, D, and E carries two crewmen to hit ground targets as well as other planes. The 64-foot-long jet can fly at a top speed of 1,875 miles per hour, and carries a variety of missiles.

The 2nd Brigade of the 82nd also got a new nickname: "The Trip Wire," meaning that if Saddam's thousands of tanks and hundreds of thousands of men moved into Saudi Arabia, the 2nd Brigade's job was to slow them down with a few dozen tanks and a couple of thousand men.

The first U.S. troops on Saudi soil immediately began securing the Dhahran Air Base and preparing a nearby port for a landing by U.S. Marines. They also discovered that they were the first elements of a new operation—*Operation Desert Shield.*

A few pages back, we talked about CENTCOM and the DIA coming up with a project called Internal Look 90 before the invasion of Kuwait. The scenario it projected for putting U.S. troops onto the Arabian Peninsula was now in full swing.

> **Desert Lore**
>
> According to Colin Powell, his staff and that of CENT-COM commander Gen. Norman Schwartzkopf came up with several names for the operation to defend Saudi Arabia. Peninsula Shield and Crescent Shield were rejected before they settled on Desert Shield. Schwartzkopf suggested that once offensive operations started, Desert Shield be changed to Desert Storm.

Be Our Special Guest

On August 2, 1990, Saddam issued an order forbidding U.S. citizens or any other foreign nationals from leaving Iraq or Kuwait. Military personnel, civilian businessmen and their families, oil workers, relief agency employees, embassy personnel, and others found themselves trapped. On August 12, the border between Kuwait and Saudi Arabia was finally closed, and a British citizen trying to cross into Saudi was shot and killed.

On August 20, Saddam began a full-scale project of protecting Iraqi industrial and military installations from Allied air attack. All Americans, British subjects, and others who had been captured in Kuwait were taken to Baghdad. They included everyone from eight American oil workers captured the first day to women and children.

They were then taken to facilities ranging from airfields and chemical plants to power-generating stations and suspected chemical warfare research laboratories. More than 100 Americans, along with hundreds of other foreign nationals, were being used as human shields to prevent attack. The Iraqi government referred to the hostages as "special guests."

> **Heads Up!**
>
> "Americans ... are held against their will in Iraq. Saddam calls them guests. They are held in direct contravention of international law. I don't believe Adolf Hitler ever participated in anything of that nature."
>
> —Pres. George Bush, November 1, 1990

At the time, I was a reporter in Baghdad where other journalists and I were treated to some of the more surreal photo opportunities in the history of Saddam's media manipulation. We were allowed to interview many of the "special guests." On videotape, they would tell us they were being treated well. Once the cameras stopped rolling, the hostages would whisper to us to pass along information to their families and, if we could, get them out.

One of the photo ops backfired badly. Saddam himself was videotaped tousling the hair of a British boy who was being held with his family. The image of a dictator like Saddam laying his hands on an eight-year-old child caused an eruption of outrage around the world. By the end of August, Saddam agreed to release the hundreds of women and children he was holding. The male hostages remained in place.

Meanwhile, the trickle of U.S. and Allied forces into Saudi Arabia was increasing.

The Least You Need to Know

- The United States had to balance different interests among many countries to form the coalition.
- Osama bin Ladin's hatred for the U.S. presence in Saudi Arabia set the stage for later terrorism.
- The Iraqi occupation of Kuwait was brutal and led to resistance from Kuwaitis.
- The first U.S. troops weren't numerous enough to prevent an Iraqi invasion of Saudi Arabia.
- Saddam Hussein used hostages to prevent Allied air strikes on Iraq.

Chapter 8

Building Up, Holding Tight

In This Chapter

◆ American troops pour into Saudi Arabia

◆ Culture clashes become inevitable as the Saudis encounter the twentieth-century West on their own soil

◆ The Iraqis dig into their Kuwaiti positions

◆ Diplomacy and oil take center stage

In August 1990, the United States found itself having to deploy thousands of troops and millions of tons of equipment halfway around the world as fast as possible. Iraq seemed poised to make a run into Saudi Arabia, with only a pair of U.S. F-15 squadrons and the tanks, men, and helicopters of one 82nd Airborne brigade to stop them.

"Amateurs talk tactics but professionals talk logistics," is one of the favorite sayings of the Army Forces Command, the Military Airlift Command, the Transportation Command, and every other branch of the military that moves people and equipment. They were about to face their biggest challenge.

The First Troops Arrive

Take a look at any big city phone book, and you'll get an idea of the size of *OPLAN 1002-90*, CENTCOM's working plan to defend the Arabian Peninsula. The daunting details can be summed up easily: It would take more than four months to get enough people and equipment in place to drive Saddam out of Kuwait.

When the first 82nd Airborne troops got off their C-141 transport in Dhahran, they found a modern air base, the home of Saudi Squadron 16. Their job was to secure the base and its X-shaped twin runways, as well as prepare the nearby port of al-Jubayl for the arrival of the Marines. Meanwhile, the first 48 F-15s were arriving at various Saudi military bases.

Gulf Lingo

OPLAN 1002-90

(Operations Plan 1002, also just called "ten-oh-two") grew out of the INTERNAL LOOK exercise in the summer of 1990. It predicted that to get more than 200,000 troops and their tanks, trucks, and bullets to Saudi Arabia would take 17 weeks and would involve almost all of the United States' airlift and sea-lift capabilities.

Heads Up!

"The nature of the current crisis [is] such that even vast financial interests could not be deemed likely to affect the integrity of the services the Government may expect from its chief foreign policy officers."

—President Bush memo to Attorney General Dick Thornburgh, August 8, 1990

The first American general to set up shop in Saudi Arabia was not a tactician or strategist. He was Gen. William Pagonis, who arrived in Riyadh with his staff to oversee logistics. Pagonis knew that if the Iraqis moved in force, they could be in Riyadh within a week. But while he geared up the machine that would move the military, and while the Eight-Deuce wondered how much resistance they could offer to 100,000 of Saddam's troops, the Bush administration had to deal with a different issue.

Conflicts of Interest?

On August 8, 1990, President Bush addressed the nation to explain why he was sending American troops to Saudi Arabia. That same day, he drafted a statement for the attorney general, asking for a waiver from federal conflict-of-interest laws. The president wanted to make sure that he would be able to deal with the Persian Gulf crisis using all of his advisors. Many of them, especially Secretary of State James Baker, had interests in the oil industry, and a strict reading of federal law would prevent Baker from advising Bush about Saudi Arabia, Kuwait, and Iraq, because of their oil.

The president himself had been in the oil business since 1952 and had met Texas oil executive James Baker in the early 1960s. At the start of Desert Shield, Baker had interests in Amoco, Exxon, Texaco, and more than a dozen oil well leases. They were deemed not to be a conflict of interest.

The Arabs Join

On August 10, the Arab League met for the first time since its headquarters had been moved back to Cairo. They hotly debated whether to condemn Iraq and just how far they should go. Finally, they voted to send a Pan-Arab military force to Saudi, but it wasn't unanimous. Pakistan, Egypt, Syria, Saudi Arabia, and Morocco led the fight for the troops; Iraq, Libya, and Yemen opposed it.

This presented Saddam with a new problem—he could no longer sell the war as a fight between Arabs and the West. But Saddam, the secular opportunist, could use Scripture to try and convince other Arabs that it was blasphemy to fight alongside nonbelievers. Sections of the Koran indicate that Muslims should not fight using non-Muslims as allies. In Book 19, section 4472, Muhammad refuses to let a courageous soldier join a military campaign because the soldier did not believe in Allah.

Coincidentally, this was the same justification used by Osama bin Ladin to oppose Western troops in Saudi. The culture shock experienced by many Westerners in Saudi Arabia played into the theory.

Culture Shock

Dropping Western troops raised on hamburgers, rock and roll, and television into a rich, insular Islamic country is asking for trouble. Most of the time, though, nothing happened, mainly because of the briefings on Saudi culture and society the U.S. military provided to its personnel.

The different standards, though, resulted in one persistent urban legend with no con-firmed basis in fact: that an air force (or marine) officer had an affair with a Saudi woman, leading to the officer being shipped back stateside and the woman being beheaded. I did, however, witness one very real incident in which a female network cameraperson and I went shopping at a mall near Dhahran. She was hit in the back with a stick carried by one of the mutwa, the Saudi religious police force that patrols public places to enforce obedi-ence to strict Saudi religious codes. Her crime was that she wore a short-sleeved shirt. The woman, strapping and healthy, punched the mutwa and knocked him to the ground. It was a minor incident, defused quickly, but it became a metaphor for expatriate life inside a country like Saudi Arabia.

The Magic Kingdom

To understand the dilemma faced by the Saudis, and the problems encountered by for-eigners in the kingdom, you have to understand Saudi Arabia. A few pages back, we talked about the founding of Saudi Arabia and how the country's guiding principles are rooted in the fundamentalist philosophy of Wahabism.

Saudi Arabia practices *Sharia*—strict Islamic law. It extends well beyond the law, and applies to day-to-day living, since to a devout Muslim, Islam governs every aspect of life. Saudi Arabia, Iran, Sudan, and to a lesser extent, Libya, practice Sharia. Although much has been made in the West about how Saudis drink and carouse when they're abroad, to a Saudi, observing strict Islamic law is a duty only while in Islamic nations, not while in nonbelievers' countries.

American and Allied troops in Saudi Arabia quickly discovered how Sharia affected everyday life. Westerners isolated inside oil company living compounds (like those run by Aramco) or in military barracks or embassies weren't bound by the tenets of Sharia. But once they stepped outside into the real world of the Kingdom of Saudi Arabia, they found that …

- Women were not allowed to go out in public unless they were accompanied by a male.
- Women were not allowed to drive vehicles.
- Women and men could not dine together in restaurants unless they were specially licensed "family" restaurants.
- Women were required to wear an *abaya*—a black covering—even in scorching temperatures. Saudi women also wore black veils. Westerners often referred to Saudi women as BMOs—black moving objects.
- The mutwa religious police would strictly enforce dress and appearance codes.
- Alcohol, of course, was strictly forbidden.
- Crimes ranging from murder and sedition to homosexuality were punished by beheading. Women, however, were not beheaded. They were executed either by pistol shot or by being stoned to death.

To understand how all this has become part of the fabric of everyday Saudi life—and how it plays into the hands of terrorists who operate under the flag of Islam—you have to understand fundamentalism's relationship to the Saudi royal family.

> **Who's Who**
>
> The Ulema in Saudi Arabia are religious scholars and leaders. They also serve as judges, attorneys, and officials at mosques, as well as make up the powerful Council of the Assembly of Senior Ulema. They are consulted about every policy undertaken by the Saudi government.

There are, more or less, 30,000 royal family brothers, nephews, and distant cousins in Saudi. They are the official guardians of Mecca, the city toward which a billion Muslims worldwide turn and pray five times every day.

In 1979, there was a brief and bloody uprising in Mecca, when fundamentalists took over the shrine. The royal family managed to put it down, but had to forge a much closer relationship with the *Ulema*, the Saudi holy men and clerics who oversee so much of Saudi life.

The royal family, aware of fundamentalist unrest in other Islamic societies, poured millions of dollars into the *madrassas*, strict Islamic schools run by the scholars. Those schools existed not only in Saudi Arabia, but in Pakistan and other Muslim nations, and aimed to spread the fundamentalist Wahabi-style philosophy of Islam.

All of this would come to a head in later years, with the rise of Osama bin Ladin and the Saudi hijackers who slammed jets into the Pentagon and the World Trade Center in 2001. But as American troops arrived in the sweltering summer of 1990, they found themselves in a kingdom teetering precariously among modernization, fundamentalism, and 100,000 Iraqi troops just across the border.

The Iraqis Fortify

On the Iraqi side of the border, Saddam's army began to dig into its positions. It also began to redeploy its forces slowly, indicating that it had no intention of moving into Saudi Arabia, but rather it intended to make Kuwait a fortress and defend it.

Almost as soon as the border with Saudi Arabia was sealed on August 12, Republican Guard units began pulling back. They were eventually replaced with seven divisions of infantry and one division of armored infantry, strung out along the Kuwaiti border from the Persian Gulf all the way west into Iraq. Three Republican Guard armored divisions were placed in reserve in central Kuwait, with another three poised to reinforce the infantry just north of the Iraq-Kuwait border.

This brought total Iraqi troop strength in Kuwait to around 200,000. Saddam, as usual, played both ends against the middle. On one hand, the Iraqis told the charge d'affairs at the surrounded U.S. Embassy in Kuwait that the occupation of Kuwait was "irreversible." On the other hand, Iraq's ambassador to Washington indicated the situation was temporary.

> **Heads Up!**
>
> "The Iraqi forces will be withdrawn as soon as the situation has settled down …. [W]e hope this will be a matter of a few days, or a few weeks at the latest."
>
> —Muhammad al-Mashat, Iraqi ambassador to the United States, August 1990

As the Iraqis solidified their hold on Kuwait, the United States was quickly moving forces into the Saudi region. In addition to the F-15s from Guam and Diego Garcia, a squadron of F-16s from the United States arrived in Saudi. The F-16 Fighting Falcon entered service in 1975. Originally designed only to take on other fighters, it was modified for ground support. It carries a single pilot, can reach a top speed of 1,500 miles per hour, and can be armed with a variety of missiles and heavy bombs. The aircraft carrier USS *Independence*, a venerable warhorse that had seen duty in the 1962 Cuban Missile Crisis, Vietnam, and the invasion of Grenada, became the first carrier to enter the Arabian Gulf since 1974.

The Iraqis, meanwhile, told all foreign embassies in Kuwait to evacuate by August 24. "Evacuate," in this case, meant being taken as hostages to Iraq. The United States and other embassies battened down for what would be a long siege. Meanwhile, the relatively poor Iraqis "liberated" almost everything they could from the relatively rich Kuwaitis. If it wasn't bolted down—and even if it was—someone carted it back north of the border.

Heads Up!

"We saw hundreds of cars from Kuwaiti car dealerships being transported on Iraqi HETs (heavy equipment transporters), T-72s (tanks) towing boats from the Kuwaiti yacht basin, and military trucks loaded down with booty."

—Col. Fred Hart, *The Iraqi Invasion of Kuwait: An Eyewitness Account*, U.S. Army War College, 1994

The little human intelligence the United States had on the ground in Kuwait and the spy satellite photos merely showed a hubbub of movement by the Iraqis. There was still no way for the United States or the Saudis to know what Saddam was planning next. Taking Winston Churchill's dictum as a guide—"Pray for peace but prepare for war"—the United States had no choice but to assume the worst.

Moving the Earth

Early in August, U.S. Forces Command issued a summary report with speculation about what Iraq might do next. Options included …

The Machines

The Patriot Antimissile and Antiaircraft System (mim 104 Patriot) was first produced in late 1981. Each launcher, mounted on the back of a trailer, contains four of the 17.5-foot-long missiles. Each missile can reach three times the speed of sound and carries a 200-pound warhead. First developed as an antiaircraft weapon, the Patriot became an antimissile system in the Gulf War.

- Invading eastern Saudi Arabia to seize oil facilities and ports.
- Attacking U.S. and coalition ships as they passed into the Persian Gulf.
- Using missiles with chemical or conventional warheads to bombard airfields and ports.

The Iraqis sitting still and doing nothing was not among the possibilities discussed. So FORSCOM set a goal: Within five weeks, move more than 50,000 soldiers, more than 650 tanks, 150 attack helicopters, and 50 *Patriot Antimissile Systems* into Saudi Arabia.

The bulk of the burden fell onto the Military Sealift Command, the MSC. While jets could carry small numbers of troops, and even some light armor, the huge M1A1 Abrams battle tanks, heavy artillery, and tons of fuel and supplies needed to sustain them had to be moved by ship.

Problems began to pop up. The 1st Calvary Division, for example, was supposed to be on station in Saudi Arabia by September 15, 1990. But due to a shortage of ships that could get equipment from Houston to Saudi, the date was moved back by a month.

The MSC, unlike most of the military, depended largely on civilians to get the job done. The command either leased civilian vessels from U.S. companies, or used its own ships crewed not by sailors, but by civilian mariners. While military ships were designated USS (United States Ship), the MSC's hybrids bore the prefix USNS (United States Naval Ship).

There had been warnings for years that America's sea-lift capability was being hamstrung by a shortage of both vessels and mariners. At the start of Desert Shield, for example, the average age of a member of the U.S. Merchant Marine was over 50. There was also a shortage of roll-on/roll-off ships, the kind where vehicles could drive into and off of the vessels without being hoisted onto a deck or into a cargo hold.

Despite shortages and miscues, much of the sea-lift operation went surprisingly well. For example, the transport ship USNS *Capella* arrived in Savannah, Georgia, on August 11. By August 13, it was headed toward Saudi Arabia, loaded with 88 heavy tanks, 10 attack helicopters, various antiaircraft guns and missiles, 100 advance troops of the army's 24th Mechanized Division, and 38 armored fighting vehicles. These vehicles are sort of minitanks that can carry infantry. The Bradley, for example, has an antitank missile launcher and a 25-millimeter cannon, travels on tanklike treads, and can carry a crew of three plus six soldiers.

The sea-lift and airlift operations outlined in OPLAN 1002 were starting to move. The only question in the minds of operational planners was whether Saddam would hold off long enough for all the materiel to arrive.

> **Heads Up!**
>
> "This no-notice war spotlighted two major inadequacies … that required correction: greater numbers of roll-on/roll-off ships were needed, and force readiness required improvement."
>
> —Capt. Robert Kesteloot (Ret.), former director of strategic sea lift, 2001

The Oil Equation

As we've noted before, the United States' primary domestic concern over oil in the region focused on Saudi Arabia, which supplied the United States with a large percentage of its oil. Internationally, the United States was worried about the flow of oil through the Arabian Gulf, since that oil largely powered the economies of Europe and Japan.

In August 1990, there was a glut of oil on world markets. When the United Nations slapped sanctions on Iraq and occupied Kuwait, it took oil from both countries off the world market. In a strict supply-and-demand world, that shouldn't have caused a price spike, because of the oversupply.

But oil markets, like most of human activity, are powered by psychology. And the invasion caused a sharp spike in prices, along with scattered panic buying, especially when it seemed Iraq might seize Saudi oil fields. So the U.S. economy was shoved into a recession, a downtown whose effects wouldn't become apparent until after the Gulf War.

Despite the sudden run-up in prices, there was no increased exploration for oil in the United States. In fact, the Federal Reserve in September 1990 noted that oil drilling was declining in the "oil patch" of Oklahoma and West Texas. U.S. oil companies had long since decided to move much of their exploration overseas, where they could drill unhampered by American labor and environmental regulations. U.S. officials, though, initially said the rationale for assisting Saudi and Kuwait was to protect U.S. jobs.

> **Heads Up!** _____
>
> "The economic lifeline of the industrial world runs from the Gulf .... To bring it down to the level of the average American citizen, let me say that means jobs. If you want to sum it up in one word, it means jobs."
>
> —Secretary of State James Baker, August 1990

As we'll see in the next chapter, the Bush administration faced a bit of a public relations problem selling U.S. intervention to a public that was skeptical of the oil industry and specifically of oil-based regimes in the Middle East.

But as Desert Shield began, the U.S. economy began to contract, consumer confidence plunged, consumption of consumer goods dropped, oil prices rose, and the stock market's Standard and Poor's 500 Index had dropped around 8 percent.

There were other reasons that the Iraqi invasion weakened the U.S. economy. Inflated real estate markets were collapsing and the savings and loan crisis led to the insolvency of a large number of financial institutions. Going to war is an expensive business, and the United States found itself mobilizing as a recession was starting.

But the nature of America's allies helped take off the financial edge. By the time the Gulf War ended, the United States had spent around $80 billion (in 2001 dollars). But in the end, the war only cost about $5 billion in real dollars, since the wealthy oil states of the Gulf reimbursed the United States for most of the cost of the war.

For the U.S. troops deploying to the Gulf, however, this was all so much megabookkeeping. The diplomatic and military temperature was rising as fast as the mercury in the scorching Middle East.

The Least You Need to Know

- ◆ The United States rushed troops and equipment to the aid of Saudi Arabia.
- ◆ Iraqi troops began to dig in to their Kuwaiti positions, looting as they went.
- ◆ The culture of insular Saudi Arabia not only was strange to U.S. troops, it also provided the basis for many later terror acts.
- ◆ The movement of troops and weapons to the Middle East was one of the largest logistical operations ever undertaken.
- ◆ The politics of oil remained central to the conflict.

Chapter 9

Countdown

In This Chapter

- ◆ The first shots of Operation Desert Shield are fired
- ◆ Concerns grow about Iraq's possible use of chemical weapons
- ◆ Diplomats take one more shot at averting an all-out war
- ◆ The overall strategy for a war begins to emerge, just as a public relations campaign to sell the war effort begins

The United States was now committed, full bore, to leading an international coalition. In an astonishingly short amount of time, the Bush administration had marshaled support at the United Nations, among Arab countries, and in the NATO alliance. The first U.S. and Egyptian troops had arrived in Saudi. An impressive flotilla of U.S. sea power was on its way to the Gulf.

But there was confusion as to what exactly the end goal was going to be. Keeping oil flowing through the Persian Gulf was a given. And the United States had made it clear that it intended to defend Saudi Arabia should the Iraqis push across the border. But beyond that, things were murky. Would force be used to expel Saddam from Kuwait? Would the United States go beyond that and attack Iraq? Could there be a negotiated settlement? And how hard would the United States strike back if its ships, planes, or troops were attacked? In this chapter, we look at what happened as the goals became clearer, and as the clock ticked down.

Blockade Running

On August 6, the United Nations passed Resolution 661, putting sanctions on Iraq and occupied Kuwait. On August 11, joint chiefs chairman Gen. Colin Powell issued orders from the Pentagon calling for a "quarantine" of Iraq and Kuwait. The word *quarantine* had last been used in the Cuban Missile Crisis of 1962, and was largely viewed as a synonym for *blockade*.

> ## Heads Up!
>
> "All States shall prevent the import into their territories of all commodities and products originating in Iraq or Kuwait exported therefrom after the date of the present resolution."
>
> —U.N. Resolution 661, August 6, 1990

The word made diplomats nervous because Resolution 661 never mentioned what sort of force might be used to enforce the sanctions. The Soviets used their seat on the U.N. Security Council to make it clear that they felt no force could be used, and that their old ally Iraq would have to comply voluntarily with any sanctions.

The word *quarantine* lasted less than a day, quickly replaced by Powell's office with *interception*. But in his Tampa headquarters, CENTCOM commander Gen. Norman Schwartzkopf had other ideas. Powell had once described being around Schwartzkopf as like being around "… a hand grenade with the pin pulled."

By the time President Bush authorized the U.S. Navy (aided by the Coast Guard) to start intercepting Iraqi shipping on August 16, Schwartzkopf's own orders for maritime intercept operations were ready to go. He called the plan Operation Stigma, and it left no doubt that military force was to be used to stop Iraqi ships.

About the same time those orders went out, a ghost from World War II was thundering through the Mediterranean heading toward the Persian Gulf. In a war that would see the emergence of twenty-first-century smart bombs, pinpoint missiles, and gee-whiz technology, the plated steel and 16-inch guns of the battleship USS *Wisconsin* would play a vital role.

The USS *Wisconsin* (BB-64) was first launched exactly two years after Pearl Harbor— December 7, 1943. Weighing 52,000 tons and almost as long as nine football fields, the Wisconsin saw action in the Pacific during World War II and Korea, and was mothballed in 1958. She was recommissioned in 1986, served in the Gulf War, and was decommissioned for the final time in late 1991. She is now berthed in Norfolk, Virginia.

No matter what anyone called the job the USS *Wisconsin* performed in the Gulf War— quarantine or interception operation—this was now a blockade.

Intercepts, Shots Fired

The first test came on August 17, when the cruiser USS *England* encountered two Iraqi cargo ships. They radioed that they were empty, and failed to stop. CENTCOM ordered that they be allowed to go on to Iraq, since they carried no cargo. That sparked the first of many flaps between Schwartzkopf and Powell.

Powell angrily told Schwartzkopf to stop ships, empty or full. The next day, the USS *England* intercepted a Chinese ship coming from Iraq. Wary over offending the Chinese, CENTCOM ordered that the ship be allowed to sail on to China.

 Heads Up!

"Let them (the empty Iraqi ships) go. There's no use starting World War Three over empty tankers."

—Gen. Norman Schwartzkopf, *It Doesn't Take a Hero,* Bantam Books, 1993

The rest of that same day, August 18, was a study in confusion. The destroyer USS *Scott* stopped a ship bound for Jordan, and it agreed to return to Sudan. But both Sudan and Jordan filed diplomatic protests.

The frigate USS *Reid* then tried to stop an Iraqi tanker that refused to halt. The *Reid* fired warning shots at the ship, but it still forged ahead. The ship's commander contacted the CENTCOM naval commander, who contacted CENTCOM in Tampa. CENTCOM called Powell at the Joint Chiefs of Staff, and the joint chiefs called the National Security Council, which in turn, called President Bush. The decision was made to let the Iraqi ship go. The Bush administration decided to get a new resolution from the U.N. specifically authorizing the use of force. They got it: Resolution 665. Adopted August 25, 1990, it authorized Allied naval forces to use "such measures commensurate with the specific circumstances" to halt shipping to and from Iraq and Kuwait.

The first shots had been fired.

Jordan's King Hussein, under pressure from Pro-Saddam Palestinians in Jordan, supports Saddam in public while trying to broker a solution to the crisis.

The Sieve in Jordan

King Hussein of Jordan, as we detailed a few chapters back, supported Saddam out of political necessity—more than half of Jordan's population was Palestinian, not Jordanian, and those Palestinians were firmly in Saddam's corner. In addition, before the invasion, Iraq was Jordan's biggest trading partner to the tune of $400 billion a year in two-way commerce.

Iraq imported three-quarters of its food, and paid for it by oil exports. Iraqi oil was squeezed off through the Gulf, and the pipelines running into Turkey and Saudi Arabia were shut down. So the 100-mile-long border between Iraq and Jordan and the Amman-to-Baghdad highway became just about the only way to get anything into or out of Iraq.

The United States knew the importance of that route, and tried a carrot-and-stick approach with King Hussein. The carrot was an offer of additional economic aid if Jordan went along with the embargo. The stick was a threat to blockade almost-landlocked Jordan's only port, Aqaba, a city of 100,000 squeezed between Israel and Saudi Arabia.

King Hussein felt the squeeze in many ways. The United States was threatening him, while thousands of Palestinians demonstrated daily in Jordan in support of Saddam. The worst problem, though, came from the 750,000 refugees—mostly Indians, Palestinians, Pakistanis, Bangladeshis, Egyptians, and Filipinos—fleeing Iraq and Kuwait who ended up in refugee camps in Jordan. At the Sha'alan refugee camp, one Pakistani doctor welcomed me and my TV camera crew by saying, "Welcome to hell, population 100,000 and growing."

King Hussein refused the U.S. offer of extra aid, but also promised to keep Iraqi exports from flowing through Aqaba. The Gulf States cut off aid to Jordan, Jordan's trade with Iraq was crippled, and the Hashemite Kingdom had to deal with hundreds of thousands of refugees. Jordan's economy became a basket case, and the king turned a blind eye to the trailer trucks filled with goods for Iraq that rumbled down the rutted highway toward Baghdad. As we'll see shortly, King Hussein would make one final try to save his economy and negotiate a settlement.

Chemical Weapons Worries

The Allies had good reason to worry about Iraq's possible use of chemical or biological weapons. The United States, Germany, and other countries had allowed Iraq to import chemical, biological, and nuclear material, legally, for years. In 1986, for example, the United States allowed 26 separate shipments of toxins ranging from anthrax to botulism sent to Baghdad. In addition, France, Britain, the Soviet Union, Switzerland, Germany, and the United States had been shipping so-called dual-use chemicals to Iraq since the 1970s. Iraq had managed to obtain plenty of chemicals from the West because of their dual-use nature. For example, hydrogen cyanide is a deadly chemical gas, and is also used as a pesticide. Triethanolamine is used to make nerve gas, but is also an industrial solvent.

The Pentagon also knew that the standard chemical protective suits issued to American troops were ineffective against some of the chemicals Iraq had used against Iran, chemicals spread in finely powdered dust. Days after the invasion, the U.S. military formed the Dusty Agent Working Group, trying to come up with a fix. Their suggestion? U.S. troops should wear ponchos or raincoats over their chemical suits to try and keep the deadly agents out.

Available stocks of chemical protective suits were shipped from Europe to Saudi Arabia within two weeks of the invasion. The CIA was busily sending out a series of Threat Reports, noting that Iraq had stepped up its production of mustard gas, sarin, and other general purpose nerve weapons.

As the buildup continued, including chemical suits and gas masks, diplomats from various nations prepared to give peace a final chance.

> **Heads Up!**
>
> "The Iraqis are capable of delivering CW [chemical warfare] agents by mortar, a variety of tube artillery, surface-to-surface rockets, air-to-surface rockets, and aerial bombs."
>
> —Defense Intelligence Agency message to CENTCOM, August 29, 1990

Heated Diplomacy

August 24 was the deadline the Iraqis set for closing all embassies in Kuwait. The U.S. Embassy closed, but 30 personnel stayed behind, stocked with all the water and precooked food embassy personnel had been able to scrounge up. Around 1,000 U.S. nationals, including the embassy's marine guards, were taken to Baghdad, where they became de facto hostages.

The buildup, meanwhile, continued at astonishing speed. By the last week in August, more than 200 U.S. aircraft—including *B-52* bombers—were stationed in Saudi Arabia. Some 40,000 U.S. troops were on station, along with 7,000 Kuwaiti soldiers who had managed to escape, 5,000 Egyptians, 3,000 soldiers from the Gulf States, 8,500 French troops, 1,000 Moroccans, 1,200 Syrians, and 45,000 men of the Saudi Army. In addition, some 70,000 Turkish troops were poised along their border with Iraq. The British Royal Air Force had arrived with several squadrons of jets. And the battleship *Wisconsin* had sailed into the Arabian

> **The Machines**
>
> The B-52 Stratofortress bomber entered service in 1955, making it a good deal older than any of its crew. Updated with fresh engines, avionics, and weapons systems every few years, the B-52 is projected to last in service until about 2045. The B-52 carries a crew of six and up to 70,000 pounds of missiles, mines, and bombs.

Gulf to join a quickly expanding armada. If Iraq tried to move into Saudi Arabia now, it would face not only a fierce fight in the south, but would also have Turkish troops pushing into Iraq from the north.

Several parties decided it was time to give peace a chance. Again.

Jordan Tries

The day after Iraq invaded Kuwait, King Hussein of Jordan had flown to Baghdad and had received Saddam's astonishingly transparent agreement to withdraw from Kuwait. The king had tried to hammer together what he called "an Arab solution," but the video of the king embracing Saddam in Baghdad didn't sit well with the Egyptians, the Syrians, or the Gulf States.

The king then flew to Maine and met with President Bush at the president's vacation home. As usual, the beleaguered king was trying to play both ends against the middle. His reception at Kennebunkport was only a few degrees warmer than frosty.

Heads Up!

"I think he'd [King Hussein] like to find some way to be helpful, and he reiterated his interest of making everything in an Arab context. But I had an opportunity to tell him my views."

—Pres. George Bush, August 16, 1990

On September 5, King Hussein flew back to Baghdad, only to be sandbagged. Hussein wanted to see if withdrawal from Kuwait was negotiable, as Saddam had indicated in August. Saddam called in members of his General Staff and dryly asked them what the military opinion would be on withdrawal. The generals practically broke into tears, begging Saddam not to even consider such a move. The king dropped the issue, unaware that Saddam had made even discussing withdrawal an offense punishable by firing squad.

The French Connection

America's oldest ally had sent the Foreign Legion to Saudi Arabia and had condemned the invasion in the U.N. But as always, the French insisted on going their own way, suspicious of Anglo-Saxon motives. France, after all, had helped Saddam build roads, bridges, airports, factories, and the nuclear reactor that the Israelis bombed in 1981. French Pres. Jacques Chirac had even once called Saddam "a personal friend." Nicknamed "the bulldozer" for his headstrong ways, Chirac had served as a member of the National Assembly, premier twice, and mayor of Paris. He was elected president of France in 1995, championing a policy of conservative nationalism.

In early September, the French began to urge a policy of moderation, trying to use their long-standing ties with Iraq to negotiate a peaceful settlement. Despite sending thousands of troops to Saudi Arabia, Defense Minister Jean-Pierre Chevenement was dead set against any military action. In fact in 1991, he resigned rather than lend his name to military operations against Iraq.

Despite that, Foreign Minister Roland Dumas warned the Iraqis that time was running out for them to withdraw from Kuwait. He was ignored.

Jesse

Veteran civil rights activist the Rev. Jesse Jackson became involved in the effort to free Iraqi "guests." His supporters said it was evidence of Jackson's humanitarian concerns, while his detractors said it was evidence of Jackson's thirst for publicity.

On September 1, Jackson visited Baghdad, meeting with Saddam Hussein as well as several of the hostages. Whatever Jackson's motives, his results were solid. Eleven ill men were released, and the same day more than 500 women and children were allowed to leave. Some of the hostages, though, were less than impressed with this and other diplomatic efforts.

> **Heads Up!**
>
> "No legal basis exists today for armed intervention against Iraq or even to liberate Kuwait."
> —French Defense Minister Jean-Pierre Chevenement, September 5, 1990

> **Desert Lore**
>
> As recounted by Col. Fred Hart, many of the "special guests" saw the diplomatic trips to Baghdad to get hostages released as nothing more than political theater. Some of the hostages began referring to the parade of dignitaries as "Bargaining for Bodies."

With Friends Like These

The Kuwaitis, meanwhile, weren't doing themselves any favors in the diplomacy department. By early September, stories were circulating in the Western media about rich Kuwaitis living in splendid exile in posh hotels throughout the Middle East and Europe while their maids, drivers, and nannies from Pakistan, Egypt, and Sri Lanka were raped and tortured by Iraqi soldiers. As we'll see in the next chapter, many Palestinians working in Kuwait were only too glad to betray their former masters and collaborate with Iraq.

Nine days after the invasion, the exiled emir and his family hired what was then the largest public relations firm in the world, Hill and Knowlton, to put out their side of the story. Even that didn't help much when it came time for a delegation of U.S. senators to visit Saudi Arabia at the start of September.

In his book *The Commanders* (Simon and Schuster, 1991), journalist Bob Woodward details how the delegation visited U.S. troops and Saudi rulers, but were refused a meeting with the emir. The arrogance of the Kuwaitis stunned the delegation. According to Woodward, Sen. William Cohen of Maine later told President Bush, "We visited the Kuwaitis, we saw the Kuwaitis, and we realized the Kuwaitis as willing to fight—until every U.S. soldier has dropped."

Schwartzkopf's Strategy

By this time, CENTCOM had shifted its operations to Riyadh, and Norman Schwartzkopf had set up his command center in the Saudi capital.

In Schwartzkopf's case, *command* was a verb. Burly, bearlike, and bullying, the general demanded complete and total control over every aspect of the operation. In fact, according to journalist William Arkin writing in the U.S. military newspaper *Stars and Stripes*, Schwartzkopf even tried to ban intelligence agents from the DIA from the area because they'd been operating out of Jordan without his knowledge.

Since early August, CENTCOM planners had been devising an air campaign against Iraq. At the beginning, it was merely designed to strike Saddam's forces and Baghdad in case the Iraqi army crossed into Saudi. But joint chiefs Chairman Powell wanted it expanded to cripple the Iraqi military. Some overeager air force general staffers concluded that the plan, preliminarily called *Operation Instant Thunder*, could cripple Iraq within a week.

Gulf Lingo

Operation Instant Thunder was the code name given to the initial plan to strike Iraq from the air. It eventually morphed and expanded into the air campaign used in Desert Storm.

Schwartzkopf was many things, rude and overbearing among them. But he was also, first and always, an infantryman. His tours of duty in Vietnam had convinced him that overwhelming ground force was the key to winning any conflict. On that, he and Powell were in complete agreement.

Air Power First

In the early days of Desert Shield, Schwartzkopf was concerned with protecting his troops and trying to make sure they could delay and survive any massive Iraqi onslaught. Air power, in that scenario, would have been used to destroy Iraqi tanks and blast advancing Iraqi infantry.

But as Allied forces moved into Saudi Arabia in greater numbers, Schwartzkopf began to refine the plan that would eventually become Desert Storm. In its rough draft, it consisted of four parts:

- ◆ Strike deep into Iraq, hammering Saddam Hussein's command and control facilities, industrial infrastructure, airfields, radar installations, and communications facilities.

- ◆ Destroy antiaircraft guns, missiles, and radar in occupied Kuwait.
- ◆ Blast Iraqi ground troops with constant bombardments to reduce their fighting capability significantly.
- ◆ Launch a ground campaign against a weakened and demoralized Iraqi army.

Schwartzkopf was a boots-on-the-ground kind of commander, but he'd outlined a four-part campaign, and three parts were to be carried out from the air.

Overwhelming Force

Back when OPLAN 1002-90 was devised, it called for more than 200,000 U.S. troops to defend Saudi Arabia. This was a continuation of a doctrine first formulated under Secretary of Defense Caspar Weinberger in the Reagan administration, and which was strongly supported by Colin Powell. In fact, the idea soon became known as the *Powell Doctrine*.

The Powell Doctrine, as it's popularly known, says that American troops should never be sent into combat unless they have overwhelming superiority against an enemy. In addition, any use of U.S. forces must have total political support and a clear exit strategy.

Both Powell and Schwartzkopf served in Vietnam, and both blamed the debacle there on the lack of political support in Washington. First and foremost, they believed there should be unambiguous support for the mission, and clearly defined goals. Second, there had to be a plan for removing American troops, and not turning them into a semipermanent occupation army. And finally, there had to be enough firepower to destroy any enemy convincingly and in the shortest amount of time possible. It was a theory of total war that went all the way back to *Ulysses S. Grant* in the American Civil War.

There was going to be no Vietnam-style incrementalism in the Arabian Gulf. Schwartzkopf and Powell disagreed on many things, but they were of a single mind when it came to this—punish Iraqi troops from the air, sea, and land until they had no options but to retreat, surrender, or die.

> **Desert Lore**
>
> Ulysses S. Grant became known as "Unconditional Surrender" Grant during the Civil War for his fierce approach to fighting. His strategy was always to overwhelm the enemy with superior firepower, stretch out Confederate lines until they were too thin to resist an assault, and to always be on the offensive.

The General Takes Prisoners

By late September, the vise was tightening around Iraq. In addition to the sea and land blockade, the United Nations approved an air blockade of Iraq. At the same time, U.S.

intelligence continued to issue reports on the possible use of chemical weapons by Saddam's forces. One DIA message noted that the Iraqis notified their own troops that chemical weapons were about to be used by shooting off red and green flares.

On September 26, General Schwartzkopf became the first among the Allies to take Iraqi prisoners. He was inspecting the terrain along Saudi Arabia's border with Iraq when his convoy encountered an Iraqi army truck that had crossed the border. Inside were two Iraqi soldiers, who immediately surrendered and said they had come south looking for food and water.

The incident told Schwartzkopf and his staff that the Iraqis were poorly supplied and that the troops dug in facing Saudi had something of a morale problem. The Americans also found that the Iraqi soldiers gas masks were still encased in packing material, showing that the troops hadn't even tried them on yet.

Schwartzkopf began to suspect that the much-vaunted Iraqi army was a good deal less than it seemed. But as the clock continued to tick, he wasn't taking any chances. More and more troops and equipment kept rolling into Saudi Arabia.

The Least You Need to Know

- ◆ The initial naval blockade of Iraqi shipping was mired down in strategic and diplomatic confusion.
- ◆ The United States and its allies were concerned about Iraq's possible use of chemical weapons.
- ◆ The French, the Jordanians, and Jesse Jackson—along with many others—attempted to find some sort of diplomatic solution to the crisis.
- ◆ The U.S. doctrine was going to be to use overwhelming military force against Iraqi positions.

Chapter 10

Last-Minute Moves

In This Chapter

- ◆ Public relations spin takes center stage in Washington, while U.S. troops encounter the realities of desert living

- ◆ The Iraqis continue to reinforce their positions in Kuwait, and find many foreign workers there willing to collaborate with them

- ◆ The Allied coalition works out its plans for striking Iraq and Kuwait while diplomats take one last shot at defusing the crisis

- ◆ Iraq gets a final deadline for pulling out of Kuwait, and ignores it

On September 1, 1939, a few months before Nazi Germany invaded Poland to start World War II, the Nazis and the Allies made military moves, prepared for an eventual war, and traded diplomatic notes. In a pun on the German tactic of blitzkrieg, this period was known as the *sitskreig*, also called "The Phony War."

The period from October 1990 through January 17, 1991, was much the same in the Persian Gulf region. The Iraqis and the Allies glared at each other across the border between Kuwait and Saudi Arabia. Both sides reinforced their military positions. Both sides used the media to sell their side of the story. But Saddam continued to pillage Kuwait and refused to withdraw. It was time for a real war in the desert.

Doubts at Home

As we noted in the last chapter, many Americans were dubious about going to war to support wealthy Arab sheikdoms, especially with memories of Arab oil embargoes in 1973 and 1978 fresh in their minds. At first, the Bush administration's secretary of state, James Baker, tried to frame the conflict in terms of oil and American jobs.

President Bush, an old oil man himself, saw it in far less parochial terms. As a combat veteran of World War II, the president believed it was a simple struggle of good versus evil, of democracy versus a totalitarian invader. Iraq was an international bully and had to be taught a lesson.

Selling the Shield

The Kuwaiti government in exile knew it had an image problem, so it hired the public relations firm of Hill and Knowlton to sell its story to the Americans. It's estimated the firm was paid around $11 million for its work as it sent out press kits and helped set up witnesses for congressional hearings. The head of the firm's Washington office, Craig Fuller, had been chief of staff to Bush when he was vice-president. The company had clout and access. Hill and Knowlton, in late 1990, was the world's largest public relations firm. After the Gulf War, the firm shrank due to layoffs, recession, and the lack of Kuwaiti money.

The high point for the firm and the Kuwaiti government came during congressional hearings in October. A 15-year old Kuwaiti girl, only known as Nayirah, tearfully testified that she had seen Iraqi soldiers in Kuwait City invade a hospital, dump babies out of incubators, and steal the incubators for shipment to Iraq. The babies, she sobbed, died.

The media, public, and politicians reacted with outrage. It was an astonishing story. It was also a total fabrication. After the war, it was revealed that Nayirah was actually Nayirah Nasir al-Sabah, a member of the Kuwaiti royal family, and that her father was Kuwait's ambassador to the United States. The hospital incident was a lie, made up by the Kuwaitis and Hill and Knowlton.

Iraq Uses the Media

Iraq's media manipulation, by contrast to Kuwait's, was ham-handed but effective. I was in Baghdad during this period, and saw how bugged hotel rooms, the dour Iraqi internal security apparatus, and censors in news work spaces led to the worst form of censorship: self-censorship.

Journalists, often intimidated by armed guards and constant badgering by Iraqi officials, occasionally left critical details about Saddam's regime out of their stories. However, there were ways to get around the problem. At the time, I was working for *CNN*. A skeleton staff remained at the otherwise empty U.S. Embassy in Baghdad, and they let Western journalists use their secure phones, which bypassed the listening government operatives in the Iraqi telephone company.

Wary that our stories would be censored as we fed them from the Iraqi government-run satellite uplink, we would file our audio directly to our newsroom on the secure telephones. To avoid having our pictures censored, we would insert what we in TV called a flash frame in each story.

Desert Lore

CNN (Cable News Network) was founded in 1980 by Atlanta billionaire Ted Turner. It was the first global TV news network. During the Gulf War, billions of people in hundreds of countries watched its coverage. CNN is now owned by the AOL-Time Warner media conglomerate.

Video feeds 28 images every second. One image lasts 1/28th of a second, invisible to the naked eye, and is therefore called a flash frame. In one case, for example, we interviewed members of the Kuwaiti Resistance who had fled to Baghdad and were hiding out, waiting to be smuggled out of Iraq. We fed a voice track to CNN's Atlanta headquarters on the secure embassy phone, and then inserted a single video frame of the resistance fighters somewhere in our stories. The Iraqi censors at the satellite feed point would realize we had interviewed a resistance fighter and would stop the video tape. They would then fast-forward past the offending part and allow the rest of the story to feed.

But by using the complete audio track fed by phone, and by freezing the single frame of video and using it, videotape editors in Atlanta were able to assemble a complete story, uncensored. The Iraqis finally figured out the trick, since they were watching CNN along with the rest of the planet. It was one of the reasons I was declared persona non grata and expelled from Iraq in late September, 1990.

Living in the Desert

Living in the Saudi Arabian desert is not like walking in the sand at your favorite beach. The sand in Saudi is usually the consistency of talcum powder, and can easily work its way into aircraft turbines, tank and armored personnel carrier gearboxes, and the eyes, ears, and throats of individual troopers.

In addition, the Arabian Peninsula is home to all sorts of bacteria, viruses, and animals that created difficulties for U.S. troops beyond the cultural difficulties we've mentioned previously. The biggest problem is one familiar to anyone who has ever traveled abroad— serious intestinal problems, including diarrhea, stomach cramps, and nausea. Most of those symptoms are caused by the shigella bacterium, and at one point or another, two-thirds of the U.S. troops deployed in Saudi suffered from what became known as Saddam's Revenge.

Desert Lore

General Schwartzkopf's General Order One forbade pornography, body-building magazines, alcohol, display of religious symbols, or almost anything else that might offend the Saudis.

Then there was the problem of the troops being in a strictly Islamic country. For a short while, some Saudi religious leaders demanded that all trash from the U.S. troops be shipped out of Saudi Arabia immediately. There was also Schwartzkopf's *General Order One*, which ruled, among other things, that no crosses or any other non-Islamic religious symbols could be worn or displayed, and that all Jewish religious services would have to be held aboard ship and not in Saudi Arabia itself.

This was the first major overseas combat deployment in U.S. history that featured a large number of females in regular military roles. American women in uniform presented a problem for the Saudis, given the repressed position of women in Saudi society. For example, women in the U.S. armed forces regularly drove vehicles of all kinds. But Saudi law forbade women from driving. So according to the Saudi religious decree issued just for Desert Shield, U.S. women were not females when they were driving.

Heads Up!

"U.S. female military personnel in uniform are not women when driving military vehicles."
—Saudi religious decree, September 1990

Living conditions varied, depending on what part of Saudi which unit was stationed in. If, for example, you were helping maintain supplies at the port of al-Jubayl, you slept in a mammoth warehouse, with barely adequate bathroom facilities and no privacy. For some in logistics and support units, it was like living in a combination aircraft hangar and prison.

Then there were the forward-deployed units, having to make do in the middle of a desert that seemed to support only snakes, scorpions, and desert rats. Only the Bedouin tribesmen had been able to take this hostile Mars-like environment and make a home in it. The Bedouins are nomadic tribes who have lived in the deserts of the Arabian Peninsula, North Africa, and Syria for centuries. They are known for their horsemanship, fierceness as warriors, and for their hospitality. They often raise and herd either sheep or camels.

The experience of the 82nd Field Artillery of the U.S. Army's 1st Cavalry Division is relatively typical. When at its base, or AA (assembly area), the soldiers either slept in army-issue tents, or in tents available from the local Bedouins. As one soldier noted, that meant two kinds of living conditions: "bad or worse." The Bedouin tents were woven wool and could easily burst into flames. That meant no smoking in them, and no heaters to guard against the bitterly cold desert nights.

Water was a constant worry, since the average person could dehydrate within hours unless he drank several gallons of water every day. Tanker trucks full of drinkable water made available by the Saudi government helped solve the problem, along with endless cases of bottled water. As for food, it was either standard Army MREs—Meals, Ready to Eat—or local mutton, canned food, or whatever else was available.

Forward deployed units, whether Special Forces or Marine Reconnaissance, had even more rudimentary surroundings. They would sleep burrowed into the sand itself, sleeping bags tightly zipped and sealed to prevent scorpions or any other unwelcome visitors from making themselves at home. Fires in the far desert were strictly forbidden, for fear of attracting snipers. So morning coffee consisted of a packet of instant coffee emptied between the cheek and gum and washed down with a slug of bottled water. What it lacked in taste it more than made up for in caffeinated jolt.

Across the border in Iraq and Kuwait, Iraqi grunts were also digging in, albeit in a much more primitive way.

The Iraqis Fortify Kuwait

As the crisis went on, the Iraqis pulled their elite Republican Guard units back toward northern Kuwait and into Iraq itself. The number of troops in Kuwait doubled, but the forces were now made up largely of conscripts. The same was true of many of the Iraqi units facing the coalition across the border between Saudi and Iraq.

Why? It seems in hindsight that Saddam realized that, sooner or later, his forces would be facing a massive assault by the coalition. And the canny dictator was in no mood to sacrifice his elite units when he could use draftees. So hundreds of thousands of conscripts, mostly from towns and cities in Iraq's north and south, were shipped out to the unfamiliar desert. In northern Iraq, Saddam had faced uprisings from the Kurds. In southern Iraq, he faced opposition (admittedly disorganized) from Shia Muslims. So he took young men from both of those politically unreliable areas and dropped them into Kuwait and his barren desert facing Saudi Arabia. After all, why not have the Allies help him depopulate areas that had always been a problem?

So Iraq began fortifying Kuwait, under the assumption that the same battle rules that had worked in the war with Iran would work against the Allied coalition. The Iraqis fully expected the

> **Heads Up!**
>
> "He (the Iraqi soldier) broke down in tears. He told me he was only fourteen and that he had to join the army to protect the lives of his mother and his sisters. His orders were to kill and bring back valuables. He had no choice."
>
> —Prasanti Rao, Indian from Kuwait describing his encounter with an Iraqi draftee in 1990, *National Post* newspaper (Canada) June 30, 2001

Allies to follow standard terrain in any attack, meaning that the main highway leading north from Saudi to Kuwait would be a primary defensive stronghold, along with the Wadi al Batin, a dry riverbed running into southwest Kuwait.

The Iraqis also used defensive obstacles that had proven effective against Iranian attacks, namely sand bulldozed into wall-like berms and trenches that could be filled with oil or gasoline and ignited. The occupying army also found some allies among the estimated 350,000 Palestinians who lived in Kuwait. A small minority of the Palestinian population collaborated with Iraq, helping Saddam's forces keep basic infrastructure like electric generating plants and port facilities operating. Other foreign workers were also pressed into service by Iraq.

> **Heads Up!**
>
> "I feared I would be tortured and I feared for my two children."
>
> —Jordanian Abdal Ruhman al-Hussaini, newspaper writer in occupied Kuwait, May 1991

Iraqi troops were also busy placing explosive charges on hundreds of oil well heads throughout Kuwait. Saddam fully intended to give "scorched earth" a new meaning in case of war.

Targeting the Triad

CENTCOM's strategy for attack was taking shape. It would begin with the air campaign, and that campaign was coming into focus, but not without difficulty and confusion. Everyone agreed that the first part of the "triad" to be targeted would be Saddam Hussein's political and command structure. This included everything from military communications centers to various Ba'ath Party offices, since the military and the political were pretty well inseparable in Iraq.

The second-tier targets were supposed to be industrial. But Schwartzkopf and the Bush administration were becoming concerned over increased CIA and DIA cable traffic indicating that Iraq was capable of arming missiles and artillery shells with both chemical and biological warheads.

So the second-level targeting was changed to concentrate on Iraq's nuclear, biological, and chemical facilities, like those in the town of Salman Pak. Salman Pak is a facility south of Baghdad, along the Tigris River, used as Iraq's primary research facility for chemical and biological weapons. The fenced compound contains a villa used by Saddam Hussein. Despite numerous media reports about Salman Pak, it was not added to the list of coalition air targets until the last minute.

The third part of the targeting would be aimed at Republican Guard emplacements. While the air campaign was still designed to hammer all potential enemy troop concentrations, the Republican Guard divisions were moved higher on the target priority list simply because they were the most professional troops, with the best armor, best equipment, and best chance of causing trouble for coalition ground troops.

That was the plan, and it was a secret, that is until October 9, when the Air Force chief of staff, *Gen. Michael Dugan*, talked to reporters. Dugan told them the initial air campaign would be to "decapitate" the Iraqi leadership and target Saddam himself, and that it would be followed by a massive aerial assault. Defense Secretary Cheney and Joint Chiefs Chairman Powell went ballistic and fired Dugan, or more correctly, forced him to retire.

> **Who's Who**
>
> Michael Dugan was born in New York State in 1937. A West Point graduate, he flew 300 combat missions over Vietnam and became Air Force chief of staff in July 1990. He was forced to retire at the end of that year because of his media comments.

Enter the Jedi

The CENTCOM staff assisting Schwartzkopf had all sorts of expertise. But shockingly, when it came to planning a ground campaign against Saddam, they drew a blank. To be charitable, CENTCOM in the early days was far too busy figuring out how to delay an Iraqi thrust into Saudi to concentrate on an eventual ground attack on Iraq and Kuwait.

On September 18, three majors and a colonel, all graduates of the U.S. Army's School for Advanced Military Studies, arrived in Riyadh. Set up by the U.S. Army in 1984 and based at Fort Leavenworth, Kansas, this school provides graduate-level seminars on tactics and strategy for officers of not only the army, but also the navy, air force, and marine corps. In the Gulf War, their job was to plan for ground thrusts into occupied Kuwait and Iraq itself. Given their secret mission and their arcane knowledge of strategy and tactics, the four soon became known as "The Jedi Knights." It was a term of both respect and derision from the rest of Schwartzkopf's staff.

At first, the four Jedi had limited options because of the lack of sufficient coalition troops. Their initial plan was what football coaches call "straight up the gut"—a frontal assault into Kuwait from the south. But by late October, the Pentagon had decided to shift the Army's *VII Corps* from Europe to Saudi. The VII Corps's job had always been to stop any Soviet thrust into Europe. Now their tens of thousands of men and thousands of tanks were available to the Jedi.

> **The Machines**
>
> The Army's VII Corps in the Gulf consisted of the 1st Armored Division, the 3rd Division, and the famous 1st Infantry Division, also known as "The Big Red One." They would spearhead the ground assault into Iraq and then into western Kuwait.

With the additional resources available, the colonel and three majors of the Jedi devised an audacious plan for a ground assault, a plan that involved moving mammoth numbers of troops and tanks quickly into Iraq, then wheeling them around to punch into Kuwait from the west. Desert Storm had been born.

Diplomacy's Last Dance

By mid November, reserve and National Guard forces were being mobilized. In the end, they would amount to 70 percent of the army's Gulf forces. Ships, planes, and troops from around the world were arrayed in the desert. The U.S. Marines and the Saudi army staged a huge combat exercise just south of the Kuwait border.

On Thanksgiving—November 22—President and Mrs. Bush, Secretary of State Baker, and a host of other dignitaries arrived in Saudi Arabia for a Thanksgiving meal photo op with the troops. That same weekend, families of some troops, worried about reports of Iraqi chemical and biological weapons, formed the Desert Shield Association. Their job was to keep independent track of any reports of chem or bioweapons use, and document their effects on the troops. It was the first hint of the controversy to follow about the effects of chemical and biological agents on allied personnel.

Who's Who
Tariq Aziz was born Michael Yuhanna in Iraq in 1936. A Christian, he changed his name to Tariq Aziz, which means "glorious past." An English literature major, he rose through Ba'ath Party ranks to become deputy prime minister in 1979. He also served as foreign minister and is personally close to Saddam Hussein.

As November ended, the U.N. passed Resolution 678, authorizing the use of force unless Iraq withdrew from Kuwait by January 15, 1991. On the last day of November, Secretary of State Baker and Iraqi Foreign Minister *Tariq Aziz* met in Geneva, Switzerland. The same day, President Bush invited Aziz to Washington for talks.

Aziz agreed, but insisted the talks be tied to the Palestinian-Israeli conflict. Washington viewed the demand as a smoke screen, and refused. The Aziz-Baker meeting in Geneva lasted six hours. There were more diplomatic moves to come. But the Geneva meeting was the last real chance to stop the war.

The Last Holiday

As December began, the Bush administration was facing fierce opposition at home from Democrats in Congress who felt a war with Iraq would be a bloodbath and who opposed the president's unilateral military moves. Dozens of them even went to federal court to force the president to get congressional approval before committing any troops to combat. The case was tossed out.

Meanwhile, inside Iraq, U.S. and British intelligence monitored several missile firings. The missiles were aimed away from Saudi and coalition troops, but the message was unmistakable. Saddam had already warned the Saudis that he would hit them with missiles if they allowed their soil to be used to launch an attack on Kuwait. American intelligence believed that the Iraqis had made several attempts to mount chemical and biological warheads on their *SCUD missiles*. It was believed all the attempts had failed, but no one could be sure that Iraq would not rain chemical or biological agents down on coalition troops with their SCUD arsenal.

Meanwhile, the aircraft carrier USS *Saratoga* was steaming toward the Gulf region. The "Sara" docked in Haifa, Israel, in late December for shore leave. Haifa was a good liberty port, with plenty of bars, clubs, and restaurants to cater to young sailors headed toward the war zone. Because the seaport had long been a stopover for U.S. ships, it had an active USO chapter that had planted 241 trees in a memorial park to remember the 241 marines and sailors who died in the Beirut barracks bombing in 1983.

> **The Machines**
>
> SCUD was the NATO designation for the Soviet-made SS-1 family of artillery missiles. The Iraqis had purchased several variants from the Russians and Chinese. Roughly 34 feet long, each SCUD weighed around 10 tons and had an effective range of less than 200 miles.

It was almost midnight on December 21 when the Israeli ferry tender *Ein Tuvia* picked up 102 sailors from Haifa to ferry them back to the Saratoga. A few of the swabbies were in handcuffs, picked up by the Shore Patrol for being a shade too celebratory. As the tender pulled from the dock and rumbled into the harbor, it began to list. It capsized and sank in 65 feet of water in less than 20 seconds, apparently because valves to vent seawater had been accidentally left open and allowed the Mediterranean to swamp the boat. Twenty-one sailors drowned. It was the beginning of what would be a hard-luck cruise for the venerable *Saratoga*.

Christmas Day in Saudi Arabia found the Bob Hope show performing for the troops. Armed Forces Radio played Christmas music. Some troops got a hot turkey and all the trimmings. In the deep desert, others made do with cold MREs. CNN and other networks broadcast footage of American troops celebrating a Christian holy day on the Islamic soil of Saudi Arabia. At his family's home in Jeddah, Osama bin Ladin watched the videotape and was outraged.

Meanwhile, the flurry of diplomacy became a blizzard. As Vice President Dan Quayle visited U.S. troops in Saudi Arabia on New Year's Day, Iraq rejected Egypt's demand that it withdraw from Kuwait. A week later, the foreign ministers of three major Islamic nations—Turkey, Iran, and Pakistan—issued the same demand.

For moments on January 7, it looked as if Iraq were staging a surprise attack into Saudi Arabia. U.S. radios in northern Saudi squawked a warning used by allied forces during storm—"Red Air! Red Air!"—as army and marine gunners prepared to fire on incoming Iraqi aircraft. Instead, it turned out a half dozen Iraqi helicopters had scooted across the border as their crews sought asylum.

On January 9, Baker and Aziz met again in Geneva, a meeting President Bush had called "the final chance" to stop a war. Baker found Aziz had a grasp of realpolitik when it came to the Middle East. The suave Iraqi foreign minister placidly told the American secretary of state that Saddam had no fear of a war because "… no Middle East nation has ever entered into a war with Israel or the United States and lost politically."

Heads Up!

"… [I]t is said by some you do not understand just how isolated Iraq is and what Iraq faces as a result …. [U]nless you withdraw from Kuwait completely and without condition, you will lose more than Kuwait. What is at issue here is not the future of Kuwait … but the future of Iraq. The choice is yours to make."

—Letter from Pres. George Bush to Saddam Hussein, January 9, 1991

Heads Up!

"The Americans were piss poor when it came to the enemy's order of battle. In January, they thought Saddam had 35 divisions in Kuwait at first, this gradually rose to 40 then 43. It really didn't reinforce our faith in the intelligence-gathering process."

—Quote from an SAS commando in *SAS Gulf Warriors*, by Steve Crawford, Simon & Schuster, 1994

For Saddam, withdrawing from Kuwait would mean losing face as the new Saladin of the Arab Nation. He and his foreign minister knew they had no chance against the well-armed and -trained coalition forces. But the issue was not victory—it was Arab honor. That much became clear when Baker gave Aziz a letter for Saddam from President Bush. Aziz read it and calmly said he would refuse to deliver it to Baghdad, since he considered it "insulting."

Meanwhile, the U.S. Defense Department issued a statement putting Iraqi troop strength in the region at 540,000. This didn't impress some of the Allies, most notably the British, whose Special Air Service (SAS) commandos were specialists at gathering ground-level intelligence on enemy strength. The SAS consists of highly trained commando units skilled at infiltration, behind-the-lines operations, counterterrorism, and hostage rescue. The SAS is considered by many to be the world's premier special forces organization. The British suspected that the Americans, relying solely on satellite photos rather than human spies on the ground, were seriously over-estimating Iraqi manpower and capabilities.

On January 12, the U.S. Congress voted on a resolution supporting the use of force against Iraq. It wasn't exactly an overwhelming statement of confidence, passing 52 to 47 in the Senate and 250 to 183 in the House of Representatives, with the majority of Democrats in both houses opposing military action.

The U.N. deadline for Iraq to withdraw from Kuwait by January 15, 1991, came and went. On Wednesday,

January 16, it was 3 P.M. in Washington D.C. as the crews of nine Apache attack helicopters and one Blackhawk helicopter boarded their aircraft in the desert darkness.

Adjusting their night-vision goggles, the crewmen, all from the Army's 101st Airborne Division, slowly guided the helicopters off their landing pads. Joined by a squadron of search-and-rescue helicopters from the U.S. Air Force, they pulled up and headed north, toward Iraq. They were flying low, barely clearing the tops of some of the sand dunes that rolled across the desert like silent ocean waves.

It was 11 P.M. in Saudi Arabia.

The Least You Need to Know

◆ While Kuwait tried to "spin" its side of the media story, Iraq attempted to control information getting out of Baghdad.

◆ Living conditions in the desert were harsh for coalition troops.

◆ As Allied forces increased in Saudi Arabia, Allied planners hatched a daring plan to defeat Iraq in a combined air and ground campaign.

◆ Iraq ignored the U.N. deadline for leaving Kuwait, and all diplomatic efforts to resolve the crisis failed.

Part 3

Desert Storm— The Air War

The air war over Iraq was much more than video-game images of targets exploding. In this section, we look at the stories of the people who dropped bombs, and the people who found themselves underneath them. We also look at an Iraqi military move into Saudi Arabia, and the audacious Allied strategy for pushing Iraq out of Kuwait.

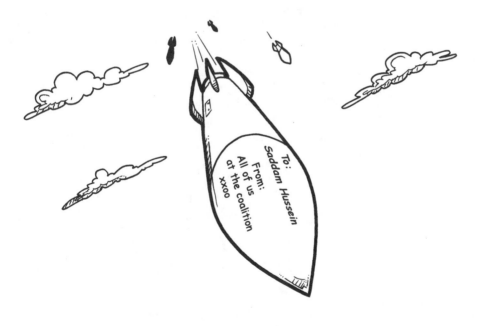

Chapter 11

January 17 to January 21, 1991

In This Chapter

◆ The first air strikes blind Iraq's radar to enable coalition jets to bomb Baghdad and other targets

◆ Iraq retaliates by firing SCUD missiles into Saudi Arabia and Israel

◆ The first of many controversies erupts about Iraq's chemical arsenal and about the effectiveness of the Patriot missiles

◆ Television makes it seem that the war is being broadcast live, while most action actually takes place away from the cameras

The Gulf War has been called the world's first war that was televised live. That's not exactly accurate. The difference between image and reality is a discussion that goes all the way back to Socrates and Plato. The images of antiaircraft fire bursting above Baghdad and of panic in Saudi and Israel as the first air raid sirens sounded were dramatic. But the reality of the war usually took place far from any cameras.

The video game nature of the conflict was amplified by Allied military briefings showing grainy green images exploding like so many video arcade aliens. But the reality of the air war was far from antiseptic. Death and fear and the smell of combat always are.

Hellfire Paves the Way

The desert is cold at night. So as the four massive MH-53 helicopters from the 20th Special Operations Squadron lifted off, the pilots could see their breath forming small puffs of fog inside the cockpits. It was 11 P.M. on January 16. Just behind them, eight Apache attack helicopters and a Blackhawk helicopter tilted their noses forward, picking up speed as they scooted across the Saudi desert into Iraqi airspace.

> **Desert Lore**
>
> The 101st Airborne Division, also called "The Screaming Eagles," is based at Fort Campbell, Kentucky. The 101st gained fame during World War II by holding out against the Nazis in Bastogne, Belgium while surrounded during 1944's Battle of the Bulge.

The Special Ops troops were along as insurance, just in case the attack helicopters crashed or were shot down. The Apaches and the Blackhawk belonged to the *101st Airborne Division*, and they were about to break the silence of the desert night with the first shots of Operation Desert Storm.

After hours of dune-top low-level flying, the helicopters reached their targets, an array of early warning radar stations in the Iraqi desert. There were two targets, 35 miles apart, so the attack Apaches peeled off into two attack teams. The attack teams maintained total radio silence until 10 seconds before they opened fire.

At 2:30 A.M. on January 17,1991, the Apaches cut loose with a volley of 27 Hellfire missiles. The AGM-114 Hellfire is an air-to-ground missile designed to be fired from attack helicopters. Each missile is around $5^{1}/_{2}$ feet long, weighs 100 pounds, and can strike ground targets ranging from tanks and artillery pieces to radar and other stationary installations.

Sixteen separate radar installations at each of the two sites vanished in the explosions and concussions. With the early warning radars now piles of twisted metal, a 20-mile-wide-air corridor was now open straight into Baghdad.

New Weapons

At almost the precise moment the Apaches were hitting their radar targets, the first Tomahawk cruise missiles ever fired in combat were being launched from the cruisers USS *Bunker Hill* and USS *San Jacinto*. More than 100 of the missiles would be fired in this first evening, grinding along at below the speed of sound toward targets in Iraq and Kuwait.

Also for the first time, the F-117 Stealth Fighter was used in combat. The bat-winged planes, designed to be almost invisible to radar, used their laser and radar-guided bombs and missiles to strike targets in Baghdad, including the Defense Ministry and the main telephone exchange. To make sure the super-secret fighters were based out of harm's way, they flew from the far southern Saudi city of *Taif*.

Hundreds of jets from the United States, Britain, France, Kuwait, and Saudi Arabia were in the air, but none flew a more unusual mission than the B-52 bombers flying from Louisiana. Seven of the B-52s flew what became the longest continual combat air mission in history, flying 14,000 miles nonstop over 36 hours. But it wasn't just the length of the flight that was unusual, it was the weapons they carried.

Until the Gulf War, air-launched cruise missiles (ALCMs) were armed with nuclear warheads and were designed to be used against the Soviets. But unknown to everyone except the bomber crews and top Pentagon planners, the Barksdale B-52s carried *cruise missiles* armed with conventional warheads. The missiles were so secret that the air force didn't even acknowledge their existence for months. Most of them hit their planned targets. Some did not. One ALCM slammed into a civilian apartment building in the southern Iraqi city of Basra.

Gulf Lingo

The city of **Taif** (or al-Taif) is in the mountain highlands of southwest Saudi Arabia, near the holy city of Mecca. It was chosen as the base for the Stealth Fighters because it's some 600 miles from Iraq, well out of the range of SCUD missiles.

The Machines

There are several varieties of cruise missiles. The sea-launched cruise missiles (SLCM) and air-launched cruise missiles (ALCM) were both used in the Gulf War. The subsonic missiles find their targets by means of terrain maps programmed into their onboard computers.

The carrier USS *Saratoga*, still reeling from the pre-Christmas loss of 21 sailors in Haifa, suffered even more losses as the air war began. Fighter Squadron 81, the Sunliners, was based aboard the Saratoga with their F-18s. Around 4 A.M., one of the fighters was hit by either a SAM missile or antiaircraft fire over western Iraq. The pilot, Lt. Comdr. Michael Speicher, born in 1958 in Missouri, managed to eject. His body was never found. After he vanished over Iraq, the Pentagon first listed him as missing in action, then changed it to killed in action. In 2001, the Defense Department again changed the designation to missing. His body has not been recovered, and some Gulf War activists are convinced he is an Iraqi prisoner.

In the United States, the first reports of bombs falling over Baghdad came from ABC News, quickly followed by CNN. The problem was that there were no falling bombs, at least not yet. The Iraqi capital's air defenses, alerted when their early warning radar went dead, sprang to life, arcing tracer and missile fire into the night sky. But they were firing at nothing, since the first jets and Tomahawks had yet to arrive.

Meanwhile, well out of sight of the cameras, the systematic destruction of Iraqi ground forces was starting. High-altitude B-52 runs pounded Republican Guard positions, while smaller aircraft struck at airfields, tanks, artillery, and troops in Iraq and Kuwait. By the end of the first 24 hours, more than 2,000 missions had been flown, and hundreds of cruise missiles launched. The Pentagon liked to brag that Saddam was hit with more tonnage in the first day than the Iranian air force dumped on Iraq in nine years.

> ## Heads Up!
>
> "This is an historic moment. We have in this past year made great progress in ending the long era of conflict and cold war. We have before us the opportunity to forge for ourselves and for future generations a new world order."
>
> —Pres. George Bush, address to the nation, January 16, 1991 (Washington time)

For those of us in Saudi Arabia, that first night was punctuated by air raid alarms and warnings from army and marine guards that Iraqi missiles were incoming, possibly loaded with chemical warheads. None of us had any way of knowing that these were false alarms and that the launches detected by U.S. satellites were actually antiaircraft missiles.

Just before dawn, unconfirmed reports of chemical weapons being used were filed by troops in northern Saudi Arabia. As conventional Iraqi rocket and artillery fire was launched against a Saudi oil refinery in the city of Khafji, allied forces were ordered to go to MOPP-1, their highest level of chemical and biological attack alert, which involves troops putting on gas masks, protective rubber gloves, protective boots, and chemical protective suits.

> ## Heads Up!
>
> "This is war, with all that the word implies. Afterwards, the enemy planes began their intensive bombings of the airfield we have been assigned to defend …. I am very worried for my relatives. I know they are alone out there. And I know how afraid they are."
>
> —Iraqi lieutenant's diary entry, January 17, 1991, reprinted in newspaper *Le Midi Libre* (France), March 23, 1991

Iraq Strikes Back

Saddam had repeatedly threatened to strike at Israel if war broke out, and around 2 A.M. on January 18, he did. But the SCUD-B missile, described by one reporter as having "… the aerodynamic characteristics of a falling bathtub," spirals into the Mediterranean Sea.

That one may have been a range finder, because it was followed with seven SCUD launches against Israel within a half-hour. Allied jets throughout the air war tried to target Iraqi missile launchers, and had a fair degree of success with stationary facilities. But the mobile launchers often managed to elude the coalition planes, especially in open stretches of desert. The Iraqis obviously knew their missiles couldn't be guided so much as aimed in a general direction. They also knew their warheads contained neither chemicals nor biological agents, but relatively small amounts of conventional explosives. So why launch an inaccurate spread of missiles at Israel?

Because Saddam's strategy was to hit Israel, killing and injuring civilians. His hope was that Israel would strike back at Iraq, turning the conflict into an Arab-Israeli war and destroying the coalition. Three of those seven missiles augered into the desert. But two SCUDs hit Tel Aviv, while another pair hit Haifa. The next few days would see a rain of SCUD strikes in Israel, including one that injured 45 people. There was fierce debate inside Israel's cabinet about striking back at Iraq, but in the end, assurances from President Bush and Secretary of State Baker convinced the Israeli government to hold its fire.

The Patriot Paradox

The same night that the SCUDs fell into Israel, one of the missiles was arcing toward the Dhahran Air Base in eastern Saudi Arabia, home of many of the coalition's planes. A Patriot missile was launched, intercepting the SCUD. It was great publicity for the Patriot, although not altogether accurate.

True, the Patriots did strike many incoming SCUDs. But they often hit the incoming missile in the fuel tank, not the warhead, which meant that the SCUD warhead was often blown loose from the body of the missile and then fell to earth and exploded anyway.

During the Gulf War, much of the Patriot's effectiveness was unquestioned. It was only later that investigations revealed that the Patriot system had not been nearly as accurate as advertised.

> **Desert Lore**
>
> A 1992 probe by the U.S. House of Representatives Government Operations Committee concluded that the Patriot missiles may have hit as few as 9 percent of the SCUDs they tried to intercept. One of the problems seemed to be that the rickety SCUDs often broke up in flight, and the Patriots hit debris, not the SCUD itself.

Shifting Targets

In the first five days of the air war, Iraq launched 33 SCUD strikes against Israel and Saudi Arabia. Israel's defense minister, Moshe Arens, and the chief of staff of the Israeli Defense Forces, Gen. Dan Shomron, urged Prime Minister Yitzhak Shamir to launch retaliatory strikes against Iraq.

Knowing that was precisely what Saddam wanted, President Bush telephoned Shamir and repeatedly assured the grizzled veteran of three full-scale wars with the Arabs that the Allied air forces would take care of the SCUD launchers.

After January 18, the coalition's air power was aimed at a new primary target, the 60 or so SCUD launchers inside Iraq. Thirty of them were thought to be in fixed sites, like the Wadi Amij facility in western Iraq and the Uum Quasr airbase near the southern city of *Basra.* But the other half of Iraq's SCUD launchers were mobile, mounted on Soviet-made

Gulf Lingo

Basra (or al-Basrah) is a city of one million people in southern Iraq. It sits on the Shaat-al-Arab waterway, the broad delta that flows into the Persian Gulf, formed by the union of the Tigris and Euphrates Rivers. It was the site of repeated battles during the Iran-Iraq War, and was bombed repeatedly by the Allies during the Gulf War.

MAZ-543 launch vehicles. Each MAZ rode on 16 large tires and a chassis made to withstand cross-country travel in rough terrain, meaning they could be driven to the exact center of nowhere, launch their missiles, and then disappear before Allied jets could spot them.

At the same time the decision was being made to shift the focus to SCUD launchers, a raggedy cold front staggered into Iraq, Kuwait, and northern Saudi Arabia. Starting on January 18, clouds and haze obscured targets, which meant that pilots couldn't guide their precision munitions precisely, which meant that hundreds of air strikes were aborted. But between the start of the air war and January 21, around 200 air missions were aimed specifically at SCUD sites. In addition, a battery of the Patriot missiles was hurriedly shipped from a U.S. base in Germany to Israel.

First Blood

The air war was a largely antiseptic video game affair, unless you were involved in it. Despite their sleek, high-tech appearance, an attack jet has little room for creature comforts. The cockpit can be either bitterly cold or a solar oven as sunlight steams through the canopy. It smells of grease and aircraft lubricants and metal. The ejection handle silently reminds you that you're sitting on top of enough explosive to blow you up and away from a speeding jet in case something goes wrong. And then, of course, there's the nagging suspicion that somewhere down below you, either in the night's blackness or the scorching tan desert whose contours grow even more fuzzy from the heat, people are trying to kill you.

Heads Up!

"The bombing and enemy raids began very early today. Air-to-ground missiles began to explode at 3:30 A.M. I am very worried for my relatives. O God! Protect. O God! Save us all."

—Iraqi lieutenant's diary entry, January 21, 1991,reprinted in newspaper *Le Midi Libre* (France), March 23, 1991

Then there was the scene on the ground, anxiously scanning the skies for Allied jets you knew you would never see and never hear until their bombs and rockets crashed down on your position. The worst part was always the concussion, the shock wave from the explosion that could rupture eardrums and could toss pieces of dirt, machinery, and men into the air like dry leaves.

We already talked about Michael Scott Speicher, the first airman shot down and (presumably) killed. But the next evening, January 17/January 18, Iraqi missile and antiaircraft fire became more effective. Three

A-6 Intruders were hit by ground fire within minutes of each other. One, from the USS *Saratoga*, managed to limp back to a Saudi base. But the other two, one from the *Saratoga* and one from the aircraft carrier USS *Ranger*, disappeared from the radar screens. Lieutenants Jeffrey Zaun and Robert Wretzel from the *Saratoga*, and Lieutenants William Costen and Charles Turner from the *Ranger* were taken prisoner.

Meanwhile, marine Col. Clifford Acree and CWO Guy Hunter were also captured when their twin-propeller AV-10 attack plane was shot down. The coalition lost several aircraft, including two F-16s, an F-15, and a radar-jamming F-4 "Wild Weasel." Allied pilots shot down 17 Iraqi fighters.

On January 21, another jet from the *Saratoga*, an F-14 Tomcat, was shot down. Its two crewmen bailed out over southwest Iraq, and a rescue attempt was mounted immediately. As helicopters carrying U.S. Special Forces troops converged on the area, an A-10 Warthog tank killer attack jet found the location and began blasting Iraqi vehicles in the area. One of the F-14 crewmen was taken prisoner, but the other was snatched from the ground and rescued under heavy Iraqi fire.

> ## The Machines
>
> The A-6 Intruder, built by Grumman, entered service in 1963 and was retired in 1997. With two crewmen sitting side by side, the bulbous-nosed attack plane was homely and nicknamed "SkyPig" among other things. The A-6 could reach a top speed of 650 miles per hour and carry 18,000 pounds of various bombs and missiles.

> ## Heads Up!
>
> "It is a clear violation of the Geneva convention for the protection of prisoners of war, and it will have very, very strong repercussions not only throughout the United States but throughout the world if these violations continue."
>
> —Speaker of the House of Representatives Thomas Foley, January 21, 1991

POWs

The evening of January 20, television viewers worldwide saw the steely faces of Allied pilots the Iraqis had captured, including Americans, Kuwaitis, Britons, and Italians. *Lt. Jeffrey Zaun*, an A-6 pilot from the *Saratoga*, was dirty and bruised. His face was bruised, his jaws puffy. The Iraqis claimed he had injured his face while ejecting. The United States suspected that the pilots were being tortured and warned the Iraqis that they would be held responsible for any maltreated POWs.

The Iraqis generally ignored the protests and instead said they would take POWs to possible target sites, resurrecting the "human shield" ploy. There was no evidence, however, that any Allied pilots were actually held at target sites.

Who's Who

Jeffrey Zaun, born in 1963 in New Jersey, was a navy lieutenant when he was shot down. He was released in March 1991, and said that he had never been tortured, and that he had, indeed, injured himself while ejecting. He also said he hit himself in the face several times to prevent the Iraqis from using him on TV again.

Durrah

The Durrah oil platforms sat about 50 miles out in the Arabian Gulf off the coast of Kuwait. The Iraqis seized them the day of the invasion, using them not only as lookout and communications posts, but also as firing platforms. Allied pilots reported repeated incoming fire from light antiaircraft guns and shoulder-held missiles fired from the platforms.

Before dawn on January 19, Allied forces made the first substantial face-to-face contact with the Iraqis on the Durrah platforms. It was also the first operation test for the combined commands that were to prove so vital in the ground phase of Desert Storm.

The Machines

The Kiowa AH-58 (now designated the OH-58) is a single-engine helicopter that entered service in 1968. It has a targeting radar array mounted on top of the rotor mast, and carries a variety of missiles as well as radar jamming devices. The Kiowa can be used for surveillance, attack, or transport.

The guided missile frigate USS *Nicholas* was given the job of taking out the Durrah platforms. On board was Helicopter Anti-Submarine Squadron 44, a.k.a. "The Swamp Foxes," a navy unit whose mission was not only to detect submarines, but to go after surface targets as well. Also on board were a detachment of navy SEALs, and a pair of *Kiowa AH-58* U.S. Army attack helicopters. A Kuwaiti naval patrol boat was alongside.

The Kiowas assaulted the Durrah platforms with Hellfire missiles and rockets that exploded into a rain of antipersonnel darts. The SEALs then stormed the platforms as the Swamp Foxes and Kuwaiti craft provided supporting fire. When it was over, 23 Iraqis were captured, the first combat POWs of the war. Five Iraqis were killed.

Where Are the Chemicals?

U.S., British, and Israeli intelligence all feared Iraq's chemical and biological weapons arsenal. CIA memos to CENTCOM before the war started noted an "extremely sophisticated" production capability for chemical agents ranging from sarin to mustard gas, and for biological agents like anthrax, cholera, and botulism. On January 17, the Israeli government was so worried that it ordered gas masks distributed to the general population.

That same day, a Saudi army chemical detection unit stationed just south of the Kuwaiti border reported that it had detected "traces" of chemical weapons. U.S. troops stationed just west of that area were ordered to go to MOPP-1, with full chemical suits and protective masks, gauntlets, and boots. At almost the same time, chemical and biological detection alarms went off near the civilian airport serving Dhahran.

The next night, those same alarms sounded again at the same airport. American armored units stationed just south of the border with Iraq sent CENTCOM headquarters in Riyadh a message confirming detection of chemical weapons contamination. At this point, the trickle of chemical detections became a steady stream, largely due to reports from the Czech coalition contingent. Czechoslovakia's contribution to the Gulf War consisted of several chemical and biological detection units stationed north of the Saudi city of Hafir al Batin, just south of the Iraqi border.

On January 19, three separate Czech units detected low levels of an unidentified nerve gas in the air in the area where the French Foreign Legion and U.S. armored troops were stationed. Later that same day, French units reported their monitors had also detected tiny amounts of nerve gas and blistering agents in roughly the same area.

On January 20, the Czechs reported that they confirmed mustard gas residue near King Khalid Military City, a large air base south of Hafir al-Batin used by Allied warplanes. The next day, a French armored division went to MOPP-4 because chemical detection alarms went off. Over the following few days, traces of sand in the Hafir al-Batin region tested positive for mustard gas.

The official CENTCOM position was that no chemical weapons had been fired at any Allied troops by the Iraqis, and that either the chemical detection alarms had malfunctioned, or the chemical detection units had picked up tiny traces of fallout from coalition air strikes against the Iraqi chemical weapons facility at Salman Pak.

Hearts, Minds, and Eyeballs

As we noted before, ABC News was the first TV organization on the air with word that Baghdad was being bombed, or that, at least, Iraqi antiaircraft guns and missiles were being fired. But CNN soon owned the story, and the reasons why provide some insight into the nature of the televised war, and on efforts to control the media and put "spin" on a story even as bombs fell.

The first night, CNN was on the air for 16 hours from Baghdad before Iraqi censors shut them down temporarily. Other networks from around the world were only able to report for less than an hour before their signals went dead. The reason? Engineering genius and bureaucratic foresight by CNN. Many TV operations brought portable satellite uplink dishes to Baghdad but were unable to use them the first night of the war because of Iraqi restrictions and fears that their electronic signals would be targeted by Allied planes.

So the first coverage out of Baghdad of the bombing was via a medium Edward R. Murrow would have recognized from his days broadcasting from the top of a London hotel during the blitz of 1940 and 1941: radio. The networks were sending the world word of the war via telephones. But even that coverage ceased after the first Allied bombing run, when a laser-guided smart bomb punched through the roof of the Iraqi telephone exchange building and leveled it. All of the city's telephone switching equipment went dead, and all of the city's telephones went silent.

> ### Who's Who
>
> Peter Arnett, a native of New Zealand, won the Pulitzer Prize for his Associated Press Vietnam reporting. He left CNN in 1999. John Holliman was a veteran space reporter. He died in a car crash in 1998. After his death, NASA named an asteroid in his honor. Bernard Shaw, a former marine, was an anchor for ABC News and CNN. He retired in 2001.

All, that is, excerpt those being used by CNN correspondents *Peter Arnett, John Holliman, and Bernard Shaw*. The trio described the bombs falling to the world because CNN had foreseen the telephone system being targeted and had negotiated with Iraq for permission to use a series of low-powered "repeater" transmitters strung along the desert toward Jordan. The phones were turned into low-powered radios, with the signals being bounced from one repeater to the next and finally uplinked to the rest of the planet by technicians in Jordan. None of the rest of the world's TV networks used diplomatic perseverance or engineering know-how like CNN. In granting the permission, the Iraqis may have felt CNN would tell their side of the story more sympathetically than other news organizations.

But Arnett became a controversial figure during the war because of his reports from Baghdad that sometimes seemed to parrot the official Iraqi government line. As we'll see in the next chapter, that criticism reached a crescendo about a week into the war with his coverage of Allied bombing of what the coalition claimed was a chemical weapons plant and what the Iraqis said was a baby milk processing plant.

In fairness to Arnett, CNN's unspoken credo was to soft pedal any criticism of a host government for fear of being expelled. As one network executive put it, "It's better to have to open a window a crack than shut completely." That was part of the rationale for CNN not objecting when the Iraqis expelled me from the country for my stories on fugitive Kuwaiti resistance fighters: The network's mission in Iraq, they reasoned, was far more important than standing on principle over any single story.

The Allies, meanwhile, were working on their own media spin. The military tried to keep reporters on a short leash by restricting them to "pools," where selected journalists would travel with military units. But the pool assignments were few and far between, access to the countryside was restricted, and most of the information came from printed handouts and the daily CENTCOM briefing, complete with bomb and missile damage video from jet cameras.

On January 21, veteran CBS News correspondent Bob Simon and his three-man crew got through the Saudi countryside roadblocks by flashing their media ID cards as if they were U.S. military IDs. Their reasoning was that the real story was closer to the front, not in an air-conditioned briefing room. Simon, producer Peter Bluff, and cameramen Roberto Alvarez and Juan Caldera were captured by Iraqi troops near the Saudi-Kuwait border.

The military blamed Simon and his crew for being "hot dogs." The media blamed the military for forcing journalists to risk capture if they wanted to be near the real story.

The Least You Need to Know

- Early air strikes against Iraq were overwhelming successes, executed with pinpoint precision.
- Several Allied pilots were taken prisoner as Iraq launched SCUD missiles into Israel and Saudi Arabia.
- There were disputed reports of chemical use by Iraq, which would feed into postwar controversy.
- Both sides fought for hearts and minds through the media, especially television.

Chapter 12

January 22 to January 28

In This Chapter

- The first ground fighting of the war occurs unexpectedly
- Iraq rains more SCUDs into Israel, and an international firestorm erupts over bombing of an alleged baby milk factory
- The first Kuwaiti territory is liberated and the first oil well fires are ignited
- The air campaign changes targets, aiming to destroy elite Republican Guard units

Sigmund Freud supposedly once commented, "Of course a cigar is a phallic symbol. But it is also, occasionally, a cigar." The same can be said of an unexpected ground engagement: It was a grab for glory, but was also a heroic fight. And the same for a baby milk factory: It processed infant formula, but may also have been used to produce chemical weapons.

Any chest-thumper who says war is simply right versus wrong, good versus evil, has probably never been shot at in combat. Larger certainties are wrapped in smaller ambiguities on the battlefield. This chapter is about that sort of gray area, what strategists call "the fog of war."

The First Ground Action

The 3rd Armored Cavalry Regiment (ACR) is known as "The Brave Rifles," a slogan forged in action like the storming of Chapultepec castle in Mexico in 1847, Sherman's March to the Sea in 1864, the surrender of Geronimo in 1866, and the first push into Germany in 1945. George Patton had once commanded the 3rd ACR, a fact not lost on its commander in 1991, Col. Douglas Starr.

One of Starr's fellow officers later claimed that staff meetings would normally start with someone saying, "When do we get to kill something?" The 3rd ACR was stationed as part of the 18th Airborne, just south of the Iraqi border, so it wasn't surprising to some that it was a unit of the 3rd ACR that engaged in the first ground action of the Gulf War.

> **Heads Up!**
>
> "Brave Rifles! Veterans! You have been baptized in fire and blood and have come out steel!"
> —Gen. Winfield Scott to the Regiment of Mounted Riflemen (later the 3rd Armored Cavalry), Contreras, Mexico August 20, 1847

What was surprising to some was that in the predawn hours of January 22, the regimental commander himself would lead a patrol by the 3rd Platoon, I Troop of the 3rd ACR's 3rd Squadron. This sort of action was well beneath the operational responsibilities of a regimental commanding officer. The platoon's Bradley Fighting Vehicles mounted the top of some sand ridges about 6:30 P.M. and spotted a platoon-sized patrol, apparently Iraqi border guards.

For the first time, the Bradley was used in combat as its 25-millimeter rapid-fire cannon tore into the Iraqi vehicles. The half-dozen GIs inside the Bradley dismounted and laid down more fire. At the end of the engagement, three members of the 3rd Platoon were slightly wounded, while three Iraqis were killed and six captured. Colonel Starr was able to report the first ground action of the war with I Troop.

In a little less than a month, I Troop and Colonel Starr would be involved in one of the war's uglier incidents, complete with charges of fratricide, falsified medal recommendations, and an eventual Congressional investigation.

Baby Milk

The same day Colonel Starr and I Troop engaged the Iraqis, CNN's Peter Arnett reported Iraqi government claims that the Allies had bombed a baby milk factory in the Abu Gharib area of Baghdad. Abu Gharib, in the Baghdad suburbs, had been long identified as a production area for chemical and biological weapons. It's also the site of an infamous prison where many of Saddam's opponents have been tortured and executed. The

TV images of the flattened building were immediately used as propaganda fodder by Saddam, who claimed that the United States was indiscriminately bombing civilian targets.

The bombing immediately became a test of wills and of media savvy between Iraq and the United States. In 1996, President Bush said he had personally ordered the air strike after seeing satellite photographs of chemicals being hauled into the building. CENTCOM also noted the structure was painted in camouflage, indicating it was a military installation. The Iraqis claimed the paint job had been done early in the war with Iran.

Iraq paraded destroyed cans of infant formula before the world's media. The United States steadfastly maintained the facility had been used in chemical and biological weapons production. It wasn't until 1995, when one of Saddam's sons-in-law defected, that U.S. intelligence admitted the bombing was based on faulty intelligence. Other buildings in the area were used for chemical storage, but not the infant formula plant. The main Iraqi biological research facility was actually 60 miles southwest.

> **Heads Up!**
>
> "It is not an infant formula plant. It was a biological weapons facility, of that we are sure."
>
> —Gen. Colin Powell, January 23, 1991
>
> "It would have been impossible to transform this (plant) into the making of chemical products."
>
> —Michel Wery, director of French company that built the plant, February 2, 1991

Oil As a Weapon

The Persian Gulf managed to support an astonishing variety of marine life, despite the carnage of nine years of war between Iran and Iraq and the leaks and pollution from dozens of offshore oil platforms and thousands of oil tankers. Some unspoiled coral reefs still existed in parts of the Gulf, alive with colorful coral polyps and luminescent fish. Dugongs—the huge Arabian Gulf sea cows, first cousins to the manatees of Florida—would splash and roll lazily in some areas, feeding off vegetation.

CENTCOM was concerned about possible environmental damage to such a sensitive area, so it was no surprise when General Schwartzkopf went ballistic when he found out about the incident of January 22. U.S. Navy jets pounded an Iraqi tanker, but the resulting explosions fractured the hull, sending crude oil roiling into the Gulf. Schwartzkopf threatened to court-martial everyone involved, but later calmed down.

Contrast that with the Iraqi military, which began setting Kuwaiti oil wells afire the very same day the Iraqi tanker was attacked. They began in the south of Kuwait in the Wahfra fields, and worked their way toward the Iraqi border. Fires were also set at a pair of Kuwaiti refineries.

Desert Lore

The CIA reported that captured Iraqi documents showed that Iraq's troops had been ordered to destroy Kuwaiti oil wells long before the invasion, and had practiced detonations on dummy wellheads inside Iraq.

Clouds of raw petrochemicals released by the burning crude immediately began to spew into the atmosphere. At first, only dozens of wells were ignited. But before the ground war started, hundreds had been detonated and set ablaze. The heat in the center of each burning wellhead created a white-hot "halo" as wide as several football fields. Soot shot up volcanically, creating a rain of black, sticky carcinogens across Kuwait, the Gulf, parts of Saudi Arabia, and as far east as Iran. It fell like vaporized motor oil, thick with raw metals like nickel, rancid with sulfur, atomized.

Some wells, though, tapped methane, and they burned like welders' torches, ripping into the sky with a jet of sun-hot burning gas, heated to 2,000°F at the center. When the crude was too thick to burn, it leaked, oozing lakes covering 30 acres into the sand. Kuwait's crude oil is 2.5 percent sulfur by weight, with significant amounts of nickel, nitrogen, and vanadium. It contains up to 30 parts per million of hydrogen sulfide and is classified as "moderately" toxic. Over 100 million metric tons were spewed into the air from the Kuwait oil fires.

Saddam had threatened a scorched earth policy, regardless of its effect, and he was living up to his promise. But why? If the idea behind invading Kuwait was to siphon off its oil to fatten Iraq's coffers, why destroy all that black gold? Because Saddam Hussein, after one week of bombing, knew that the Allies would drive him out of Kuwait. He knew that saving face and instilling fear were often as important as victory in Arab opinion. And he was willing to poison the air over thousands of square miles.

But that wasn't enough, so on January 24, oil valves were opened into the Arabian Gulf from the Kuwaiti refinery at Mina al-Hamadi, a town on the coast just north of Saudi Arabia. Large pipes ran under the Gulf from the refinery to the Sea Island Terminal about 10 miles offshore where tankers would be pumped full of refined crude. Oil began to gurgle into the Gulf from eight different locations at Sea Island as outflow valves were opened, vent valves were opened on loaded tankers, and fires were set at a pair of pumping stations. The next day, American satellites spotted the oil slicks, the largest of which was nine miles long. On January 26, another slick appeared, this one a half mile wide and eight miles long.

Heads Up!

"The war in the Persian Gulf threatens to turn that environmentally fragile region into another wasteland."

—James Ridgeway, *Village Voice*, March 6, 1991

In the end, the slick was larger than the area of New York City. It choked, soaked, and killed tens of thousands of birds, cut off endangered turtles from nesting habitat, and created a sheen of oil across thousands of square miles. As it drifted south, it threatened the intake valves for the huge desalinization plant in the Saudi city of Khafji.

On January 27, Allied planes staged one of the most precise bombing runs in the history of aerial warfare. CENTCOM obtained blueprints for the refinery and terminal facilities, and discovered that by blasting away one transfer pumping station, the flow of all of the oil into the Gulf could be stopped. The attack succeeded. A larger environmental disaster had been averted, but only after an estimated 250 million gallons—the largest oil spill in history—had been pumped into the Gulf by Iraq.

Qarah

Fourteen miles off the Kuwaiti coast, Qarah Island was a little slice of the South Pacific dropped into the Arabian Gulf. Made of coral piled up on the seabed, Qarah rose out of the 70-foot-deep turquoise waters, sheltering green turtles, moray eels, and several species of sharks. It was tropical paradise duty for the several dozen Iraqi soldiers and sailors stationed there, observing jet and ship movements and servicing the shallow-water Iraqi mine laying boats that were seeding the Gulf.

Like so much in warfare, the liberation of the first captured Kuwaiti territory of the war happened almost by accident. Early in the morning of January 24, a pair of A-6 Intruders from the carrier USS *Theodore Roosevelt* blasted an Iraqi mine layer and a nearby patrol boat. Near Qarah, a second mine layer began turning in a panicked zigzag course, playing cat-and-mouse with another A-6. As the boat's commander tried to escape from the Intruder's rocket and cannon barrage, he hit one of his own mines. Kiowa helicopters from the *guided missile frigate* USS *Curts* were scrambled to pick up survivors.

The *Curts*, like other frigates, carried army helicopters operating under navy command. As the Kiowas approached the remains of the mine layer and its 22 crewmen in the water, they started to take incoming fire from the Iraqi garrison on Qarah. The helicopters returned fire, and the *Curts* maneuvered close enough to blast the coral atoll with its 76-millimeter guns.

The Machines

The first U.S. Navy guided missile frigate was launched in 1977. The navy currently operates 35 of them. They are designed for antiaircraft and antisubmarine work, not for surface fighting. Each carries an array of missiles and up to two helicopters. Each frigate is roughly 450 feet long and carries a crew of 300. No new frigates are planned, and the class of ships will eventually be retired.

Heads Up!

"The high point for me was when I saw the Kuwaiti flag flying over its own territory."

—Commanding officer, USS *Curts*, February 1991

At the same time, Navy SEAL commandos aboard the destroyer USS *Leftwich* sped to the island by helicopter and engaged the garrison in a quick firefight. Three Iraqis were killed, 51 were taken prisoner, and the SEALs—always prepared—whipped out a Kuwaiti flag and ran it up a makeshift flagpole. The first tiny parcel of Kuwait had been liberated.

Death from Above

As the second week of the air campaign got underway, doubts were already beginning to appear concerning CENTCOM's daily video game briefing sessions. Russia's Interfax News Agency reported that Russian intelligence estimated that 90 percent of the bombs and missiles had missed their targets during the first week. Some of the air war's biggest successes, though, never made it onto the satellite uplinks.

On January 22, an Iraqi convoy of around 70 vehicles was spotted by airborne radar heading into Kuwait from Iraq. An AC-130 Spectre gunship, armed with a cannon, and several *A-10 Warthog*, or *Thunderbolt*, tank killing jets were vectored to attack. Fifty of the vehicles were smashed.

The Machines

The A-10 Thunderbolt is commonly called the Warthog because of its ungainly appearance. The single-seat fighter has two bulbous turbofan engines halfway between its wings and twin tail fins. The cockpit is lined with titanium and can take numerous direct hits from ground fire. The Warthog flies low and slow and pulverizes armor with a 30-millimeter seven-barreled cannon that can fire 4,200 rounds a minute.

On January 24, Desert Storm's host country got a morale boost when a Saudi Air Force F-15 shot down a pair of Iraqi fighters. It was the first multiple kill by a single pilot since the war started. Meanwhile, both the DIA and CIA were reporting indications that Iraq was preparing a chemical attack using its air force rather than missiles.

At an airfield near Baghdad, a squadron of Iraqi bombers was suspected to be ready for a mission using chemicals, so F-117 Stealth Fighters were dispatched at night, using "bunker buster" guided bombs to tear through the hardened hangars sheltering the planes.

A new wrinkle appeared when Allied radar spotted two dozen Iraqi aircraft of all kinds—including civilian Iraq Air passenger jets—heading east into Iran on January 24. CENTCOM was concerned that Iraq might have reached a secret deal with Iran to launch an aerial "second front" against the Allies, but Iran announced it was impounding all the Iraqi jets until hostilities ended. By the 28th, 80 Iraqi jets had landed in Iran.

CENTCOM also issued an announcement that "air supremacy" had been achieved over Iraq. That meant Phase Three of the air war was set to commence: targeting Republican Guard positions with B-52s.

Carpet Bombing

If smart bombs and missiles are used for precision, old-fashioned dumb bombs are used for mass destruction and raw terror. After the Gulf War, the Pentagon estimated that of 88,500 tons of ordnance dropped on Iraq and Kuwait, 81,080 tons—92.5 percent—were *not* precision guided. And 27,500 tons of those "dumb" bombs were dropped by B-52s.

There were 27 of the lumbering bombers used in the war, and while they sometimes launched the still-secret air-launched cruise missiles, they were most effective when they were dropping conventional bombs in massive, tight patterns, using several B-52s flying what became generically known as *arc light missions.*

The effectiveness of that first week of bombing in the Gulf War was exaggerated, especially at the time, but was still good enough to ground Iraq's air force, suppress most of its antiaircraft, and open the way for Phase Three of the air war. As we'll see in the next section, targeting SCUD launch sites became the primary mission of the one- and two-crewman aircraft.

Gulf Lingo

Operation **Arc Light** began in Vietnam in June 1965 with 27 B-52s flying a saturation bombing mission over Viet Cong positions, dropping 750- and 1,000-pound bombs. Arc light has since become a synonym for any B-52 saturation mission, where bomb patterns overlap to create an uninterrupted swathe of destruction.

But CENTCOM gave the air force the job of demoralizing and destroying the Republican Guard. It did it with conventional bombs, with some incendiary bombs, but most of all with a nasty bomb-within-a-bomb, the CBU-87/B cluster bomb, a 950-pound bomb. Inside are packed 202 BLU-97/B bomblets. Each bomblet weighs $3\frac{1}{2}$ pounds and contains shrapnel, an antitank warhead, and an incendiary charge.

Each CBU 87/B could spray out more than 200 deadly minibombs packed with explosives, incendiaries, and shrapnel, and each B-52 could carry 40 of the huge bombs, containing more than 8,000 bomblets. Each small bomblet would explode dozens of feet over the heads of cowering troops, sending razor-sharp shards of metal spinning in every direction while the antitank warhead and incendiary charge would punch straight down with enough muscle to turn a small tank or armored personnel carrier into a charcoal briquette. One B-52 could pulverize an area equal to more than 27,000 football fields, shredding metal and flesh while scooping out tons of dirt, sand, and rock like a giant plow.

The biggest mission flown against the Republican Guard dropped 450 tons of the cluster bombs, enough to destroy the surface area of Rhode Island. One of the first missions involved a strike against Republican Guard positions in southern Iraq, which pounded an ammunition storage facility so hard that the Air Force claimed it produced "… the largest nonnuclear explosion ever recorded."

SCUDs Again

If the tautological definition is correct and the object of terrorism is to terrorize, then Saddam Hussein was using SCUD missiles as terror weapons. They had almost no tactical value, since their cranky inertial guidance systems might or might not place the missiles within five miles of where they were aimed. But they had potential *strategic* value precisely because they were flying pieces of junk.

They could be excellent terror weapons because of their very uncertainty. No one knew for certain where they might land. No one knew for certain that they wouldn't contain chemical warheads. No one knew for certain where the warheads might fall if a Patriot intercepted a SCUD through the fuel tank. Saddam could keep the Saudis and their American allies uneasy, and could infuriate the Israelis, hoping to goad them into a unilateral counterattack. So the nuisance weapons became psychological weapons.

It began before dawn on January 22, when a SCUD was lofted toward Tel Aviv. Just north of Tel Aviv sits the industrial suburb of Ramat Gan, population 122,000, home of Israel's biggest stadium. It holds the distinction of being hit by SCUD missiles more than any other Israeli municipality. In one of the war's biggest ironies, the population of Ramat Gan is largely made up of Iraqi Jews. On January 22, a warhead fell and detonated on top of an apartment building. Three Israelis died, but the Shamir government, trying to calm public opinion in response to pressure from Washington, emphasized that they were elderly and died of heart attacks.

That same night, the Iraqi's launched seven SCUDs toward Saudi Arabia. One warhead landed near Dhahran, and another near Riyadh. The rest either fell into the desert or exploded in midair. The next night, another SCUD was launched at Israel, with five more aimed at Saudi. All of the warheads went off in midair except for one missile that splashed into the Gulf.

General Schwartzkopf called joint chiefs Chairman Powell that night, January 23, and emphasized that the missiles were having no tactical effect, but were

Heads Up!

"The destruction was horrifying. The whole area looked like a battlefield. Everything was scorched and uprooted. Cars were burnt out. People wandered around with the remains of their broken belongings."

—Account of Ramat Gan on January 22, 1991, Israeli newspaper *Mishpacha*, February 1991

creating fear and uncertainty. The DIA and CIA were both reporting that Iraq "probably" had been unable to mount either chemical or biological warheads on the SCUDs. But again, no one knew for certain.

Powell authorized reemphasis on going after SCUD launch sites, and within 24 hours, 200 missions had been flown against real or suspected SCUD launch platforms. Another 100 missions followed, and for the first time since the war started, a full day and a night passed with no SCUD launches.

The reason might have come on January 25, when a barrage of eight SCUDs was launched against Tel Aviv and Haifa. Seven of the missiles were listed as intercepted, but one warhead slammed into Ramat Gan, killing one person. Meanwhile, one person died in Riyadh when a patriot intercepted a SCUD less than 50 feet off the ground. The blast knocked down walls and broke windows blocks away.

The next night, six SCUDs were aimed at Tel Aviv and Haifa, with warheads once again striking the unlucky Ramat Gan, while a pair of missiles launched at Saudi Arabia was intercepted. Despite the Allies averaging more than 50 missions a day against SCUD sites, coalition intelligence estimated that the vast majority of SCUD launch sites and mobile SCUD launchers were still operational.

The next day, Sunday January 27, was the largest secular holiday in the United States, Super Bowl Sunday. After a day of quiet, Saddam chose halftime of the Giants-Bills game to launch two nuisance missiles, one that burrowed into the Israeli desert near Haifa and another that was intercepted by a Patriot barrage over Riyadh.

> **Desert Lore** _____
>
> A Gallup Poll released in the United States on January 27 showed 45 percent of those polled thought the United States should use nuclear weapons if Iraq used chemical or biological weapons against Americans.

Weapons of Mass Distraction

Iraq's NBC capability—nuclear, biological, chemical—was a primary target in the air war's second week. The United States targeted a pair of Iraqi nuclear reactors in the town of Tuwaitha. One, made by the Soviets, generated five megawatts, while the other, built by the French, was rated at 500 kilowatts. The Allies had also gone after a gas centrifuge, used for enriching uranium, also at Tuwaitha, as well as a fuel rod storage assembly plant. No radiation leaks were ever reported from the strikes, although *New Scientist* magazine reports at the time that more than 40 pounds of enriched uranium from the reactors was missing, possibly buried in the rubble.

Heads Up!

"We've gone after factories where Iraq has produced chemical and biological weapons and continued working on nuclear weapons …. [W]e have targeted that nuclear facility they have very carefully. … I can confirm for you that the two operating reactors they had are both down. They're gone. They're finished."

—Joint Chiefs of Staff Chairman Gen. Colin Powell, January 23, 1991

Gulf Lingo

BDA (bomb damage assessment) is used by the military to estimate how much destruction has been caused over a specific area. Often more art than science, BDA can use reconnaissance photos, satellite images, or, most reliably, infrared photos. A new generation of optical lasers may be even more precise.

On the chemical front, DIA reported that there were serious disruptions throughout the chain of research, development, manufacture, and delivery of chemical and biological weapons in Iraq, but that it was still possible that some form of chemical ordnance had been delivered to front-line units. The good news was that thanks to a special warhead aboard the Tomahawk cruise missile, most of Iraq's electrical generating capacity was knocked off-line, meaning no power for weapons laboratories. Indeed, during the Gulf War, some Tomahawk cruise missiles carried warheads loaded with spider-web-thin carbon graphite filaments. The warhead would ignite, and the filaments would spread, shorting out electrical transformers, generators, and substations. A new, highly classified generation of these "soft warheads" are designed to spread filaments out over a wider area even more effectively.

When the cruise missile warhead, called a Kit-2, exploded, carbon graphite strands would shoot in all directions, short-circuiting power lines, generators, and any other electrical equipment they touched. CENT-COM could relax about contradictory *BDA*—bomb damage assessment—as long as the electricity was out to potential weapons of mass destruction facilities. Within a few days, 85 percent of Iraq's electric grid had been knocked off-line.

But CENTCOM's attention was about to turn, very quickly, toward the small northern Saudi city of Khafji. Iraq was about to strike into Saudi Arabia for the first time.

The Least You Need to Know

- The Allies' drive to disable Iraq's chemical and biological capabilities was enmeshed in the controversy over bombing an Iraqi baby formula plant.
- Iraq's army used ecological terrorism as a weapon by causing mammoth oil spills and igniting Kuwaiti oil wells.
- With air supremacy achieved, the coalition began to target Iraq's Republican Guard with punishing air strikes.
- Saddam Hussein used SCUD missile attacks as much for their psychological as military impact.

Chapter 13

January 29 to February 4

In This Chapter

- The only Iraqi ground offensive of the war erupts, killing American marines
- An American patrol is trapped inside the city while airpower pulverizes Iraqi reinforcements
- Two Americans are captured, including a female POW
- The United States suffers its biggest loss of the air war and retaliates with a terrifying weapon

My introduction to Khafji came while we were being "Saudi-ized," mediaspeak for being led on an escorted tour by Saudi military officials. It was night, and our nervous Saudi hosts were endeavoring to show us how their army had liberated the captured city. They were almost right, discounting the occasional sniper round that ricocheted off nearby walls.

The Saudis kept telling us to keep our TV camera lights off, so we generally stumbled around in the dark. Turning a corner on one of the debris-littered streets, my foot kicked something that felt like a wet sandbag. I clicked on my tiny flashlight with the red lens, and saw the head of an Iraqi soldier, mouth wide open under a bushy mustache, staring back at me. There was no trace of his body.

Crossing the Border

The modified Boeing 707 cruising slowly between Kuwait and western Iraq on the night of January 29 had the look of a jet the Beatles might have flown into Idlewild in 1964 or John F. Kennedy's Air Force One. In a war dominated by futuristic weapons, the air force E-8 (the military designation for the modified 707) had an anachronistic, early '60s look. It was actually the air force's newest and most experimental system, simply called *J-STARS*.

The J-STARS plane, bristling with electronic devices, had arrived in Saudi three weeks before for a shakedown cruise. Its main job was to spot SCUD missile launchers in western Iraq by pinpointing the launcher's radar signals. But they occasionally had spotted something else. On the night of January 22, they had scanned 70 or so vehicles moving toward the Kuwaiti border with Saudi. On January 25, another 80 Iraqi vehicles were spotted just north of the Saudi border. And on January 28, J-STARS reported "moderate to heavy" Iraqi military vehicle traffic along the Saudi border with Kuwait.

> **The Machines**
>
> J-STARS—Joint Surveillance and Target Attack Radar System—was first used in the Gulf War. Mounted inside a modified 707 are 17 separate encrypted radio channels, direct satellite uplinks, and a variety of radar systems. J-STARS radars can scan for miles, picking up ground, air, and ocean-going targets.

> **Heads Up!**
>
> "We didn't think they (the Iraqi army) were going to do anything because they hadn't done anything in so long."
>
> —Gen. Thomas Olsen, deputy air force commander in the Gulf, 1995

All of those reports were forwarded to CENTCOM in Riyadh and were given the "f-squared" treatment—file and forget. CENTCOM believed the Iraqis would not mount a ground offensive, and that on the off chance they did, it would run down the Wadi al-Batin. The heavy troops of the U.S. Army had been moved several hundred miles west, leaving a token force of U.S. Marines and the Saudi army facing Iraqi troops across the Kuwaiti border near the Gulf.

Saddam's planners hoped to use the same tactic they had used against Iran—attack, draw the enemy into a counterattack, and then spring a trap on them. Iraq's theory was that they could lure the Allies into chasing them into Kuwait, where they could be engaged in a potentially costly land battle among Iraqi defensive emplacements.

Iraq's plan called for pushing into Saudi Arabia like three prongs of a pitchfork:

- Iraq's 5th Mechanized Division was to drive straight down the coast and roll through Saudi defenders, taking the Saudi town of Ras al-Khafji.

- The 3rd Armored Division was to push in just west of the 5th, then make a sudden turn toward the Gulf and seize the Saudi town of Mishab, below Khafji.

◆ The 1st Mechanized Division would jab into Saudi even farther west to guard the movement's right flank.

On top of that, Iraqi commandos were to approach from the Gulf to sabotage Allied positions south of Khafji. The strategy was to attack and withdraw behind Kuwait's reinforced berms and then catch pursuing coalition troops in a crossfire. Around 9:30 P.M. January 29, the J-STARS flashed a message that reinforced Iraqi units were moving into Saudi Arabia.

Khafji Falls

General Schwartzkopf had ordered the U.S. Air Force's Tactical Air Control Center to go after SCUDs and the Republican Guard. So on the night of January 29, they were up to their ears in complicated missions and weren't paying much attention to J-STARS' reports of Iraqi maneuvering.

The U.S. Marines of Task Force Shepherd, however, knew immediately. The three marine companies, along with a headquarters unit and an antiaircraft battery, spotted a battalion of *T-62* tanks and armored personnel carriers lumbering toward them out of the desert darkness.

At 8 P.M., the marines began to fight off the tanks with their only heavy weapon at hand, the TOW antitank missile. They also radioed for air support. Within half an hour, the first planes arrived, peppering the Iraqis with cannon and rocket fire from a pair of AC-130 Spectre gunships, a pair of F-16s, another pair of F-15s, and four of the A-10 Warthog tank killing planes. About the same time, *Gen. Charles Horner*, the CENTCOM air force commander, arrived at the Tactical Air Control Center and ordered heavy air reinforcements sent north immediately.

After four hours of resistance from the marines and pounding by attack jets, Iraq's 1st Mechanized Division broke off the attack and retreated into Kuwait. But during the attack, 11 marines died at the hands of the ultimate military oxymoron, "friendly fire." The two light armored vehicles carrying the marines were struck in the darkness

The Machines
The T-62 battle tank was produced by the Soviets from 1961 until 1975. Armed with a 115-millimeter cannon, the T-62 can reach a top speed of a little over 30 miles per hour on paved roads. The tank carries a crew of four.

Who's Who
Charles "Chuck" Horner was born in Iowa in 1937. After almost dying in a 1962 training flight, Horner flew more than 100 combat missions in Vietnam. During Desert Storm, Horner commanded all Allied air forces. He retired as commander of the U.S. Aerospace Command.

and confusion by artillery fire and a missile from an A-10. One of the prongs of Saddam's pitchfork had been broken, but at a high cost due to fratricide, or "friendly fire" incidents.

Of the 146 U.S. combat deaths during Operation Desert Storm, 35 died in "friendly fire" incidents. Of the 480 wounded, 72 were wounded by their own troops.

> **The Machines**
>
> The tube-launched, optically tracked, wire-guided (TOW) missile system entered service in 1970. Usually fired from a launcher on a vehicle, the TOW can pierce armor at a distance of over two miles. Each missile is a little over four feet long.

While that fight was going on, the lead elements of the 3rd Mechanized Division were rolling to northern Saudi Arabia, straight into the Marine's 2nd Light Infantry Battalion. They immediately radioed for air support while fighting off around 50 Iraqi tanks with *TOW missiles*. By this time, the air commanders knew something was up, so the marines immediately received help from flights of A-10s, F-16s, F-18s, and A-6s.

Around 2 A.M., the Iraqis finally gave up and began retreating. Nearby, a single marine light armored vehicle and its crew tried to fight off a dozen tanks. The marines shot, dodged, and fired again, retreating slowly until air support pulverized the Iraqi column. As dawn broke, the 3rd Mechanized Division was in full retreat toward Kuwait, leaving burned-out tanks and armored personnel carriers in their wake.

Just to the east, Iraq's 5th Mechanized Division was roaring down the four-lane highway linking Kuwait with the Saudi seacoast town of Ras al-Khafji. Since Khafji was within artillery range of Kuwait, all of its 15,000 people had been evacuated right after the invasion. The only things left in town were deserted buildings, a couple of journalists hiding out inside a beachfront motel, dead sea birds from Saddam's oil slick, a desalinization plant, and two six-man squads of U.S. Marines.

Standing between Iraq's 5th Mech and Khafji was the Saudi National Guard and some troops from the Gulf nation of Qatar, and what happened next depends on which version of history you believe. One version is that Iraqi tanks approached the Saudi positions with their turrets and cannon pointed backward, which the Saudis took as a sign of surrender. That was logical, given the small numbers of Iraqi defectors who had been dribbling across the border. But then, this version continues, the Iraqi tankers wheeled their guns around and opened fire. The surprised Saudi and Qatari troops made a hurried withdrawal.

> **Heads Up!**
>
> "General bin Sultan (commander of Saudi ground forces) predictably blames the Americans for Iraqi occupation of the town. In reality the problem was that the light Saudi forces in the area left the battlefield."
>
> —retired U.S. Army Col. Norville de Atkine, *Middle East Quarterly*, December 1999

The other, less charitable explanation is that the defenders ran and scattered in panicked disarray. The Arab defenders of Khafji retreated safely behind marine lines. A British colonel told me a few days later, "If that

had been my sector, I would have ordered my men to open fire on the bastards."
Whatever happened, the Saudis later claimed CENTCOM had ordered their retreat.
CENTCOM denied it. Iraqi tanks rolled into Khafji shortly after midnight on the morn-
ing of January 30.

*Three carrier-based U.S.
F-14 Tomcats fly in formation over Iraq.*

Fighting Back

The Khafji incursion found the majority of coalition strength—the U.S. Third Army, the
XVIII Airborne, and VII Corps—well west of the action. The Jedi Knights had worked
out the backbone of the coming ground offensive, an audacious movement of troops far
west into Saudi Arabia, then driving into Iraq and
storming into Kuwait from the west. CENT-
COM was in no mood to shift its armor into
reverse, so it decided to leave the Khafji situation
up to the marines and the Saudis. CENTCOM
also deduced, correctly, that Saddam was looking
for a headlong counterattack and headlong pursuit
and decided not to oblige him.

The problem with all this was that Khafji itself
was on the coast, and that area along the Gulf was
under the operational control of Gulf coalition
troops, specifically the Saudis. With his pride
already injured, *Gen. Prince Khalid bin Sultan*, top

> **Who's Who**
>
> Prince Khalid bin Sultan bin
> Abdulaziz was born in 1949
> and is the son of Price Sultan, the
> Saudi Arabian defense minister.
> Khalid received both military
> training and a pair of master's
> degrees in the United States.
> After the Gulf War, he fell out of
> favor with King Fahd, his uncle,
> and was relieved of his duties as
> military commander.

commander of the Saudi army, started making demands, which once again turned this into a war of battlefield diplomacy as much as battlefield operations.

General bin Sultan, for example, angrily called General Horner at the Tactical Air Control center and demanded that extra planes be diverted to support a proposed Saudi counterattack. CENTCOM had little use for the Saudi plan, since the marines had decided the best way to fight the Iraqis was to cut their supply lines and starve the few hundred Iraqi troops out of Khafji without actually going into the city. But General bin Sultan said that if he didn't get air support the afternoon of January 30, he would pull Saudi planes from coalition control.

The Airpower Decision

To CENTCOM, it seemed that Iraq was trying to engage Arab forces as much as possible, with the 5th Mechanized driving against the Saudis and the 3rd Mechanized heading toward an area controlled by Syrian and Egyptian troops. General Horner quickly decided that airpower, for the first time in the history of warfare, could break the back of an armored offensive.

Before dawn on January 30, Allied airpower went to work. "Kill boxes" had been designed for Allied jets, each about 30 kilometers on a side, an area of about 350 square miles. Specific units were assigned to specific kill boxes inside Kuwait and Iraq, with orders that anything on the ground or the air was likely hostile. The orders were simple: Every eight minutes in daylight and every 15 minutes at night, coalition planes cruised through their own kill box. Anything that moved on the ground was fair game.

Heads Up!

"I myself, one captain in one airplane, was engaging up to a battalion of Iraqi armor on the ground."

—Capt. Ron Givens, A-10 Thunderbolt pilot, 1992

Horner succeeded. Running everything from B-52s to A-10 tank killers through the boxes, the Allies managed to rip the 1st and 3rd Mechanized Divisions to pieces, before the Iraqis even had a chance to deploy antiaircraft missiles. As elements of the 5th Mechanized attempted to reinforce the troops inside Khafji, they were blasted by airpower ranging from the lethal AC-130 gunships to marine corps Harrier jump jets. Dozens of tanks and hundreds of POWs were taken from the three bent prongs of Saddam's pitchfork after only a few hours.

Saudi Counterattack

Marine corps *Gen. Walter Boomer* commanded the 1st Marine Expeditionary Force in the Gulf. Gen. John Admire commanded the 3rd Marine Regiment. Both men had served in Vietnam combat, and both brought three lessons from the triple-canopy jungles of

Southeast Asia to the powdery deserts of Saudi Arabia—a marine commander should always be at the front, with his troops; properly organized, infantry and light antitank weapons can be surprisingly effective against enemy armor; and, most important, treat your allies—in this case the Saudis—like full combat partners, not second-class warriors.

Who's Who
Walter Boomer was born in North Carolina in 1939. He joined the U.S. Marines in 1960, served several combat tours in Vietnam, and eventually became assistant commandant of the marine corps. He commanded all marine forces in the Gulf, and retired from the service in 1994. He is now CEO of a firm that makes plastics for computers and communications equipment.

The marines agreed that an overall ground push toward Khafji was needed. They disagreed, however, with the Saudi plan to wade into the city and fight house-to-house. Before dawn on January 30, as the battle was raging in several locations, General Admire stood along the coast road in a conference with a Saudi colonel and Qatari major. He told them he had 12 marines trapped in Khafji, and that they could hold out on their rooftops for 48 hours maximum before being discovered.

The Arab forces decided to attack, with marines backup. As the two trapped marine recon teams radioed Iraqi positions from their rooftop hideouts, the Arabs and marines conducted a probing attack to the edge of Khafji. They then withdrew, and as the recon units reported on how Iraqi troops were redeploying, the Saudis and Qataris attacked in force, with assistance from the marines.

There were mishaps. A Qatari tank accidentally shelled Saudi armored vehicles, and a marine helicopter opened fire on a Saudi unit by mistake. Only one Saudi soldier was killed, and the attack pressed forward. North of Khafji, the Iraqis kept trying to punch tanks across the border and kept running into coalition airpower. Twenty-eight Iraqi tanks were left smoldering after just one of those engagements.

A Female POW

No female American service personnel had been taken prisoner by an enemy force since the fall of the Philippines to the Japanese in 1941 and 1942. That was about to change as the fight around Khafji was heating up. And it all started on a stretch of highway that was a combination of a scene from a Mad Max movie and a particularly bad Los Angeles rush hour.

The Trans-Arabian Pipeline ran from the Gulf coast of Saudi across the desert to Jordan. About 100 yards north of the pipeline, the Trans-Arabian Pipeline Road was built, a stretch of highway that everyone called Tapline Road and which was the main artery for anything going by car or truck across Saudi Arabia east to west. Even before the Iraqi offensive, Tapline Road was chaos, with U.S., French, and British military vehicles clogging the road, often dodging convoys of 18-wheel trucks and passenger vehicles ripping along the highway at a reasonable Saudi cruising speed of over 80 miles per hour.

Army Specialists Melissa Rathburn-Neely and David Lockett had come to Saudi as part of the 233rd Transportation Company out of Fort Bliss, Texas. Lockett, 23, was from Alabama, while Rathburn-Neely, 20, was originally from Michigan. They were heading east along the Tapline Road, delivering supplies to troops in the area, when they made a wrong turn and their Humvee was suddenly faced with Iraqi troop columns heading toward Khafji.

A second Humvee traveling with them managed to speed away and the troops inside radioed for help. By the time a marine patrol supported by Cobra helicopter gunships arrived on the scene, they found an empty Humvee flipped on its side, the wheels still turning. Lockett and Rathburn-Neely had been captured. Both were released at the end of the war, and Rathburn-Neely later said she had not been mistreated in any way by her captors. But the image of an American female soldier in Iraqi hands kept floating through the minds of CENTCOM commanders.

Moving In

By midday on January 30, it was clear the Iraqi troops inside Khafji were cut off from reinforcements and supplies. Allied airpower had destroyed repeated Iraqi attempts to move south with men and armor. Navy and marine jets had sunk boats loaded with Iraqi special forces troops attempting to land in Khafji.

> ## Heads Up!
>
> "The Arab forces led a forceful counterattack. Within 6 to 12 hours, we destroyed 93 Iraqi armored and personnel vehicles. We captured more than 600 prisoners, including a brigadier general and five colonels."
>
> —Gen. John Admire, Commander, 3rd Marine Regiment, 1996

The Iraqi 5th Mechanized Division had been thought to be just below the Republican Guard in terms of the quality of its equipment and troops. That turned out to be dead wrong. The 5th Mech was unable to sustain any kind of organized defense of Khafji, although they did manage to repulse one Saudi attack around 6 P.M. But the Arab forces regrouped and attacked again, and by the next day, January 31, Khafji was effectively back in Allied hands.

The Death of Spirit 03

The serial number stenciled on the plane's tail section was 69-6567. It's call sign was "Spirit Zero-Three."

Spirit 03 was a Spectre gunship, one of the modified C-130 Hercules four-engine propeller planes that could circle a target and pulverize it with fire from the cannon and Gatling gun on the ship's left side. The 14 men inside Spirit 03 were part of the 16th Special Operations Squadron based at Hurlburt Field Air Force Base near Florida's Atlantic coast.

The crews of several of the gunships attached to Special Ops units had been complaining, quietly but persistently, about dangerous missions they felt exposed them and their ships to hostile fire unnecessarily. So it became standing policy for pilots and commanders to conduct a "sanity check" before each mission. Spirit 03's last mission might have failed that test.

Maj. Paul Weaver, Spirit 03's pilot, had been banking left over Iraqi positions in the darkness before dawn on January 31, blasting the Iraqi 5th Mech in Khafji. Major Weaver's co-pilot, Capt. Tom Bland, was the baby of the crew at age 26. Aft, watching over the sensors that revealed targets below, was the crew's old man, 43-year-old S.M. Sgt. Paul Buege. Night was the Spectre's best friend. Despite its impressive firepower and sophisticated sensor and radar arrays, the four-engine propeller plane could make a top speed of only 300 miles per hour, full throttle, which made it a fat target for ground missiles.

Around 6 A.M., just as Spirit 03 was due to end its patrol, 28-year-old S. Sgt. Damon Kanuha, the flight engineer, took a radio call from the marines below them. They needed an Iraqi FROG missile launcher taken out as soon as possible, fearing that it had chemical warheads. The sky around Spirit 03 was already streaked with yellow and pink as night faded into the crepuscular light before dawn. Major Weaver decided to stay on station, despite the daylight dangers, and go after the missile launcher. He polled the crew. Most said they wanted to stay.

Spirit 03 vectored toward the missile position. Using their 105-millimeter howitzer sticking out of the tail, along with the 40-millimeter cannon and Gatling gun, they made short work of the missile site. Below them, an Iraqi soldier hoisted a surface-to-air missile launcher to his shoulder, easily targeting the slow Spectre.

The Iraqi missile hit near the inboard engine on the right wing. The metal supporting the wing torqued, howled, and collapsed as the wing tore away and Spirit 03 spiraled into the Persian Gulf. No one survived. The 14 men on Spirit 03 had 18 children. The oldest was 17. The youngest was six months.

Daisy, Daisy

More than 700 Iraqi prisoners were rounded up in the days immediately after Khafji was retaken. But the air force was still smarting over the loss of Spirit 03, so they prepared to use a weapon that had a devastating effect both militarily and psychologically—the "Daisy Cutter."

Officially known as the BLU-82, the Daisy Cutter had been around since Vietnam. The bomb, at 15,000 pounds, was far too large to be carried by any bomber. So it was mounted on a sledlike device and slid out the rear door of a cargo plane. Once it left the plane, the BLU-82 would separate from the sled, and a parachute would open, lowering the mammoth bomb to the ground relatively slowly.

A three-foot-long probe stuck out from the bomb's snout, which detonated the device just before it would have landed on the ground. Inside the huge bomb canister would be packed several tons of a jellied mixture of aluminum powder, ammonium nitrate, and polystyrene soap. The effect upon ignition is biblical in its destruction.

Everything—people, vehicles, buildings, trees—within several hundred yards of the explosion would be vaporized. Blast overpressures of 1,000 pounds per square inch are created, forcing a concussion wave outward at the speed of sound that would level anything in its path. Everything for an area of three acres would be flattened; every living thing in an area of 120 acres would die from the shock wave. Furthermore, the Daisy Cutter produced a mushroom cloud that looked like a mini–atomic bomb.

Heads Up!

"We're not sure how you say 'Jesus Christ' in Iraqi."

—Col. Mike Samuel, CENTCOM Special Operations Commander, February 1991

"The Yanks have just nuked Kuwait!"

—Radio message from British SAS reconnaissance team, February 1991

The first Daisy Cutters to be dropped were in the area just north of Khafji, on top of Iraqi positions in Kuwait where remnants of the offensive force that had tried to invade Saudi had retreated and dug in. First, a modified C-130 would circle the area and drop leaflets, warning the troops below they were about to be hit with "the most powerful bomb ever made."

A few hours later, a BLU-82 would be ejected from the rear of a similar plane. After the war it was estimated that the 11 Daisy Cutters dropped during the Gulf War resulted in ten times as many defections as casualties.

Special Ops

After the Desert One hostage rescue fiasco in Iran in 1979, it became clear the U.S. military needed to pay more attention to commando and special operations units. In 1989, the unified U.S. Special Operations Command (USSOC) was established at MacDill Air Force Base in Florida—also CENTCOM headquarters. The USSOC had the job of tying together special operations units from the military's four branches:

◆ The U.S. Army Special Operations Command, based at Forth Bragg, North Carolina, included Airborne Rangers, Army Special Forces (the "Green Berets"), the 160th Special Operations Aviation Regiment (the "Night Stalkers"), and Psychological Operations (PSYOPS) units.

- The U.S. Air Force Special Operations Command, headquartered at Hurlburt Field, Florida, included the 16th Special Operations Wing (which often flew the Spectre gunships and dropped the Daisy Cutters); the 352nd Special Operations Group based in England; the 353rd Special Operations Group in Korea; and the 720th Special Tactics Group.

- The U.S. Naval Special Warfare Command, based at Coronado (San Diego), California, had responsibility for navy SEAL (sea, air, and land) commando units, including the supersecret SEAL Team Six, also called the Naval Special Warfare Development Group. It was also in charge of shallow-water Special Boat Units.

- The U.S. Marine Corps had numerous special operations capable units, all trained by the Special Operations Training Group in Okinawa, Japan. Each Marine Expeditionary Unit is trained to be capable of special operations, and also contains a Maritime Special Purpose Force, which can infiltrate and rescue personnel behind enemy lines. Other Special Ops marine units included the Fleet Antiterrorism Security Team and Direct Action Platoons.

In Desert Storm, U.S. special operations units worked with British Special Air Service (SAS) and Special Boat Service (SBS) commandos. The fact that the teams were inserted inside Iraq and helped hunt down SCUD launchers, as well as provide critical intelligence and rescue capability for downed pilots, was a tribute to the top British officer in the Gulf War, *Gen. Sir Peter de la Billiere.*

The British commando veteran convinced Schwartzkopf, who was always skeptical of special operations, that the SAS and U.S. Special Forces should be used inside Iraq. Most of their missions were successful. Some were not.

> ### Who's Who
>
> Peter de la Billiere was born in England in 1934. His naval officer father was killed in 1941. Peter joined the British Army as a private, rose through the ranks, served in Korea, Asia, and the Middle East, became a commando, and eventually commanded the SAS. He commanded all British forces during the Gulf War, was knighted, and retired in 1992.

Bravo Two Zero

The night the air war started, Sgt. Andy McNab (a cover name) and his eight-man SAS squad were helicoptered into Iraq near the Amman-Baghdad Highway. With the radio call sign "Bravo Two Zero," their job was to slice the fiber-optic cables that linked many of the SCUD launch sites. Each man carried 210 pounds of equipment and supplies to sustain the unit in the desert.

The eight-man squad was dropped and found a cave to use as a base camp. Things went wrong immediately. The radios were tuned to the wrong frequencies. The fiber-optic switching boxes were not where intelligence guessed they were. The weather was the coldest in the region in decades, old enough to freeze diesel oil. And a shepherd boy spotted Bravo Two Zero. He told Iraqi soldiers in a nearby village, who mounted a patrol.

McNab and his men had one option: escape, evade, and try to make it to the Syrian border, almost 100 miles away. Two of the troopers froze to death in the desert night. A third died in a firefight with the Iraqis, an engagement that left at least 60 Iraqi soldiers dead. The patrol became separated, and McNab, along with three others, was captured. Only commando Chris Ryan (another cover name) escaped into Syria.

> **Desert Lore**
>
> The Delta Force is officially the U.S. Army's 1st Special Force Operation Detachment-Delta, and is headquartered at Fort Bragg, North Carolina. Until the terrorist attacks of September 11, 2001, they and SEAL Team Six were the only military units devoted to counterterror operations outside the United States. Delta Force is organized in three squadrons, with expertise in specific areas of infiltration.

The four survivors of Bravo Two Zero were taken to Baghdad and tortured repeatedly. McNab's teeth were broken in a beating, so an Iraqi dentist was summoned to drill into McNab's good teeth and expose the nerves. All four were repatriated after the war. McNab became a best-selling author.

SOF in Black and White

While the SAS was infiltrating the area between the Amman-Baghdad Highway and the Saudi border in western Iraq, the U.S. *Delta Force* and the 160th Special Operations Aviation Regiment—the Night Stalkers—were trying to perform similar missions north of the highway, all the way to the Syrian border.

> **Who's Who**
>
> Wayne Downing was born in 1939 in Illinois. His father died in combat when Wayne was six. Downing joined the army, served in Vietnam, and personally accepted the surrender of Gen. Manuel Noriega in Panama in 1989. After the Gulf War, Downing commanded the entire U.S. Special Operations Command. He came out of retirement in 2001 to advise Pres. George W. Bush on fighting terrorism.

Two of the major special operations units in the region were White SOF (special operations forces) and Black SOF. The White SOF contingent was relatively large. In it were 7,000 combined army, air force, and navy commandos. Their job was to react immediately and rescue downed Allied pilots, as well as infiltrate, sabotage, and hook up with any dissident Iraqis or Kuwaiti resistance units.

But Black SOF has never been formally recognized as ever having existed. It was under the command of *army Gen. Wayne Downing*. Downing's units were later credited with shutting down the SCUD war for good. But neither the army nor the CIA will reveal any details of their activities.

The Least You Need to Know

◆ The Iraqi assault on Khafji took Allied commanders by surprise. The offensive was crippled and then destroyed by airpower.

◆ For the first time since World War II, an American servicewoman was taken prisoner.

◆ The shooting down of a U.S. Spectre gunship was avenged by using the mammoth BLU-82 "Daisy Cutter" bomb.

◆ British and U.S. Special Forces were active inside Iraq long before the ground war started.

Chapter **14**

February 5 to February 12

In This Chapter

- ◆ Allied air power continues to go after both individual ground targets and Republican Guard units
- ◆ American troops attempt a move to fake out the Iraqis
- ◆ The defense secretary and chairman of the Joint Chiefs of Staff travel to Saudi Arabia
- ◆ Half-century-old naval vessels prove their worth in a high-tech war with brute force

Interservice rivalries are as old as warfare itself. Ramses' charioteers probably thought they were the real force behind Egypt's might, while Alexander the Great's infantry probably felt jealous of the cavalry as their army conquered the known world. The Gulf War was no different as the ground and air forces snarled at each other.

But Desert Storm introduced something new: precision bombing. Until now, pursuing tanks, artillery pieces, armored personnel carriers, and mobile missile launchers with laser- and radar-guided munitions had been unavailable. This new capability led ground commanders—including supreme commander General Schwartzkopf—to complain that the air force was off operating on its own. The air commanders, not surprisingly, replied that they were saving the lives of ground troops.

Is a Ground War Necessary?

Quietly but persistently, the question of whether a ground war was necessary was asked (mostly by Air Force officers) as phase three of the air war moved to a new level. The military targeted Iraqi ground troops and emplacements, while the Allied air forces were attacking and destroying individual Iraqi weapons on the ground. The KTO, *Kuwait Theatre of Operations*, became an independent shooting match for the pilots.

> **Gulf Lingo**
>
> The KTO, Kuwait Theatre of Operations, was often used to refer to Iraqi targets inside Kuwait itself. In a more general way, it meant Kuwait, Iraq, and waters of the Persian Gulf, as well as parts of Saudi Arabia and Bahrain.

General Schwartzkopf's corps and divisional commanders began complaining, quietly but bitterly, that the air force wasn't concentrating enough on Iraqi troop positions but was instead expending smart bombs and missiles on individual pieces of hardware. They pointed out to the CENTCOM chief that pilots were using their *HARM missiles* not on Iraqi antipersonnel ground missile launchers, but against antiaircraft missiles.

Cheney and Powell to the Gulf

The argument over air power versus ground power soon became academic, as Defense Secretary Cheney and Joint Chiefs Chairman General Powell left for Saudi Arabia on February 7. The Bush administration was committed to a ground war, and the two power brokers wanted to see about preparations for themselves. The tension between the two was often almost palpable.

> **The Machines**
>
> The AGM-88 HARM (High-Speed Antiradiation Missile) entered the U.S. arsenal in 1984. The 14-foot-long missile is "fire and forget," meaning it hones in on the slightest bit of radiation from a radar installation once fired. HARM missiles, usually fired by F-16s, have a range of around 30 miles.

Cheney was a rock-ribbed conservative politician, and a hawk when it came to Iraq. He wanted Saddam taken out sooner rather than later, and viewed Powell as a general who had become too cautious through years of driving a desk. Powell, for his part, was a career soldier who had seen combat in Vietnam and who had little patience with someone whose entire view of war was based on theory, not from seeing men wounded and dying. Surprisingly, though, the two men managed to work well together despite the tension.

When they arrived, Cheney and Powell immediately went into Riyadh meetings with Schwartzkopf and his staff. They were updated on the Jedi Knights plan for the rapid movement of troops west, then wheeling and hitting Iraq and Kuwait once the ground war started. They were also briefed on how long it would take to reduce the effectiveness of Iraqi troops with the air campaign; they were told it would last until late February at least.

When the two men returned to Washington, they immediately went to the White House. President Bush, perhaps remembering his days as the youngest fighter pilot shot down in World War II, agreed to give the air campaign the time it needed.

Desert Lore

George Bush enlisted in the navy when he was 18. On September 2, 1944, he was flying his 58th combat mission when his Avenger torpedo bomber was shot down near the Japanese-held island of Chichi Jima. He was rescued from the ocean by the submarine USS *Finback*. He was 19 years old.

The Colonel's Maps

On February 5, U.S. Marine Corps Col. Mark Swanstrom traveled from Saudi Arabia to Washington. Colonel Swanstrom was the chief engineer for the 2nd Marine Division. The 1st and 2nd Marine Divisions' job was to divert the Iraqis once a ground war began by trying to slam through the Iraqi lines in southern Kuwait, then attempting to push due north while the surprise maneuver from the west hit Kuwait from that direction.

The marines knew the Iraqis had been laying mines and putting oil into trenches in front of their positions, as well as constructing sand berms. Berms were originally used as earthen dams. In Kuwait, sand berms were bulldozed into place by Iraqi troops to protect the front of their defensive positions. Each berm was roughly three to five feet wide and up to 10 feet high.

To get through these formidable defenses, the marines needed good maps, so Colonel Swanstrom met with representatives from both the DIA and U.S. Army Intelligence. Using a combination of satellite images and photos taken by overflying planes, the intelligence agencies provided the marines with maps of Iraqi defensive positions. Within three days, Colonel Swanstrom was back in Saudi Arabia and every U.S. Marine company commander soon had a copy of the maps.

The Battleships

The Komodo dragon is an evolutionary throwback, a direct descendant of the dinosaurs. In the same way, the two American battleships in the Persian Gulf—the USS *Wisconsin* and the USS *Missouri*—were throwbacks, directly descended from the dreadnoughts of the American and European navies that plowed through the oceans at the turn of the 20th century.

The Machines

The USS *Missouri*, BB-63, nicknamed the Mighty Mo, was launched in 1944. The ship was hit by Japanese kamikaze planes in the battle of Leyte Gulf. On September 2, 1945, Japan formally surrendered on the deck of the *Missouri* in Tokyo Bay. The ship saw action in Korea, was decommissioned in 1954, then was recommissioned in 1986. The *Missouri* retired after the Gulf War, and is now a floating museum and memorial at Pearl Harbor, Hawaii.

Modern strategists thought the day of the battleship was over by the end of the Korean War. But the Reagan administration reactivated three of the battlewagons in the mid 1980s—the *Iowa*, the *Missouri*, and the *Wisconsin*—outfitted them with new missiles and radar, and gave them a singular job. In the event of war with the Soviet Union, their job was to park themselves at the entrance to the Baltic Sea and bottle up the Soviet fleet for as long as possible.

In the Gulf War, two battleships—the *Wisconsin* and the *Missouri*—were used simultaneously for the first time since World War II, and for the last time in military history. The dreadnoughts were no longer prowling 10,000-fathom blue water preparing to engage an enemy over the horizon, but were instead cruising relatively shallow Persian Gulf waters and terrifying the enemy like a pair of seagoing B-52s.

On February 5, for example, the battlewagons launched cruise missiles, but the *Missouri* unlimbered its massive battery of nine 16-inch guns and reduced an Iraqi artillery emplacement in Kuwait to shrapnel. In the 48-hour period ending February 6, the Mighty Mo fired 112 16-inch shells, the equivalent of what would have been fired to support a World War II Pacific landing. Five artillery sites, a command bunker, and a radar installation were destroyed, the massive shells echoing overhead with a sound like the fabric of the sky itself tearing.

Desert Lore

The Mark 7 16-inch battleship guns fired two projectiles—a high explosive weighing one ton, and a 2,700-pound armor-piercing round that could penetrate 30 feet of concrete. Each shell could travel up to 22 miles. Gunners inside the turrets breech-loaded each projectile, carefully followed with cylindrical silk bags packed with gunpowder.

Many of the strikes were guided by the first combat use of UAVs (unmanned aerial vehicles), pilotless drones that came into wide use as the war against terrorism erupted after September 11, 2001. Guided by a UAV, for example, the *Wisconsin* on February 7 destroyed boats and piers, blasted artillery emplacements, and wrecked radar sites in Iraq and Kuwait. The *Missouri*, meantime, shifted to a support role for the marines, and on February 12 fired 60 of its massive shells at Iraqi positions while protecting a marine reconnaissance incursion into southern Kuwait.

The Wadi al-Batin Strategy

As we noted a few chapters back, the Wadi al-Batin—the dry riverbed running from Saudi into Kuwait—was thought by most Iraqi strategists to be where part of the main Allied punch would center. After all, the Iraqis themselves had used the wadi to shield some of their troop movements during their ill-fated move on Khafji.

CENTCOM let the Iraqis think they were right. The troops of VII Corps faced the Iraqis near the wadi, and VII Corps commander *Gen. Fred Franks* wanted to make sure the Iraqis thought that the major assault would come straight down the wadi's throat. So on February 7, the 1st Cavalry Division and VII Corps artillery began pouring fire into the

wadi. Franks had three reasons for doing it: 1) convincing the Iraqis the wadi was the main invasion road; 2) giving his own artillery valuable live fire practice; and 3) blasting away any Iraqi artillery in the wadi region.

On February 7, 1st Cavalry artillery opened up with a high-tech weapon, the *Copperhead* projectile. A forward artillery-spotting vehicle popped up its periscope and aimed a laser beam at a 40-foot-tall Iraqi observation tower. The tower, located in the flat terrain, had an unobstructed view for almost 20 miles in every direction. A 155-millimeter howitzer 10 miles away fired one Copperhead that destroyed the tower.

While that action continued, the Iraqis decided to reinforce the area around the wadi. One-hundred-millimeter antitank guns were quietly being dug into the soft sand sides of the dried riverbed. This move would have deadly consequences in a few days.

The activity around Wadi al-Batin was vital when it came to deceiving Iraq about CENTCOM's true intentions. If Iraq had had active intelligence inside Saudi Arabia, spy satellites, a few planes with cameras, or even some soldiers to infiltrate and report back, Baghdad might have had some hint about Allied tactics. But they had none of the above.

Who's Who

Fred Franks was born in Pennsylvania in 1938. A West Point graduate, Franks was wounded in combat in Cambodia in 1970. He rose from platoon to regimental commander, and commanded U.S. and British VII Corps forces during Desert Storm. He retired in 1994, wrote a best-selling book in collaboration with Tom Clancy, and now teaches military history and theory.

The Machines

The M712 Copperhead is the grandfather of all "smart" artillery ammunition. Four and a half feet long and 138 pounds, the Copperhead is fired from a cannon, pops out fins like a rocket, and follows the forward spotter's laser beam to within inches of any target.

Preparing the Forward Pass

Call it the "Hail Mary" or the "forward pass," the football analogy to the placement of Allied troops before the ground war started was apt. The idea was to "go long," or to move as many troops and as much materiel as possible as fast as possible west along the Tapline Road. Fuel depots near the road made sure Humvees, tanks, artillery, missile launchers, trucks, ambulances, helicopters, and anything else powered by internal combustion could keep moving until they were all poised like a 300-mile-long knife blade aimed at Iraq's belly.

The thrust, it was becoming clear, would be into Iraq's Sahra al-Hijarah desert, mostly trackless and empty dirt, sand, dunes, and scrub that shared several hundred miles of border with Saudi Arabia. At points, the Tapline Road was only a couple of miles from the frontier, so it automatically became the MSR—Major supply route. Its code name was MSR Dodge.

For the maneuver to work, three conditions had to be met. First, Saddam had to be completely ignorant of one of the largest mass movements of troops and equipment since World War II. Second, he had to be convinced that the Allies were going to hit him not from the west, but from the south, with marines and Arab troops along the coast, and the 1st Cavalry Division up the Wadi al Batin. Part of that also involved making him think a huge D-Day or *Inchon*-style amphibious landing was possible from the east. Third, the men and women in logistics had to perform heroic feats to keep gasoline, water, spare parts, bullets, and bandages flowing.

Logistical Base Charlie was a microcosm of what it took to prepare the forward pass. At one point, the border between Saudi and Iraq takes a sharp turn due north. The Saudi town of Rahfa sits just a couple of miles west of Iraq, just north of the Tapline Road. Logistical Base Charlie was set up just southeast of town, close to the road and even closer than Rahfa to Iraq. Once the air war had started, the U.S. Army's 20th Engineer Battalion had 48 hours to construct Charlie and get it up and running. They beat the deadline.

The acronyms around Charlie were thick as sand fleas. There were several ASPs (Ammunition Supply Points) and RRFs (Rapid Refueling Points supplied by the TPT, Tactical Petroleum Terminal) that helped gas up planes on the FLS (Forward Landing Strip, where fuel was hauled) by a fleet of HEMTTs (Heavy Expanded Mobility Tactical Trucks). The least glamorous units in any armed forces—the quartermasters—oversaw all of

Gulf Lingo

Inchon is a harbor city on the Yellow Sea in South Korea. On September 15, 1950, 70,000 American troops landed behind enemy lines and stormed the area, driving quickly to retake the capital of Seoul from the invading North Koreans, and trapping the entire North Korean invasion force by slicing their rear supply and communications lines.

this activity. Literally, the "masters of quarters," the quartermasters' designation came from the 1500s. Before 1686, the British army called them "Harbingers," as in units that went in front of an army to arrange supplies and lodging. The U.S. Army created a separate Quartermaster Regiment in 1986.

The 102nd Quartermaster Detachment ran the day-to-day operations of Charlie. Their main job was rapid refueling of 101st Airborne Division and other helicopters that used the RRFs. Up to 20 helicopters of all kinds could be refueled at once, and often were, since the 101st was staging recon and other operations inside Iraq, using Charlie as a hopping-off point. At its busiest, Charlie ran 38 separate bases, from fuel to ammunition.

Charlie also supplied the earth movers and road graders needed to scrape out two-lane roads, which had to be capable of handling heavy equipment moving up to 30 miles an hour without shaking the combat hardware to pieces with ruts, rocks, and potholes. The 937th Engineering Group constructed a series of the roads connecting Tapline Road with the various *phase lines*, the points where ground troops were to stop and wait, out of sight of the Iraqis, for the ground war to start.

A road grader driver's seat and a diplomat's desk chair had one thing in common this week: The war was being fought by the people in both of them.

Gulf Lingo

Phase lines in the Gulf War had code names ranging from Abilene and Apricot to Razor and Vermont. They were map lines just inside Saudi Arabia, on low ground and out of sight of Iraqi observation towers, from which troops would launch the ground war assault.

Diplomatic Rhetoric

President Bush met reporters on February 5, and found that Desert Storm was proceeding quietly enough so that he didn't mention the war until the sixth paragraph of his opening statement. Bush had chosen to ignore a tentative peace overture from Iran that offered to use Tehran as an intermediary because there wasn't a proposal in it for Iraq to withdraw from Kuwait by a specific date. Many in Washington believed the U.S. government secretly feared that Iraq might give up before a ground war, and that President Bush looked at a quick and effective ground campaign as a way to exorcise all of America's Vietnam ghosts.

It's an interpretation Bush and his advisors have always scoffed at.

Bush used this news conference to issue a veiled warning to the Iraqis that any use of chemical weapons might be met with a U.S. nuclear response.

The next day, Jordan's King Hussein ripped into the United States and the Allies in a speech broadcast throughout the Middle East. A few hours later, Secretary of State James

Baker came out with the administration's view of a postwar Middle East. Among Baker's five points was one the administration hoped would defuse future conflicts in the region: a comprehensive Arab-Israeli peace.

Heads Up!

" … he ought to think very, very carefully about doing that (using chemical weapons). Very, very carefully. And I will leave that up to a very fuzzy interpretation … I would not discuss options ahead of time one way or another."

—Pres. George Bush answering a reporter's question about the United States possibly using weapons of mass destruction in response to chemical weapons, February 5, 1991

By February 7, the Bush administration, which was fuming at King Hussein, began a comprehensive review of all U.S. aid to Jordan. Meanwhile, the international community began to glean the implicit threat that America's nuclear arsenal might be brought to bear if Saddam used his chemical stockpiles. Baker, with an eye toward the criticism and toward appeasing the coalition's Arabs, suggested that the entire Middle East be made a nuclear-free zone. He hoped it would take the edge off the president's hint and placate Arabs worried about Israel's nuclear arsenal. The French, meantime, said any use of weapons of mass destruction—nuclear, biological, or chemical—would be "barbarian."

Red Star Setting

Several hundred miles north of Iraq, the Soviet Union was disintegrating. Only a few years earlier, Desert Storm would have been almost impossible to launch because of the Soviets' influence in Iraq. Any military move against Saddam would have been a modern version of the Berlin Airlift or the Cuban Missile Crisis—it could have brought the world to the brink of nuclear war as the Americans and Russians went eyeball-to-eyeball.

The Berlin Wall fell in 1989, and formerly Communist East Germany united with West Germany in October 1990, right in the middle of Desert Shield. Between 1989 and 1990, the Soviet Union's European satellites had all deserted Communism—Poland, Czechoslovakia, Hungary, Yugoslavia, Bulgaria, Romania, and the Germans conquered after World War II all left the Soviet orbit.

Opposition parties and limited free markets had been allowed inside the USSR itself since 1990. The stage was set for the total dissolution of the Soviet Union and for the collapse of Western Communism, which came in December 1991. But in February, the Soviets still existed, albeit weakened and distracted. Anti-Israeli forces in the Arab world, from the PLO to Hezbollah, had lost their Soviet backing. And from Havana to Baghdad, the Kremlin was pulling back from its allies.

The Soviets were almost complete nonplayers in the region. But they still commanded some 20,000 nuclear warheads, and as Al Capone once noted, "A loaded gun and a kind word get you so much farther than just a kind word."

Soviet leader *Mikhail Gorbachev* was determined to exercise his country's waning influence and try and prevent any American-led military campaign less than 500 miles from his own unstable borders. So on February 5, he sent Foreign Minister Eduard Shevardnadze to Tehran, hoping to bring in the Iranians as intermediaries. The Iranians agreed, but their overture went nowhere.

A few days later, Gorbachev reacted to the constant aerial pounding of Iraq by saying he thought the constant pummeling of bridges, highways, electrical plants, and water supplies went well beyond what the United Nations required, and was punishing the Iraqi population. He also urged Saddam to take a "more realistic" view of the situation.

In a last-ditch move to put out the diplomatic fires, Gorbachev dispatched veteran diplomat Yevgeny Primakov to Baghdad to meet with Saddam. The Russian got more double-talk. The Iraqi leader told Primakov that any cease-fire was off the table, and 24 hours later told him he'd consider thinking about withdrawing from Kuwait if the bombing stopped. Nevertheless, the Soviets invited Iraqi Foreign Minister Aziz to Moscow for personal meetings with Gorbachev. Aziz agreed, feeling that world opinion might be slowly turning in Iraq's favor because of what diplomats called the CNN Factor: video of civilian damage inside Iraq.

> ### Who's Who
>
> Mikhail Sergeyevich Gorbachev was born in 1931. An attorney, he joined the Communist Party in 1952 and by 1985 became general secretary of the Communist Party. He was president of the Soviet Union in 1990 and 1991, favoring *glasnost* (openness) and *peristroika* (change). He oversaw the dismantling of the Soviet state, retired to private life, and now heads the Gorbachev Foundation.

Collateral Means Civilian

Throughout history, military leaders have commented on the slaughter of war. We get the phrase "pyrrhic victory" from the Greek king Phyrrus, who leaned on his lance after a particularly bloody battle against Rome and said, "Another victory like this and we are finished." Confederate Commander Robert E. Lee noted, "It is good war is so horrible lest we should become too fond of it." Union Gen. William Tecumseh Sherman was more to the point: "War is hell."

The Pentagon seemed to be more indebted to George Orwell, though, when it coined a new term in the Gulf War—"collateral damage"—to refer to bombs and missiles that missed and hit nontargeted, usually civilian, areas. The bloodless phrase was being given flesh and bone by Iraqi propaganda tours conducted for overseas TV operations. A blasted apartment building in Basra; the baby milk factory; flattened homes in Nasiryah; video of Iraqi civilians either in hospitals or being pulled from the rubble—it was all having a slow but cumulative effect.

Kurds in Iraq's north, always firmly opposed to Saddam, reported to Washington that at least 800 of their civilians had died in Allied air strikes. When he met with British Defense Minister Thomas King at the White House on February 12, the president, according to British reports, seemed worried that continuous publicity surrounding civilian casualties was damaging international support. But the worst was to come within 24 hours.

Inside Saddam

Why? Why would any rational leader subject his country to constant bombing and his army to almost certain destruction? Why would Saddam Hussein spill oil into the Arabian Gulf, ignite Kuwaiti oil fields, and order his forces to dig in opposite superior forces armed with the latest technology? Why would he sit and watch as Allied air power cut off electricity, smashed bridges, destroyed highways and railroads, blasted water plants, and push his country into the early nineteenth century? Why would he allow the coalition blockade to cut off food and medical imports?

U.S. intelligence had no firm answers. Indeed, at one point, General Schwartzkopf became enraged at a "fuzzy" psychological profile of Saddam offered by the CIA. The problem was that Allied analysts misread Saddam as seriously as the Iraqi dictator misread the West.

Saddam had become Nietzsche by way of Saladin and Stalin. He had a will to retain power, a vision of Pan-Arab grandiosity, and a ruthlessness unfathomable to most descendants of the Enlightenment, an eighteenth century movement that emphasized science and rationality. The iron-willed small-town boy who became Saddam Hussein never read John Milton's *Paradise Lost*, but his foreign minister had. And the English literature major inside Tariq Aziz could easily recognize his boss in Milton's Lucifer, bellowing that it was "… better to rule in Hell than serve in Heaven."

Saddam expected to win by losing and cared absolutely nothing for the damage being done to his people. A rearrangement of military command here, a few promotions in the Ba'ath Party there, and Saddam cemented loyalty to him in the structure of Iraq's ruling elite, which was the only thing that mattered.

He would save face among the Arab Nation by being defeated by a vastly superior force rather than surrender to the West in advance. And if his read of American psychology was accurate (which it turned out not to be), he might even be able to salvage a victory by inflicting heavy casualties on U.S. forces and causing an outcry among the American population.

Even if that didn't work, he would still gain prestige—he thought—by going down fighting against the Allied behemoth. Besides, he and the rest of the al-Tikritis were making a handsome profit on food, fuel, and medicine, since any of the embargoed material that made it into Iraq couldn't be smuggled in without Saddam's participation, and without Saddam controlling its price and distribution.

As usual, other Iraqis were about to pay the price for Saddam's ambition.

The Least You Need to Know

- ◆ Allied air power was thoroughly dominating the skies over Iraq and Kuwait, destroying troops and infrastructure.
- ◆ The Allies prepared to deceive the Iraqis by convincing them that the main thrust into Kuwait would come from the south.
- ◆ At the same time, one of the largest movements of people and equipment in military history was taking place, preparing to strike into Iraq and Kuwait farther to the west.
- ◆ Diplomatic efforts to avoid a ground war continued, although without much hope of success.

15

February 13 to February 19

In This Chapter

- Hundreds of Iraqi civilians die when U.S. "bunker busting" bombs slam into an air raid shelter
- The Russian-sponsored negotiations to avoid a ground war continue
- The air campaign increases in tempo, targeting troop concentrations
- The Battle of the Ruqi Pocket occurs before the ground war ever breaks out

Military strategist James Dunnigan once wrote: "Bombing ground targets from the air is an art, and there's always been a shortage of artists." That rather blithely explains everything from on-scene mistakes to bad intelligence and is as close as any explanation for the horror that resulted when an air-raid shelter packed with Iraqi men, women, and children was incinerated in mid February by a bomb dropped by an American fighter plane. The difference between the air-raid shelter bombing and the atrocities committed against civilians by Iraqi forces was that the bombing was a mistake, since Allied intelligence reported that the shelter was a command bunker. But Saddam's forces had systematically targeted civilians among Kurds, Kuwaitis, Iraqis, and Iranians for years. Intent was the distinction, but it was a distinction without a difference to the families of the dead and injured.

al-Amerieh

It was 2:30 A.M. on February 13, and the weather front that had slipped across northern Saudi Arabia and Kuwait causing rain and fog had lowered temperatures in Baghdad to near freezing. Uum Gaida, a 34-year-old housewife, couldn't sleep, which wasn't surprising since she was packed inside a bomb shelter with several hundred other people from the al-Amerieh neighborhood nine miles west of downtown Baghdad.

Due to the pounding bombs had given Baghdad's infrastructure, the shelter was one of the few places in the neighborhood with electricity, heat, and running water. But the Allied bombing seemed to be scaling back in the area, so Gaida took her restless eight-year-old son with her and decided to go back to her apartment to try and do some laundry in the cold water she had stored in her sinks. She also just wanted to get some air.

Her girls, one 13, one six, were sleeping, and she decided to let them get some rest. So she trudged through the dark streets with the boy, hoping that maybe the familiar routine at home would help calm her so she could come back to the shelter and get some rest.

At almost the same time that the shelter's six-inch-thick doors were creaking shut behind Gaida, a pair of F-117 Nighthawk Stealth Fighters were lifting off from Taif, Saudi Arabia.

What the Iraqis called the al-Amerieh shelter, CENTCOM called the al-Firdos bunker, and two days before, on February 11, it had been added to the master attack plan. Contractors from Finland had built the shelter during the Iran-Iraq War. The Finns had constructed 25 air-raid shelters in and around Baghdad during the early days of the Iran-Iraq War. Some were hardened against direct hits, even nearby strikes by nuclear weapons, and U.S. intelligence had long suspected many of them were command bunkers. The Finnish contractor gave the United States the al-Amerieh shelter plans so smart bombs could target the relatively weak area around a ventilation shaft. A high-ranking Iraqi officer, spying for the CIA, told U.S. intelligence that the Iraqi army and secret police agencies were using the shelter as an alternate command center, and that top officials and sophisticated communications equipment were in the lower levels of the hardened shelter.

> **The Machines**
>
> The GBU-27 (Guided Bomb Unit) follows a laser beam fired from a Stealth Fighter and "rides" it down to its target. The guts of the GBU-27 is a one-ton bomb capable of blasting through steel-reinforced concrete. Once released, tail fins deploy, helping guide the bomb to within inches of where it's aimed.

Only the F-117s were allowed to bomb Baghdad, and for good reason. They had earned their Arabic nickname of "*shaba*," or ghost, by hammering Baghdad nightly without suffering a scratch themselves. The pair of *shabas* winging toward Baghdad were armed with a weapon carried only by the F-117, the *GBU-27* laser guided bomb.

The two Nighthawks reached their station over western Baghdad around 4:30 A.M. The first GBU-27 was launched, aimed straight at the ventilation grid on the shelter's reinforced roof. As accurate as advertised, the bomb burrowed into the steel and concrete and went off, blowing a ten-foot-wide hole in the roof. Debris rained down inside the shelter, and the blast shook Uum Gaida in her apartment several blocks away.

Within a minute, the second Nighthawk released the second GBU-27, and it easily zipped toward the gaping chasm in the roof. The second bomb flew through the opening and went off inside the shelter. The six-foot-thick concrete walls and half-foot-thick steel doors of the shelter became a crematorium.

Inside a steel mill blast furnace, temperatures run around 1,500°F. The temperatures inside the shelter were five times that great. Human beings simply vaporized. Days later, Uum Gaida found the shadows of children's palm prints burned into the concrete. No one could tell her if they belonged to her two girls. Between 400 and 500 people had died.

At first, CENTCOM trumpeted the raid, airing video of the precise hits by the laser-guided bombs, claiming that the bunker was an Iraqi command-and-control center. There were, indeed, some scattered intelligence reports that the shelter might have served that purpose during daylight hours, but not at night.

When it became clear what had happened, General Powell was appalled. He went to the White House to justify the targeting of the shelter. And he notified the *Black Hole*—the supersecret planning center in Riyadh—that henceforth no missions, not even one, would be flown over Baghdad without the express approval from the chairman of the joint chiefs.

Until the shelter was bombed, 25 specific missions were approved against Baghdad itself. After the incident, there were only seven missions. Powell took the heat from his protesting commanders because of a larger goal—to prevent the coalition from falling apart if there was another disaster like this one.

> **Gulf Lingo**
>
> The **Black Hole** was the nickname given to the CENTCOM planning center in Riyadh that plotted targets and tactics for the air campaign. It got its name because it was in a cavernous, poorly lit basement.

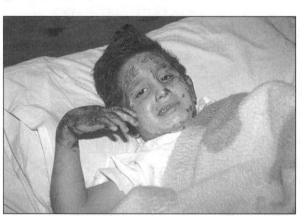

A burned Iraqi child recovers in a hospital after the bombing of the al-Amerieh shelter.

Fallujah

If ever one city represented the "fog of war," it was al-Fallujah, located about 50 miles west of Baghdad on the banks of the Euphrates River. On one hand, Fallujah was home to storage facilities for Iraq's nuclear program, a fact that would become apparent after the Gulf War when weapons inspectors discovered uranium there. It was also home to a facility that manufactured chemical agents including mustard gas. And as a DIA memo to CENTCOM noted, it was also being used to produce biological weapons.

U.S. intelligence also estimated that the chemical operation at Fallujah could produce up to 1,000 tons a month of both sarin and V.X. nerve gases. Those three facilities for nuclear, chemical, and biological weapons—code-named Fallujah I, II, and III by the United States and Project 9230 by the Iraqis—were near the top of Allied priority targets.

> ## Heads Up!
>
> "... [A] bunker in which botulinum toxin is stored ... is located in a fenced area at Fallujah .... [N]early 80 percent of the facility at Fallujah is underground .... [T]hese underground facilities for processing may be for weaponization."
>
> —Defense Intelligence Agency Intelligence Report 2-201-0768, January 1991

Since Fallujah was also home to an Iraqi air force base, it was doubly a target.

But Fallujah was also a city of more than 200,000 people, with the usual assortment of civilian bridges, buildings, streets, and marketplaces. And February 13, the same day as the al-Amerieh shelter bombing, the British Royal Air Force flew a formation of Tornados to target bridges and part of the weapons complexes in the city. The Tornado fighter-bomber was designed by a team from Britain, Germany, and Italy, and is used by several air forces around the world. The swing-wing two-seat aircraft entered service in 1979. At 54 feet in length, the jet can carry nine tons of missiles and bombs, and has been measured at a top speed of over 1,400 miles per hour.

One of the Royal Air Force's laser-guided bombs was released as the plane's laser designator illuminated one of the Euphrates bridges. For some reason, the bomb refused to track directly along the laser beam, and instead wobbled and fell out of control several blocks away. It smashed into a marketplace, killing 130 civilians.

Iraq immediately rushed foreign TV crews to the site to record the wailing civilians and the devastation. The Royal Air Force, to its eternal credit, conducted an immediate investigation and released the cockpit video of the bombing three days later. The British, with typical forthrightness, decided that killing civilians by accident was bad enough without trying to cover it up. Saddam, for his part, never apologized for placing high-priority military installations next to civilian areas.

Diplomatic Options

Unexpectedly, Soviet President Gorbachev's effort to mediate the end of the war had "legs," as Washington insiders say, which meant it looked like it might go someplace. Gorbachev had invited Tariq Aziz for talks in Moscow following Soviet meetings with Iraqi officials in Baghdad. After those initial meetings, Iraq issued a statement on February 15 saying Saddam would agree to withdraw from Kuwait and abide by the U.N. resolutions, but only if all offensive military action was halted immediately. President Bush rejected the offer.

Gorbachev knew his weakened nation was in no position to challenge the might of the United States. By sending Yevgeny Primakov to Baghdad, Gorbachev had picked someone who had known Saddam for two decades, and thereby increased the chances that the Soviets could at least remain players in the region. Saddam listened politely, indicated he might think about withdrawing from Kuwait if the bombing stopped, and dispatched Tariq Aziz to Moscow.

We don't know if Aziz believed it himself, but we do know he went to the Soviet Union armed with the Ba'ath Party dogma that death was preferable to dishonor and that the Allies didn't have the stomach for a ground war. His Russian hosts later remarked that they had told Aziz that Iraq was facing utter devastation, and that he had merely nodded and lit another cigarette.

Gorbachev had come up with a four-point plan that insisted, first and foremost, that Iraq withdraw from Kuwait. He also pushed Aziz to accept a framework that would not have required progress on Palestinian-Israeli relations, even though the Gorbachev proposal still mentioned the desirability of an overall settlement between the two.

> **Heads Up!**
>
> "There's no evidence of any withdrawal ... it's a cruel ploy. What he did was to reiterate some conditions and add some new ones, and it's totally unacceptable to everybody."
> —Pres. George Bush February 15, 1991

> **Desert Lore**
>
> The four main points of the Gorbachev peace proposal of February 1991 were: Iraqi withdrawal from Kuwait; a commitment from the Soviets to assure Saddam was left in power and Iraq's borders were left intact; a statement by the Soviets opposing any sanctions of any kind against Iraq; and the beginning of talks aimed at a broader Middle East peace, including Israel-Palestinian relations.

Aziz flew into Moscow on February 17. He returned to Iraq 16 hours later, promising that Saddam would fully consider all the implications in the proposal. The United States didn't believe him and we don't know if he believed it, either.

We do know that Washington took the negotiations seriously enough to postpone the ground war. It had originally been scheduled to start on February 18. But on the off chance Aziz and Gorbachev might come up with something, G (for ground) day was pushed back to February 21. A combination of diplomacy and the need for more air strikes would eventually push G-day back even more.

Air War Tactics

As the aerial campaign continued, Phase Three, which involved targeting Iraqi ground troops, shifted into high gear. While most of the damage was being done in the south from planes launched from Saudi Arabia or from aircraft carriers, significant strikes were being conducted in the north, from a NATO air base in Turkey.

The northern front operation was called Operation Proven Force, designed to pressure Iraq by bombarding targets in the northern half of the country. Proven Force targets included biological and chemical weapons facilities, but they also provided a deterrent to Saddam in case he decided to park any of his elite army units in Kurdish country to the north.

At the same time, a certain amount of controversy was being generated about *bomb damage assessment*. British estimates of Iraqi capabilities, for example, had been consistently higher than American figures. General Schwartzkopf, not wanting to see a Vietnam-style replay of inflated enemy casualty figures, took an unusual step.

On February 13, CENTCOM intelligence analysts were instructed to keep counting all of the damage photographed by overflying recon planes, but to discount pilot reports of damage, counting sometimes only half of what pilots told debriefers was hit. The reasoning behind the move involved something far more important than avoiding public relations embarrassment. CENTCOM wanted to make sure that Iraqi ground forces were degraded by at least half before staring a ground war.

Gulf Lingo

BDA, bomb damage assessment, is the technique used to estimate damage done to enemy facilities from the air. It's usually accomplished by photo reconnaissance missions, often flown by remodeled fighter jets such as the F-4 or the F-111.

Meanwhile, U.S. Army commanders started grousing, loudly, about air strikes. They felt too much air force and navy firepower was being expended on behind-the-lines Republican Guard units, or on Iraqi forces dug in across from the U.S. Marines and Arab forces, and not enough tonnage was being dropped on Iraqi troops farther west, where the VII and XVIII Army Corps would be attacking. Besides, they noted, marine airpower was only being targeted at Iraqi units in marine sectors.

General Schwartzkopf had an answer that may have placated the army brass, but it certainly didn't satisfy them completely. Since the Iraqis were effectively blind when it came to intelligence gathering, Schwartzkopf didn't want to provide them a seeing eye dog by heavy bombing that might tip them off as to where the surprise attack would come. So he said yes, Iraqi artillery, infantry, and armor across from western Army positions would get more air strikes, but no, they wouldn't be as heavy as his ground commanders wanted.

The Ruqi Pocket

To keep the deception going, the Iraqis had to be convinced that the main ground attack would come from the south, up the Wadi al Batin or straight into southern Iraq. So a series of skirmishes, feints, raids, and shoot-outs that eventually became known as the Battle of the Ruqi Pocket began, named for the tiny Saudi settlement of al-Ruqi. Al-Ruqi is a small Saudi town just south of the Neutral Zone between Iraq and Saudi, a diamond-shaped patch of land claimed by both countries. In the Koran, the phrase "al-ruqi" means a prank or a joke.

The deception began in earnest on the afternoon of February 15, with combat engineers and artillery from the 1st Cavalry's 2nd Brigade deciding to make life interesting for Iraqis nearby.

Berm Busting

At around 2 P.M. on February 15, elements of the 1st Cavalry began moving in tanks and Bradley Fighting Vehicles toward a rolling series of sand berms that separated Iraq from Saudi. Close behind were 155-millimeter self-propelled howitzers. Also along for the ride was a psychological operations (psy-ops) unit with cassette players and loudspeakers.

Before the initial operation, the psy-ops unit began playing tapes of heavy equipment grinding and straining through the sand to make the Iraqis think a huge number of troops were closing in on the area. The combat engineers crept forward and placed charges under the berm, and at 4:30 P.M., the howitzer batteries opened fire for precisely seven minutes, plastering assigned targets on the Iraqi side of the berm.

Once the firing stopped, the infantry scooted through the holes in the berm and secured a roadway on the Iraqi side. It was a small hole in a giant berm, but the smoke, shelling, and psy-ops prerecorded noise convinced the Iraqis that a major incursion might be underway. It was enough, as it turned out, to tie down the better part of an Iraqi division.

Operation Red Storm

As the holes were blown in the berm, the 1st Cavalry's 82nd Field Artillery had more work to do. As their guns cooled from the afternoon berm breach, they turned their *155-millimeter howitzers* hard right, driving 10 miles or so east for another feint at the

Iraqis, this one designed to make them think the Wadi al-Batin was still the main highway for the ground war.

This maneuver was designed to tie up the better part of another Iraqi division, and it started a little after midnight with artillery cascading dozens of shells down on Iraqi radar, observation, and troops positions within a three-minute span. As soon as the howitzers let up, there was a frontal probe as Apache attack helicopters from the 11th Aviation Brigade flew low and fast up the wadi, blasting Iraqi forward artillery emplacements. At the same time, a precoordinated air strike pounded the actual Iraqi troop concentrations several miles ahead with antipersonnel cluster bombs.

> **The Machines**
>
> The M-109 self-propelled howitzer, to the uninitiated, looks like a tank. Looks are deceiving, since a tank might carry, at most, a 120-millimeter cannon, while the 155-millimeter weapon in the M-109 is heavy artillery. It can travel at 35 miles an hour and heave a 100-pound shell more than 16 miles.

With no intelligence, no communications network to relay orders from Baghdad, and no technology that came even close to what the Americans had, all that the several thousand Iraqi soldiers could do was sit and wait for the main attack that was sure to come from their front. Four days later, the U.S. forces would move up the wadi again, with bloodier results for both sides.

SCUDs Again

Between February 13 and February 18, 10 SCUD missiles were launched, which was 11 too many for CENTCOM planners. The military had concluded that the missiles were nothing but nuisance weapons, lacking almost any tactical value. But as before, the missiles had strategic value on the diplomatic front because they kept landing in Israel, outraging Israeli civilians, who kept complaining to the Israeli government, which in turn kept raising hell in Washington.

The F-14 Tomcats flying off the decks of U.S. carriers had dual roles. They were designed to clear the skies of Iraqi jets—by now a moot point—and they were used for photo reconnaissance. Using a pod called TARPS—Tactical Air Reconnaissance Pod System—the F-14s were able to deliver high-quality infrared and regular recon photos to CENTCOM. On February 13, Joint Chiefs Chairman General Powell ordered at least one TARP mission every day should be flown over suspected SCUD launch sites south and west of Baghdad.

At the same time, Allied Air Force Commander General Horner was under additional pressure to get rid of more SCUDs. U-2 spy planes were retasked to photograph suspected SCUD sites. As always, orbiting spy satellites from the *Defense Support Program* spotted SCUD launches immediately and relayed the word to CENTCOM. But Horner, Powell, Schwartzkopf, Cheney, and the president wanted the launches stopped, not detected.

The same problem plagued anti-SCUD defenses throughout the war: A lot of damage, at least psychologically, could be caused by even nonexplosive missile parts raining down on neighborhoods in Israel and Saudi. And the SCUD tended to fall apart in flight, sometimes even without being hit by a Patriot, which meant a lot of pieces were going to fall to the ground.

As Maj. Stephen Finch, air defense officer, XVIII Airborne, described February 2, 1991, "These SCUDs are really badly constructed and they sometimes even break up as they come in …. [Y]ou may have five pieces of things coming in, and they all have the same trajectory, so at that point missile control will see them as five missiles coming in even though its one warhead and four parts."

Desert Lore

The Defense Support Program (DSP) is a series of sensors mounted on satellites designed to spot missile launches and nuclear detonations. In use since 1970, there were five DSP satellites in orbit during Operation Desert Storm.

During the day, the homely and almost-indestructible A-10 Warthogs were given free rein to pound anything on the ground that even remotely looked like it could be used to launch a SCUD. At night, Horner let it be known that the F-15s patrolling Iraq were to blast different highway overpasses in Iraq before heading back to base, just in case the missiles and their mobile launchers were hiding underneath.

On February 14, Saddam sprang a surprise. Apparently convinced by the Allied feints that the main assault was going to head up the Wadi al-Batin, the Iraqis launched five SCUDs simultaneously around 11:30 P.M. They were aimed in the general direction of Hafr al-Batin, a town in northern Saudi that served as a headquarters locus for Egyptian, Syrian, British, and American troops. They were also angled toward a target 30 miles away: *King Khalid Military City*, home to up to 65,000 troops.

Most of the SCUDs disintegrated, which was lucky, since there were no Patriots anywhere near the section of Hafr al-Batin where the debris landed. A pair of F-15s on patrol shot down two of the SCUDs, while the rest fell on their own. This particular launch caused CENTCOM brass to go ballistic, since all five came from the area around Taji, a city 17 miles north of Baghdad that was home to a good deal of Iraq's missile research. Taji had been hit repeatedly from the air, and no SCUDs had been launched from there before, which meant that more mobile launchers had escaped the Allied pounding.

Gulf Lingo

King Khalid Military City (KKMC) was constructed by U.S. Army and Air Force engineers in the 1960s and '70s. The sprawling octagonal base, less than 75 miles from Iraq in northern Saudi Arabia, can house and supply an entire division.

Two nights later, five more SCUDs were launched. The one aimed at Saudi Arabia splashed harmlessly into the Persian Gulf. Four were fired at Israel from a dry riverbed in western Iraq. One was destroyed by Patriots over Haifa. At least two, perhaps three, SCUDs landed in the barren desert northwest of the Israeli town of Dimona. That sent shivers up the backs of CENTCOM planners, since Dimona is home to Israel's nuclear reactors, which provide power and may also be an integral part of Israel's nuclear weapons program.

Israel again said it would strike Iraq if the attacks continued. CENTCOM once again redoubled its efforts to find and disable SCUD launchers. On February 18, General Horner ordered a new wrinkle: F-15s would begin dropping mine clusters at night around areas where mobile SCUD launchers were suspected to be operating. CENTCOM had decided if it couldn't pinpoint all SCUD launchers, it could at least impede their mobility.

Making It Up As You Go Along

The Hentzen Paint Company started business in Milwaukee in 1924. By 1991, now Hentzen Coatings, it specialized in high-technology paints and coatings for military uses. The family owned company may have saved countless lives in the Gulf, because it developed a special paint to avoid "friendly fire" deaths.

After the accidental deaths of seven marines by friendly fire in January 1991, CENTCOM decided that air force pilots needed a reliable way to tell friend from foe. They envisioned a special paint that would fluoresce when detected by infrared sensors in Allied warplanes. Hentzen said it could develop it quickly, and by February 15, more than 50 tons of the special paint was being distributed to ground commanders to smear on tanks, armored personnel carriers, trucks, Humvees, and anything else on the ground that might look Iraqi from the air.

Saddam had said the fight for Kuwait would be "the mother of all battles." It was actually the mother of invention, since equipment was often being modified on the fly for desert use. The *Washington Post*, for example, told the story of U.S. Army Sgt. John Hall, who normally worked out of the U.S. Army's weapons lab in Fort Belvoir, Virginia. Hall shuttled back and forth between Belvoir and Saudi, sleeping with the troops, listening to their needs and gripes, and then rushing back to Virginia to see what could be done.

Some of the stuff he brought back to Saudi was run-of-the-mill, such as special adapters allowing soldiers wearing chemical masks to drink from larger water jugs. But some of it was top-secret, such as experimental computer software and special ammunition.

The *Post* also noted that something as simple as shoveling sand into a sandbag for fortifications became an exercise in the unexpected:

"The Saudi sand, fine as dust, began leaking out of bags, according to a Defense Logistics Agency official. He said the agency recently received an urgent request for sandbags made of more tightly woven cloth, 75 million of them."

Allied troops in charge of trucks, armored-personnel carriers, and tanks wrote home asking to be shipped pantyhose after they had bought every pair at malls in Dhahran and Riyadh. They had been using plastic tie-down straps and a section of pantyhose as filters for air intakes. When Iraq invaded Kuwait, there wasn't one production facility making desert boots for the U.S. military. By mid-February, four contractors had made half a million pairs.

Helicopter parts and spares were shipped to Saudi from everywhere but the Korean Peninsula, where helicopter units were the only ones not cannibalized. The administration couldn't risk running short of helicopters in case the North Koreans chose early 1991 to make an offensive move. Almost every spare part that existed for the U.S. fleet of M1A1 tanks was in the desert. F-15s were kept flying by taking other jets apart as spares. Some analysts admired the ingenuity of the buildup, but were appalled at the make-it-up-as-you-go-along nature of the preparations.

In the end, through ingenuity and cannibalization of machinery, the tanks kept rolling and the jets kept flying. February 18, the original date for the start of the ground war, came and went, delayed because of diplomacy and because CENTCOM didn't think Iraq was yet softened up enough.

> **Heads Up!**
>
> "Had the Gulf War lasted longer, the lack of a coherent industrial response ... would have resulted in disastrous shortages of critical spare parts, consumable items, certain ammunition, and other items."
>
> —James Blackwell, Center for Strategic and International Studies, November 1991

The Least You Need to Know

♦ Despite the general accuracy of the intense Allied bombing, around 500 people died when U.S. Air Force planes bombed what seemed to be a civilian shelter, and another 130 civilians died when British planes accidentally bombed a marketplace.

♦ The original starting date for the land war—February 18—was pushed back because of peace talks between Iraq and the Soviets.

♦ The Allied strategy of convincing Iraq that a main offensive would come from the south succeeded in tying down thousands of Iraqi troops.

♦ Mobile launchers for SCUD missiles proved elusive targets, but SCUD launches became rarer as the Allied air campaign intensified.

Chapter 16

February 19 to February 23

In This Chapter

- ◆ A final raid up the Wadi al-Batin ends in tragedy for three U.S. soldiers
- ◆ The air campaign takes aim at Iraq's elite Republican Guard units
- ◆ The start of the ground war is delayed once again
- ◆ The Soviet-sponsored peace plan fails and the way is paved for the start of ground action

These five days in February saw pressure growing to get the ground war started. In their memoirs, both Powell and Schwartzkopf alluded to frustration in Washington that G-day kept being pushed back, first from February 18 to February 21, and then to February 24. As we've noted, there were two reasons for the delay: The Soviet talks with Iraq were continuing, and many Allied commanders didn't believe Iraq's army had been reduced enough in size and effectiveness.

There was also a feeling in Washington that the United States needed to have the ground campaign come off almost flawlessly, with a decisive result. The ghosts of Vietnam, the marine barracks bombing in Beirut, and the Iranian hostage humiliation had been partly exorcised by successful military operations against Libya in 1983, Grenada in 1985, and Panama in 1989. George Bush had a chance to crown the Ronald Reagan legacy of renewed American confidence with a victory based on diplomatic sophistication, overwhelming military force, and—for a change in world opinion—the moral high ground. For that to happen, the days to come were vital.

He Said What?

David Lamb is one of the best journalists and writers around, a skeptical, thoughtful man who has covered Africa and the Middle East for the *Los Angeles Times* since the 1970s. When General Schwartzkopf sat down with him for an interview on February 19, each was in the presence of a master of the other's profession.

Over an hour and a half, Schwartzkopf catalogued the damage Allied air strikes were doing to Saddam, destroying around 100 Iraqi tanks a day. He said that if a ground war started, he expected the Iraqis to hurl chemical shells at coalition troops. He called the Iraqi Khafji offensive "a joke." Schwartzkopf insisted he wasn't underestimating the enemy or their capabilities. And then he said, "Iraq's military is hurting, and hurting very badly. Our assessment of them is that they are on the verge of collapse."

The next day, the headline "Iraq's Army on Verge of Collapse," or a variation on the theme, appeared in hundreds of newspapers across the globe. The White House issued no public rebuke, since Schwartzkopf was clear in the interview that he still respected Iraq's capabilities. But privately, officials at the White House, State Department, and Pentagon winced.

With the full-scale ground war due to start in days, the Bush administration didn't need any Vietnam-style predictions of victory to come back and bite them. The ground fighting, though, had already started.

Desert Lore

The 5th Cavalry Regiment and its predecessor unit fought in the Mexican War, the Civil War, the Indian wars, the Spanish-American War, the raids against Pancho Villa into Mexico, World War II, the Korean War, Vietnam, and Desert Storm. Its commanders have included Robert E. Lee and John "Blackjack" Pershing.

Wadi of Blood

It was called Operation Knight Strike, and officially was a "reconnaissance in force." Unofficially, it was a thumb in Saddam's eye, and a way to tie down anywhere from two to four Iraqi divisions. It was set to start the night of February 19 and continue into February 20, and involved artillery from the 1st Cavalry firing support while members of the 1st Cavalry's *5th Cavalry Regiment* were supposed to attack up the Wadi al-Batin. They were to take prisoners, destroy whatever Iraqi equipment and installations they found, and scoot back into Saudi Arabia. That, at least, was the plan.

Nicknamed the Black Knights, the 1st Battalion 5th Cavalry was to spearhead the thrust, pushing ahead in Bradley Fighting Vehicles and tanks. On the night of the 19th, the artillery began softening up the target area, pounding the wadi with 155-millimeter shells and rockets. Several Iraqi observation posts disappeared completely beneath the withering fire.

By early morning on the 20th, Knight Strike was ready to roll. The 5th Cavalry's 1st Brigade (known by its shorthand designation, the 1-5) roared up the wadi, with Bradleys in front, tanks behind, and the mobile artillery pieces following. The artillery soon peeled off and set up firing positions to support the thrust, which was going to cut several miles inside Iraq. Communications problems began to crop up immediately.

First, the low-power FM radios used for combat communications began to cut in and out. Then, for some reason, communications with the battalion's command center went down completely. Not only did that mean the artillery units couldn't coordinate fire with battalion commander Col. Randy House, it meant they were unable to contact the *Close Observation Lazing Teams (COLTs)* whose job it was to travel forward with the troops and "illuminate" targets with tiny laser beams that would guide in the shell and rocket fire.

Gulf Lingo

A COLT (Close Observation Lazing Team) is usually platoon-sized. It's equipped with laser-beam range finders and radios. The COLT will fire a laser at a target, radio for artillery fire, and hold the beam on target long enough for the shells and missiles to follow the laser and destroy the target.

The only thing troopers could hear on their radios was the angry voice of Colonel House demanding that something be done to restore communications. Meanwhile, the 5th Cavalry moved ahead without any supporting artillery fire and even without cover from smoke shells. One of the COLT members then saw Iraqi antitank missile emplacements dug into the sides of the wadi. He spotted the array of *AT-12* missiles, and tried to direct U.S. artillery to fire at them, but his radio was only working sporadically.

The AT-12s opened up, hitting a pair of U.S. armored personnel carriers (APCs) that had stopped to pick up surrendering Iraqis. Three GIs died, and seven were injured as the missiles ripped their APCs apart. Colonel House ordered whatever artillery could hear him to start firing, and they did. The smoke from the high explosive and antipersonnel rounds peppering the side of the wadi mixed with blowing dust as medical helicopters flew toward the destroyed APCs.

Meanwhile, the 5th Cavalry's 1st Brigade's task force continued to advance, led by Alpha Company. Across the border inside Iraq, Alpha was soon face-to-face with an entire Iraqi battalion, some in their tanks and armored personnel carriers, but most of them dug into trenches, facing the rapid U.S. advance like misplaced World War I doughboys.

The Iraqi conscripts never knew what hit them as Alpha Company called in supporting fire and the gunners, outraged over the wadi ambush and angry over communications failures, poured it on with antipersonnel shells that exploded about 50 feet over the heads of the cowering Iraqis. Shrapnel whistled down in an unending angry torrent on the uncovered trenches. The death toll was probably in the hundreds, although no one stopped to count. Dozens of Iraqis surrendered.

As night began to fall, Alpha Company and the rest of the 1-5 task force pulled out and withdrew back in Saudi. At a cost of three U.S. dead and seven wounded, they had wiped out an entire Iraqi battalion, kept up to four Iraqi divisions from moving, and caught the attention of one entire division of Republican Guard troops to the north. That kept thousands of Iraqi soldiers focused immediately on the south, and prevented them from reacting to the mass movement of Allied personnel and armor to the west.

The Eagles Strike

If the Jedi Knight's plan for a "forward pass" of troops and equipment was like a street football game, then the 101st Airborne was the kid the quarterback told to "go long, real long, real, real long." The 101st was some 300 miles west of the Gulf, but they weren't the farthest out in the desert. Some 30 miles to their west, the French 6th Light Armored Brigade and elements of the 82nd Airborne were out "where the buses don't run"—the extreme left flank of the Allied movement.

The 101st "Screaming Eagles," like the 82nd and the French, were supposed to do two things once the ground war started: They were to set up a blocking line to prevent any Iraqi reinforcements from showing up from the west, and they were to sweep across Iraq, bypass Kuwait, and cut off any retreat for Republican Guard troops.

> **Who's Who**
>
> Bernard Janvier gained even more fame—or infamy—after the Gulf War when he commanded U.N. peacekeeping forces in the former Yugoslavia. In 1995, Janvier was widely blamed for standing aside and allowing Serb troops to massacre hundreds of Bosnian men, women, and children in the city of Srebrenica.

On February 20, with G-day approaching, the tempo of cross-border raids was stepping up across the entire front. The troops were becoming restless, but their commanders were having it even worse. There was a coalition within the coalition out on the left flank, with 101st Airborne Comdr. Gen. J. H. Binford Peay, 82nd Airborne Comdr. Gen. James Johnson, and French 6th Light Armored Comdr. Gen. *Bernard Janvier* often butting heads and outsized egos.

Around 7 A.M. on February 20, elements of the 101st headed into Iraq supported by eight attack helicopters. The idea was to see exactly what troops and equipment the Iraqis had distributed in their sector, as well as to go after any emplacements and machinery they found.

The dozen transport helicopters swung deep into Iraqi territory, immediately spotting about 100 soldiers, a collection of trucks, and several antiaircraft guns.

After killing the soldiers and destroying the equipment, the unit swung farther north toward what their maps identified as Objective Toad. Toad was a military complex on a small ridge just west of the Iraqi village of Thaqb al-Hajj, some 40 miles north of the border. It consisted of 15 bunkers housing radar and communications equipment, staffed by more than 400 troops from Iraq's 45th Infantry Division. As the 101st attacked from the ground using TOW missiles, more air support in the form of a flight of A-10 Warthogs was called in to augment the attack helicopters.

As the bunkers were blown to bits, Iraqi soldiers began scurrying out of their trenches and foxholes with their hands up. There were dozens at first, then 100, then several hundred. By the time the firing stopped, the 101st found itself in possession of 402 Iraqi prisoners, including a major who was a battalion commander, along with two cases of documents.

The problem now was how to get more than 400 POWs out of Iraq as quickly as possible. Seventeen helicopters were dispatched into Iraq, packed with the prisoners, then flown low and fast back to Saudi Arabia. The mission was an astonishing success, and word of it was quickly picked up by several media outlets, including the "combat pool" of journalists assigned to the 101st.

General Schwartzkopf had ordered the coordinated assaults to confuse Iraq's command-and-control, or at least what was left of it. But not surprisingly, the mercurial Schwartzkopf was also upset, fearing that his surprise plan for an assault on Iraq's right flank might have been revealed by the 101st's deep incursion. But Iraqi communications were so badly mauled by that time that apparently no word of the 101st assault ever percolated up the Iraqi chain of command.

Border Crossings

If Saddam was going to take cross-border raids as a hint of where he would be attacked, he would have concluded he was about to be attacked everywhere. Just west of the 101st incursion, the 82nd Airborne pushed about three miles into Iraq, knocking out a series of antiaircraft guns and hauling off three prisoners. Other units of the 82nd killed 18 Iraqis while destroying four command bunkers.

Just to the east, on February 20 the 6th Cavalry of the 1st Air Cav struck inside Iraq at 8 A.M., just about the same time as the other strikes. In a combination of air strikes and ground action, they took out several antiaircraft guns, 20 five-ton trucks, two hangars, and set off ammunition storage areas that contained almost 3,000 artillery shells.

Meanwhile, even farther east, the 24th Infantry Division was conducting raids of its own, knocking out antiaircraft guns and a radar site. The French 6th Light Armored Division pushed almost 40 miles into Iraq at about the same time, pursuing several moving targets across the desert. The French managed to take out any reinforcement capabilities for the Iraqi 45th Infantry.

Near the Gulf, U.S. Marines began moving forward slowly, infiltrating small teams into southwest Kuwait. The Iraqis were facing movement, incursions, and incoming fire across a front more than 300 miles long.

Softening Up the Guard

Despite the coordinated raids and the softening up of Iraqi front line positions, the focus of the air campaign remained aimed at the Republican Guard. On February 19, there were six Republican Guard divisions perched just outside Kuwait:

- The Tawakalna Division (comprised of armored infantry) was the farthest south, but was still well north of Kuwait City, inside Iraq. This division might end up blocking any thrust into Kuwait from the west.

- The Medina Division, just to the Tawakalna's north, was heavily supplied with the latest T-72 tanks.

- The Adnan Division, almost due north of the Medina, was armored infantry. Those first three divisions would form a "front line" through which any Allied advance into Iraq would have to pass.

- The Hammurabi Division, which many Allied planners believed to be the best of the Republican Guard, was set just east of the first three divisions.

- The Nebuchadnezzar Division was just north of the Hammurabi.

- The Al Faw Division was just north of the Nebuchadnezzar, and helped form a solid "second line" behind the first three divisions.

> **Heads Up!**
>
> "They were bombing the Republican Guard less than a 100 meters from me. As the shelling ended, I could smell something very bad ... I made it back to my base and found everything had been destroyed. Tanks were smashed and metal was lying everywhere."
>
> —Amran Abed Ali, Iraqi draftee, quoted in the *Toronto Star,* February 14, 1999

Farther north, a seventh Republican Guard unit, the Baghdad Division, was stationed closer to the Iraqi capital. Because they all were dangerous, CENTCOM planners had decided all of them needed to be hit constantly from the air. Whether it was B-52s flying punishing Arc Light missions, or the ungainly A-10 Warthogs swooping low to destroy armor, the Allies hit the Republican Guard units almost hourly.

In fact, by February 20, CENTCOM intelligence analysts concluded that no unit of the Iraqi army, including the Republican Guard, was capable of mounting any offensive operations. Defensive operations would be a different story.

Iraq Reacts

The cross-border raids and the bombing were having an effect. By this week of February 19-23, 1991, the Allies had captured around 2,500 Iraqis, and the stories they told were remarkably similar—the Iraqi army had low morale, was short of supplies, and was almost completely cut off from any communications with the Iraqi command-and-control structure. The Iraqi 36th and 48th Infantry Division's draftees seemed to have the least stomach for what was to come, with up to half of each unit, according to the prisoners, ready to desert.

But what was happening strategically with Iraqi forces? Were they just sitting, waiting to be pounded from the air and then attacked on the ground? Surprisingly, the answer seemed to be yes, although Saddam was making preliminary moves. In hindsight, they don't seem to make a lot of sense, but remember: The Iraqi dictator still apparently believed that diplomacy could avert a ground war, and that even if a ground assault did take place, he could win Arab public opinion by fighting and losing rather than by negotiating a peace.

The Kuwaiti resistance was an important if less than 100 percent reliable conduit of information to CENTCOM. Days before the ground war, the Kuwaitis reported out that a 24-hour curfew had been imposed on the residents of Kuwait City. They also reported that elements of Iraq's 19th Infantry Division seemed to be pulling out of the Kuwaiti capitol and that reinforcements from a Republican Guard division had been sent into Kuwait. Mundanely, they reported that the Iraqis had been reduced to commandeering civilian vehicles to move troops and equipment. Ominously, they sent word that Iraqi troops were starting to move out of Kuwait City, carrying looted booty and Kuwaiti hostages with them.

On February 19, the Iraqis began a wholesale ignition of Kuwait's oil wells. By the time the ground war started, more than 250 oil wells were ablaze in Kuwait, and three times that many would eventually go up in flames. Tactically, there was almost no reason to unleash that kind of environmental havoc, since the burning oil fields themselves were in isolated areas and posed no threat to any advancing Allied troops.

Desert Lore

The Kuwait oil well fires, burning from February to November 1991, increased global carbon dioxide emissions by 5 percent. *Scientific American* estimated that, at their height, the fires pumped out as much sulphur dioxide as all the industries and automobiles in Italy, Germany, France, and Great Britain combined.

Strategically, burning the wells was a way for Saddam to show the Arab Nation that he was a man of his word. He had threatened to set fire to both Israel and Kuwait in the event of a war. He was Gilgamesh, Nebuchadnezzar, and Saladin, destroying everything in his path. In fact, semisolid lakes and ponds of oil and tar still dot much of Kuwait's landscape, cooked into a gelatin-like consistency by the desert heat.

Marines Offshore

Because of constant maneuvers and the presence of a U.S. Navy and Marine Corps flotilla off the coast, Iraq's high command had always expected an invasion along Kuwait's coast. The beaches of Kuwait, from the border to Kuwait City, had been fortified. The marines had stormed beaches from Tripoli and Guadalcanal to Iwo Jima and Inchon, and this promised to be as difficult as any of them.

A few dozen feet offshore, the Iraqis had placed steel girders, giant chunks of cement, and mines, all designed to take the bottoms off of landing craft. Between the high- and low-tide lines on the beach itself, concertina wire had been looped over shallow mines to slow and disable any troops that made it ashore. In the countryside, there were bunkers and fortified trenches behind the beach. In urban areas running up the coast toward Kuwait City, buildings overlooking the beach had been turned into high-rise bunkers, bristling with small arms, antitank weapons, light artillery, and mortars.

The defense of the coastline tied up at least five infantry divisions on the front along the coast, backed by artillery and a mechanized division in reserve. Friends of mine who pulled duty in the journalists' combat pools on shipboard with the marines reported that briefings estimated dead and wounded of at least 10 percent among the attackers on landing day.

That day never came. The 17,000 men of the 4th and 5th Marine Expeditionary Units (MEUs) were aboard 31 amphibious assault ships, equipped with 115 assault amphibious landing craft. They were backed with 136 assault and landing helicopters and 19 AV-8B Harrier jump jets. They would never be used, but their presence was more effective than any beach assault, for they kept more than 100,000 Iraqi troops out of the battle, tied down watching the beaches.

Part of the Allied strategic deception involved scooting Navy SEALs and marines as close to shore as possible in small raiding boats. Another feint involved *Faylaka Island*, an island poised like a pointing finger at the very entrance to the large bay where Kuwait City sat. CENTCOM made repeated plans for raids on the island to further convince the Iraqis that the marines were about to invade from the Gulf.

But the raids on the island were called off on February 18, when two U.S. ships—the USS *Princeton* and the USS *Tripoli*—hit mines in the area and sustained significant damage.

CENTCOM decided there were better ways to spook the defenders than risk expensive ships near a phantom target.

On February 23, the Iraqis, and the world, got a peek at twenty-first-century unmanned warfare. The USS *Missouri* plastered Faylaka Island with giant one-ton shells. An unmanned drone aircraft, a Pioneer UAV (Unmanned Aerial Vehicle) was launched from the *Missouri*'s sister ship, the battleship *Wisconsin*, to take a look at the damage.

The 14-foot-long Pioneer, looking and sounding like a giant model plane, would grind along, its 27-horsepower two-cycle engine producing a distinctive buzzing sound like a huge lawnmower. A video link on board sent real-time pictures back to the ship and allowed the sailor manning the joystick controls on board to "pilot" the plane. The sailors intentionally swooped the plane low and slow over the island, a signal to the battered Iraqis that another round of shelling was about to be unleashed from the battleships somewhere over the horizon.

The three sailors manning the flight console on the *Wisconsin* looked at the grainy black-and-white picture on their video monitor and didn't know what to do. They made another pass with the drone and finally had to report to the bridge that several dozen Iraqi defenders were waving white flags. A contingent of marines was sent ashore quickly to gather up the prisoners. For the first time in history, troops had surrendered to an unmanned vehicle. That particular Pioneer—tail registration number 159—is now on display at the Smithsonian Institution's Air and Space Museum in Washington, D.C.

> **Heads Up!**
>
> "Sir, they want to surrender. What should I do with them?"
>
> —Pioneer flight controller to USS *Wisconsin* Capt. David Bill, February 23, 1991

Peace Is Not an Option

While Allied troops were parrying and feinting, the tempo of the diplomatic fencing match was picking up. Tariq Aziz returned to Baghdad on February 19, carrying the Gorbachev peace plan. President Bush, meanwhile, had been apprised of the details by Gorbachev, and said bluntly that the Kremlin proposal wasn't even close to the Allied demand—a total, immediate, and unconditional withdrawal of all Iraqi troops from Kuwait.

The Russians protested that Saddam had, indeed, agreed to an unconditional withdrawal immediately. The Americans responded that the rest of the plan—calling for no postwar sanctions, no overthrow of Saddam, and no incursions into Iraqi territory—amounted to conditions that were out of the question.

After the war, the Bush administration would explain its failure to remove Saddam from power by saying the U.N. resolutions called for Iraq to get out of Kuwait, not for Saddam to be overthrown. But in these last few days before the ground war started, it had become clear that getting rid of Saddam was, indeed, one of the White House's top priorities.

The *Washington Post* quoted a top administration official saying that the president had decided leaving Saddam in power would be "... an endless headache." Behind the scenes, the administration was concerned the Soviet initiative might succeed in allowing Saddam to withdraw from Kuwait on his own terms. Secretary of State James Baker told Congress the United States hoped the Iraqis themselves would rise up against their dictator.

G-day was still set for February 21. But on the 20th, Soviet envoy *Yevgeny Primakov* said any ground war had to be delayed to give Iraq a chance to respond to the Gorbachev plan. In public, the Bush administration said all the plans for a ground campaign continued on track. In private, Bush told Gorbachev that he would delay until noon February 23 Washington time, 9 P.M. Kuwait time. No more delays after that, Bush said. Period.

Who's Who

Yevgeny Primakov was born Yevgeny Finklestein in the Ukraine in 1929. His parents were Jews, but Primakov doesn't practice the religion. Majoring in Middle East studies, he became a journalist and intelligence agent in the Mideast. Primakov met Saddam Hussein in 1970. He was a Kremlin foreign policy advisor, and headed intelligence operations after the fall of the USSR. He became premier of Russia in 1998.

February 21, the day the ground war had been scheduled to start, Aziz flew back to Moscow and immediately into meetings with Gorbachev. There had been some minor tinkering, and the linkage between Iraqi withdrawal and progress on Israeli-Palestinian talks had been dropped. Gorbachev telephoned Bush with the details. Bush was unimpressed. As political cover at home, Saddam delivered a half-hour broadcast speech that night, making more bellicose demands, vowing not to surrender, and making only a passing mention of the Moscow plan.

The Soviets trumpeted the fact that Baghdad had agreed to the plan. Iraq, meanwhile, issues a terse statement that it has signed off on the Gorbachev proposal and that a cease-fire would start the next day, February 23. President Bush then repeated in public what he had told Gorbachev in private, that at noon February 23 Iraqi troops had better be withdrawn from Kuwait City.

Lunchtime on the 23rd came and went in Washington, while the dinner hour passed in Baghdad, and Iraqi troops were still in Kuwait. Saddam issued a final defiant statement. The president prepared to go on nationwide radio and TV at 8 P.M. Washington time.

The Final Pounding

Air strikes had been running over Iraq and Kuwait since January 17. But there had never been a plastering delivered like the one on February 23. For the first time, more than 3,000 missions were flown in a 24-hour period. In this last day of the air war, more than 400 tanks, Jeeps, trucks, and armored personnel carriers were obliterated.

So what was left of the Iraqi army? Plenty. CENTCOM had tempered its earlier battle damage assessments under pressure from both British and U.S. intelligence, which had repeatedly said Schwartzkopf's staff was being "too robust" in their estimates of what had been destroyed. As ground troops prepared to jump off from their points of departure, the scorecard looked roughly like this:

- ◆ 1,700 Iraqi tanks destroyed—2,700 tanks still operational.
- ◆ 1,500 artillery units destroyed—1,700 artillery pieces still operational.
- ◆ 950 armored personnel carriers destroyed—2,000 armored personnel carriers still operational.
- ◆ No estimates of the number of dead and wounded Iraqi troops were issued.

On the ground, engineers from Allied units began blasting holes in the defensive sand berms on the Iraqi and Kuwaiti borders. Even before the noon Washington time deadline had passed, scattered ground action had begun. Elements of the U.S. Army's 1st Infantry Division destroyed a dozen Iraqi tanks. The 1st Cavalry's 2nd Armored Cavalry Regiments punched through the berms in their sector and pushed 12 miles into Iraq, encountering only scattered infantry resistance.

Out on the Allied left flank, the 101st Airborne inserted special forces teams inside Iraq about the same time other Special Ops units were moving into Iraq and Kuwait. The French 6th Light Armored shoved its way inside Iraq and seized high ground from which they could nail down and protect the Allied right and block any Iraqi reinforcements from the west. Out in the Gulf, the *Missouri* and the *Wisconsin* opened their heaviest barrage of the war on southern Kuwait.

Navy SEAL teams in fast boats skidded in toward the Kuwait shoreline, running parallel to the shore, opening up on coastal defenses with rockets and machine gun fire. They set explosive charges on timers, so by the time they exploded on the beaches, the SEALs were long gone. They tossed marker buoys out of their boats, as if setting up beaches for landing craft.

Before dawn on Sunday, February 24, the weather was cloudy with scattered showers along the coast, merely overcast farther west. A desert winter chill hung in the air. The ground war was minutes away.

The Least You Need to Know

- Raids by Allied forces had been increasing in frequency and tempo to keep the Iraqis off balance.
- Iraq began to shuffle troops around, despite heavy damage, and set fire to hundreds of Kuwaiti oil wells.
- The Soviet-sponsored peace plan delayed the start of the ground war, but was unsuccessful because of the conditions attached to it.
- As the final deadline for Iraqi withdrawal from Kuwait passed, the full-scale ground war was set to be launched.

Part 4

Desert Storm— The Ground War

Desert Storm was one of the quickest and most decisive military campaigns in history. At least that's what we've been told. This section reveals many of the previously hidden truths about the Gulf War. Individual tales of bravery, terror, and sacrifice show that, as always, the real story of any conflict is the story of the individual soldier. We also examine how the seeds of today's terrorism and the war against it were sown in the sands of Desert Storm.

Chapter 17

Opening Salvos

In This Chapter

- ◆ The ground war is preceded by Special Forces infiltration into Iraq and Kuwait
- ◆ The U.S. Marines begin their movement into Kuwait from the south
- ◆ Another move is made up the Wadi al Batin, pinning down even more Iraqi divisions
- ◆ While one terrorist who will strike the United States sits and fumes, another terrorist attacks with U.S. forces

The desert campaign against Iraq lasted only 100 hours. It was quick but, as history has shown, far from decisive. It achieved victory, but allowed thousands of elite Iraqi troops to escape. It drove a despot from Kuwait, but allowed him to stay in power. It was a major strategic triumph that ended up shrouded in confusion and controversy.

The big picture of the ground war often overshadows individual stories of heroism, sacrifice, and courage. It has also obscured stories of fear, confusion, and panic. In this chapter, and the chapters that follow, we'll take a close look at the units, incidents, and individuals involved in what became simply and universally known as the ground war.

Infiltration

Special Forces troops—whether British or American, marine, army, navy, or air force— had been infiltrating Iraq and Kuwait long before any ground war started. They were the first Allied troops inside enemy territory. Their raids, and the intelligence they provided, were key components of Desert Storm. Before the air war began, CENTCOM's Special Forces branch, SOCCENT (Special Operations Command, CENTCOM) began to train Kuwaitis and Saudis in infiltration techniques. But, as we've noted in previous chapters, special forces units of the British and American armies did the lion's share of the work.

One of the most daring missions came courtesy of Britain's SBS, or Special Boat Service. On January 22, a unit of 36 SBS commandos boarded two helicopters to fly barely above the sand dunes to within 35 miles of Baghdad. Infiltrating deep inside Iraq, their job was to disable a major fiber-optic cable that provided the Iraqis with command and communication information. The helicopters landed in an area crawling with Iraqi troops. They disengaged the helicopter's rotors but kept the engines running while the three dozen British commandos scurried out, located the cable, and planted 400 pounds of explosives. They lifted off and detonated the blast, taking out almost 150 feet of the precious fiber-optic network and crippling Baghdad's ability to communicate with many troops and commanders.

Kuwaitis on the Rocks

U.S. Navy infiltrators repeatedly went close to the Kuwaiti coast, trying to draw fire and make the Iraqis think a major seaborne invasion was imminent. In mid February, Navy SEALs began training a 13-man Kuwaiti army unit in the basics of infiltrating along a coastline. The idea was to drop them just south of Kuwait City before the ground war, so they could link up with Kuwaiti resistance forces.

On February 21, there was a final rehearsal. SEAL advance teams scoured the Saudi shoreline, and then guided the Kuwaitis ashore from inflatable Boston Whaler–type boats. It went smoothly. So the next night, February 22, the SEALs escorted five of the Kuwaiti commandos north to an industrial beach and pier between al-Fuhayhil and al-Funaytis, just south of Kuwait City.

As before, SEAL scouts scoped the shoreline, found it free of any Iraqi troops, and brought the five Kuwaitis to a pier. The SEALs withdrew, and the Kuwaitis, their rubber boat tied under the pier, climbed to the top. For some reason, the members of the Kuwaiti resistance with whom they were supposed to rendezvous never showed. As the minutes dragged on, the Kuwaitis realized they were trapped in an industrial area probably crawling with Iraqi units nearby, so they blinked their flashlights toward the Gulf.

They scurried back down the pier's pylons, got in the small dinghy, and rowed about 500 yards offshore, where the SEAL team picked them up. There was no exchange of fire, no casualties, and as far as CENTCOM ever knew, no indications from the Iraqis that they knew about the mission.

Green Berets Under Fire

In the United States, the term "Green Beret" has almost become synonymous with "special operations." But the men of the Special Forces Groups (SFG) stand apart even from other Special Forces units. Within the U.S. Army, for example, the Airborne Rangers are an elite group of commandos trained in airborne jumps and unconventional warfare. But the members of one of the SFGs tend to be older than the Rangers, with more experience, and often fluent in the languages of the areas where they operate. Take, for example, the *5th Special Forces Group*, whose specialty is the Middle East and South Asia.

When members of the Green Berets are inserted in an area, they belong to the most basic fighting unit of the special forces groups, an Operational Detachment Alpha (ODA), otherwise simply known as an "A-Team." ODAs usually contain 12 men, but sometimes there are fewer. That was the case on February 23, when eight men from ODA 525, 1st Battalion, 5th Special Forces, flew low and fast from Saudi Arabia, crossing over and into Iraq.

Two *Blackhawk* helicopters scooted low and fast above the terrain. The ground war was set to start in a few hours, and CENTCOM wanted the Green Berets inserted 150 miles inside Iraq to keep an eye on Highway 7, a major north-south artery connecting Baghdad and Basra. CENTCOM brass didn't want to be surprised, and they wanted plenty of advance warning about how the Iraqis were preparing to react to the sudden thrust of massive armor at them from the west.

The first problem occurred when one of the Blackhawks suddenly shook, shuddered, and kept flying. The chopper was scooting so low that its rear wheel had hit the top of a sand dune. Zipping just over, and sometimes under, power lines, the

Desert Lore

The 5th Special Forces Group is based at Fort Campbell, Kentucky. Officially formed in 1961, its members won 18 Congressional Medals of Honor in Vietnam. The unit saw action in the Gulf War, in Somalia, and in the war on terrorism in Afghanistan.

The Machines

The UH-60 Blackhawk helicopter entered service in 1978, with the last helicopter delivered to the U.S. Army in 1997. It can carry up to 11 troops, and was the first helicopter to be designed for both attack and transport. It has a three-person crew. The variant used by the U.S. Navy is called the Sea Stallion.

helicopters approached the landing zone near a village just south of Baghdad. The eight men hopped out, dangerously close to the village, and trotted with their 200-pound packs through marshes and ditches to a small ridge near town. They dug themselves a pair of small caves and burrowed in, four men to a hole.

Within hours, team leader CWO Richard Balwanz faced the kind of life-or-death decision men in combat dread—not because it involved enemy troops, but because he had to decide whether to kill three children. Two Iraqi girls—the commandos guessed they were eight or nine—and a little boy who looked to be about three stumbled on the Green Berets' hiding places. Two of his men held guns on the children, while Balwanz weighed the options. They could shoot the kids, or let them go to run back to the village. Balwanz ordered the guns lowered. The children scampered for the town, and Balwanz ordered his men to evacuate and find some other place to dig in.

ODA 525's sergeant, *Charlie Hopkins*, thought they could keep the mission intact. As they began to move out, an Iraqi goat herder spotted the team. He began sprinting back to the village. The team moved through a muddy ditch, hoping to get to some trees nearby and dig in. Suddenly, popping their heads up, they saw dozens of Iraqi militiamen from the village heading toward them.

Rounds from AK-47s began to buzz past the men and thud into the walls of the ditch. Looking up, Hopkins saw the Iraqi troops were now backed by armored personnel carriers that were turning off of Highway 7 and into the marshy ground. The Green Berets estimated there were probably 200 or more Iraqis heading toward them. The men of ODA 525 silently looked at one another. Two of them half-saluted, half-waved at each other as they said good-bye. They figured their recon mission had just turned into a suicide mission.

The Green Berets returned fire. Dozens of Iraqis fell, but the men of ODA 525 had only 200 rounds of ammunition each, so they conserved and fired only when there was a clear shot. As the Iraqis kept closing in, there was a rumble overhead. A pair of F-16s on patrol were nearby, but an antenna on the team's radio that could contact the jets directly had broken off in the firefight.

The team immediately began broadcasting appeals for air support on the remaining antenna. To this day, members of ODA 525 swear it was fate that an AWACs radar plane on patrol over northern Saudi Arabia

---

Who's Who

Sergeant Charlie Hopkins, winner of the Silver Star, survived the Gulf War and retired from the U.S. Army. He was killed in the United Arab Emirates in a motorcycle accident on January 25, 2001.

Heads Up!

"We're going to have to fight right here. This is it. No place else to go. We gotta fight like junkyard dogs."

—CWO Richard Balwanz to the men of ODA 525, February 23, 1991, as quoted in the *Army Times*, February 5, 1996

picked up their signal and vectored the fighters over their position. The Iraqis retreated under the bombardment and the A-Team was able to make it to a nearby field, where they were picked up by a pair of Blackhawks. On the way back, the team members wondered if they might end up in the stockade or discharged from the service because of the mission. They all got medals instead.

The Marines Go Early

The U.S. Marines held down the easternmost part of the 300-mile-long front. Saudi and Quatari troops were located to the east of the marines, next to the Arabian Gulf, but the eastern part of the line was all generically considered to be the marines' sector. Anchoring the far east end of the line, right next to the Saudis, was the 1st Marine Division. Based at Camp Pendleton, California, the 1st Marine Division was officially formed in February 1941, but its precursors had seen service in Cuba, Haiti, and World War I. The 1st Marines spearheaded two of the most storied amphibious landings in history, at Guadalcanal in 1942 and Inchon in 1950. The division also served in Vietnam as well as in the Gulf War.

Members of the 1st Marine Division had actually started moving into Kuwait before G-day, on the 23rd, as their engineers dynamited defensive berms and marine task forces moved north. An Iraqi missile hit a Humvee that morning, killing one marine and wounding another. The division's 2nd and 3rd battalions moved north, stopping only when they entered the edge of the flaming al-Wafra oil field, awestruck at the biblical proportions of the roaring flames, gushing black smoke, and semisolid, oozing oil pits.

 Heads Up! _____

"All hands were awestruck by the ominous pall of smoke emanating from over 50 wellhead fires .... [R]umbling from the burning wells ... sounded almost like columns of armored vehicles approaching our right flank."

—Maj. Drew Bennett, 1st Marine Division, quoted in *With the 1st Marine Division in Desert Shield and Desert Storm,* History & Headquarters Division, U.S. Marine Corps, 1993

To the marines' right, the Saudi forces had moved forward too, so that by sundown on February 23, any Iraqi commanders should have been able to see that the Saudis and 1st Marines were preparing to breach defensive minefields and drive toward Kuwait City. But there was almost no Iraqi reaction at all. The advance task forces reported that the area around two large parallel minefields was lightly defended, at best.

Gen. Walter Boomer, the marine commander, had the same nagging fear that plagued all the Allied commanders: He was worried that his troops would become hung up in minefields and flaming oil-filled trenches, and would then be sitting ducks for the chemical weapons that everyone assumed the Iraqis had and were prepared to use.

Speed was the key, especially when the marines were launching an almost frontal assault on an area where intelligence indicated there were five Iraqi infantry divisions, two armored divisions, and a mechanized infantry division dug in among mines, oil trenches, bulldozed berms, and blazing oil fields. The best friend of this kind of movement was the *MCLC: the Mine Clearing Line Charge*. The MCLC (pronounced "Mik-Lik") was, simply put, a small rocket towing a line of explosives. The line would be fired out across a minefield and ignited. It would set off any mines in the area, and clear a lane through which vehicles and troops could move.

While many of the other troops along the front began the full-scale attack around 4 A.M., the marines started moving shortly after midnight, clearing minefields using MCLCs. But the early morning fog and dust began to create havoc with movements as soon as the sun came up. Task Force Grizzly from the 1st Marines and the 1st Marines 2nd Battalion engaged Iraqi tanks around 5 A.M. and drove them off, but suddenly began taking fire from behind.

Peppered with tank rounds and artillery, one marine died, three more were wounded, and a pair of tanks went up in flames before they discovered that another task force to their east and slightly behind them, Task Force Ripper, was firing at Iraqis and had mistaken their fellow marines in the distance in front of them for the enemy. The shelling finally stopped after a series of heated radio transmissions.

Meanwhile, Ripper had run into resistance from Iraqi troops behind a second set of fortifications. Unlike the first set, which was clearly delineated with concertina wire, this was the second berm-and-trench arrangement and had no wire surrounding it; it was also steeper and deeper than the first. That meant the marines had to be concerned with their armored vehicles plunging into the unmarked trench and getting hung up.

Ripper and Task Force Papa Bear, just to the east, were about to encounter an unexpected problem that realized General Boomer's worst fear about bringing the rapid advance to a grinding halt. The problem started just before noon on February 24. Ripper had just cleared out Iraqi resistance from the second deep trench and opened a series of lanes through a large minefield when Iraqis began to surrender. They weren't giving up in ones or twos, but by the dozens, and soon, by the hundreds. The marines were dumbfounded.

Heads Up!

"POWs started to appear from everywhere … they surrendered to the tanks in our sector. POWs were blowing us kisses, waving American flags, and asking us for food and water."

—Gunnery Sgt. Paul Cochran, 3rd Tank Battalion, 1st Marine Division

"Progress was slowed by the multitude of surrendering Iraqi soldiers. Literally thousands of Iraqis emerged, begging for food."

—Capt. John McElroy, Task Force Papa Bear historian, 1st Marine Division

The surrendering Iraqis jammed the mine-free cleared lanes, hands up, many grinning, others asking for food. The trickle of surrendering Iraqis became a torrent and then a flood. Marine tanks, personnel carriers, and Humvees were stalled inside the lanes, mobbed by surrendering Iraqis like rock stars at a concert that was out of control.

Marine commanders had to hustle to bring order out of the chaos, especially since isolated pockets of dug-in Iraqis continued to fight with mortars and tanks. The marines finally had to admit that they didn't have enough personnel to handle the crush of surrendering enemy. They began herding the Iraqis into a single cleared lane and trying to move them to the rear with one armed guard for every few hundred Iraqis.

The 1st Marines finally began to move again, with a new set of marching orders: Surrendering Iraqis were not to be captured, merely disarmed and sent walking toward the rear while the marines plowed ahead. To the west, the 2nd Marine Division had breached its berms around 4 A.M., ripping into Iraqi positions with artillery fire, at one point pouring almost 1,500 rounds into 40 separate Iraqi positions in 15 minutes, a rate of almost 100 shells a minute. That meant that, on average, a shell was exploding on or near an Iraqi position every six-tenths of a second.

One thing was driving Gunnery Sgt. Martin Cuip crazy. Line charges were failing to ignite all over the place. Sergeant Cuip repeatedly trotted into minefields with his team, set explosive charges, and ignited them, despite mortar and machine gun fire. He opened three lanes for the tanks that way.

Low visibility from haze and the oil fires made matters worse, especially since the marines were wearing their antichemical MOPP gear. They didn't wear the masks and protective gloves, but

The Machines

The TPz1 Fuchs chemical detection vehicle is made by the German firm Rheinmettal Landsysteme. The "Fuchs" became "Fox" in the mouths of its U.S. military customers. Each six-wheeled armored vehicle is equipped with sensors and instruments to detect a wide range of chemical, biological, and radiation hazards.

the chemical suits didn't do much for mobility. At midmorning it got worse, when a *Fox chemical detection vehicle* picked up traces of mustard gas.

The marines were ordered to MOPP 4, which meant they had to wrestle on their gas mask hoods and rubberized elbow-length gloves. Luckily, they were allowed to remove the masks and gloves after less than an hour. Seeing through the small goggles of the gas mask hood was difficult enough. Between the masks and the gloves, fighting would have been almost impossible.

Where fighting did erupt, it was the noncommissioned officers who made the difference, as they had since the days of Alexander the Great. Sgt. Bill Warren led his squad from A Company, 1st Battalion, 8th Marines, in an assault on a concrete building under fire from Iraqi antitank rockets and machine guns. Sergeant Warren repeatedly exposed himself to enemy fire as he led 3rd Squad through a breach in a fence and into the building. All the Iraqis inside abandoned their weapons and ran into the desert. Just to the west, Gunnery Sgt. John Cornwell was guiding his tank platoon into a fight with a succession of dug-in Iraqi tanks, artillery pieces, and bunkers. They were all destroyed in a half-hour of rapid movement and firing.

U.S. Marines tanks roll toward Kuwait City.

Tiger, Tiger

Between the 1st and 2nd Marines was an armored brigade from the U.S. Army under U.S. Marine Corps command. This was the 1st Brigade from the 2nd Armored Division, the Tiger Brigade. The Tigers would survive combat in the Gulf and politics and budget cuts at home. After the Gulf War, the 2nd Armored Division was deactivated, but the Tiger Brigade was transferred, intact, to the 1st Cavalry Division, to become the Greywolf Brigade.

Detaching units from one branch of the service to serve under another branch temporarily is as old as warfare itself. But it usually hasn't been to the liking of the U.S. Marines. The marines have historically been reluctant to surrender autonomy. During the air war, for example, marine commanders made it clear that marine air power would mainly be directed at softening up areas in front of marine positions.

At the same time, it became apparent early on in Desert Shield that the marines would have problems sharing operational boundaries with the U.S. Army. Preliminary plans called for the marines to operate next to the army, and to be able to depend on army armored units for firepower more robust than the marines' Sheridan tanks could provide. But in the end, Arab forces were inserted between the army and the marines. Some believed the Allied Arab forces were put to the west of the marines to keep them from arguing too much with the army.

But that shift left the marines in the 1st and 2nd Divisions without the workhorse of the Gulf War: the *M1A1 Abrams tank*. The Tiger Brigade supplied plenty of those and gave the marines the punch they would need to drive toward Kuwait City and cut off any escaping Iraqis.

> **The Machines**
>
> The M1A1 Abrams battle tank entered service in 1985. It carries a four-person crew, weighs 70 tons, and can travel at up to 40 miles an hour. Its main armament is a 120-millimeter cannon. The inside of an Abrams is said to resemble a space ship because of the array of video monitors and computers.

Operation Deep Strike

Just on the other side of the Pan-Arab forces, west of the marines, the 1st Cavalry Division was still poised at the Wadi al-Batin, preparing to once again make the Iraqis think that the main thrust was going to come up that historic invasion route. Operation Knight Strike a few days before had confounded the Iraqis and caused them to place an entire mechanized infantry division astraddle the wadi, with two infantry divisions nearby and an entire Republican Guard division in position to plug the wadi. That kept tens of thousands of Iraqi troops looking the wrong way.

At noon on G-day, the 1st Cav's Blackjack Brigade did it again, this time pushing up the wadi supported by Apache attack helicopters and howitzers from the 82nd Field Artillery. The gunners on the howitzers were amazed that they were able to pour fire in the daylight into Iraqi positions for more than an hour without any kind of moves from the enemy at all.

By 2 P.M., the 1st Cavalry was moving up the wadi in force, supported by so much artillery fire that various batteries were in constant danger of running out of ammunition.

The defensive berm between Saudi Arabia and Iraq was breached around 5 P.M., and in the gathering darkness, the 1st Cavalry, its air support, and the trailing artillery pieces pushed ahead. As the light grew dimmer, mist and settling oil smoke cut vision down to almost zero. The advancing troops became more worried about obscured minefields or unexploded U.S. shells than they were about Iraqi resistance.

The relatively smooth movement continued throughout the day, and into the evening. As it became night, the U.S. artillery kept up a constant pounding on Iraqi positions. Operation Deep Strike was designed to be like a dentist's drill: Keep going until you hit a nerve, then pull out. The 1st Cav had yet to hit a nerve. But they would.

The Big Red One

The U.S. Army's *1st Infantry Division*—the famous Big Red One of World War II—was perched just to the west of the 1st Cavalry. Technically, British forces, led by the legendary "Desert Rats" of Britian's 7th Armored Division, were stationed next to the 1st Cav. But the British troops were being held as a ready reserve. The plan on G-day was for the 1st Infantry to punch through Iraqi defenses, then British troops would follow, pushing deep into Iraq.

Desert Lore _____

The U.S. Army's 1st Infantry Division was formed in 1917, and saw service in France in World War I. The unit went through North Africa, Italy, the Normandy Invasion, Belgium, and Germany in World War II, and was the first army division to land in Vietnam. The nickname "Big Red One" comes from the red numeral *1* on the unit's shoulder patches. It is the oldest continuously serving division in the U.S. Army.

The 1st Infantry's job was to slash through the sand berms and past Iraqi soldiers dug in to World War I–style trenches. The tactic was for the Big Red One to clear lanes for heavy armor, then wheel to the east and punch into Kuwait as the British armor rolled through the holes created by the Americans.

Facing the 1st Infantry was Iraq's 26th Infantry Division. Actually, *facing* isn't as accurate as *cowering*. The conscripts of the Iraqi 26th had been hammered mercilessly from the air. Their communications had largely broken down, but like most of the Iraqi forces, they were expecting the major Allied push to be where the marines, Saudis, and 1st Cavalry were attacking, straight into Kuwait's underbelly. They had no idea that a 300-mile-long front of U.S., Arab, British, and French forces was going to drive due north and then turn and pivot east.

They also had no idea that the 1st Infantry Division had been practicing a maneuver designed to keep the men and machinery moving and not get bogged down by trying to root Iraqi soldiers out of their trenches. While in Saudi Arabia, engineers would dig trenches approximately the width and depth of the ones the Iraqis would be jammed into. By rigging blades on the front of tanks, or using combat earth movers, they were able to half fill the trenches with sand in one parallel pass. They discovered that by having two vehicles follow each other, they could almost fill the trenches to the top with sand.

A tactical decision had been made to bury enemy troops alive. It was a decision that neither the public nor the rest of the media would discover until September 12, 1991, when the New York newspaper *Newsday* reported:

> "... three brigades of the 1st Mechanized Infantry Division—"The Big Red One"— used the grisly innovation to destroy trenches and bunkers being defended by more than 8,000 Iraqi soldiers, according to division estimates."

> **Heads Up!**
>
> "A thought occurred to me, we could actually use these plows to fill in the trenches. In fact, I had tested it myself. I got down in the ditch myself and had two tanks plow toward me just to see what it did. I learned several things and one I learned is that it happens very quickly."
>
> —Col. Lon Maggart, 1st Infantry Division, *Frontline*, Public Broadcasting System, 1996

At 6 A.M. on February 24, the 1st Infantry's 1st and 2nd Brigades drove through two dozen holes punched in a defensive sand berm. They soon advanced and began taking small arms fire from the trenches. Thousands of demoralized Iraqi troops surrendered within hours. Others didn't, and Colonel Maggart's innovation was put to use.

The tanks would turn parallel to the trenches and quickly fill them with sand. The Iraqis who weren't able to surrender or get out were buried, some still firing off impotent rounds from their rifles at the unyielding tank armor. A decade later, the Iraqi government news agency claimed bodies were still being discovered. The Iraqis claimed thousands of troops were buried. Given the number of troops that surrendered, the actual number could only have been in the dozens, not thousands. But no one knows.

Two Believers

The Bradley Fighting Vehicle carries a three-person crew: the commander, the driver, and the gunner. The gunner operates the Bradley's 25-millimeter cannon, the M242 "Bushmaster" chain gun that can fire three rounds per second over a distance of a mile and a quarter. The gunner also has to be able to operate the TOW missiles that can be mounted on the Bradley, as well as the 7.62-millimeter machine gun.

At Fort Benning, Georgia, one sergeant training with The Big Red One stood out as a Bradley gunner, scoring almost a perfect 1,000 on his gunnery examination. In Saudi

Arabia, he got the reputation of being at least the best gunner in Charlie Company, maybe the best gunner in the entire 216th Infantry. His Bradley, part of 1st Platoon, C Company, went by the radio call sign "Charlie 11." The sergeant, being a fan of classic rock, nicknamed it "Bad Company."

On February 24, the gunner, Sgt. Timothy McVeigh, rode Charlie 11 through the breached berms with the rest of the units from the 1st Infantry Division. For taking out several Iraqi tanks over the next few days, McVeigh would win the Bronze Star. His performance and that of Charlie 11 was so good, in fact, that when General Schwartzkopf accepted the surrender of Iraqi generals at the end of the ground war, Sergeant McVeigh's Bradley was one of those chosen to guard the CENTCOM commander.

Years later—after his failure to qualify for the Special Forces, his honorable discharge, his resentment at the U.S. government following the siege of the David Koresh Cult at Waco, and after his truck bomb killed 169 American men, women, and children in the Murrah Federal Building in Oklahoma City—McVeigh wrote an essay for an antigovernment website called *Media Bypass*. It read, in part:

> "… the people of the nation [the United States] approve of bombing government employees because they are 'guilty by association'—they are Iraqi government employees. In regard to the bombing in Oklahoma City, such logic is condemned."

McVeigh wrote those words in 1998. He was executed in 2001. He was responsible for the second-worst loss of life to a terror attack in American history. But the cauldron of the Gulf War was where his survivalist, antigovernment views began to simmer. McVeigh was already attracted to militia-type groups. But he was rejected by the Special Forces in 1992. Four federal agents and 80 members of the Branch Davidian cult died in the siege at Waco in 1993. Those two events caused McVeigh to swear revenge against the U.S. government. On February 24, 1991, that same government guided McVeigh to kill Iraqi soldiers. He would learn the art of killing on his own later.

About 700 miles southwest of Charlie Company's position, a Saudi family drama was playing itself out. Osama bin Ladin, the seventh son of Saudi construction billionaire Mohammad Awad bin Ladin, had returned home from leading and financing Muslim holy warriors fighting against the Soviets in Afghanistan. Osama was seething over the Saudi royal family's rejection of his august plan to drive off the invading Iraqis with an army of holy warriors. He was livid over "infidel" Americans trampling the holy soil of Saudi Arabia. And he was living in an extremely modest two-story house in Jeddah, where guests and devotees slept on the floor or on the ground, in circumstances more like his late father's early impoverished days.

In his groundbreaking book *Holy War Inc.* (Free Press, 2001), journalist and terrorism expert Peter Bergen notes that even during Desert Shield and Desert Storm, Osama bin Ladin was rallying Saudi fundamentalist clerics to his side:

"Bin Ladin's opposition to the presence of American troops was echoed by two prominent religious scholars, Safar al-Hawali and Salman al-'Auda, who were subsequently jailed by the Saudis. In a sermon delivered n 1991, al-Hawali observed: 'What is happening in the Gulf is part of a larger Western design to dominate the whole Arab and Muslim world.'"

As we'll see later, resentment grew to hatred, and that hatred led to Osama bin Ladin leaving Saudi Arabia to form the terror network that would kill almost 3,000 people on September 11, 2001.

During McVeigh's trial for the Oklahoma City massacre, it was alleged that a fellow soldier and conspirator, Terry Nichols, might have met with Osama's allies—or perhaps even with Osama himself—in the Philippines in 1992. That has never been proven. What we do know is that the closest the two brothers under the skin, bin Ladin and McVeigh, ever got to each other was the 700 miles between the rundown house in Jeddah and Charlie 11.

The Least You Need to Know

◆ Before the ground war started, Allied commando teams had been regularly infiltrating Iraq and Kuwait.

◆ The U.S. Marines made surprisingly fast progress in their initial drive into Kuwait from the south.

◆ As the 1st Cavalry Division made another feint into Iraq and Kuwait, the 1st Infantry Division was plowing into Iraq, sometimes literally burying enemy troops.

◆ The two worst terrorists in American history, Osama bin Ladin and Timothy McVeigh, were both in Saudi at the same time. Their Gulf War experiences helped form the basis for their actions to come.

Chapter 18

The End Run

In This Chapter

◆ French forces move deep into Iraq to nail down the Allies' far left flank

◆ The 101st Airborne makes the biggest move in its history

◆ The 82nd Airborne moves deep into Iraq and then changes direction

◆ Iraqi commanders try to react to the surprise coalition tactics

The CENTCOM strategy against Iraq was audacious and complex. As we've seen, troops on the extreme right flank—the Saudis and the marines—launched frontal assault into the underside of Kuwait. Just to their west, the 1st Cavalry tore northward up the Wadi al-Batin, a move designed solely to fool the Iraqis that this was the main attack. But everything west of them was supposed to be a precisely orchestrated maneuver that swept into Iraq and Kuwait like a windshield wiper, with troops punching north and then sweeping east. The strategy was designed to attack Iraq's elite Republican Guard divisions in a surprise move from the west, then trap and destroy them.

Just to the west of the 1st Cavalry, the U.S. 1st Infantry Division breached the defensive berms, clearing a path for them and British forces to move north then pivoting east. Just west of them, the U.S. 1st and 3rd Armored Divisions, and the 3rd Armored Cavalry Regiment, were to do the same, but push even farther north, then turn east. All these units were under the U.S. Army's VII Corps. But troops even farther west held the key to the entire operation.

This was the area controlled by the U.S. XVIII Airborne Corps. How well they functioned as the outer part of the wiper blade would determine how well the ground war would go. Their job was to secure the left flank, cut off any escape routes, then turn and hit Republican Guard units above Basra, in southern Iraq.

The French Spearhead

On April 30, 1863, 35-year-old Capt. Jean Danjou and 64 French Foreign Legionnaires found themselves facing more than 2,000 Mexican rebel troops at a hacienda owned by the Camerone family near Puebla, located about 75 miles southeast of Mexico City. Captain Danjou, who wore a wooden hand to replace the one shot off in the Crimea, and the rest of the French were trying to prop up the ruler of Mexico, the Emperor Maximilian. They were failing. The legionnaires fought for hours, killing hundreds, until only five legionnaires were left. Legend has it that the five fixed bayonets and rushed the Mexicans in a suicide charge.

To this day, every April 30, Captain Danjou's wooden hand, recovered from the battlefield, is displayed in its ceremonial box at French Foreign Legion headquarters near Marseilles. Grizzled tattooed veterans see it and weep. The hand is a symbol of the legion's determination to keep fighting even against hopeless odds.

Then, like now, only the officers were French, so Captain Danjou was the sole Frenchman among the 65 honored foreign legion dead. Today, more than half of the French Foreign Legion's 8,000 men are from Eastern Europe alone. The legion's deal is simple: If you're the one out of seven applicants accepted, and if you survive what may be the world's most grueling military training without dropping out or killing yourself, and if you can last five years in the ultraelite commando unit, you become a French citizen. With Gaullic logic, the Foreign Legion considers itself the most French of all fighting units, even with almost no Frenchmen on its rolls.

In the past, the legion has sometimes attracted unsavory recruits. Today it refuses to accept anyone with a criminal record. In the Gulf War, the legion was the linchpin of the French contribution, since most other units were filled with draftees short on military expertise. At least once, though, their old reputation returned to haunt them, when the U.S. 82nd Field Artillery in January accused the legionnaires of cutting padlocks in the 82nd's storage area and stealing tents, cots, food, and just about anything else that wasn't bolted down.

But the *French Foreign Legion*'s 2nd Parachute Infantry Regiment and 1st Cavalry Regiment, along with the French 6th Light Armored Division, had one of the most important jobs of the entire war. Both had to push more than 100 miles inside Iraq on the extreme left of the Allied line. While the 6th Light Armored was to seize high ground and station themselves to fight off any possible Iraqi reinforcements from the west, the legionnaires were to take the Iraqi air base at as-Salman, just east of the 6th Light Armored's defensive line.

At 7 A.M. on G-day, the units started moving. The 6th Light Armored, supported by its own squadron of *Gazelle* helicopters, along with attack helicopters of the U.S. Army, pushed ahead, coming under fire from dug-in tanks and taking them out almost immediately. As they approached an Iraqi troops concentration, the unit split and attacked in a pincers movement.

The 6th Light Armored took the objective with no killed or wounded, but had a problem then becoming common among all the Allied forces. They had between 800 and 1,200 prisoners from Iraq's 45th Infantry Regiment, and the milling Iraqi POW's were starting to slow the division's advance. By managing to shove the Iraqis aside under minimal guard, the French continued their northward thrust.

Desert Lore _____

The French Foreign Legion has only been used inside France itself three times: during World War I and World War II, and currently in the hunt for suspected Islamic extremists.

The Machines

The SA341J Gazelle was produced by an Anglo-French team and entered service in 1970. Used by British and French forces, the one-crewman, four-passenger observation chopper can reach a top speed of near 200 miles an hour.

Planners had initially thought it might take two days to secure the left flank and capture the as-Salman airfield. But by 6 P.M., the Foreign Legion had the airfield surrounded.

The Eight-Deuce

The U.S. 82nd Airborne Division was becoming rusty in the Saudi sand. The division is proud of the fact that every soldier in the Eight-Deuce, from cooks to computer specialists, is parachute-qualified. But the 82nd had been in Saudi since the Iraqi invasion of Kuwait and there hadn't been a single practice jump. Instead, the paratroopers had become ground troops with the job of being the most westerly American soldiers on the line.

A task force from the division's 2nd Brigade was fighting alongside the French, just to the west. The 82nd's job was to seize a two-lane highway that ran from the border to the Iraqi airbus at as-Salman. The road was going to become a major supply route, with troops, tanks, ammunition, and fuel moving north to the air base—once it was captured, of course.

But after reaching al-Salman, the division was supposed to conduct the most complicated maneuvers of any unit in the war. From as-Salman, the 82nd was to head almost due east in Iraq. That meant they would be crossing the paths of the 24 Mechanized Infantry, the

3rd Armored Cavalry Regiment, and the 1st Armored Division as they headed due north. Doing so could be a dicey proposition, given the rash of friendly fire deaths and injuries. The 82nd had no desire to be mistaken for an Iraqi unit and pounded by Allied artillery and air power as they crossed in front of other advancing coalition forces.

But if that weren't difficult enough, the division was supposed to move east and then suddenly turn north again. The objective this time was to ben Iraqi airfield near the town of Talil. But the problem here was that at the same time the 82nd was to turn north, the 24th Mechanized and 3rd Armored Cavalry were to be changing directions themselves, and heading east. That meant the Eight-Deuce would be crossing in front of them *again*. It was a series of tricky movements that depended on precise timing and constant communication with other units to prevent a disaster.

Before the war had even started, the Bush administration was so worried about possible SCUD launches that the military briefly considered a plan to airdrop the 82nd into western Iraq. That, at least, was the proposal floated by Defense Secretary Dick Cheney in October 1990. The plan was dropped, not because of unwillingness on the part of the 82nd, but because CENTCOM Commander Gen. Schwartzkopf told Cheney the plan was impossible because of logistics. It was decided, instead, to infiltrate special forces units to find and destroy the missile launchers once the air war started.

So the 82nd hadn't jumped, but instead trained as mechanized infantry. Once G-day came, they pushed up the highway much faster than anyone had thought they would. The way north was littered with burning Iraqi equipment that had been blasted by jets and artillery as well as with, as usual, thousands of bedraggled Iraqis wanting nothing more than to surrender. The 82nd beat back disorganized counterattacks on their flanks and, by nightfall, had secured the road all the way to as-Salman.

> **Heads Up!**
>
> "We're here for more than the price of a gallon of gas. What we're doing is going to chart the future of the world for the next 100 years. It's better to deal with this guy now than five years from now."
>
> —Sgt. J. P. Kendall, 82nd Airborne Division, quoted by Pres. George Bush, January 16, 1991

The Screaming Eagles

If the 82nd was annoyed at having to move on the ground, just to their east, the 101st Airborne Division was uneasy about traveling by air. The weather on the morning of February 24 was cold, rainy, and windy. The combination of blowing sand, fog, and dank mist from the burning oil wells made flying an iffy proposition, especially for helicopter pilots who, unlike the jet jockeys, couldn't get above the lousy conditions.

These conditions presented more than a minor problem, since the 101st was about to make history. The CENTCOM plan called for the Screaming Eagles to mount the largest heliborne assault ever attempted, even in the helicopter-rich environment of Vietnam. Hundreds of choppers were to airlift thousands of troops over 100 miles inside Iraq to a position along an east-west highway code named FOB (Forward Operating Base) Cobra. After refueling at Cobra, the 101st was to scoot another 60 miles north and seize Highway 8, in the middle of the legendary Euphrates River valley. The 101st's audacious move would put them on the banks of the Euphrates, where soldiers had been fighting and dying for thousands of years before the first words of the Bible were written.

First, though, they had to get there. And to do that, they had to seize FOB Cobra. The first helicopters from the 101st's assault team were supposed to lift off just before dawn. But at 3:30 A.M., a two-man Kiowa scout helicopter crashed because of the weather. Both men aboard escaped with burns, but the Kiowa burned to a cinder. The 101st's liftoff kept being delayed because of almost zero visibility.

Finally, at around 7:30 A.M., 66 Blackhawk helicopters and 30 Chinook heavy-lift choppers took off with an engine noise the 101st hadn't heard since the days of massed C-47 jump planes in World War II. The first helicopters landed at Cobra at 10 A.M., and within two minutes, the 426th Supply and Transportation Battalion was on the ground, hauling fuel and fuel bladders out of the helicopters to set up refueling points. At the same time, Capt. John Russell took his infantry company north, calling in air strikes and artillery on dug-in Iraqi positions about a mile north of Cobra. They took the bunkers within half an hour and rounded up more than 300 prisoners. Included among them was an Iraqi officer, Maj. Samir Ali Khader, who confirmed that the one company of U.S. soldiers had just eliminated an entire battalion of Iraq's 45th Infantry Division.

Meanwhile, more than 700 trucks, refueling vehicles, Humvees, tanks, and armored personnel carriers began to tear along a road being carved into the desert by the 101st engineers who struggled to stay ahead of the column with their road graders. Flights of Apache attack helicopters followed behind the main assault force, and began landing at Cobra within an hour of the arrival of the first troops.

Within two hours, more than 40 refueling stations had been set up at Cobra, enabling the Apaches to gas up and head north toward Highway 8. Meanwhile, hundreds of other helicopters began ferrying GIs and equipment to Cobra, which would become a vital refueling base for the entire XVIII Airborne Corps.

If the Iraqis were going to attempt to reinforce either their troops in Kuwait or their Republican Guard units, they would have to move south on Highway 8 from Baghdad. And if any of the Republican Guard units hoped to escape the

Desert Lore

The largest aerial helicopter assault in history was led by the 101st Airborne's 327th Infantry Regiment. Forward Operating Base Cobra was named in honor of the 17 men of C Company (Cobra Company) of the 327th who died in Vietnam in 1965 and 1966.

Allied onslaught, they would be forced to move north on Highway 8. By noon, air strikes and the predatory Apaches had effectively closed the highway near the city of as-Samawah.

As it began to grow dark, the 101st sent teams of men north in Blackhawks. They landed and secured an area controlling the highway, even pushing a mile or so north to seize the south bank of the Euphrates.

So far, so good. The French had nailed down the left flank and blocked it to keep any Iraqi troops from moving overland to the rescue. The 82nd Airborne and the French had taken the Iraqi airfield at as-Salman. And the 101st had set up a major refueling depot 100 miles inside Iraq and then proceeded north to slice a major highway. To many of the troopers, it seemed everything was moving on fast forward. Like the marines to the east, the army in the west had taken all of its objectives hours—and even a full day—ahead of schedule.

The 24th Mech Rolls

The 24th Mechanized Infantry Division, stationed on the line just east of the 101st Airborne, had started life in paradise. The 24th Infantry Division had been formed in Hawaii in 1921, and for the next two decades guarded the Hawaiian Islands against attack. On December 7, 1941, the men of the 24th watched in amazement as hundreds of low-flying Japanese fighters zipped over their positions to attack Pearl Harbor. The division had seen brutal fighting both in the Pacific under Gen. Douglas MacArthur and in Korea, where they fought rear-guard holding actions against rapidly advancing North Korean infantry.

> ### Who's Who
>
> Barry McCaffrey entered West Point at age 17. He served combat tours in the Dominican Republic and Vietnam. After he retired as commander of the 24th Mechanized Infantry, he was appointed head of the Office of National Drug Control Policy by President Clinton. He was criticized for attacking retreating Iraqi troops at the end of the Gulf War.

In the Gulf, the 24th was fated to be involved in the most violent battles of the war, and would eventually be embroiled in controversy about what its troopers did—or did not do—to Iraqi troops. The 24th Infantry had morphed into the 24th Mechanized Infantry, with an emphasis on speed, maneuverability, and firepower. The 24th Mech was commanded by a man who would be heavily criticized by the end of the war: *Gen. Barry McCaffrey.*

The 24th Mech's task was to drive north into Iraq, parallel to the 101st, then make a sweeping right turn, pushing east and then southeast. The 24th was to bypass Kuwait completely and drive toward the Iraqi city of Basra, cutting off the escape route of any Iraqi troops withdrawing from Kuwait and blocking the Republican Guard units from retreating north.

Successfully moving supplies, tanks, and attack vehicles from the supply areas to the attack position required a miracle in itself. The 24th was short of the mammoth number of loading and transport vehicles needed and, because the roads north to the staging area were just graded strips of sand, it also found itself without enough off-road trucks to handle the job. To move everything into attack position, the 24th needed more than 3,000 heavy equipment transporters, 500 flatbed trucks, and 450 equipment-hauling trailers. Since they had nowhere near that, the 24th borrowed vehicles from the nearby Arab armies, from the Saudis, and even got transport help from former Warsaw Pact countries that weren't contributing troops, but did lend entire transport battalions to the 24th. At one point, the logistics units formed what they dubbed "Saudi Motors," and began leasing hundreds of heavy transporters and off-road heavy rigs from private Saudi owners.

The earliest the 24th had been told to expect to move out was 8 P.M. on G-day. In fact, they were assured, the unit probably wouldn't even move at all until the next day, February 25.

But reports were flooding CENTCOM with intelligence from the various fronts, indicating that Iraqi forces were in chaos. Seven of Iraq's infantry divisions in front of the U.S. Marines in the east, as well as a mechanized infantry division and an armored division, had either surrendered or had been wiped out. Farther west in Kuwait and along Kuwait's border with Iraq, intelligence estimated two Iraqi infantry divisions and an armored division were no longer fit to fight.

General Schwartzkopf decided to move up the assault plans, and suddenly, the 24th found itself ordered to move out at 3 P.M. on February 24. General McCaffrey decided to push ahead in a "battle box" formation, a fast-moving version of the giant boxes used by Roman legionnaires. A reinforced company was put 5 to 10 miles in front, acting as scouts.

Each front corner of the box was anchored by units of Bradleys or M1A1 tanks. The rear corners were secured by a full company each. On each flank, a company was strung out to protect the outside edges. The ammunition, water, and fuel vehicles were trucked safely in the middle of the box. The box was 5 miles wide and 20 miles deep, meaning it covered about 100 square miles. General McCaffrey's command covered an area about the size of the city of Fresno, California, and it was moving due north across the desert at around 25 miles an hour.

The 24th used night vision goggles, Global Positioning Satellite receivers, and other high-tech tools of the trade to keep moving forward with poor visibility. By midnight, the mass of troops and armor had pushed more than 75 miles inside Iraq.

The Third Armored Cavalry's Screen

A few chapters back, we talked about how the 3rd Armored Cavalry Regiment (ACR) became involved in one of the first ground actions of the war, long before the official ground war started. As we'll see shortly, the 3rd Armored Cav's stint in the Gulf War would end with deadly consequences and controversy about alleged cover-ups, as well as charges that troopers in the 3rd ACR had been exposed to Iraqi chemical weapons.

As the ground war started, the 3rd ACR's job was to protect the 24th Mech's right flank. The 3rd ACR was near the center of the Allied line. To their west, as we've seen, was the 24th Mech. Just to their east, in VII Corps territory, was the 1st Armored Division. The 3rd ACR was to move up and down its line of advance, to make sure there were no surprises to the 24th's right flank. Like the other units, the 3rd ACR was ordered to penetrate well over 100 miles into Iraq, then wheel right and attack east-southeast, joining the 24th Mech and the 1st Armored in a push toward Basra and the Republican Guard.

With more than 200 tanks and 16 Apache attack helicopters, the 5,000 men of the 3rd ACR were a formidable independent attack force. Like most of the other Allied attackers in the first day, they met almost no resistance in their initial assault. That would change soon enough.

An Army Falls Apart

At dawn on February 24, Iraq had the fourth largest army in the world, at least on paper. By midnight, they had the second largest army in Iraq. Allied units had gone twice as far as they thought they would have been able to, even in their most optimistic scenarios. Iraq's III and IV Corps, the ones with the responsibility for defending Kuwait itself, were in a shambles.

By midnight of the first day, the Allies had taken almost 15,000 Iraqis prisoner. Between desertions, surrenders, aerial strikes, and the rapid movement of Allied ground troops, large sections of Iraq's armed forces were out of the fight for good within the first 24 hours.

Heads Up!

"We're going to go around, over, through, on top, underneath, and any other way it takes to beat 'em."

—Gen. Norman Schwartzkopf, briefing for media, February 24, 1991

Iraq's III Corps, for example, were supposed to defend southern Kuwait and Kuwait City. But five of its infantry divisions—the 7th, 8th, 14th, 18th, and 29th—could no longer be classified as fighting forces. On top of that, III Corps' 5th Mechanized Infantry and 3rd Armored Division had been so badly mangled by air strikes that they were next-to-useless. The big story from III Corps, though, was the sheer volume of troops surrendering. The survivors from units that had been pounded from the air for weeks were giving up in the thousands, all of them telling stories that were more or less the same.

The units had been demoralized by the aerial bombardments, they said. Food, water, and medicine were in short supply. There was plenty of ammunition, but almost no one left with the will to use it. Battalion commanders talked freely about how their communications lines were down, and that they hadn't been able to communicate with brigade, division, or corps headquarters for weeks except by courier.

Back toward Kuwait City itself, Iraq's 11th, 15th, and 19th Infantry Divisions were mostly intact, along with three brigades of Iraqi Special Forces troops. But they were looking the wrong way, prepared to fight off the marine assault from the Persian Gulf, but it would never come.

Farther to the west, Iraq's IV Corps had the task of defending western Kuwait and the Saudi-Iraqi border. Here again, several units were already completely out of the fight, with the 20th and 30th Infantry Divisions eliminated, and the 6th Armored Division crippled.

The Iraqis were fighting blind. With no air force and little, if any communications left, they could react to what was directly in front of them, but had no idea of the size, scope, and direction of the coalition advance. Despite the damage, Baghdad's ministry of information continued to crank out communiqués. One, issued late in the day on February 24, packed a novel's worth of fiction into a few lines:

> "Our forces have wiped out an enemy paratrooper assault …. [T]he heroic 3rd and 1st Divisions are grappling in an epic confrontation against the onslaught … our forces repulsed and contained the enemy attacks and foiled their objectives. The 3rd Division burned and destroyed hundreds of enemy tanks and vehicles and inflicted large numbers of casualties."

The communiqué was making fact out of what had not materialized. First, even though the Iraqis had been expecting a paratrooper assault on their airfields by either the 82nd or 101st Airborne, it never happened. Second, the Iraqi 1st Division was the Republican Guard Hammurabi Division, and the 3rd Division was the Guard's Tawakalna Division, and neither of them were anywhere near Allied troops. Yet.

But it wasn't as if the Iraqis were sitting still. At 9:30 P.M. Iraq's 12th Armored Division ordered its brigades to set up a screen in front of Republican Guard units. That, alone, says a lot about what had happened to Iraq's military capabilities, since the 12th Armored was a second-line unit. Stationing themselves in the desert west of the Kuwait border, units of the 12th Armored turned southwest. Just behind them, units of the Tawakalna Republican Guards eased themselves slightly down the back side of a rise just west of the Wadi al-Batin.

The tactic seemed solid enough: They would wait on Allied troops approaching them from the west, then ambush them from the rear of the slope as coalition armor mounted the top of the high ground. The Medina Republican Guard Division was to be held just to the rear, with the Adnan Republican Guard Division to the north. The Allies, the Iraqis thought, would be slowed by Iraq's 12th Armored Division, and then would run headlong into three divisions of Saddam's best-trained troops as they crossed the *Sahra al-Hijarah*—the desert of stones.

Much farther east, Iraqi troops were set to try a desperation ploy against the advancing marines. Units of Iraq's 3rd Armored and 8th Mechanized Brigades had hidden themselves among the belching flames and thick smoke of the Burgan oil field inside Kuwait. They were poised to try and smash the frontal assault from the south with a surprise attack from inside the collection of flaming oil rigs.

But those were just about the only Iraqi countermoves. The push into the burning oil field was a desperation gamble designed by field commanders on the spot. Only the arrangement of Republican Guard units behind Iraq's 12th Armored Division seemed to have any semblance of forethought to it, designed apparently by the commander of all Republican Guard units, *Gen. Ayad Flayeh al-Rawi.*

Day one of the ground campaign ended with even the most optimistic CENTCOM planners shaking their heads. They had no idea their troops could range so far and so fast with so little opposition. They feared that would change soon. They were right.

> **Gulf Lingo**
>
> The area of southeastern Iraq from which the Allies were advancing from the west is a desert region called **Sahra al-Hijarah.** The only road anywhere in the region runs east from the town of al-Busayyah into Kuwait.

> **Who's Who**
>
> Ayad Flayeh al-Rawi commanded all Republican Guard units during Desert Storm. He survived the Gulf War, became governor of Baghdad Province, and was appointed minister of youth and sports in 1999. He has been a close ally of Saddam Hussein's for decades.

The Least You Need to Know

- ◆ French troops, led by the legendary French Foreign Legion, quickly secured the extreme left flank of the coalition's line.

- ◆ While the U.S. 82nd Airborne moved north paralleling the French, the U.S. 101st Airborne conducted the biggest helicopter operation in the history of modern warfare.

- ◆ The 24th Mechanized Division and the 3rd Armored Cavalry Regiment moved north quickly into Iraq with only token opposition.

- ◆ As shell-shocked and demoralized Iraqi troops surrendered, a few elite Iraqi units managed to form some sort of strategy.

Chapter

19

Moving In

In This Chapter

- ◆ The U.S. Marine Corps engages in the biggest tank battle in its history in the middle of a flaming oil field
- ◆ General Schwartzkopf becomes enraged at the slow progress of some U.S. troops
- ◆ Britain's famed "Desert Rats" return to battle while U.S. troops capture a major Iraqi highway and wheel east
- ◆ A SCUD missile slams into a barracks in Saudi Arabia, killing 27 Americans

There are lots of terms to describe things going wrong. One of the military's favorites is FUBAR: fouled up beyond all recognition. (Of course the word isn't really "fouled," but it's as close as we'll get here.) Then there's Murphy's Law: Whatever can go wrong will go wrong at the worst possible time. But when it comes to weather making a mess of plans and equipment, the Bedouins have the best word: *haboob*, which loosely translated means "the worst of everything all at once."

Day two of the Ground War, February 25, began with miserable weather that only got worse. Late February on the Arabian Peninsula is the *Shammal*, the season of the north winds, when chilly winds gust 30 to 40 miles an hour. The winds, in turn, can stir up massive sandstorms called *Khamsins*. *Khamsin* literally means "50," for the number of days the storm season lasts. Add winds, sand, rain, sudden desert thunderstorms, ground fog, and heavy smoke from oil fires, and you get the sort of *haboob* faced by Allied troops.

Out of the Flames

The Burgan oil field in Kuwait stank like a combination of burning tires, drained crankcase oil, and rotten eggs. Troopers from the 1st Marine Division coughed up black particles as the tires and treads of their Humvees and tanks splashed through reeking oil. The roar from dozens of burning wellheads sounded for all the world like armored vehicles moving in all directions. The only light in the February 25 predawn darkness came from the ghastly glow of flames arcing into the air as gas from the oil wells burned off. It was damp, foggy, foul, and completely miserable. One marine in a Humvee later said that even with his night vision goggles, he could barely make out the end of the barrel on his .50-caliber machine gun.

The 1st Marine Division was just preparing to take the nearby Jaber airfield without much of a fight. A few T-62 tanks had been engaged and destroyed, but the entire Iraqi 56th Mechanized Infantry Brigade had surrendered at the first possible opportunity.

Heads Up! _____

"The smoke clouds from the burning oil wells were closing fast, reducing my visibility to less than 1,500 meters. All of a sudden my loader, Lance Corporal Rodruigues, yelled, 'We got a T-62 out there! Look! Gunner! Sabot! Tank! Range 1,100 meters!' The first explosion was small but then its ammo began cooking off. I counted 14 secondary explosions."

—Lt. James Gonsalves, 3rd Tank Battalion, 1st Marine Division, quoted in *With the 1st Marine Division*, USMC History Division, 1996

But commanders of the 1st Marines were worried about reports that kept coming in from the prisoners, that the Iraqis were going to attack "… out of the flames." To the marine brass, that could only mean one thing: Iraqi forces were out there, somewhere, hidden in the flaming oil fields. But they also had a hard time believing it, given the hellish conditions.

The commander of the 1st Division, Gen. James "Mike" Myatt, had climbed through the reserves, tours in Vietnam, and stints with the joint chiefs to become the youngest general in U.S. Marine Corps history at age 46 in 1987. Now he had a problem. On one hand,

Iraqi prisoners and enemy radio traffic hinted that some sort of counterattack was coming. On the other, the airfield wasn't completely secure and there were reports of Iraqi artillery on the far side of the airstrip. He played it safe, reinforced the marines in the oil field, and decided to send a battalion into the flaming mess to root out any hidden Iraqis as soon as dawn broke on February 25.

Counterattack

Iraq's 3rd Armored Brigade and 8th Mechanized Brigade were equipped with the kind of armor usually reserved for Republican Guard units, namely Soviet-built T-72 and T-62 tanks. They had managed to hide enough tanks in the flames of *Burgan* to launch a counterattack, but they were just as blind as the marines.

A little after 4 A.M., the first Iraqi units blundered into the left side of the 1st Marine Division. A few minutes later, the main Iraqi attack stumbled upon the marines' right flank in the oil field. Tankers began to exchange fire at point-blank range through the gloom, smoke, and dust. The marines didn't need to elevate their gun barrels at all, since the Iraqis were close enough to fire straight into them.

In civilian life, he was Ralph Parkinson of Yakima, Washington. But since his marine reserve unit had been activated, he was Captain Parkinson, commanding Company B, 4th Tank Battalion, U.S. Marine Reserves. Just before 6 A.M., he spotted a column of top-of-the-line T-72 tanks moving straight for his position in the swirling muck. He didn't have time to radio anyone up the chain of command, not with the Iraqis on top of him. He ordered the barrels of his company of M1A1 tanks level and opened fire. The darkness was split by the barrel flashes from the U.S. and Iraqi tanks, creating a strobe effect like dozens of flashbulbs going off in the blackness. Within half an hour, 34 of the Iraqi tanks were burning hulks.

In the meantime, Company D of Marine Task Force Shepherd spotted a column of Iraqi tanks moving south, following a power line parallel to the marine positions. Company D was mounted on several Bradleys, each armed with the 25-millimeter chain gun and TOW antitank missiles. The Iraqis had a good deal more firepower, but Company D had the mobility. They trailed parallel to the Iraqis, picking off a truck and five tanks in the column's rear.

The sting from Company D pushed the Iraqis along into a defensive line set up by Marine Task Force Ripper. The Iraqis collided with Ripper just at dawn, and the fire between the T-62 and T-72 tanks and the marines' tanks and TOWs was withering, as the units were almost nose-to-nose. A dozen of the 20 Iraqi armored personnel carriers and tanks were disabled, and the rest scattered back into the haze.

Oops, We Surrender

The 1st Marines 1st Battalion began to probe the oil field around 7:30 A.M., but quickly became bogged down by thick haze and oozing slop. The marines, meantime, wheeled their artillery around, aiming it at the oil field rather than at the air base. Within 10 minutes, more than 750 high-explosive and shrapnel-spreading artillery rounds were going off in and around the Iraqi tanks.

About the same time, marine Col. Rich Hodory, commanding the marines' right flank, decided to hold a staff meeting. He wanted to make sure everyone completely understood General Myatt's orders to redeploy in order to fend off the counterattack. The problem was that, even in daylight, visibility was less than 100 yards, and many of the unit commanders never even found their way to the regimental headquarters that had been set up in the flaming oil field. Colonel Hodory found himself briefing the stragglers as they managed to find his position.

Just after 8 A.M., Hodory was bent over a table, explaining the situation on the oily map spread out in front of him when he heard a rumble that sounded more like armored vehicles than burning oil wells. He looked up. Less than 50 yards away, an Iraqi T-55 tank and three armored personnel carriers suddenly appeared out of the petroleum fog. The marines froze. The T-55's cannon barrel was aimed straight at the colonel's Humvee.

Instead of firing, the tank just sat. An Iraqi officer—a brigade commander, as it turned out—appeared out of the haze and walked toward them, hands up. Since he had accidentally found some marines, he asked if it might be possible to surrender. He said neither he nor his companions were interested in fighting anymore, but that some of the other units still out in the fog had plenty of fight left in them.

> **The Machines**
>
> The standard ammunition used by NATO countries for rifles such as the U.S.-made M-16 and the Israeli Galil is 5.56 millimeters. Those sorts of rounds zipping through the marines' command post indicate either the Iraqis had purchased NATO-type weapons on the open market, or that the marines were taking return fire from their own men.

Colonel Hodory barely had time to shake off his amazement when suddenly cannon and machine gun fire began to blast around and through the command post. Marine Maj. John Turner, who was at the command post, later wrote: "We had main gun rounds, machine gun tracers, and even *5.56-millimeter* (small arms) fire coming through the command post. I remember hitting the deck for the first time during the war and saw tracer rounds going through the command post east to west at knee height."

Colonel Hodory wasn't the only one in that fix. The battalion commander, Col. Michael Kephart, had just started to brief company commanders when his battalion headquarters was peppered with machine gun fire.

The battalion's Company I was dug in nearby, and opened fire on the unseen Iraqis with Dragon and TOW antitank missiles. The Iraqis, surprised by the sudden return fire, faltered.

Company C encountered a line of armored personnel carriers and tanks and opened up with its missiles, knocking out 18 of the Iraqi attackers. As the firing continued, the fog began to burn off, just enough for spotter planes to zero in on the Iraqi positions. Marine air strikes backed by the army's Apache helicopters began picking off tanks and personnel carriers. The burning oil field was soon littered with burning wreckage. By 11 A.M., the largest tank battle in U.S. Marine history was over. The Iraqis lost 50 tanks, 25 armored personnel carriers, and over 300 prisoners. No marines were killed or wounded.

Feeling Feint

Just to the west of the marines, the 1st Cavalry's Blackjack Brigade continued pounding its way up the *Wadi al-Batin*. The feint was designed to make the Iraqis think a main avenue of attack would be up the dry riverbed, and it seemed to be working. By the time the desert was painted sickly yellow by the early morning sunlight filtered through fog and haze, the brigade was at the Iraqi's fire trenches.

The trenches had been gouged out of the sand, stretching miles toward the horizon in front of the Blackjack Brigade. Hastily assembled pipes had leaked millions of gallons of oil from nearby fields into the moat. Suddenly smoke began to shiver down the trench, from one end to the other. Then hissing flames erupted on the oil's surface, sending black and gray clouds billowing into the fetid sky.

It was just the reaction the 1st Cav had hoped for. As they had done all night, they fired their Multiple Launch Rocket Systems (MLRS), launching hundreds of rockets into Iraqi positions on the other side of the flaming oil. They called in Apache helicopters to skid low over the rising wall of soot and hammer the Iraqis. They unlimbered their 155-millimeter howitzers and sent more explosives into the enemy positions. If it was an assault like a dentist's drill, the fire trenches were the nerve the 1st Cav had hoped to hit.

Around noon, the Blackjack Brigade began a quick withdrawal, heading back down the wadi to join the rest of the division. The fake attack had been a complete success, pinning down four Iraqi divisions, trying to see the oncoming Allied attack across the fire trenches. The Apache pilots reported that at least five Iraqi tanks and one antiaircraft piece had been destroyed, and that Saddam's army was staying burrowed inside its bunkers.

Gulf Lingo

In the nineteenth century, a sizable number of biblical scholars thought that the ancient river that had once flowed through the **Wadi al-Batin** was one of the four rivers the Bible mentions as watering the Garden of Eden.

There wouldn't be much time to rest on the laurels of this success, because the 1st Cav was about to get a new mission, one of the most complex in the unit's long history.

Schwartzkopf Explodes

After the war, General Schwartzkopf wrote in his best-selling autobiography, *It Doesn't Take a Hero* (Bantam Books, 1992), that it was all the fault of the VII Corps that the Republican Guard wasn't destroyed. Army Gen. *Frederick Franks* commanded the VII Corps—the 1st Cavalry, the 1st Infantry, the British, the 1st and 3rd Armored Divisions, and the rest of the units just west of Kuwait. Schwartzkopf wrote that he was ready to replace General Franks on February 25 because, in his estimation, he wasn't aggressive enough.

> **Who's Who**
>
> Frederick Franks was born in Pennsylvania in 1938. A West Point graduate, he served in Vietnam and Cambodia. After retiring from the U.S. Army in 1994, Franks became a consultant and author, collaborating with author Tom Clancy on *Into the Storm: A Study in Command.*

A certain amount of General Schwartzkopf's complaint was self-serving, since the failure to wipe out the Republican Guard haunts American military and foreign policy to this day and is one of the few blemishes on Schwartzkopf's tenure as head of CENTCOM. On the other hand, General Franks has been criticized for his caution by people other than Schwartzkopf.

Franks was, and is, a military intellectual. He taught at West Point and, after leaving VII Corps, ended his career by formulating strategy at the Army's Training and Doctrine Command. General Franks was thoughtful, deliberate, and a man admired by those who served under him. At the same time, like Union Gen. George McClellan during the Civil War, General Franks was more worried about taking casualties and exposing his units to attack than he was about attacking the enemy forcefully. On the night of February 24, Franks ordered the entire VII Corps advance to stop for the evening so he could consolidate his forces.

On February 25, Schwartzkopf looked at a map of unit advances so far and went ballistic. The left flank was doing just fine. The French had secured the left part of the line, the 82nd and 101st Airborne Divisions were striking deeper and faster than planned, and the 24th Mechanized Infantry was tearing up the road into Iraq. The right flank was also in good shape, with the marines and Saudis making plenty of headway into Kuwait and tying down Iraqi forces.

The problem was in the center—Franks's center. Schwartzkopf's strategy called for the marines on the right to pin down Iraqi troops in Kuwait, while the XVIII Airborne Corps units on the left would sweep into Iraq and cut off escape routes. But Schwartzkopf wanted the Republican Guards attacked and destroyed. That job fell to Franks's VII Corps in the center. And the map showed that General Franks's units were lagging well behind both the left and right flanks.

As freezing rain began to fall all across the front in the early morning, Schwartzkopf contacted General Franks and blistered him. CENTCOM intelligence indicated Iraq's III Corps inside Kuwait was all but collapsing. Why weren't the British troops across the line yet? Why wasn't the 1st Infantry Division farther along? What was holding back the armored units? Schwartzkopf bellowed that if the mustachioed professorial Franks didn't start moving fast, he might find himself relieved of command in the middle of a war.

That afternoon, Franks issued new orders to his three heavy divisions. Via e-mail, he told them to swing around to the east, pivot clockwise, and smash into the Republican Guard units. Some of the war's biggest battles were to result from that order.

Desert Rats Redux

In the scorching North African summer of 1942, all that stood between the Nazis' vaunted Afrika Corps, led by Gen. Erwin Rommel, and the rich oil fields of Libya was the battered and exhausted British Eighth Army, including the 7th Armored Brigade.

If they failed, the Nazis would not only get the oil, they would sweep across North Africa, hit Egypt, and take not only the fertile Nile River Delta, but the vitally important Mediterranean port of Alexandria as well.

At that point, Gen. Bernard Montgomery took over the Eighth Army. They held and then routed Rommel at the battle of El Alemein in Libya, and became known to history as "The Desert Rats." In the Gulf War, that name was continued by the only Eighth Army unit still in service, the 7th Armored. But it was also granted, by extension, to any unit fighting alongside them. Soon, many of the troopers in Her Majesty's 1st Armored Division were proudly sporting the Desert Rat insignia: a black patch embroidered with a brown rat sitting on its hind legs. Nowhere else on the battlefield was such a homely emblem given such respect.

The Desert Rats were finally able to move out at 10 A.M. on February 25. The first unit of the 7th Armored Brigade to carry the Desert Rats insignia forward was the Queen's Royal Irish Hussars. Maj. Vincent Maddison guided the first tanks and armored personnel carriers across the phase line, and the regimental commander, Col. Arthur Denaro, waved his troops on, his voice crackling over the radio headsets: "Move now! Tally ho! Move along now!"

Heads Up!

"If anyone attempts to surrender, do not engage; any enemy vehicles trying to get away, engage."
—Orders to British 1st Armored Division, February 25, 1991

The advance started with British verve, but came to a grinding halt within half an hour. The U.S. 1st Infantry Division, which had cleared the berms through which the Desert

Rats passed, had taken so many Iraqi POWs that the roads were now clogged with prisoner convoys. It was a metaphor for the problems in VII Corps that caused General Schwartzkopf to blow his stack.

At noon, the unit was finally able to move out. The Irish Hussars sped through the desert and didn't encounter their first Iraqi until 4:30 P.M., when a lone straggler was picked up in the desert waving a white flag. The Desert Rats continued east in driving rain and cold until midnight. They were on the eve of their fiercest fighting since the days of El Alemein.

Turn, Turn, Turn

On February 25 the Allied forces began a huge turning movement, toward the Iraqis both guarding the Kuwaiti border and north of the border inside Iraq itself. General Schwartzkopf had decided that the primary objective—to find and destroy the Republican Guard units—needed to be pursued harder now that everyone except the VII Corps units was running ahead of schedule by at least a full day.

As we've noted, General Franks responded to the tongue lashing by Schwartzkopf by calculating time and distance on the back of a wet envelope at his command post. Pushing water drops off a plastic map overlay, he used a grease pencil to sketch out the turning maneuver. It was *FRAGPLAN* 7, one of a grab bag of contingency plans drawn up before the ground war started.

The plan assumed that the Republican Guard units would not maneuver, but would remain dug in pretty much where they were. Almost 150,000 troops and thousands of vehicles would turn to the right like a giant wheel, with the British as the hub and the American infantry and armored divisions moving like huge spokes.

Desert Lore

FRAGPLAN 7 called for three heavy divisions to wheel around and hit the Republican Guards. At the time it was issued, General Franks only had two: the 1st and 3rd Armored Divisions. Luckily, the 1st Infantry Division was able to become the third, since it had breached the berms with almost no losses.

To VII Corps' northwest, General McCaffrey's 24th Mechanized Division was already straddling Highway 8 in the Euphrates River Valley. Moving at just under an average of 20 miles per hour, the 24th Mech wheeled 26,000 troops and more than 8,500 tanks, trucks, and artillery pieces into a sweeping right turn, moving toward the Iraqi city of Basra and the hope of cutting off all escape for any Republican Guard units.

Meanwhile, the 101st Airborne was ready to grip the Euphrates Valley in its fist. But first they needed a place to land. Before dawn, a helicopter dropped off Lieutenant Jerry Biller and his scout platoon into the rain, wind, and complete darkness of Iraq, just south of the Euphrates. Biller and his men, wading through marshy mud in the gusting cold, had no idea whether they might end up dead, or prisoners, since they were the only Allied troops for miles in any direction. But they needed to find a flat, relatively isolated field where an entire airborne division could land. They found it.

By 3 P.M., more than 500 paratroopers had secured Highway 8, while 20 miles south, everything from armored assault vehicles to artillery and antitank weapons was being ferried in and then sent north to hook up with the brigade along the highway. It had taken the 101st less than 30 hours to mount the biggest helilift operation in the history of warfare and cut off both any Iraqi escape routes from the battle zone and supply routes into it.

The 101st was as far north as any Allied troops were going to go. To their south, coalition troops began to sweep to the right like a hand on a mammoth clock.

U.S. military personnel inspect the remains of the Dhahran, Saudi Arabia building where 27 G.I.'s died in a SCUD attack.

Disaster in Dhahran

Greensburg, Pennsylvania, population 16,000, sits a little more than 30 miles east of Pittsburgh on U.S. Route 30. It has two colleges, an art museum, a train station where the daily Philadelphia-to-Pittsburgh Amtrak run stops, and the Westmoreland County Fair every summer. It was founded before the Revolutionary War, and was originally called "Newtown," but Benjamin Franklin's Postal Service asked for a name change in 1786, since a lot of other Pennsylvanians had named their settlements Newtown also.

City leaders decided to rename it Greensburg, after Revolutionary War Gen. Nathaniel Green, who was instrumental in defeating the Hessians and British at the Battle of Trenton under George Washington's command. As far as we know, Green never set foot in the town.

The U.S Army Reserve's 14th Quartermaster Detachment, which specializes in water purification, is based in Greensburg, Pennsylvania. The 14th had been mobilized one day before the air war began, and was sent to Fort Lee, Virginia, learning about the latest state-of-the-art purification techniques and devices, vital in the desert, where water is precious. They arrived in Dhahran, Saudi Arabia, on February 19, having spent six days training in desert operations.

At 8:30 P.M., the familiar air raid sirens warbled in Dhahran, sounding not so much like a wail as a car theft alarm that wouldn't shut off. In the first days of the air war, Dhahran had been peppered with SCUD attacks, most of them aimed at the *Dhahran Air Base.*

Gulf Lingo

The **Dhahran Air Base** was well known to the Iraqis, since the Saudis had allowed Iraq to use it to refuel their jets during the war with Iran. The Iraqis knew not only its precise location, but the runway, fuel depot, and hangar layouts.

The missiles had either shaken apart in flight, fallen harmlessly into the Persian Gulf, or been intercepted by the two Patriot missile batteries at the airfield.

A warehouse near the airfield had been converted for use as a barracks, since every usable hotel room and apartment in the immediate area had long since been requisitioned by the Saudi armed forces or the Allies. The 14th, along with other Quartermaster units and just about anyone else who had recently arrived in eastern Saudi Arabia was housed in the makeshift barracks.

As the missile arced through the haze and reached its apogee, the radars of both four-missile batteries should have been acquiring it. But one of the batteries was down for maintenance, and wasn't even operational.

The other Patriot battery, everyone thought, was working just fine. But an undetected software glitch had sent faulty signals to the radar unit. It sat there, silent, aimed skyward but not seeing anything. The first hint for the Patriot crews that something was wrong was when they heard the explosion around 8:35 P.M.

The SCUD had begun to wobble and shake on its way down through the clouds and wet, unstable atmosphere. Finally, the stress had become too much, and the missile broke into a dozen or so pieces. The warhead detached, intact. The warhead, it was later estimated, contained anywhere from 700 to 1,100 pounds of high explosive. It crashed through the roof of the converted warehouse and went off.

The roof was peeled back. Girders, steel, cement, and glass went flying in all directions at hundreds of miles per hour. The walls collapsed. As medics and nearby soldiers arrived, they found 28 bodies in the rubble and 99 more wounded, some of them in severe shock.

At 8:30 P.M. on February 25, the 14th Quarter-master Detachment consisted of 69 men and women. By 8:40 P.M., 14 of them were dead, and 43 were wounded, some critically.

In dead and wounded, the 14th suffered casualties of 81 percent, one of the highest totals for any unit in the history of the U.S. Army.

Later that night, I broke the news of the attack to a three-man squad from Task Force Ripper as they paused at the edge of the burning Burgan oil field. The sergeant just stared at me, his eyes bloodshot from the oil fumes, his face covered with oil and soot. He looked past me, through the belching oil fires, north, toward Kuwait City, toward Iraq, toward Baghdad. "Time to go to work," he said quietly. The three of them walked off, into the oil smoke.

> **Heads Up!**
>
> "They were all of us—a high school football star, a lover of country music, future homemakers of America, secretaries and salesmen, hunters and fishermen, postal workers and volunteer fire-men, friends and lovers, fathers, sons, brothers, and two of our daughters."
>
> —Pennsylvania Gov. Robert Casey at a memorial service for the 14th Quartermaster Detachment, March 2, 1991

The Least You Need to Know

- The U.S. Marines fought off a surprise counterattack that came out of a burning oil field.
- CENTCOM Comdr. Gen. Schwartzkopf was outraged that General Franks's VII Corps hadn't made better progress.
- The 101st Airborne Division vaulted all the way to the Euphrates River and cut off any Iraqi escape to the north.
- A SCUD missile slammed into a barracks in Saudi Arabia, killing 28 Americans and wounding 99 more.

20

The Going Gets Tough

In This Chapter

- ◆ Iraqi troops fleeing Kuwait City with loot are slaughtered along the highway connecting Kuwait City to Iraq
- ◆ The 24th Mechanized Infantry encounters stiff resistance from Iraqi troops
- ◆ Allied troops of the VII Corps slam into the Republican Guard
- ◆ A battle named after its map coordinates—73 Easting—rages

Around 1991, a new religious cult was appearing in the Euphrates Valley, on the same ground the 101st Airborne and 24th Mechanized Infantry was about to traverse. The cult leader's father, Terah, was unhappy about his son's rejection of the family's religion. Terah was an old man, and his son was getting older, too. This is how hot-blooded young men act, Terah was said to have fumed, not how a mature man behaves.

But the son had a calling, so he dragged his family across the Euphrates and set out for God knows where. The whole thing is summed up by the voice the son said he'd been hearing: "Get thee out of thy country, and from thy kindred, and from thy father's house, unto a land that I will show thee." The year was around 1991 B.C.E. The son was Abraham, or Ibrahim, or Abram, father of Islam, Judaism, and Christianity. The ancient city of Ur, from which he started, was near the modern air base at Talil, just across the river from the city of as-Nasiriyah, Iraq. Abraham's tracks were about to be followed by a new kind of war chariot.

Saddam Radio

On February 26, Saddam Hussein, making a virtue out of necessity, went on Baghdad Radio to announce that Iraqi troops were pulling out of Kuwait and that the withdrawal would be completed within 24 hours. But he made it clear he was not bowing to international diplomatic pressure. Kuwait, he growled, is part of Iraq and will be part of Iraq again.

Then the secular Saddam once again played the religion card for the Arab nations. He said that Constantinople didn't fall to the Muslims in the first try, but that it took many battles before the Christian city was conquered for Islam and renamed Istanbul in 1453. The implication was clear: Saddam, the new Saladin, had led the first of many battles against the Christian invaders. The speech conveniently omitted mentioning who had invaded whom to start the war in the first place.

The Bush administration reacted immediately, dismissing the speech as pure propaganda, and warning Iraqi troops that the war was continuing, on schedule, and that the alternative to surrender would not be pleasant.

 Heads Up!

"It should be borne in mind that Constantinople was not conquered in the first battle. The result was achieved in other battles."
—Saddam Hussein, radio speech, February 26, 1991

"He is trying to claim victory in the midst of a rout …. [T]he coalition will continue to prosecute the war with undiminished intensity …. [T]he liberation of Kuwait is at hand."
—Pres. George Bush, February 26, 1991

Highway to Hell

Kuwait City is orbited by a series of ring roads. The Sixth Ring Road is the outermost, and it intersects with a divided six-lane superhighway with a wide sand divider between the three lanes on each side. It runs west from Kuwait City until it hits the town of Jahra. Unlike Kuwait City with its palatial homes, Jahra is a jumble of cheaply built one- and two-story cement homes used by the Palestinian, Indian, Pakistani, Egyptian, Sri Lankan, Filipino, and other foreign workers who keep Kuwait City running.

At Jahra, the highway turns north, and narrows from six lanes to four. The center divider disappears, and the two northbound and two southbound lanes are separated by concrete dividers. The highway slopes gently uphill for 30 miles toward the border post between Iraq and Kuwait on the al-Mutwa Ridge.

Kuwaiti resistance fighters had been sending word to CENTCOM for two days that Iraqis were burning and looting the city, fleeing north toward Iraq with hostages, weapons, and booty of all kinds. Around 1:30 A.M. on February 26, U.S. Marine combat air patrols spotted a traffic jam going north in the darkness from Kuwait City toward the Iraqi border.

To the pilots on the Harriers and F-18s attached to Marine Air Group 11, the jumble below them before dawn on February 26 looked like the worst big-city traffic jam imaginable. Trucks, tanks, limousines, taxis, ambulances, armored personnel carriers, delivery vans, 18-wheel tractor trailers, police cars, passenger cars, you name it, were snarled and gridlocked in a surreal jumble of military and civilian vehicles.

Marine Air Group 11 Commander *Col. Manfred Rietsch* was informed, as was the nearest navy aircraft carrier squadron, the VA-155 "Silver Foxes," flying A-6 Intruders off the deck of the USS *Ranger*. Just as they were notified, marine pilots reported a parallel road, running from the north end of Kuwait Bay up the coast, was also packed with vehicles.

> ### Who's Who
>
> Manfred Rietsch was born in East Germany and immigrated to the United States in 1956. He joined the U.S. Marine Corps and became one of its most legendary pilots in Vietnam. He flew 66 combat missions in the Gulf War, the most of any pilot. He retired in 1994.

The marines and the navy began guiding planes toward the jumbled mass. They swooped low over the convoy, dropping 500- and 1,000-pound bombs. The marine Harriers and F-18s and Navy A-6s began running shuttle missions from their bases or the carrier, striking the Iraqi targets at will every few minutes.

Colonel Rietsch in his F-18 orbited the area, acting as forward air controller, or FAC. The marine jets alone flew 300 individual missions. Antipersonnel bombs were mixed in with the high-explosive ones. The panicked Iraqis either died where they sat, or tried to break free and drive out into the desert. A pair of tanks and some armored personnel carriers that got loose were chased down by Marine Corps Maj. Jurgen Lukas in his F-18. In his combat notes, he wrote:

"I rolled in on the lead tank and dropped two Mk-83s [1,000-pound bombs]. One hit short but the second hit the top of the tank. After that, the column dispersed in all directions and we easily picked off most of the rest, ending our attacks with multiple strafing runs."

The bombing went on for hours. Smoke and flames from the burning vehicles could be seen for miles. No one has ever estimated the death toll on the ground, but British and American burial teams shoveled thousands of body parts and the few intact bodies they could find into mass graves in early March.

As a reporter, I drove out along the highway five days after the attack. In a quarter century of covering conflicts of all kinds, I have never witnessed anything to approach it. Vehicles of all kinds were packed with looted goods. One truck contained a jumble of smashed color TVs. Another, stolen from the Royal Kuwait Botanical Garden, was flipped on its side, with two ragged date palms dangling from the back. An armored personnel carrier was on top of a crushed ambulance, looking like they were mating. A T-55 tank was still smoking where it had tried to crash through the concrete barriers, and a pair of Chevrolets loaded with rolled-up Persian carpets lay on their sides. The Iraqis had apparently taken everything they could grab from homes, offices, and industrial sites throughout the city, and piled whatever vehicles were available with the loot.

> **Desert Lore**
>
> There had been other battles at the town of Jahra before the Highway of Death. An ocher-colored rectangular mud building squats near the highway. This is the Red Fort, where invaders from Saudi Arabia were fought off by Kuwaiti and British troops in 1920.

Behind the melted windshield of a truck, an incinerated body, a black mummy with burned matchsticks for fingers and its mouth peeled back over yellowed teeth, grinned at me. The devastation went on as far as I could see, both up and down the highway, and out in the desert, for miles stretching to the horizon. The air was filled with the acrid smell of burned rubber and the foul sweetness of raw meat left out in the sun. British Royal Navy Comdr. Gareth Derryck had been among the initial Allied officers to visit what was now known as *The Highway of Death*. He had said, simply, "It must have been the nearest thing to hell that can be imagined."

The world wouldn't see video of the carnage until the day after the attack, on February 27. As we'll see, the public and media reaction caused the Bush administration to push for an end to the war as quickly as possible.

Iraqi vehicles and corpses litter the "Highway of Death" in northern Kuwait.

The Battle of the Euphrates

The 101st Airborne had secured Highway 8 and sent thousands of troops fanning out across the region to guard the Allies rear to the northwest. Besides armed soldiers, the 101st sent teams carrying medicine and water into nearby villages. The Iraqis living in the marshlands near the Euphrates were Shia Muslims, always suspected and often persecuted by Saddam and the Sunni Muslim majority in Iraq. But they still believed some of the regime's propaganda, including stories that American troops were cannibals with a particular fondness for children. Captain Paul Floyd of the 101st later recalled that women screaming, "Please don't eat us!" met American patrols at some villages.

With their rear flank secure, the tanks and troopers of the 24th Mechanized Infantry Division were able to concentrate on rolling down Highway 8 toward Basra. General McCaffrey's forces, though, had two problems to solve first. One, there were Iraqi airfields at Tallil and Jalibah, near the Euphrates, that had to be seized. Two, the 24th Mech had come so far so fast that they had outrun their supplies, with some of the 500-gallon fuel tanks on the M1A1s down to a little over 100 gallons.

It became clear that the two Iraqi air bases had to be neutralized before anything else. As always, the weather would have something so say about that. On the night of February 25, a sandstorm added to the rain and wind.

The Worst So Far

For most of the night, the 24th Mech had been slogging through swamps, marshes, and previously dry riverbeds now running with water and turning to mud from the rains. The troopers had nicknamed it "The Great Dismal Swamp," but mucking through the slop had an upside. Highway 8, the Tallil and Jalibah airfields, the Republican Guard's Nebuchudnezzar Division, and the Euphrates River were all north of them. The Iraqis had apparently never considered an attack through the bogs south of their positions, so they'd never laid any mines in them.

Around 2 P.M. on February 25, three Brigades of the 24th Mech were ready to attack. The Tallil air base was almost right on top of the ruins of Abraham's ancient city of Ur. That was the left side of the 24th Mech's line. The Jalibah air base, some 40 miles to the east, was the far right. The plan was for the 197th Brigade to hit on the left and seize at least the edge of Talil, the 1st Brigade to punch through the middle, slice Highway 8, and mop up any Iraqis, and the 2nd Brigade to hit the highway, head east fast, and overrun Jalibah.

For half an hour, artillery softened up the spot where the 1st Brigade would slice the highway in the middle of the line. But for the first time, the Iraqis stood and fought, and fired back with gusto. Iraq's 47th and 49th Infantry Division, along with Republican Guard commandos, opened fire with antitank guns and artillery. First dozens, then hundreds of artillery rounds began to pour down on the 1st Brigade as it tried to cross the highway in the wind, rain, and sand.

Heads Up!

"The storm which wears away the country covered Ur like a cloth,

its people's corpses littered the approaches,

in the streets and roadways bodies lay.

The country's blood now filled its holes like metal in a mold, Bodies dissolved, like butter left in the sun"

—Lament for the City of Ur, Sumerian poem, circa 2000 B.C.E.

But the troopers began to notice that the shells were falling in tight patterns over just a few selected spots. They saw some old 55-gallon oil drums scattered around the fields, and saw the Iraqi gunners were zeroed in on them. Apparently they had been using the drums as reference points for artillery practice, and were still firing at them. The American tanks and armored personnel carriers could avoid being hit if they avoided the oil drums.

But the firing between the U.S. tanks and the Iraqi emplacements roared on for four hours in the pelting rain. The Iraqis should have had an advantage, dug into rocky outcroppings and collapsed wadi banks and with a clear field of fire at the Americans. But their aim was terrible, and resistance finally collapsed as it was growing dark when U.S. artillery could finally zero in.

Chemical Dump

While the firing went on, part of the 1st Brigade pushed ahead, crossing Highway 8 and driving for a canal just north of the road. They were headed for an area known on their maps as *"Objective Gold."* Iraqi troops began to put up a fight, but Col. John Craddock used his M1A1 tanks to either blast them out of their positions or send them scurrying into the weeds choking the silted canal.

Colonel Craddock and his men found a flat fenced area covering several acres. Stored aboveground, and in concrete bunkers, were thousands of rounds of artillery ammunition, rockets, rocket-propelled grenades, and even a large cache of 500- and 1,000-pound bombs belonging to the Iraqi Air Force.

Desert Lore _____

Objective Gold was the Iraqi ammunition dump at Khamisiyah. As we'll see later, destruction of this ammo dump after the war ended may have exposed thousands of American troops to chemical fallout.

The colonel and his men had no way of knowing that General McCaffrey had been notified in a flash message from XVIII Airborne Corps head-quarters that there were "... possible chemicals at Objective Gold." They would find out later.

Commando Ambush

Battalions belonging to the 18th Infantry Regiment, attached to the 24th Mech, had no idea what they might face, since intelligence on Iraqi units in the Euphrates Valley was spotty at best. There would be a three-pronged attack along the 24th Mech's line, and the 18th Infantry—part of the 197th Brigade—would be on the left, aiming to take at least a corner of the Tallil air base.

The 18th Infantry Regiment was rattling along in its outdated *M-113 armored personnel carriers*, since the unit hadn't yet gotten the newer Bradley Fighting Vehicles, when General Eric Olsen, the commander, decided to send out a task force to scout ahead. The scouts started taking fire from the darkness. Two troopers fell, wounded, and the scout platoon's commander, Lt. Larry Aikman, began asking for artillery fire to clear out the Iraqis. But artillery units hadn't caught up with the rapidly moving troops yet, so General Olsen himself went forward with a team of scouts and a tank company, blindly moving toward the Euphrates in the pelting rain.

The Machines

The M-113 Armored Personnel Carrier entered service in 1956. In use in more than 50 countries, the M-113 started out armed with a .50-caliber machine gun, but has since been armed with everything from a 106-millimeter recoilless rifle to the Vulcan anti-aircraft system.

The general soon found the scouts, and came under heavy fire from the dug-in 3rd Commando regiment of the Republican Guards. Using grenade launchers, M1A1 tanks, machine guns, and, finally, artillery, they engaged in a firefight that ranged through the mud for more than two hours. The troopers then stormed the bunkers, one at a time, and found 50 Iraqi dead, and several hundred more who wanted to surrender.

We Were Just Leaving

After dark, troopers from the 1st Brigade bundled themselves against the cold and blocked Highway 8, secure in the knowledge that to their northwest, the 101st Airborne had also breached the highway, blocking it to stop any Iraqi reinforcements from rolling south. Around 10 P.M., they heard rumbling down the highway, like trucks and tanks headed their way.

They tensed. Anything approaching them in force from that direction couldn't be friendly. Scouts were dispatched down the road on foot on either side of the highway. Using night-vision goggles, they spotted an Iraqi convoy—trucks and heavy equipment transporters carrying tanks—rolling rapidly toward the 24th Mech's roadblock. It wasn't an attack, since the tanks were secured to the backs of the mammoth transporters. They were simply following each other down the highway.

It was an entire brigade of the Republican Guard's *Hammurabi* Division, driving northwest on Highway 8, leaving the potential battle zone near Basra and lumbering back toward the comparative safety of Baghdad. They didn't discover that American troops had sealed the most direct road to Baghdad until the 24th Mech opened up with tanks, artillery, and TOW missiles, incinerating the tanks, trucks, transporters, and everyone in them.

> **Desert Lore**
>
> Despite being mauled twice by the 24th Mechanized Infantry, elements of the Hammurabi Republican Guard Division survived the Gulf War. As of early 2001, one Hammurabi brigade had been stationed near Iraq's western border with Syria and Jordan.

Dragon's Roar

General Schwartzkopf was still fuming on February 26 that General Franks's VII Corps still hadn't swung to attack the Republican Guard. Given the mammoth logistics in the turn-to-the-right maneuver, though, Franks's corps was running only about 10 hours behind schedule, which might have been understandable to another commander, but not to Schwartzkopf.

One thing Franks had been waiting for was the 1st Cavalry Division. Exhausted after their feint up the Wadi al-Batin, the 1st Cav's troopers weren't given much time to rest.

Instead, they were regrouped and shoved west, into the 1st Infantry Division's sector and then through the holes in the berms punched by U.S. Army's 1st Infantry Division, known as the Big Red One, discussed in Chapter 17.

Moving as fast as they could, the 1st Cavalry was still well away from the action when Franks ordered VII Corps to go after the Republican Guard. Franks intended to attack along a front with three divisions pushing due east. In the south would be the 1st Infantry Division and the British armored units, heading for the Tawakalna Republican Guard Division. The 3rd Armored Division would anchor the center of the line. And in the north, the 1st Armored Division—"Hell on Wheels"—would drive the attack against the Adnan Republican Guard Division.

The same terrible weather that gummed things up for the 24th Mech inside Iraq created problems farther south, too. Sand was blowing steadily, rain would fall, first lightly and then in sheets, and darkness was complicating matters even more. But Franks couldn't wait any longer.

At the radio sign "Dragon's Roar," the 1st Armored in the northern part of the line aimed itself due east and advanced against the Republican Guard. In the very center of their line was the M1A1 Abrams tank designated tank I.D. number D-24, from Delta Company, *1st Battalion, 37th Armor*. Sgt. Anthony Steeded and his crew had been voted the best tank crew in the entire U.S. Army, and were going to represent the U.S. in the Canadian Army Trophy Competition for tank gunnery. The crew of D-24 got the honor of being the center of the entire line.

> **Gulf Lingo**
>
> The **1st Battalion, 37th Armor,** has been deactivated and reorganized several times. In its latest incarnation following a U.S. Army reorganization in 1997, the 4th Battalion of the 67th Armor became 1st Battalion, 37th Armor. The unit is based in Friedberg, Germany.

The attack began at 7 P.M. The 1st Armored Apache attack helicopters zipped across the battlefield toward the Adnan Republican Guard Division. Despite the darkness and swirling sand and wind, six of the Apaches managed to knock out 38 top-of-the-line T-72 tanks, along with more than 70 transport trucks and at least a dozen armored personnel carriers. It was becoming clear that the night-vision goggles worn by the U.S. helicopter and tank crews would make the difference on a night when visibility was often close to zero.

Just to the south, Sergeant Steeded and the crew of D-24 were about to prove why they deserved those gunnery awards. As the U.S. 1st Armored Division pushed east in the darkness, most of its units managed to scoot to the north of the dug in Republican Guards. But Sergeant Steeded's 1st Battalion managed to run right into the Tawakalna Republican Guard's 29th Brigade. That's the unit we mentioned two chapters ago that had taken the time to dig into an ambush position on the down slope of a rocky, rutted rise. For the first time in Desert Storm combat, an Iraqi unit would take out America's top tank, the M1A1.

Not only was the U.S. 37th Armor's 1st Battalion surprised by the dug-in Iraqi positions, they also found themselves outnumbered by a brigade-sized force of the latest T-72 tanks. One of the 37th Armor tanks was stopped in its tracks when it hit a mine. Four others were destroyed when they topped the rocky rise and came in the sights of the Iraqi tankers dug in on the slope beneath them.

Like the rest of the 1st Battalion tankers, Sergeant Steeded and his crew used their thermal-imaging night-vision goggles to spot the Iraqis after the surprise wore off. They began to muscle their way through the Iraqi positions, moving, pivoting, firing, reloading, then moving and firing again.

The *kaarump* of exploding shells mixed with the *whoosh* of burning fuel, the diesel rumble of tank engines, and the faint screams of the wounded and dying from the Iraqis. Two and a half hours later, the Americans suffered no deaths and had only lost the five tanks originally knocked out of action. The Iraqis lost 76 T-72 tanks, 84 armored personnel carriers, eight howitzers, half a dozen command and control vehicles, three antiaircraft guns, and so many trucks that the tankers gave up counting after 100. The Iraqi dead and wounded were never estimated, but probably numbered at least in the hundreds.

The Battle of 73 Easting

The 1st Armored Division was pushing its attack on the far north of the Allied line when Sergeant Steeded encountered the dug-in Iraqi tanks. South of them, in the middle of the VII Corps offensive, the 3rd Armored Division was approaching the center of the Tawakalna Division's line. And in the south, the 1st Infantry Division was pushing toward the left side of the Iraqi line.

In front of the 1st Infantry were the tanks from the 2nd Armored Cavalry Regiment. At the north end of the 2nd Armored Cav's line was the regiment's 2nd Squadron—Cougar Squadron. Part of Cougar Squadron was a tank company, G Troop. They were called Ghost Troop. There were 150 men in Ghost Troop, half of them in M1A1 tanks, half in Bradley Fighting Vehicles. They had put chemical "glow sticks" on the rear of their vehicles as they moved east, so the 1st Infantry could see them in the blizzard of sand and rain that was gusting from the south.

Ghost Troop had been sporadically encountering Iraqis for a few hours. They had destroyed three tanks and seven armored personnel carriers as they pushed east to a grid line on their map, a line identified as 73 Easting. They arrived at 73 Easting around 4:30 P.M. They were about to be swarmed, surrounded, and outnumbered.

Twenty-nine-year-old Capt. Joe Sartino, Ghost Troop's commander, arranged his Bradleys and tanks in a straight line. They were on a rise across a wide flat wadi from Iraqi units, which were starting to hit them with more and more accurate fire. Ghost Troop was silhouetted against the hazy sunset as they gunned down Iraqi infantry trying to advance across the wadi. But artillery and tank fire from the Republican Guard became more accurate, and soon antipersonnel rounds were bursting in air above the U.S. positions, raining hot sharp shrapnel on the tanks' armor.

One shell hit a Ghost Troop Bradley as 23-year-old Sgt. Nels Moller was trying to unjam his machine gun. Moller toppled backward, dead. Captain Sartino's tank tracked and blasted the Iraqi T-55 tank that fired the fatal round. It was dark by now, and the howling sand and rain cut visibility to only a few dozen yards. Through the night-vision sight in his tank, Lieutenant Garwick could see nine burning Iraqi tanks scattered in front of him. The thermal imaging showed two more headed straight for him. They exploded in roiling fireballs under fire from the M1A1's cannon and the TOW missiles on the Bradleys.

Ghost Troop watched in amazement as dozens of Iraqis at a time would jump off their armored personnel carriers and run, firing, straight at the Americans, mowed down as they came. More airbursts clattered down on the U.S. vehicles. Ghost Troop couldn't believe it, but even more tanks were trying to swarm directly on top of their position.

Heads Up!

"Those guys were insane. They wouldn't stop. They kept dying and dying and dying. If the rest of their army had fought as hard as the Tawakalna fought, we would have been in trouble."

—Lt. Keith Garwick, Ghost Troop, 2nd Squadron, 2nd Armored Cavalry, quoted in *The Stars and Stripes*, March 1991

Desert Lore

Immediately after the battle of 73 Easting, Army engineers and technicians photographed every inch of the battlefield and interviewed all of the participants, using each vehicle's tape-recorded audio log of battle action as a guide. The results were digitalized, and now a computer simulation of 73 Easting is used to train army tankers at Fort Knox, Kentucky.

The Iraqi troops and machines kept hammering the flat wadi, seeming to aim at G Troop. Looking out the back of his Bradley, SP Chris Harvey looked around and was amazed. Later, he said, "All I saw were things burning. For 360°, nothing but action."

Occasionally the rain and sand would stop blowing for a moment, just enough for unit commanders to see even more tanks on the far horizon, grinding down the wadi straight toward them. They called for rocket and artillery fire as far down the dry riverbed as they could shoot. Apaches that could be spared from elsewhere zoomed in to blast tanks.

Why were Iraqis apparently falling all over each other to sweep across Ghost Troop's position? The Troop coordinates—73 Easting—turned out to be the junction of two Iraqi divisions willing to stand and fight. The Tawakalna Division and the Iraqi 12th Armored Division outnumbered and outgunned Ghost Troop, but the Americans held. After the war, CENTCOM concluded that troops at the border of the two divisions were actually trying to get away from the fighting, and the fastest route out—through the wadi—meant that to escape, they would have to roll through G Troop.

The fighting went on for four hours. Around 8 P.M., Captain Sartino's tanks were running out of shells, his Bradleys were running out of TOW missiles, and some of the machine guns were already out of ammunition. Behind them, suddenly, Hawk Troop, a company made up entirely of M1A1s, rolled up. The added firepower finally stopped the Iraqi surge. The explosions became less frequent, then stopped altogether.

Ghost Troop had destroyed 29 tanks and 24 armored personnel carriers. After the shooting stopped, more than 1,300 Iraqis surrendered to them. There was no Bull Run or Shiloh Creek to name this battle after, no Normandy Beach, no city like Khe Sanh, no island like Iwo Jima. There were only rocks and sand and a north-south line drawn on a map and labeled 73 Easting.

The Least You Need to Know

- ◆ Thousands of Iraqis probably died as Marine Corps and navy jets attacked along what became known as the Highway of Death.
- ◆ The Battle of the Euphrates saw the 24th Mechanized Division seize part of the Euphrates River valley and destroy a brigade of Republican Guard troops and equipment.
- ◆ VII Corps wheeled due east on February 26 and hit units of the Republican Guard head-on.
- ◆ In the Battle of 73 Easting, the 2nd Armored Cavalry fought off fierce resistance from Republican Guard units.

Chapter 21

Endgame

In This Chapter

- ◆ Friendly fire incidents kill British and American soldiers amid charges of at least one cover-up
- ◆ The U.S. Marines fight off the Republican Guard at Kuwait's airport, while the battles of Medina Ridge and Norfolk punish the Iraqis
- ◆ Kuwait is liberated and a cease-fire is declared
- ◆ Iraq's army is defeated, but much of it is poised to escape

Our TV crew beat the Allied troops into Kuwait by 14 hours. It was an accident. We had dodged minefields, burned-out Iraqi vehicles, and shell fire from battleships offshore to arrive in Kuwait City the night of February 26. We encountered a marine recon team from Task Force Ripper, riding in their armed dune buggies, who told us they were going to check out the situation at the abandoned U.S. Embassy. We were surrounded, hugged, and kissed by a dozen Kuwaiti resistance fighters, armed with AK-47s they told us came from Iraqi soldiers, "who no longer needed them." We heard the concussion of explosions a few miles away as the marines fought Republican Guard units at the Kuwait City airport.

We were told that troops from Kuwait, Saudi Arabia, and Qatar would ceremonially enter the city at dawn. Next to a burning Iraqi T-55 tank, we saw graffiti spray painted on an underpass. One said, "Bless you Haji (Lord)

Bush." Another read "Free Kuwait. Kill Iraq." An Iraqi soldier's torso had been blown several yards from his armored personnel carrier. It landed upright, so the open-mouthed soldier looked like he had been buried up to his chest in dirt and was trying to climb out.

Kuwaitis were starting to emerge from their fire-scarred buildings, cheering and clapping. But the war wasn't over yet. Not by a long shot.

Friendly Fire Carnage

The "fog of war" is real. On a battlefield, especially at night, with sand and rain swirling around you, explosions and chattering small-arms fire in every direction, and fear and adrenaline cooking inside you, things go wrong.

Not that special precautions hadn't been taken to cut down on the number of friendly fire incidents. Special reflective paint was used on vehicles. Global Positioning System transponders were used in tanks and armored personnel carriers to send out signals. Yet there still was a disproportionate number of deaths and injuries.

In both Desert Shield and Desert Storm, 367 American soldiers, marines, and aviators died. Of that number, 165 died because of fire from their own troops. Of all the Allied forces killed, 51 percent died from friendly fire, including the vast majority of British casualties.

We know of 28 friendly fire incidents. At the time, the Pentagon calculated they amounted to 10 times the percentage of friendly fire incidents of any other American war of the twentieth century.

Some of these incidents were the kinds of things that happen in any war. On February 26, the 1st Platoon, A Company, 27th Engineering Battalion, was clearing some of the unexploded cluster bombs dropped during the aerial pounding of the as-Salman airfield in southern Iraq. Seven of them died when a packet of the shrapnel-loaded bombs went off.

Desert Lore

An investigation into the British friendly fire deaths after the Gulf War concluded the British armored personnel carrier crews were exactly where they should have been, and that they bore no fault for the accident. The report failed to reach any conclusions about the culpability of the A-10 pilots or their air traffic controllers.

But two other incidents were more troubling. That same afternoon, the Third Royal regiment of Fusiliers, attached to the British 1st Armored Division, was slugging it out with Iraqi tanks from Saddam's 52nd Armored Division. The British were moving over ground so rocky and inhospitable that the Iraqis had considered it impassable, and had never laid any mines. Two American A-10 Warthog tank killing jets suddenly vectored in and blasted two of the British warrior armored personnel carriers. Nine British soldiers from the 8th Platoon, C Company of the Fusiliers, were killed, and another 11 wounded, some of them horribly burned.

A more troubling incident occurred around midnight on February 26 at an Iraqi airfield. It resulted in medals being awarded, charges of a cover-up being leveled, and a congressional investigation being launched. It started when the 3rd Armored Cavalry Regiment (ACR)—attached to the U.S. 3rd Armored Division—was ordered to push east toward an airfield near the town of Umm Hajul, in southern Iraq.

The problem started when the 3rd ACR slid south, across the boundary dividing the 3rd Armored Division from the 1st Armored Division. The 3rd ACR didn't know that some of the 1st Armored's engineers had dug in to their south, directly in the line of advance of the 3rd ACR's 3rd Squadron.

Charlie Company of the 54th Engineer Battalion, attached to the 1st Armored Division, was hauling ammunition forward when one of its ammunition-carrying vehicles broke down. Lt. Kevin Wessels, the company commander, decided to stay with the vehicle until a heavy-duty towing vehicle could arrive. With him were four other men, including Cpl. Lance Fielder. They dug in for the night, hoping they could be towed out at first light.

The 3rd ACR's commander, Col. Douglas Starr, had run into some Iraqis while heading south, and had personally taken charge of the operation, urging his men forward. The 3rd Squadron commander, Col. John Daly, pushed his tanks farther south, encouraged by Colonel Starr's aggressiveness. His tanker spotted vehicles ahead of them and opened fire.

They were shooting at the engineers. The engineers had seen the U.S. tanks approaching from the north, and assumed they were their towing convoy. Suddenly, the engineer's position was pelted with machine gun and cannon fire. Corporal Fielder began sprinting toward cover, but he was hit in the lower legs by machine gun fire. Moments later, he crawled toward his fellow engineers and was hit by at least four other slugs. He fell, dead.

Lieutenant Wessels began walking forward, waving his flashlight. The firing stopped and the 3rd ACR discovered its mistake, then a cover-up began. Both Colonels Starr and Daly were awarded the Bronze Star for valorous action in contact with enemy forces. Both men claimed the incident had been a firefight with Iraqis. It took a 1995 congressional probe to recommend that both colonels be stripped of the medals, and to uncover the truth—that Cpl. Lance Fielder had been killed by Americans.

> **Heads Up!**
>
> "This lie has done more harm to the military than a thousand truths would have done."
>
> —Ron Fieldler, Cpl. Lance Fielder's father, testimony before U.S. Senate committee, April 7, 1995

The Battle of Kuwait Airport

The carnage along the Highway of Death wasn't over yet. The Tiger Brigade, lead by the 67th Armored, shoved into Kuwait and seized the high ground on the Muttwa Ridge, looking down on the carnage and the jumble of vehicles. The Iraqis were still trying to get out of Kuwait City, so the Tiger Brigade's tanks opened up on the highway. Their only escape route to Iraq had been plugged, and now the Iraqis had to take punishing fire from U.S. Army tanks, which were shooting from the highest point for hundreds of miles.

Meanwhile, there was the matter of Kuwait International Airport. The 1st Marine Division, pushing toward Kuwait City, gave the task of securing the airport to a pair of marine companies driving *Light Armored Vehicles (LAVs)*.

> ### The Machines
>
> The Light Armored Vehicle system (LAV) is a sort of minitank that travels not on treads, but on six huge tires. It's armed with a 105-millimeter cannon and can reach a top speed of over 60 miles an hour.

The marines waited until dawn of February 27 to launch a full-scale assault because of the mines that had been scattered around the airport. After daylight, the LAVs punched through the perimeter fence and began to advance. The Iraqis resisted, trying to blast the Americans with rocket-propelled grenades and machine guns. After 45 minutes, the marines were able to secure the airport and capture dozens of remaining Iraqis.

Near the terminal sat the burned-out hulk of what had been British Airways Flight 149. On its way from London to India, the aircraft had landed in Kuwait City to refuel the day of the invasion. The British later claimed the Americans had bombed the jet from the air, while the Americans claimed it had been torched by retreating Iraqis. Whatever the truth, the charred 747 figured in two postwar incidents. Some passengers had sued British Airways because they had been held captive by the Iraqis. Their case was dismissed in 1996. Later that same year, a Colorado man and several Kuwaitis were indicted in the United States for taking parts off the jumbo jet and trying to sell them as new.

The Republican Guard's Last Stand

If you had been able to look down from space on Kuwait and southeastern Iraq the night of February 26 and morning of February 27, you would have seen U.S. Marines, along with Saudi, Kuwaiti, and other Arab troops driving into Kuwait City from the south. Just north of Kuwait City, you could have seen Iraqi troops being cut to pieces as they clogged the Highway of Death. Even farther north, the 24th Mechanized Division had cut the Baghdad-Basra Highway and was pushing southeast.

But 25 miles west of the Iraq-Kuwait border, the Republican Guard's Tawakalna Division was positioned in the dead center of VII Corps' advance. The Tawakalna may have been the best division in the entire Iraqi army. It was a veteran unit that had seen almost a decade of war with Iran, and was equipped with some of the best armor and machinery the Iraqis had. Its arsenal included almost 250 state-of-the-art T-72 tanks and around 300 infantry fighting vehicles, the "light tanks" like the U.S. Army's Bradley and the U.S. Marines' Light Armored Vehicle. As we saw in the last chapter, the Battle of 73 Easting was the first contact with the Iraqi unit.

If the U.S. and British units careening directly toward it were like a river, the Tawakalna was like a boulder standing right in the middle of the current. Other Iraqi units were surrendering in droves. The Tawakalna was going to stand and fight, trying to buy time for the Iraqi units behind it, to the east, to escape from Kuwait. The Republican Guard division was lined up north-to-south. Its left flank—on the south—had already been hit at 73 Easting. It was about to be overwhelmed.

The Battle of Norfolk

Phase Line Norfolk was like 73 Easting, just a line on a map. In fact, 73 Easting and Norfolk were right next to each other and, in many ways, were two parts of the same battle. The evening of February 26, Ghost Troop of the 2nd Armored Cavalry Regiment had hit the Tawakalna Division in the south, on the Iraqi's left flank. When the fighting finally subsided, troopers of the 2nd ACR were told to get back inside their vehicles, put florescent "glow sticks" on their Bradleys for identification, and hope they didn't get shot at by mistake as elements of the 1st Infantry Division poured through the hole punched by G Troop.

The concern about more friendly fire deaths was well founded. The battle of Norfolk was about to turn into the biggest tank battle of the Gulf War and, according to some, the largest tank battle in the history of warfare. In the sand, smoke, and confusion, six GIs from Bravo Company, 1st Battalion, 41st Infantry regiment, were mowed down that night by their own men. Six American M1A1 tanks and five Bradleys were destroyed by friendly fire.

But as the armored units of the 1st Infantry poured through toward the Tawakalna's left flank, American commanders had another concern. The Iraqi division was combat-hardened. It had fought in some of the bloodiest encounters against Iraq only a few years before. In contrast, almost none of the U.S. soldiers had been through anything but combat simulations. Col. Greg Fontenot commanded the 1st battalion, 34th Armor, part of

Heads Up!

"I missed the Vietnam War. One of my worst fears was always that I'd never have a chance to experience combat until I was in charge of a lot of soldiers. My worst fear came true."

—Col. Greg Fontenot, 1st Infantry Division, "Remembering the Whirlwind War," *Soldiers Magazine*, U.S. Military Academy, February 2001

the 1st Infantry. He knew as his tanks sped into the fight that only two soldiers in his entire battalion were combat veterans.

The Iraqis fought tenaciously. Red and green tracer rounds arced back and forth across the desert, and the strobe effect of cannons firing would turn the blackness into bright noon for a second at a time. Iraqi soldiers would wait until the Allied tanks ground past them, and then would pop out of the desert and try to disable the speeding M1A1s with rocket-propelled grenades. Iraqi tankers, whether in the outdated T-55s or the modern T-72s, fired with gusto but without much effect.

Two Bradleys were destroyed by Iraqi fire. Some dug-in Iraqi tanks kept their engines shut off, so they didn't show up on the Americans' heat-sensing sights. When the M1A1s were past, some of the Iraqis wheeled, powered up, and fired, only to be destroyed by tanks following along the 15-mile-wide front. Iraqi fire became so intense that the 1st Infantry Division's 3rd Brigade halted its advance and unleashed three entire battalions of 155-millimeter howitzer fire on the tenacious Iraqis.

Around midnight February 26, and as it became February 27, General Schwartzkopf was becoming even more agitated at CENTCOM headquarters in Riyadh. In the minds of Schwartzkopf's supporters, the general's anger was understandable. The XVIII Airborne Corps was making record time inside Iraq, while VII Corps was, once again, delayed in the center of the line. But to the commanders of VII Corps, especially General Franks, it seemed as if Schwartzkopf had no idea how tough the resistance had become from the Tawakalna.

But the Iraqis' bravery was no match for the determined U.S. tankers and their superior technology. By midday February 27, the entire left side of the Iraqis' line had collapsed, and the two Iraqi brigades attempting to hold it had been pulverized. Even to the north, the Iraqis kept standing their ground against a wall of tanks and artillery. But despite their often concentrated fire, the Iraqis didn't hit much of anything. The entire Tawakalna Division was being overrun and collapsing.

The Battle of Medina Ridge

Farther north, the 1st Armored Division had been pressing the attack against the Tawalkana's right flank. They suddenly found that they had also run into the Republican Guard's Medina Luminous Division. The Medina had been stationed north of the Tawalkana, but had extended their lines to the south, so as to form a longer barrier against advancing U.S. forces. The *2nd Brigade from the 1st Armored* ran into a brigade from the Medina Division that had been ordered to hold their positions, trying to screen the retreat of the rest of the Iraqi Division, as well as of the Republican Guard Hammurabi Division.

The Iraqis had hurriedly dug themselves into defensive positions, and had shut down their tank engines. Using tanks as stationary artillery had been a standard Iraqi order of battle against Iran. The added benefit against the Americans would be that, with the tanks cold, the U.S. thermal sights wouldn't pick up any heat. The thought was that, with luck, the Medina Division might be able to ambush part of the 2nd Armored.

But the plan depended too much on luck and the spotty skills of the Iraqi tankers. Once the Iraqis fired their first few rounds, the U.S. *Firefinder radar* system calculated the locations of the tanks, engines running or not. The American M1A1s, 155-millimeter howitzers, and Apache helicopters did the rest.

During the battle, U.S. tank crews looking through their heat-seeking sights toward the Iraqi positions kept noticing what they described as "floating bowling balls," hot spots that seemed suspended in midair. They realized that what they saw were the heads of Iraqi tank commanders giving off heat as they popped up through their tanks' hatches to take a look around. In many cases, the Iraqis were picked off by American tank fire from well over a mile away. By midafternoon on February 27, more than 300 of the Medina Division's tanks were in ruins.

Desert Lore

The 2nd Brigade, 1st Armored Division, had an inauspicious introduction to desert warfare, pounded and forced to retreat by the Nazis in 1942's battle of the Kasserine Pass in North Africa. In 1985, the brigade was christened "The Iron Brigade," a name originally given to Midwestern regiments who distinguished themselves in the Civil War.

The Machines

The AN/TPQ-36/37 Firefinder Radar system tracks incoming artillery shells and rockets. Within seconds, it then traces their trajectories backwards to find the weapons that fired them. Each unit can track 10 trajectories simultaneously to a maximum distance of 30 miles.

Doc Cornum

Maj. Rhonda Cornum was a doctor, a helicopter pilot, and a woman. That made her unusual enough in the U.S. military, but to the Iraqi military, she was unfathomable. On the afternoon of February 27, Major Cornum and her crew were aboard a Blackhawk helicopter, scooting low inside Iraq to attempt a rescue of air force pilot Capt. Bill Andrews.

As the Blackhawk—call sign Bengal One-Five—was within a few miles of the pilot's last radioed position, it began taking ground fire. Within a few seconds, the helicopter was spinning out of control, on fire. It hit the Iraqi desert, flipped over, and burned. Only three of the eight crew members survived.

> **Heads Up!**
>
> "And then he unzipped my flight suit and started fondling me. And I thought 'I can't believe it!' And every time I'd scream, he quit. Well next, he stopped, zipped my flight suit back up and left me alone."
>
> —Maj. Rhonda Cornum, quoted on *The Gulf War, Frontline,* Public Broadcasting System, 1996

Major Cornum was alive, but barely. Both of her arms were broken, one knee was smashed, and she had a bullet in her shoulder. The Iraqis didn't discover she was a woman until they took off her flight helmet. She was loaded into the back of a truck along with the other survivors from the crash and driven to Basra. While on the way, she was groped and sexually molested by one of the Iraqi guards, who only stopped when she screamed in pain from her broken arms.

Despite repeated interrogations in Basra, Major Cornum refused to divulge any information to the Iraqis. She was repatriated with other prisoners of war after the cease-fire.

Liberated Kuwait

By the morning of February 27, the world's major TV networks were broadcasting live from liberated Kuwait City. The Iraqis had burned or shelled most of the buildings downtown. The port and its machinery were a shambles. Animals at the Kuwait Zoo lay dead, or dying, used for target practice by the Iraqis. More than 6,000 Kuwaitis had vanished, either killed or carried off to Iraq.

Allied troops found makeshift torture chambers scattered around the city, along with piles of Polaroid photos the Iraqis had taken of their victims. Many had strips of their peeled skin hanging from their faces. Others had been grotesquely burned using electrical hot plates. Electric drills had been inserted in victims' rectums. Fingers and toes had been amputated using shears or pincers. Skulls had been crushed by placing them in a vise.

The world was seeing pictures of joyous Kuwaitis greeting Kuwaiti, Saudi, American, and British troops with hugs and celebratory gunfire. But images from along the Highway of Death were also being shown for the first time. That, coupled with the CENTCOM briefings indicating that the ground war was now an all-out rout, was starting to give the impression that this was becoming less of a war than a clay pigeon-shoot. That meant the situation had once again switched from being a military problem to a political one.

How Much Is Enough?

Public opinion in the age of mass media can shift like a sand dune in the wind. It all depends upon the pictures. On February 27, President Bush was very much aware of the impression being given by the images of smashed and burning Iraqi vehicles stretched for miles along the Highway of Death. CENTCOM Commander Schwartzkopf was still livid about what he thought was VII Corps' "slow" progress. But he also thought that 24 more hours would be enough to eliminate the Iraqi threat permanently.

Joint chiefs chairman Powell, by far the more astute politician of the two, had been pressuring Schwartzkopf to declare an end point. So when General Powell went to the White House on February 27 to brief the president, he passed along the recommendation that the fighting end in one more day. But as Powell describes the scene in his autobiography, *My American Journey*, it was President Bush who seized the initiative:

> "... the president said, 'Why not end it today?' He caught me by surprise. 'I'd like you all to think about that," he added, looking around the room. 'We're starting to pick up some undesirable public and political baggage with all those scenes of carnage.'"

At 6 P.M. Washington time on February 27, the president decided that all hostilities would cease as of midnight in Washington, 8 A.M. February 28 in Kuwait City. At least that was the way it was supposed to have worked.

Crossroads

Coordinating information on a battlefield is never easy. In the fast-changing rush of Desert Storm, it was often a nightmare. At 5 A.M. on February 28, General Franks had intended to finish off VII Corps' push by pile-driving straight east, and rolling up what Iraqi forces remained in front of him. But Franks had received word that the cease-fire would take effect at 5 A.M., and was consolidating his troops.

To Schwartzkopf, "consolidating" meant delaying. The night before, Franks had ordered the 1st Infantry Division to stop its advance around 8 P.M., and had also ordered the 1st Cavalry Division to slow its movement. Both orders came for the same reason—fear of more friendly fire casualties. Franks had also reached an agreement with XVIII Airborne Corps commander *Gen. Gary Luck* to place a three-mile-wide "sanitary zone" between Frank's VII Corps and Luck's XVIII Airborne Corps. The two generals agreed that nothing inside that zone—even Iraqi targets—was to be shot at.

All of that had slowed VII Corps' advance and, despite their phenomenal success against the Republican Guard, Schwartzkopf was still antsy. At 2 A.M. on February 28, Schwartzkopf's office informed Franks that he had been misinformed, and that the cease-fire would start at 8 A.M., not 5 A.M. In the few hours left, Schwartzkopf ordered an all-out push to the east.

Who's Who
Gary Luck was born in 1937 and became one of the most successful generals in U.S. Army history. He commanded special operations units at Fort Bragg, North Carolina, before taking the XVIII Airborne Corps to victory in the Gulf War. He retired in 1996 as commander of all U.S. and U.N. forces in Korea.

The most important objective, he said, was the crossroads at the Iraqi town of Safwan, just north of the border with Kuwait. But between concern for friendly fire casualties in the waning hours of the war, and trouble communicating with various units, the 1st Infantry Division never got the word to seize the crossroads. The push east didn't even begin until 6 a.m., and was halted for more than 20 minutes by what turned out to be a false report of friendly fire casualties. The Big Red One--the 1st Infantry Division— never did capture the crossroads by 8 a.m., leaving a small escape route open for Iraqi forces.

The 1st Armored Division, meanwhile, had a furious last hour of combat. Before the 8 A.M. deadline, they destroyed 100 more Iraqi tanks and overran the Medina Division's headquarters. When 8 A.M. arrived and VII Corps stopped for the ceasefire, they had destroyed more than 1,300 Iraqi tanks and had taken more than 40,000 Iraqi prisoners.

Almost, But Not Quite

To the north, inside Iraq, the 24th Mechanized Infantry Division had secured the two air-fields and the mammoth ammunition dump along Highway 8, and was pushing down the highway toward Basra on the late afternoon of February 27. They kept running into scattered elements of various Republican Guard units—the Adnan, the al-Faw, the Hammurabi, and the Nebuchadnezzar—but nothing organized in terms of strategy.

Apache helicopter gunships were sent ranging in front of the 24th, taking out what Iraqi armor and artillery pieces they could find. Some even veered northeast, past Basra itself, to blast Iraqi helicopters at small airstrips. As night fell, the 24th halted its advance, preparing for a mammoth push the next day that would have taken them to the gates of Basra itself.

Politically and militarily, a move like that might have made all the difference. The peoples of the floodplains and swampland surrounding Basra were Shia Muslims, not the Sunni who ruled the rest of the country. In Baghdad, they were contemptuously called "the marsh Arabs." When Iranian troops had invaded the area in the Iran-Iraq war in the late 1980s, the region was dotted with thousands of huts floating on islands made of dirt and papyrus, a method of living unchanged since the Sumerians of Ur.

> **Desert Lore**
>
> Saddam Hussein's campaign to drain the marshes and attack the Shi'ites had almost wiped out the Mi'dan—the Marsh Arabs, who were the direct descendants of Mesopotamia's founders.

Saddam had dealt with the invaders—and with the Iraqi Shi'ites—by attacking the entire area with mustard gas. He then began building a series of dams and diversion canals, draining the ancient marshes and making sure the people there would face hunger, disease, and death as the waters dried up.

The Shi'ites, the Marsh Arabs, the people of southern Iraq—all were natural enemies of Saddam. If the 24th Mech had pushed farther east, it would have likely found itself greeted as a liberating army. Basra, one of Iraq's major cities, could have risen in open revolt. The Shia in southern Iraq might have tried to declare themselves an independent state.

As we'll see later, this was precisely what many people in Washington did not want to see happen. So the 24th Mech halted its advance, content with plastering Iraqi positions with artillery during the night and until the cease-fire came at 8 A.M. The advance recon teams from the 24th even made it as far as what their maps called Phase Line Smash. Phase Line Smash was also the north-south road that connected Kuwait with Basra. The 24th Mech's scouts stopped just short of the highway and didn't cut it. It was a decision that would haunt planners for years to come.

This Way Out

Like most major cities, Basra sits at the junction of several major highways. That location would mean more than ever after 8 A.M. on February 28. First, a highway runs almost due south, and links Basra with Kuwait. Inside Kuwait, that road was now known as the Highway of Death. But north of Kuwait, inside Iraq, the road was still controlled by Iraqis, at least on the ground, all the way from the town of Safwan just north of the border into Basra. The 1st Infantry Division had failed to seize the crossroads at Safwan and the 24th Mech had stopped short of slicing the highway, so it was still available as an escape route.

But if any escaping Iraqi troops were able to go north on the road, they would find themselves in Basra. And the 24th Mech and 101st Airborne controlled Highway 8, the main highway out of Basra. But the *main* highway out wasn't the *only* highway out. Running north of Basra, another ancient path that had become a highway trailed the edge of the Shaat al-Arab waterway and skirted the foothills of the mountains forming the border with Iran. It twisted past the run-down village of al-Kumayt, where locals try to convince tourists that their settlement was the site of the Garden of Eden, and then jogged east to the city of al-Kut. From there, it would be a straight shot to Baghdad.

As the cease-fire came, the Allies had destroyed more than 3,000 Iraqi tanks and taken 70,000 or more prisoners. They had killed an uncounted number of Iraqi soldiers, variously estimated at somewhere between 15,000 and 150,000. They had smashed through two Republican Guard divisions and fought with elements of four others. They had liberated Kuwait and reduced Iraq's army from the fourth to the 22nd largest on earth within a few days of ground fighting.

They had given hope to both the anti-Saddam Kurds in northern Iraq and the anti-Saddam Shi'ites in the south. They had enraged a millionaire construction magnate's heir in Jeddah named Osama bin Ladin. They had left open an escape route for the cream of Saddam's forces.

All would have fatal consequences that would begin to develop within hours of the cease-fire.

The Least You Need to Know

- ◆ The VII Corps attack punched through heavy resistance from Iraqi Republican Guard units.
- ◆ Friendly fire losses became such a concern that they might have slowed the Allied advance.
- ◆ The Bush administration decided to declare a cease-fire sooner rather than later because of concerns about public opinion and the one-sided war.
- ◆ Allied positions at the start of the cease-fire left some Iraqi units with a means of escape.

Part 5

The Storm Doesn't End

The end of the Gulf War was supposed to have been a triumph. Instead, it was the beginning of our current war against terrorism. Osama bin Ladin's hatred for the West was refined in the furnace of Desert Storm. The presence of U.S. troops in Saudi Arabia inflamed anti-U.S. passions in much of the Islamic world. In this section, we connect the dots, and show how September 11, 2001, and its aftermath began on the battlefields of Kuwait, Iraq, and Saudi Arabia in the 1990s and earlier.

Chapter 22

Meet the Future

In This Chapter

- ◆ Retreating Iraqi troops reportedly open fire on the 24th Mechanized Division, leading to retaliation and, years later, to controversy
- ◆ The cease-fire leaves Saddam in power, which is just the way many in Washington want it
- ◆ Kurds in the north and Shi'ites in the south both attempt uprisings against Saddam and are crushed
- ◆ An ammunition dump containing chemical weapons is destroyed amid secrecy and misinformation

March 1, 1991, found corpses and burned metal scattered across Iraq and Kuwait, from 73 Easting and Phase Line Norfolk to the Highway of Death and Medina Ridge. In the most one-sided military campaign since Germany conquered France in 1940, the Allies had destroyed or captured half of Iraq's armed forces. Now the complicated part began.

How would Iraq get its remaining troops out of the combat zone? Would Saddam remain in power? Would the United States step in and support any internal uprisings? What about Iraq's stockpile of and research into nuclear, chemical, and biological weapons? How long would U.S. forces remain in Saudi Arabia? While the victors were pondering those questions, there was another urgent question they weren't even aware of: What would the effect of the Gulf War be on the man who would become the world's most ambitious terrorist?

In this chapter, we take a look at how those same questions came to plague the world again years later.

Rumaila

At the end of the last chapter, we talked about how there was one way out still available for Iraqi troops in the combat zone. They could take the road linking Kuwait with Basra, and then head north on the alternate route to Highway 8. On February 27, General Schwartzkopf told a news conference, "... the gates are closed. There is no way out of here." He was wrong.

In fact, two divisions of Republican Guard troops were fording the Euphrates on makeshift pontoon bridges. Others were aiming for a causeway that ran across the silty marshes of *Lake Hammar* just west of Basra. That road ran through the Rumaila oil field, crossed the lake on the causeway, and then proceeded north to hook up with the main highway.

The cease-fire orders to Allied troops were fairly explicit. Allied forces were free to attack any Iraqi units still inside zones controlled by the coalition. But other Iraqi troops were not to be attacked unless they fired first. If the Iraqis had the turrets and cannons on their tanks turned to the rear, it was to be assumed they were "nonhostile." That meant, in essence, that Iraqi units had a free pass to move back toward Baghdad, as long as their cannons were pointing backward.

Gulf Lingo

Lake Hammar is formed by the Euphrates River just before it joins with the Tigris River at Basra. Much of the lake and its surrounding marshes have dried up due to Saddam's policy of retaliating against Shi'ite Muslims in southern Iraq by draining their wetlands.

Needless to say, this didn't go over well with many American commanders, who had been prepared to squeeze the Republican Guard divisions into a small pocket near Basra and then annihilate them. Instead, they were ordered to stand down and watch the Iraqis move more than half their total Republican Guard strength out of harm's way.

The 2nd Battalion of the 7th Infantry Regiment (also called the 2-7), commanded by Col. Charles Ware, was the farthest forward of any of Gen. Barry McCaffrey's 24th Mech forces. Early in the morning of March 2, Charlie Company of the 2-7 reported it was taking incoming fire from a unit of the Hammurabi Republican Guard Division passing near its location. Other nearby American units said they didn't hear or see any attack, just miles and miles of Iraqis retreating toward the Lake Hammar causeway.

In May 2000, veteran journalist Seymour Hersh—who won a Pulitzer Prize for unveiling the My Lai massacre in Vietnam in 1969—wrote a series of reports for *The New Yorker* magazine detailing what happened next. According to Hersh's research, there was chaos at the headquarters of the 24th Mech. Many of General McCaffrey's subordinates didn't believe the Iraqis had opened fire and, if they did, it was probably a panicked, isolated incident.

But that wasn't the way McCaffrey saw it. He ordered the causeway cut and the Iraqis attacked. It started with one of the 24th Mech's Apaches hitting the lead Iraqi ammunition truck with a missile, blowing it sky high, causing panicked Iraqis to scatter in all directions, and blocking the causeway. U.S. tanks and artillery nearby were ordered to join the assault, with more helicopters blasting the rear of the column, so there was no way it could escape back into the Rumaila oil field. A 10-mile-long tangle of tanks, trucks, civilian cars, and heavy transporters hauling tanks and armored personnel carriers became one big target.

Hersh's article quotes several of the soldiers involved. One said, "People were all mixed up in cars and trucks. People got out of their cars and ran away. We shot them. The Iraqis were getting massacred." Another said, "The enemy wasn't firing back. They were jumping in ditches to hide." Hersh quotes a military intelligence officer who later interrogated a captured Iraqi tank commander. The Iraqi had said, "Why are you killing us? All we were doing was going home."

The final total was more than 200 T-72 tanks destroyed, along with hundreds of trucks and civilian vehicles. No one ever counted the Iraqi dead. An army investigation cleared General McCaffrey of any criminal wrongdoing.

Surrender Talks

The next day, March 3, General Schwartzkopf flew to the southern Iraqi town of Safwan for cease-fire talks with Iraqi Gen. Sultan Hashim Ahmed. Outside the tents where the ceremony took place was an honor guard for Schwartzkopf. Among the guards was Sgt. Timothy McVeigh and his Bradley, nicknamed *Bad Company*, selected because of McVeigh's accuracy as a combat gunner and *Bad Company's* record of direct hits on Iraqi targets.

What happened inside the negotiating tent paved the way for trouble to come, as the Americans set conditions for Iraq. Some of those conditions were apparently based on the hope of the United States for an uprising by part of Saddam's armed forces. That may have made sense at the moment. But what ended up happening is that the United States gave Saddam the green light to use armed attack helicopters against his own people.

Let's set the stage. General Ahmed wanted to get the most favorable conditions possible. So did General Schwartzkopf. The Iraqi opposition, based in London, had told the Americans that one Iraqi army officer who might be convinced to act against Saddam was the head of Iraq's fleet of 350 helicopter gunships. That may be why—to the astonishment of many people—Schwartzkopf said that Allied planes would shoot down any Iraqi planes inside what would be called the "no-fly zones," but that the Allies would not fire on any Iraqi helicopters.

The United States may have thought this would enable the opposition to topple Saddam. It actually enabled Saddam to slaughter his Kurdish rivals in the north as well as his Shi'ite opponents in the south.

> ### Heads Up!
>
> *General Schwartzkopf:* "So we will let the helicopters, and that is a very important point, and I want to make sure that's recorded, that military helicopters can fly over Iraq."
>
> *General Ahmad:* "So you mean even the helicopters ... armed in the Iraqi skies can fly?"
>
> *General Schwartzkopf:* "Yeah. I will instruct our air force not to shoot at any helicopters that are flying over the territory of Iraq."
>
> —Transcript of March 3, 1991, cease-fire talks, released by U.S. Dept. of Defense, 1992

Leaving Saddam in Power

The U.S. decision to leave Saddam Hussein in power in 1991 is one that still haunts the world. But we have to look at why the decision was made at the time. During the cease-fire, there was nothing between U.S. troops and the capital of Iraq except 120 miles of paved highway and the Baghdad Police Department. The Iraqi troops able to stagger home had been pounded on both the Highway of Death and the Lake Hammar Causeway. There were some undamaged Republican Guard units in the northern part of Iraq, but any movement by them could have been blitzed by Allied air power. So it was militarily possible to drive all the way to Baghdad.

> **Desert Lore**
>
> In a paper prepared for the U.S. Air War College by air force Col. Stanley Kresge in 1999, it's argued that Saddam remained in power because the United States was unwilling to do the one thing that would have guaranteed his removal: conquer Iraq militarily and occupy the country.

A captain with the 101st Airborne told me shortly after the war, "Yeah, we could have taken Baghdad and occupied Iraq. But who wanted to? It's like a dog chasing a car. Once he finally catches it, what's he going to do with it?"

There's a long list of reasons why it made perfect sense in March 1991—at least in Washington—to leave Saddam in power:

◆ The U.S. military, as we've noted, wasn't enthusiastic about occupying Iraq.

◆ The coalition partners, especially the Arab countries, would have objected to the United States actually taking over Iraq.

◆ The United States hoped that dissident elements in Iraq's military would unite with Kurdish and Shia rebels and overthrow Saddam.

◆ Public reaction to video of the carnage along the Highway of Death was so intense that there may have been almost no public support for occupying Iraq.

◆ The Allies had achieved what was called for in the U.N. resolutions—Iraq had been ejected from Kuwait. The U.N. said nothing about gunning for Saddam.

◆ There were elements inside the U.S. government that didn't think leaving Saddam in power was such a bad thing. They reasoned his military was defanged, and that neither the Kurds in the north nor the Shi'ites in the south were exactly reliable U.S. allies. Better the devil you know than the one you don't, they figured.

U.S. policy, then, was a fascinating blend of the naive and the calculating. Naive, in that there was hope Saddam could be toppled from the inside. Calculating, in that some power brokers reasoned there were worse things than leaving Saddam in power. That combination would indirectly kill thousands of people.

The South Rises

Many of the Shia in southern Iraq felt that their time had come. Saddam's troops had been routed, and American GIs were stationed inside Iraq itself. Demonstrations began on March 5, and soon had spread to three major cities in southern Iraq: Basra, Najaf, and Karbala.

Some of the protests were loud, but peaceful. But the revolt quickly became an armed rebellion. In Basra, for example, thousands of Iraqi draftees who had been mercilessly pounded by the Allies from the air and on the ground began fighting units of the Republican Guard. One conscripted crew of a T-55 tank put a round through a wall mural of Saddam in Basra, igniting a popular uprising in the city streets. As the fighting quickly spread, Saddam appointed one of his cousins well known for his ruthlessness to take charge of southern Iraq. He was *Ali Hassan Majid*.

When Majid took over security, all three southern cities were being rocked by rebellion. Ba'ath Party officials came under sniper fire, as armed insurgents were assaulting and killing Republican Guard troops. The fighting in several sections of Basra and Karbala was especially heavy. Soon reports began to filter in that the uprising had spread to the

Kurds in the north. Saddam gave his cousin orders: Put down the southern rebellion, then teach the Kurds in the north a lesson.

Majid struck back first in Karbala, which was only 50 miles south of Baghdad. Here the agreement by Schwartzkopf not to fire on helicopters came into play, since on March 6, Majid ordered helicopter gunships and artillery units to strafe the city. A hospital was shelled and almost leveled. Withering artillery and rocket fire was directed against Shi'ite mosques, including one said to hold the remains of Imam Hussein, one of Muhammad's grandsons. Hundreds of people suspected of being loyal to the rebels were herded into soccer stadiums and executed.

> **Who's Who**
>
> Ali Hassan Majid, a first cousin of Saddam Hussein, was the head of Iraqi occupation forces in Kuwait. Known as "Ali the Chemist" for his role in producing Iraqi chemical weapons in the 1980s, he is considered one of Saddam's most ruthless "enforcers."

As the survivors fled south toward the city of Najaf, Iraqi helicopters flew overhead dumping kerosene on the columns of panicked refugees. They followed a few minutes later with machine gun rounds that lit the kerosene. Opposition members who made it through the slaughter and escaped to London later reported that American jets were circling far overhead the entire time.

On March 10, more than 300 delegates from two dozen Iraqi opposition groups met in Beirut. They attempted to hammer out a common strategy against Saddam, and appealed to the Allies for military assistance. White House spokesman Marlin Fitzwater reiterated that, after the cease-fire, the United States had no desire to become involved in Iraq's internal affairs.

By March 11, Republican Guard tanks and artillery were pounding Najaf and Basra. The opposition claimed that 80 of the tanks had been allowed to roll down Highway 8 to Basra after passing through American checkpoints. Outlying villages and hamlets were burned to the ground. By the end of March, the rebellion had failed. By early April, it was utterly crushed, with thousands dead and tens of thousands more fleeing into Iran.

Killing the Kurds

Meantime, the Kurds in northern Iraq began a revolt of their own less than a week after the uprising in the south began. Leaders of the revolt hoped for help from the United States, remembering that in 1972, Pres. Richard Nixon had authorized the CIA to ship $16 million worth of arms to the Kurds inside Iraq. The shipment was requested by the shah of Iran, who hoped the Kurds could destabilize Iraq and help him in a border dispute with the Iraqis. The Kurdish rebels may have preferred to forget that in 1975, Pres. Gerald Ford cut off the aid pipeline after the shah and the Iraqis patched up their border differences.

By the middle of March, *peshmerga*—Kurdish guerrilla fighters—belonging to rival factions had managed to unite and slug it out with Iraqi troops. Major cities in northern Iraq, including *Kirkuk*, Arbil, Dahuk, and others, were under control of the Kurds. To the east, Mosul, the biggest city in northern Iraq, was under siege by the Kurds.

The Kurds remembered Saddam's campaign against them from the 1980s, when hundreds of thousands of Kurds were executed or exiled, and hundreds of towns, villages, and mosques were flattened in a campaign of ethnic cleansing that was at least as brutal as the Balkan wars in Bosnia in the 1990s.

Gulf Lingo

The city of **Kirkuk** is about 175 miles north of Baghdad, built on the site of the ancient Assyrian city of Arrapha, established about 5000 B.C.E. In A.D. 448, thousands of Christians were massacred in Kirkuk by the Persians. The city is a center of Kurdish culture.

The Kurds only had what artillery or armor they had been able to capture from Iraqi forces. They were mostly armed with AK-47 assault rifles, M-60 .50-caliber machine guns, and rocket-propelled grenades. They were, however, convinced that the Allies would come to their aid, especially since CIA-sponsored clandestine radio transmissions and broadcasts from the Voice of America radio service had been urging the Kurds to revolt against Saddam ever since the air war started in January.

Saddam's first order of business, though, was to smash the revolt in the Shi'ite south, where he already had plenty of Republican Guard units that had managed to escape destruction. By the end of March, the south was crushed into submission, so Baghdad turned its attention to the unruly north.

The Bush administration's "hands off of Iraq's internal affairs" policy sent shock waves through the Kurds' ranks. A Defense Intelligence Agency (DIA) intelligence cable from April 1991 summed up their feelings:

> "Kurdish rebels and refugees really believed that eventually the coalition force would come to help them in their fighting against Iraqi forces … Kurdish rebels and refugees felt as if they were set up and let down by the coalition force."

Saddam used helicopter gunships, artillery, tanks, and Republican Guard troops to break the back of the Kurdish uprising starting in late March. The allies had warned Saddam that they would intervene if he used chemical weapons, so unlike the 1980s, no chemicals were used against the Kurds.

Instead, rounds of the chemical white phosphorus, which incinerates the impact area and creates a poisonous cloud, fired from artillery pieces and helicopters were used to bombard cities like Kirkuk and Arbil. The lightly armed rebels had no antiaircraft capability and no way to stave off T-72 tanks. Within a few days, the rout became as one-sided as Saddam's defeat by the coalition a month before.

Kurds fled by the hundreds of thousands. Many ran toward Turkey to the north, pursued by convoys of Iraqi troops. The Turks, having fought Kurdish insurgents for years, often opened fire on the refugees at the border. Hundreds of thousands were eventually allowed into refugee camps with little food, small rations of water, and no sanitation facilities.

At the same time, hundreds of thousands of Kurds were fleeing across the snow-clogged mountain passes between Iraq and Iran. At the end, it was estimated that 800,000 men, women, and children had trudged across the Zagros Mountains into Iran, dying along the way at a rate later estimated at between 800 and 1,000 people per day. In early April, I was with a TV crew in the Zagros foothills, talking to Kurdish refugees packed into a dusty refugee camp in West Orumiyeh Province, Iran. Every family we interviewed had lost someone. Husbands had died in the fighting. Daughters had been raped and killed. Sons had disappeared when Iraqi troops rounded up all the males in a village.

But it was the stories about the children left behind that caused the parents to speak with flat dreamy voices. The families had known the trek to Iran would involve fording rivers, sleeping in the open, fighting off bandits, and climbing slowly through 8,000-foot snow-packed mountain passes. The weakest or sickest of the children had been left behind so they wouldn't slow the rest of the family's progress. One woman sat facing the mountains, two small children hovering over her shoulder, another clutched in her lap. "The baby was only six months old," she said. "He is back there, over those mountains, somewhere. I had to leave him," she repeated over and over. "I had to leave him."

Provide Comfort

Just as the video from the Highway of Death had galvanized Western public opinion to end the Gulf War, so the TV images of the bedraggled Kurds shocked the Allies' consciences. On April 5, the United Nations passed *Resolution 688*, condemning Saddam's purge of the Kurds and urging U.N. members to come to their aid. It also required Iraq to help in the aid efforts.

Desert Lore

U.N. Resolution 688 demanded that Iraq immediately stop repressing the Kurds, and allow international humanitarian groups to operate inside Iraq. The resolution also guaranteed Iraq's "territorial integrity."

Within hours, the United States announced the launch of Operation Provide Comfort, based out of the Incirlik Air Base in Turkey. By April 7, the first U.S. transport planes began air-dropping relief supplies. The pathway to hell is paved with good intentions, and so were some of the early airdrops. A combination of bad aim and faulty parachutes resulted in some crates of relief supplies crushing the waiting Kurds below.

President Bush, after consulting with Britain and France, announced on April 10 that the three Western Allies were establishing a "no-fly" zone across 19,000 square miles of northern Iraq. That meant no Iraqi aircraft of any kind—including helicopters—would be allowed to fly north of the 36th Parallel, which runs just south of the cities of Arbil and Mosul. The Bush administration claimed Resolution 688 gave them the right to establish the no-fly areas, although the United Nations never said anything about that sort of operation.

Through the summer of 1991, the United States in effect helped the Kurds carve out a more or less autonomous homeland inside Iraq north of the 36th Parallel. U.S. troops pulled out of northern Iraq in mid-July, but American forces remained stationed just across the border in Turkey as a show of force. As we'll see shortly, though, a variety of factors combined to put the Kurds at continued risk from Saddam as the years wore on. For them, the war would be far from over.

Kamisayah

In the last chapter, we talked about the 24th Mechanized Infantry's seizure of a huge Iraqi ammunition dump just north of Highway 8 in southern Iraq. Merely calling it an ammunition dump, though, is sort of like calling New York a city. It's true as far as it goes, but it fails to capture the size and scope of the place.

Located near the town of Kamisayah and the Tallil Air Base, the dump sprawled over dozens of acres, dotted with 107 concrete bunkers, each the size of a large house. Each bunker was buried into the dirt and filled with munitions of all sorts, ranging from rocket-propelled grenade rounds to 1,000-pound bombs for the Iraqi Air Force. Artillery shells and rockets were stacked in rows alongside crates of tank and armored personnel carrier ammunition, hand grenades, and mortar rounds.

As we noted in the last chapter, the 24th Mech received a message from XVIII Airborne Corps headquarters, indicating chemical weapons might be stored somewhere in the general area. It was a vague warning, forwarded to the XVIII Airborne by the CIA, so corps headquarters put out a warning about "possible chemicals near Objective Gold," which covered the entire region in and around the ammunition facility. The troops of the 24th were never told, and neither were the engineers who got the task of destroying the ammo dump. They were ordered to take the normal precautions—wearing MOPP gear, for example—but never informed of any specific threat. That might not be surprising, since American intelligence had been aware at least since 1986 that chemical weapons might have been stored at Kamisayah, but had never passed that information on to the armed forces.

The engineers and other troops were sent through the facility, going bunker by bunker, looking for any rockets or shells painted with blue, yellow, or red stripes. According to Iraqi prisoners of war, those markings indicated the munitions contained chemical weapons. They never found any striped weapons. So on March 4, the engineers set explosive charges amid the barrels and shells of one of the bunkers, known as Bunker 73. It went off with a mammoth explosion, sending a giant black cloud roiling into the sky and out over the desert, where American and British troops from dozens of various units were stationed.

Two days later, on March 6, the CIA sent a cable to CENTCOM with some disturbing information:

> "Our experience with the munitions Iraq used in its war with Iran indicates that the Iraqis did not, repeat not, mark their chemically-filled munitions ... [W]hen caches of unmarked munitions are destroyed, there is also the possibility that individuals could be exposed to chemical warfare agents."

The CIA analysts didn't know that a giant bunker full of ammunition, including 122-millimeter shells, had been destroyed 48 hours before.

A few days later, on March 12, engineers set off charges in a giant outdoor pit on the far edge of the Kamisayah facility, blowing up more 122-millimeter shells. Again, another large cloud resulted that drifted south, toward the area where hundreds of thousands of Allied troops were stationed.

It would later turn out that Bunker 73 contained artillery shells filled with sarin nerve gas. The shells found in the open pit outside of the facility had apparently started to leak the nerve agent, and were moved there by the Iraqis before the ground war started. It would be five years before the men of the 24th Mech, and all of those downwind, would discover exactly what had been blown up.

Days of Future Past

By the end of March, Operation Desert Storm was officially finished. All of the Allied POWs held by Iraq had been repatriated. Tens of thousands of troops had shipped out and returned home. Dozens of ships and hundreds of planes departed the war zone for their home ports and airfields. Minesweepers had managed to reopen the port of Kuwait City. Victory parades were held for returning veterans in cities and towns across the United States.

But March 1991 was far from the end of anything. On the contrary, it marked the beginning of a new, more dangerous era defined by numerous issues:

♦ **Terrorism:** The coalition victory in March 1991 led to anger by radical Islamic fundamentalists toward the United States. Osama bin Ladin, who had remained in Saudi Arabia throughout the war, would soon manage to sneak away and travel to the Sudan, where the basis for what we now call al-Qaida was formed. Within two years, bin Ladin's allies would bomb New York's World Trade Center. Within five years, he would mastermind the bombing of a U.S. military facility in Saudi Arabia, and the destruction of two American embassies in Africa. Within 10 years, he would strike America itself.

◆ **Instability**: In March 1991, the Soviet Union was on its last legs. It would fall within months, leaving the United States as the world's sole superpower. Old ethnic, religious, and nationalist tensions would erupt throughout the old Soviet empire, leading to genocide in Bosnia, a war with Islamic separatists in Chechnya, and an exodus of Soviet weapons and expertise all over the world. From Iraq and North Korea to Iran and terror organizations, groups and governments across the globe would soon find they had access to all kinds of training and weapons if they had the cash.

◆ **Politics:** March 1991 was actually the end of a recession and the beginning of an economic expansion that wouldn't stop until mid-2001. But it would take more than two years for that reality to reach Main Street America. Due to the economy, Pres. George Bush plummeted from a 90 percent approval rating in March 1991 to 33 percent in August 1992. He would be defeated by Bill Clinton, whose controversial administration was followed by Pres. George W. Bush, who would find himself leading a nation at war.

◆ **Gulf War Syndrome:** The destruction of the Kamisayah ammo depot in March 1991 marked the beginning of investigations into what became known as Gulf War Syndrome. Thousands of veterans from Allied nations would become ill with a series of mysterious symptoms, amid charges that they had been exposed to chemical weapons.

◆ **Saddam Remains:** Saddam Hussein was left in power to crush several uprisings among his own people. U.S. and British planes continue to fly daily over the no-fly zones in Iraq. Saddam continues to inspire, and bankroll, anti-Western groups around the world. Meanwhile, Allied economic sanctions against Iraq enabled Saddam to profit from the black market while his own people suffered and starved.

We'll look at these issues in detail in the following chapters.

The Least You Need to Know

◆ An assault on a column of retreating Iraqi troops after the cease-fire led to disagreements about whether it was necessary.

◆ The Allies stood by while Saddam used the remnants of his defeated army to crush rebellions in both northern and southern Iraq.

◆ U.S. soldiers destroyed the Iraqi ammunition dump at Kamisayah, releasing a cloud of fallout from chemical and nerve gas weapons.

◆ The end of the Gulf War marked the beginning of the twenty-first century's concern with terrorism and anti-Western Islamic fundamentalism.

23

The Roots of September 11

In This Chapter

- ◆ Osama bin Ladin's father becomes a power broker in Saudi society
- ◆ Osama, radicalized after being in Afghanistan, criticizes the presence of U.S. troops in Saudi Arabia
- ◆ The American presence in Saudi Arabia enrages Saudi fundamentalists and their allies around the world
- ◆ U.S. troops in Saudi Arabia and an upsurge in Islamic fundamentalism create a seething cauldron of hatred for the United States, and lead to a series of terror strikes

When did the modern war between Islamic terrorists and the West begin? Lots of dates come to mind, including the Islamic conquest of previously Christian areas starting in the eighth century; the Christian crusaders sacking of Jerusalem in 1099; the fall of Constantinople to Islam in 1453; the destruction of the Ottoman Empire by the Allies in 1918; the founding of Israel in 1948; the seizing of the U.S. Embassy in Tehran in 1979; the defeat of the Soviet Union in Afghanistan in 1989. But the end of the Gulf War in 1991 marked the start of a new era in fundamentalist Islam, and the beginning of the twenty-first-century version of jihad.

Terrorism against the West started long before 1991, of course. Jewish terrorists bedeviled the British in Palestine from 1945 though 1948. American embassies and facilities came under attack from radical Islamic elements as early as 1972. But Desert Storm and the presence of thousands of U.S. troops in Saudi Arabia gave fundamentalists a new reason to despise the United States. In this chapter, we'll look at how all this happened, and at how family and tribal relations intertwined with religion to create the current situation.

The Long Walk

A few chapters back, we talked about how the al-Saud family conquered most of the Arabian Peninsula in the 1920s and renamed the nation Saudi Arabia, after themselves.

On the southern end of the peninsula sits the nation of Yemen, home of the biblical queen of Sheba. The ancient incense trading routes still cross the rolling desert dunes starting in the unexpectedly fertile *Hadramout Valley*, a 30-mile-wide by 90-mile-long swath of greenery in the grim desert.

Around 1925, an illiterate bricklayer named Mohammed bin Awad bin Ladin walked out of the Hadramout, following the 2,500-year-old incense routes across the desert and into Saudi Arabia. About the same time, the al-Saud family was consolidating its hold on Saudi Arabia and starting to construct lavish palaces.

Gulf Lingo

The **Hadramout Valley** stretches between the rolling desert and craggy coastal mountains in southern Yemen. The region is filled with distant kinsmen of Osama bin Ladin, and has long been a stronghold of Islamic fundamentalism.

Mohammed bin Ladin's trek was epic. He traveled more than 1,000 miles across some of the most inhospitable country on earth, ending up in the Saudi port city of Jeddah. He became a porter, carrying baggage, suitcases, cargo, and packages to and from the port. Decades later, when he was one of the world's richest men, Mohammed kept the ragged cloth shoulder bag he had used as a porter on display under glass in the lobby of one of his own palaces.

Legend has it that Mohammed soon used his skill as a bricklayer to get a job helping construct one of the al Saud palaces. Tradition in the bin Ladin family says that Mohammed caught the eye of old Abdul Aziz, founder of the al-Saud dynasty, when Mohammed suggested construction modifications that would make it easier for Abdul Aziz to get around the palace in his wheelchair.

Mohammed bin Awad bin Ladin had arrived.

The Power Broker

In 1925, the same year Mohammed bin Ladin walked out of Yemen, King Abdul Aziz of Saudi Arabia conquered the holy cities of Mecca and Medina and consolidated his hold on the Arabian Peninsula. Legend has it that after he impressed Abdul Aziz with his design for one of his palaces, Mohammed gained favor with the royal family, and was able to set himself up as a contractor.

He supposedly underbid all of his rivals to construct one of the royal family's new palaces. Throughout it all, Mohammed kept forging close relationships with not only old Abdul Aziz, but with his sons, especially Saud, the eldest, and Faysal, the second oldest. That gave him an inside track to contracts and influence not only with the king, but with the future kings as well. By the time Abdul Aziz died in 1953, the illiterate Yemeni bricklayer was a royal favorite, with contracts to build roads, bridges, and mosques rolling in.

King Saud took the throne at the death of his father, and began an autocratic style of rule that would continue into the twenty-first century. Saud was an imperious monarch and a lousy businessman. Various government ministries were wasting Saudi Arabia's oil wealth, with almost no accountability. For the first time, there were rumblings that the Saudi royal family was corrupt and incompetent.

By 1957, Mohammed was living the comfortable life, with several wives and more than 50 children. His youngest son, named Osama, was born that year. In 1958, Mohammed bin Ladin advised Prince Faysal—next in line for the throne—as Faysal set up a plan to bring organization and accountability to the various ministries. It worked, but by the early 1960s, it became apparent that Saud was never going to cut it as a responsible monarch.

Saud was king, Faysal was prime minister, and Mohammed was close to both of them. He helped broker a deal where Saud would gracefully retire as king and let Faysal take the throne. In 1964, the transfer was accomplished in a way rare in the Arab world—without bloodshed.

There was one big problem: Saud's mismanagement had emptied most of the kingdom's treasury. Mohammed bin Ladin stepped in again and this time agreed to pay the salary of every government employee in the kingdom for six months. King Faysal was so grateful that he issued a decree ordering that all construction projects in the entire kingdom should go to the bin Ladin construction empire.

Mohammad bin Ladin went from being merely wealthy to being breathtakingly rich. But the best was yet to come. He was given the contracts to help renovate and expand the holy mosques in Mecca and Medina, as well as a license for exclusive work on the Dome of the Rock mosque in Jerusalem. When Mohammed bin Ladin died in a plane crash in 1968, his wealth was probably in the tens of billions of dollars.

> **Desert Lore**
>
> King Saud's "retirement" in 1964 in favor of his brother, Faysal, was almost unprecedented in the history of the Middle East. Mohammed bin Ladin's role in facilitating the peaceful transfer cemented his position as one of the most influential men in Saudi Arabia.

The Osama Years

Osama bin Ladin, one of 54 children, was 11 when his father died. The older sons took control of what became the Binladin Brothers for Contracting and Industry Group, a multinational holding company with hundreds of billions of dollars in contracts at any one time. The elder bin Ladin had always hosted hundreds of pilgrims during the annual Islamic pilgrimage to Mecca. The sons continued the tradition, and young Osama was able to talk with some of the most renowned scholars and clerics in the Muslim world once a year.

The older brothers had all pursued a cosmopolitan education. As exclusive universities in the United States and Europe bring the world's future leaders together as teenagers, so Victoria College in Alexandria, Egypt, puts the future leaders in the Middle East in contact with one another. Most of the older bin Ladin boys had gone there. But Osama stayed in Saudi Arabia, marrying a Syrian girl at age 17 in 1974, and graduating from a university in Jeddah with a degree in public administration in 1981.

While he was still a student, in early 1980, Osama made his first trip to Pakistan, to tour the refugee camps set up for people from Afghanistan who had fled the Soviet invasion. In Pakistan, he met with several of the Muslim religious and political leaders he had encountered over the years during the pilgrimage to Mecca, including *Mohammad Rabbani and Abdur Sayyaf.*

Who's Who
Mohammad Rabbani was an Afghan who fought against the Soviets. A strict Muslim fundamentalist, he was number two in command of the Taliban until his death in April 2001. Abdur Sayyaf, also an Afghan, is a professor and strict Muslim fundamentalist. He also fought against the Soviets and battled the Taliban in Afghanistan as a leader of the Northern Alliance.

Osama returned to Saudi Arabia and began asking for money and supplies to support the mujahadeen (holy warriors) in Afghanistan against the Soviets. His brothers and members of the Saudi royal family contributed, and Osama began shuttling back and forth between Saudi Arabia and Afghanistan, supplying the anti-Soviet guerrillas with millions of dollars. Finally, in 1982 he decided to go inside Afghanistan itself, and brought with him not only money, but bulldozers, road graders, cement mixers, and tons of heavy construction equipment supplied by the bin Ladin conglomerate.

He was soon nicknamed "The Contractor," and spent the next few years building roads, hospitals, schools, command posts, and bunkers for the anti-Soviet rebels. He also built a series of training camps for Islamic fighters, and late in 1988, organized a system for documenting the identities and whereabouts of the Arab and other non-Afghan fighters coming through the country. He set up a complex of offices to handle the paperwork and named it al-Queda, or "The Base."

After the mujahadeen defeated the Soviets in 1989, bin Ladin returned to Saudi Arabia and was treated like a combination of a war hero and rock star for his role in defeating the atheistic Soviet infidels. But he wasn't everyone's hero.

Jihad Upsets the Saudis

The Saudi government—meaning the royal family—wasn't thrilled to have Osama bin Ladin back, despite his family's close ties to the Saudi rulers. At first, that seems bizarre. Wahabism, one of the strictest sects of fundamentalist Islam, is the state religion in Saudi Arabia. The Saudi royal family personally guaranteed a dollar-for-dollar match of all the aid the United States funneled to the anti-Soviet fighters in Afghanistan. It would seem that the Saudi rulers should have embraced someone whom they had bankrolled in a victorious struggle for Islam against atheism.

But, as former Speaker of the House Tip O'Neill once observed, "All politics is local." And the al-Sauds were more concerned with their own precarious grip on power than with any worldwide jihad. Saudi Arabia, despite all of its wealth, is a weak nation. It has a population of only seven million people, compared with 21 million in Iraq and 50 million in Iran. That means the Saudi army is generally small and insufficient, as we've seen. When Islamic militants seized the Great Mosque in Mecca in 1979, the Saudis were forced to call in French commandos to storm the facility.

King Faysal had been assassinated by one of his nephews in 1975. Between that, and the rise in Islamic fundamentalism in the late 1970s, the house of al-Saud had been feeling fractures in its foundation for years. Every sermon and pronouncement in Saudi Arabia's 11,000 mosques was supposed to be cleared through official government channels. The rulers of most of the Arabian Peninsula constantly feared the kind of upheaval that had brought fundamentalists to power in Iran.

When Osama returned in 1989, he reportedly didn't intend to stay long, but to resume his trips to Pakistan and Afghanistan. But Saudi officials suspended his passport, forcing him to stay inside the country. There were two reasons. First, he was suspected of trying to smuggle weapons across the southern Saudi border into his father's ancestral Yemen, trying to begin another front for jihad inside Yemen. And second, Osama had begun giving speeches, warning of Saddam Hussein's intention to invade Saudi Arabia.

> **Heads Up!**
>
> "Arabia is rich today as it has never been before, and many simple people in this country believe that that is for one reason and one reason only—because we have been good Muslims."
>
> —Prince Turki al Faysal quoted in *The Kingdom*, by Robert Lacey, Harcourt Brace Jovanovich, 1981

Was it a lucky guess? Possibly, but it was more likely bin Ladin's ability to read politics and the possible actions of a fellow megalomaniac. What seemed to escape the CIA and the Saudis was apparently plain to Osama—that Saddam needed money badly after his war with Iran, and that the easiest way to get it would be to roll his battle-hardened troops straight through the oil fields of Kuwait and Saudi.

As we mentioned a few chapters back, bin Ladin made a proposal to the royal family days after Iraq invaded Kuwait, a proposal to use 100,000 "holy warriors" to push Saddam out of Kuwait. The offer was politely rebuffed and the Americans were called in.

According to Osama's associates, quoted on the Public Broadcasting System's *Frontline* program in 2001, "… he heard the news which transformed his life completely. The Americans are coming. He always describes that moment as a shocking moment. He felt depressed."

Saudi officials produced a pronouncement from the country's leading religious scholars certifying that they approved of the decision to invite American troops to Saudi Arabia. But bin Ladin produced his own religious scholars to oppose the presence of infidel troops.

> ### Who's Who
>
> Safar al-Hawali is dean of Islamic studies at Umm al-Qura University in Mecca. Salman al-Awdah is an author and scholar and supervises a website called islamtoday.com. Both men were arrested by Saudi authorities in 1994.

Chief among them were two young ulema (religious scholars) who had repeatedly criticized the royal family— *Safar al-Hawali* and *Salman al-Awdah.*

Both men were firebrands, and both wrote and spoke openly about the decadence and corruption of the Saudi royal family. But it was al-Hawali who got under the skin of the al-Sauds through a series of sermons concluding that Western troops were not coming to the holy soil of Saudi Arabia to protect it, or even for oil. Rather, he rumbled, they were coming to subjugate and degrade Islam.

The continuing presence of American troops in Saudi Arabia is a source of anger for many Islamic fundamentalists.

The War Months

Through his clerical allies, bin Ladin issued a *fatwa*—a holy proclamation—that called for struggle in the name of Islam, but only in the most general terms. His associates later estimated that the *fatwa* resulted in more than 4,000 additional Muslims, many of them Saudis, going to the newly liberated Afghanistan for training in various camps.

The pressure from Saudi fundamentalists against the American troops kept growing. The two young antigovernment clerics formed an organization to spearhead the drive, the *Movement for Islamic Resurgence*.

Desert Lore

The Movement for Islamic Resurgence is considered by many scholars to be as important as the Reformation or the Renaissance in the West. It refers generally to the worldwide upsurge in fundamentalist forms of Islam since the 1970s. Its roots are considered to be both political (opposition to Israel and the United States), and cultural (opposition to Western-style globalization that threatens Islamic culture). The Movement for Islamic Resurgence is just one of many examples.

By late 1990 and early 1991, the Saudi authorities had a problem. On one hand, the bin Ladins were well connected friends of the al-Saud family. On the other, Osama bin Ladin and his allies were becoming increasingly vocal. The Saudi government had already lifted Osama's passport, so they now tried to force him into a form of internal exile by limiting his movement to the area around Jeddah.

When Saudi King Fahd called together the ulemas to rubber-stamp his decision to invite American troops, he assured them the U.S. forces would leave as soon as the war ended. In March 1991, thousands of the Allied troops did leave, but thousands more stayed, forming a more-or-less permanent presence at many facilities, including King Khalid Military City. The king tried to speed up the movement of what Americans he could, going so far as to pay for several warehouses full of supplies so the U.S. forces could merely leave and not take the time to pack up their equipment.

But the pressure was continuing to build because of the foreign troops in Saudi Arabia. It was about to get worse.

Protecting the Magic Kingdom

American troops in Saudi Arabia often spoke of it derisively as "the magic kingdom," a cutting reference to Disney World. Women couldn't drive anywhere except on U.S. bases, were forbidden from being in public without a male, and had to dress in the head-to-toe *burqa* if they left American military compounds. There was no booze, and mail and packages from home were often opened by Saudi censors. They excised anything smacking of sex or Christianity, including removing lingerie ads from magazines. The more vocal of the GIs would offer pointed opinions in private—the Saudi Army was full of cowards, Saudi men were flabby and effeminate, Saudi women were shapeless "black moving objects," and Saudi society was full of hypocrites who had alcohol and Western pornography stashed behind the walls of their villas.

Heads Up!

"... America stands ready to work with (nations in the area) to secure the peace ... [T]his does not mean stationing U.S. ground forces in the Arabian Peninsula, but it does mean American participation in joint exercises."

—Pres. George Bush speech, March 6, 1991

To U.S. officials, though, Saudi Arabia was very attractive. During the Cold War, Israel was the only nation in the region where U.S. ships, planes, and troops were welcome. But Desert Storm had been won without the Israelis, and now seemed to be a good opportunity for the United States to establish a presence in the oil-rich area. Mindful of the problems the Saudis faced at home, the Bush administration played down any future plans to keep U.S. troops in Saudi.

King Fahd, on one hand, needed the American troops to guarantee Saudi security against external threats. But he also had to balance that with the growing fundamentalist uproar against the U.S. presence. He hoped that the scenes of hundreds of thousands of American troops going away would placate the increasingly vocal critics, and keep their minds off the fact that tens of thousands of the Western "infidels" remained.

But radical clerics Safar al-Hawali and Salman al-Awdah were not about to be silenced. They kept meeting with bin Ladin and his supporters, speaking to anyone who would listen about the evil being visited upon Islam. For example, in January 1991, al-Hawali delivered a sermon that said, in part:

> "It is not the world against Iraq. It is the West against Islam. If Iraq had occupied Kuwait, then America has occupied Saudi Arabia. The real enemy is not Iraq. It is the West."

By May 1991, the clerics, by now nicknamed "The Awakening Sheiks," were ready to do something unprecedented. They published a "Letter of Demands," ripping into the official Saudi clergy for approving the presence of U.S. troops, and demanding that the Saudi foreign policy be based on strict Islamic law. The regime started to round up fundamentalists, but was unable to arrest bin Ladin. He was gone.

Bin Ladin Leaves

By April 1991, bin Ladin began to figure—probably correctly—that it was only a matter of time before he would be arrested, since he had no intention of tempering his criticism over the presence of American troops. To leave the country, he would have to sneak out, and to do that, he would have to call on his family's royal connections.

Osama approached one of his brothers in the construction business and told him that he needed to return to Pakistan to "... deal with some unfinished business," and that he intended to return to Saudi Arabia as soon as it was wrapped up. The brother was close to the Saudi deputy interior minister, Prince Ahmed, and might be able to convince him to lift the travel ban and return Osama's passport, at least temporarily.

The problem was Ahmed's cousin and boss, Interior Minister Prince Nayef, who neither liked nor trusted the renegade bin Ladin. In early April, Nayef left Saudi Arabia on a diplomatic mission, leaving Ahmed in charge of the Interior Ministry. Ahmed granted Osama the right to travel.

Within days, Osama was back in Pakistan. Before leaving to go inside Afghanistan, he wrote his brother a letter, telling him the truth, which was that he was never returning to Saudi Arabia, and apologizing for straining his brother's relationship with the royal family. Inside Afghanistan, Osama found that the victory over the Communists had not united the freedom fighters under the jihad banner. Instead, the Afghan tribal factions were squaring off against one another, playing that most ancient of Afghan games, politics by murder and intimidation.

Trying to figure out what to do next, bin Ladin transferred most of his $300 million fortune out of Saudi Arabia, hiding it in a series of interlocking holding companies spread across four continents. Finally, in late 1991, he disguised himself, slipped aboard a private jet, and flew to the Sudan, where the government had declared any Muslim could enter without a visa.

The Sudan: The Beginning

The new Islamic government of the *Sudan* welcomed bin Ladin with open arms. They had declared jihad against the Christians and animists in the southern half of the Sudan, and bin Ladin helped pay for the Islamic militias fighting there. He also built roads, founded a construction company, and invested in an agricultural holding company, pumping up to $15 million of his own money into the country.

Gulf Lingo

The **Sudan** is bordered on the north by Egypt, and on the south by Kenya, Uganda, and the Congo. The northern part of the country is Muslim and Arabic, while the southern half is Christian or animist (ancestor or nature worship), and is black African. The Arab, Islamic north has been trying to subjugate the black, non-Islamic south in a civil war that has gone on for decades.

Bin Ladin brought hundreds of his supporters, Arab and otherwise, from the mujahadeen days in Afghanistan. He met daily with the newly reconstituted al-Queda in his farm outside of the Sudanese capital of Khartoum. It was there, in late 1991, in his one-story mud brick farmhouse with dirt floors, that he first declared jihad against America for "… desecrating the Holy Sites of Mecca and Medina."

Desert Lore

Three bombs went off in the Yemeni city of Aden on the night of December 29, 1992. One explosion at the Gold Mihor Hotel killed an Austrian and wounded his wife. Some 100 U.S. troops shuttling back and forth to Somalia were staying at the hotel.

A year later, by the end of 1992, there were still some 24,000 U.S. troops in Saudi Arabia. The Islamic nation of Somalia, at the tip of the Horn of Africa, had degenerated into tribal and clan chaos. The United States and U.N. decided to intervene to protect food supplies in Somalia in Operation Restore Hope. Some of those U.S. forces were stationed just across the Red Sea from Somalia in the bin Ladin ancestral home of Yemen. For the first time, bin Ladin and al-Queda would attempt to strike at an American target. A series of bombs in Yemen didn't kill any Americans. But they did set the stage for what was to come.

The Mastermind

Osama bin Ladin was taking a beating in business in the Sudan. While the Sudanese may have been more ideologically and religiously pure than the Saudis, they didn't pay their bills on time. It's estimated that by the time he left the Sudan, bin Ladin might have lost up to $45 million. Meanwhile, he was spending money on things other than Sudanese infrastructure. Later testimony from al-Queda operatives revealed that bin Ladin had been smuggling guns to fundamentalists in Yemen, bringing weapons by camel caravan to Islamic opponents of Egypt's government, and sending money and trained fighters to Somalia, Chechnya, Lebanon, Turkey, the Philippines, and Saudi Arabia.

On February 28, 1993, a truck bomb detonated in a parking garage underneath New York's World Trade Center. Six people died and 1,000 were injured. The mastermind of the plot was Ramzi Yousef, a British-educated Kuwaiti who had entered the United States on an Iraqi passport. Investigators believe he was financed by a combination of laundered money from Iraqi intelligence and cash from bin Ladin–operated "charities." In 1995, Yousef tried to hatch a plot in the Philippines to blow up a dozen U.S. airliners simultaneously over the Pacific. When Yousef was arrested in 1995, he was found in a bin Ladin–operated safe house in Pakistan.

By mid-1993, the Saudis were fed up. So on May 16, they issued an arrest warrant for Osama bin Ladin, a warrant ignored by Sudanese authorities. They also stripped him of his citizenship and, according to Saudi intelligence sources, began infiltrating teams into the Sudan with the mission of killing the renegade.

On September 30, 1993, bin Ladin issued another fatwa against Americans from his Sudanese farmhouse. Three days later, on October 3 and 4, al-Queda–trained militiamen in Somalia shot down a U.S. helicopter and in a firefight that killed hundreds of Somalis, killed 18 U.S. Army Rangers, dragging their bloated bodies through the streets.

Inside Saudi, the outpouring of rhetoric against the continued presence of U.S. troops became a torrent. According to an October 22, 2001, *New Yorker* article by investigative reporter Seymour Hersh, the Saudis became so worried about fundamentalist opposition that they began making what amounted to pay-offs to radical Islamic groups in 1994, trying to co-opt their opposition to the continuing Saudi-U.S. alliance.

> **Gulf Lingo**
>
> **Buraida** is a city of 300,000 in central Saudi Arabia. It is a center of Islamic fundamentalism, and home to both of The Awakening Sheiks. It is also a center of sympathy for Osama bin Ladin and opposition to the Saudi royal family.

In September 1994, however, the Saudis also began a crackdown, following a stunning 36-hour antigovernment demonstration in the city of *Buraida*. The Saudis arrested both of The Awakening Sheiks and dozens of their supporters.

Osama bin Ladin was about to declare full-scale war on the Saudi government and the United States.

The Birds Are on Fire

Monday, November 13, 1995, was a typical workday at the complex housing American advisors at the Saudi National Guard in Riyadh. Suddenly that morning, a car bomb exploded, and five Americans—four of them soldiers—and two Indians were dead. The Saudis arrested and tortured four Arabs who were veterans of the Afghan war. Before they were beheaded, they implicated bin Ladin.

The United States began putting pressure on the Sudan to get bin Ladin out of the country. In May 1996, the Sudanese expelled him along with hundreds of his followers and seized all of his businesses. The next month, a truck pulled up to Khobar Towers, an eight-story apartment building just outside of Dhahran, Saudi Arabia. Investigators later estimated it contained two and a half tons of TNT, so that when the truck exploded, it ripped the front off of the building. Nineteen Americans were killed, 12 of them from the 33rd Tactical Fighter Wing out of Eglin Air Force Base, Florida.

In September 1996, bin Ladin issued another fatwa, this one calling for a jihad against all Americans for their "occupation" of Saudi Arabia. By this time, total U.S. troops in Saudi Arabia numbered around 5,000. To bin Ladin, that was 5,000 too many.

By this time, bin Ladin was inside Afghanistan, supervising the funneling of thousands of Islamic extremists from throughout the world through the training camps he had built the previous decade. About the same time, mid-1996, a federal grand jury began hearing the case against bin Ladin in New York City.

> ## Heads Up!
>
> "The Americans do not understand that they are not wanted. They only understand the language of violence. It happened in Lebanon, they ran away only after there was major bloodshed. The same thing happened in Somalia. So the Saudi people thought why don't we give them bloodshed?"
>
> —Khalid bin Abdelrahman Fawaz, bin Ladin associate, quoted in November 5, 1996, in *The New York Times*

By early 1998, bin Ladin had formed a loose alliance with Islamists in Pakistan, Afghanistan, and Bangladesh, and called it "The World Islamic Front." In February, the front issued a fatwa instructing Muslims around the world to attack Americans, both civilian and military.

On August 7, 1998, truck bombs went off almost simultaneously in front of the U.S. embassies in Nairobi, Kenya, and Dar-es-Salaam, Tanzania. The carnage was unprecedented, and 213 people, most of them Kenyans, died in Nairobi, while 11 died in the Tanzania blast. A few days later, Pres. Bill Clinton ordered a barrage of cruise missiles aimed at bin Ladin's suspected hideouts in Afghanistan, as well as at a suspected chemical weapons facility in the Sudan. Bin Ladin escaped the missiles in Afghanistan, and it later turned out the factory in the Sudan was a legitimate pharmaceutical plant.

By November, a grand jury in the United States had indicted bin Ladin in the embassy attacks, and the U.S. government offered a $5 million reward for his capture. To bin Ladin, that was pocket change.

On Thursday, October 12, 2000, the 500-foot guided missile destroyer USS *Cole* put into the port of Aden in Yemen to refuel. No one paid much attention to the tiny boat with the waving Arabs on board, one of many small craft scooting about the harbor. The small boat pulled alongside and exploded in a fireball. The blast tore a 40-foot hole in the *Cole*'s side, and threatened to sink the ship. Only days of grim work by an injured but determined crew kept it from going down. The explosion killed 17 sailors and wounded 39 more. The explosion also killed the suicide bombers.

The FBI sent agents to Yemen to investigate the attack, but their work ground to a halt by August 2001. The FBI wanted to expand its investigation to include Islamic fundamentalist groups inside Yemen with connections to bin Ladin, but the Yemeni authorities refused to cooperate. American intelligence had concluded the bin Ladin organization was behind the attack.

Bin Ladin's outrage at the Saudi government's lack of Islamic zeal, his hatred of the United States for putting troops in Saudi Arabia in the Gulf War, and his determination that all Americans were legitimate targets came to a head on September 11, 2001, when more than 3,000 people died at the World Trade Center, the Pentagon, and in the crash of hijacked Flight 93 in Pennsylvania.

A few blocks from the World Trade Center, 650 children aged 5 through 12 were in class at Public School 234 on Chambers Street. As teachers led the students to safety, one child looked up at the people either falling or jumping from the Trade Center's shattered upper floors. Some of them were aflame as they spiraled down the quarter of a mile to the concrete below.

"Look, teacher," the child said, pointing, "the birds are on fire."

The Least You Need to Know

- ◆ Osama bin Ladin's father became rich through the patronage of the Saudi royal family.
- ◆ A radicalized Osama bin Ladin returned to Saudi Arabia from Afghanistan, and spoke out against the presence of American troops during the Gulf War.
- ◆ As U.S. forces remained in Saudi Arabia, fundamentalist hatred for the West increased.
- ◆ Osama bin Ladin launched an all-out campaign against the United States.

24

Iraq and a Hard Place

In This Chapter

- ◆ Saddam maintains his grip on power
- ◆ U.S. and British air strikes continue, and a CIA mission in northern Iraq fails
- ◆ Operation Desert Fox in 1998 strikes at Iraq again
- ◆ Saddam's possible role in the September 11 attacks and his continuing security threat makes him a tempting target for the United States

While Osama bin Ladin was expanding his terror network from the Sudan and Afghanistan, Saddam Hussein was busy not only surviving, but thriving in Iraq. This would have stunned the Allies in early 1991, since Saddam's army had been crushed, his elite Republican Guard units had been pounded, and both Kurds in northern Iraq and Shi'ites in southern Iraq had been emboldened to rise up.

Two chapters ago, we detailed how those revolts were crushed, and how the Allies—for a variety of reasons—lacked the will to occupy Iraq and topple Saddam. In the next few pages, we'll take a look at how and why Saddam survived the Gulf War and at why he still remains in power. The Americans and British have been striking Iraq from the air for more than a decade. As this is being written, there are rumblings that the United States may take on Saddam again as part of the war on terrorism. The dictator of Iraq has cheated death and beaten the odds before. Does he have even more political lives left?

Hanging On

By April 1991, Saddam had fairly well smashed uprisings in both the north and south. But he still had to deal with an Allied no-fly zone that had chopped off his territory above the 36th Parallel and with the presence of coalition troops in southern Iraq. But he had another problem, *U.N. Resolution 687*. On April 6, the U.N. Security Council ratified the cease-fire with the resolution and required Iraq to submit to the U.N.'s supervising the destruction of Iraq's chemical and biological weapons and its long-range missiles.

> **Desert Lore**
>
> U.N. Resolution 687 demands that Iraq "... accept the destruction, removal, or rendering harmless" of all of its chemical and biological weapons and facilities, and all of its missiles with a range greater than 150 kilometers (roughly 93 miles). It also requires Iraq to admit U.N. inspectors to oversee the program.

Trouble started almost immediately. The first inspectors arrived in Iraq on May 9. On June 28, the inspectors showed up at the al-Fallujah facility in Iraq, where suspected uranium enrichment equipment was stored. When they spotted several covered trucks preparing to leave by a back entrance, the inspectors demanded to look inside the trucks. Iraqi soldiers shoved them back, firing their weapons in the air. The United Nations reacted with "shock" and sent a special delegation to Baghdad. By July, inspectors found another nuclear facility the Iraqis had failed to list. The pattern for the next few years was being set quickly.

Meanwhile, Saddam consolidated power following the uprisings. He offered the Kurds an olive branch, promising to recognize them as an autonomous people inside Iraq. He made sure that water, electricity, and food deliveries resumed in major cities, trying to soothe the population. He appointed his son-in-law, Hussein Kamil al Majid, minister of defense. And he began a series of reorganizations and purges.

The head of military intelligence, the army chief of staff, and a dozen other top commanders were replaced. Opposition groups inside Iraq claimed that around 70 top army officers were replaced less gently in July, executed for reportedly plotting a coup and refusing to use even more brutal tactics against remnants of the uprisings. By the end of July, the last of the Allied troops withdrew from Iraqi territory.

In October 1991, a hidden anti-Saddam radio station inside Iraq, "The Voice of Rebellious Iraq," claimed there had been another coup attempt, and another 67 top officers had been tortured and killed. Although Saddam Hussein had begun the year blasted and battered by one of the most powerful military forces the world has ever seen, he ended the year perhaps more firmly in control than ever.

Iraq and Terrorism

Before we move on, we need to look back and examine Iraq's links to terrorist activity. Saddam is well-known for brutal attacks on his own people, for his crimes in Kuwait, and for his ruthlessness in the war with Iran. All of those actions served one end: more power for Saddam. But his regime also has a long history of supporting various Islamic and Arab Nationalist terror organizations. The point was the same—more power for Saddam—but used the vehicle of international terror groups targeting Israel and its supporters.

Some of the organizations with links to Iraq and headquarters in Baghdad have included:

♦ The May 15 Organization, which used to be the Popular Front for the Liberation of Palestine—Special Operations Group. Headed by Muhammad al-Umari (better known as Abu Ibrihim), May 15 bombed a London hotel in 1980, El Al Airlines offices in Rome and Istanbul in 1981, Israeli embassies in Vienna and Athens in 1981, and a Pan Am flight bound for Honolulu in 1982. That midair explosion only killed one person and the plane landed safely. May 15 is thought to have disbanded in 1984.

♦ The Abu Nidal Organization, based in Libya but with a strong presence in Iraq. Abu Nidal bombed airports in Rome and Vienna in 1985, hijacked a Pan Am airliner in 1986, and seized a Greek cruise ship in 1988. Since 1989, Abu Nidal has mainly attacked moderate Arab targets.

♦ The Hawari Group, named after its commander, Colonel Hawari, killed inside Iraq in May 1991 while being driven from Baghdad to Jordan. Their most notable strike was the midair bombing of a TWA flight over Greece, which killed four Americans but failed to destroy the plane. The Hawari Group has been quiet since 1991.

♦ The Mujahedeen-e Khalq wants to overthrow the government of Iran and replace it with a semi-Marxist state. The Iranian Air Force struck two of their training camps inside Iraq in 1997.

♦ The Palestine Liberation Front, headed by Mohammad Abbas (also known as Abu Abbas), best known for its 1985 hijacking of the cruise ship *Achille Lauro* and the murder of handicapped American passenger Leon Klinghoffer. Abu Abbas is thought to be living in Baghdad.

♦ The Popular Front for the Liberation of Palestine—Special Command, responsible for a number of anti-Western attacks in the 1980s, including the 1985 bombing of a restaurant in Spain frequented by U.S. military personnel.

In addition, Iraq's intelligence services have a long history of supporting and coordinating with various other groups, both inside Iraq and elsewhere. As we'll see shortly, there are some suspicions that Iraqi intelligence was behind the first bombing of the World Trade Center in 1993.

Bombs Away Again

As 1992 began, Iraq continued to harass weapons inspectors, ignoring impotent protests from the U.N. In February, Baghdad announced it had no intention of destroying its long-range missiles as required by U.N. Resolution 687, and asked for "continued talks." The U.N. replied that Iraq was still not complying, and that economic sanctions would remain in place until it did. By May, several U.N. teams had managed to oversee destruction of some missiles and hundreds of nerve gas warheads.

The cat-and-mouse game continued until August 26, when the U.S. announced that it was establishing a no-fly zone over southern Iraq south of the 32nd Parallel, similar to the one over the northern part of the country. One day later, U.N. guards in northern Iraq found a bomb attached to their car. Baghdad denied any knowledge of it.

Saddam meantime was finding a way to punish his enemies, despite sanctions and no-fly zones. In the north, his troops set up internal blockades to stall the delivery of food and medical supplies to the Kurds. In the south, he declared environmental war against the Shi'ites by creating the *Saddam River Project*. It drained the marshes, starved out the Marsh Arabs, and gave Iraqi tanks dry ground on which to continue their campaign against southern dissidents. Iraqi troops also used napalm against towns and dumped chemicals into the water to kill fish and birds.

Saddam also reportedly survived at least one assassination attempt in 1992, and used it to purge the military and security apparatus even more. He set up a new wing of the Republican Guard, the Golden Division, which ranked higher than any other guard elements. Its members were allowed to share in profits from black market dealings of items embargoed by the United Nations, and were given better pay, food, and medical care than any other unit in the entire Iraqi military. Their loyalty was to be to Saddam and to Saddam only.

Gulf Lingo

The **Saddam River Project** (also known as the Third River Project) is a series of canals and dikes that diverted water from the 18,000 square miles of fragile marshland in southern Iraq. The project destroyed 4,000 villages and starved countless thousands of Shi'ite Iraqis. It also killed millions of marsh animals and birds. A 1994 U.N. report called it "the environmental crime of the century."

Antiaircraft missiles and guns were steadily being moved into the southern no-fly zone. Twice in December, Allied jets shot down Iraqi fighters that had flown into the zone. As 1993 began, Iraq refused to let 70 U.N. inspectors return to the country, and ignored

U.S. demands to remove its anti-aircraft batteries. On January 13, bombs began to fall over Iraq again as 110 U.S., French, and British aircraft pounded Iraqi targets south of the 32nd Parallel. One bombing run accidentally hit an apartment building in Basra.

Saddam began to order his forces to challenge the Allies. On January 17, Iraqi antiaircraft radar began scanning coalition planes in the northern no-fly zone, and was destroyed. Later that same day, President Bush ordered 45 cruise missiles launched toward an Iraqi factory just outside of Baghdad that had been used to make components for Iraq's nuclear program. One missile, hit by ground fire, veered off course and hit the al Rashid Hotel in Baghdad, killing three civilians.

Over the next week, there were eight more incidents, including the shoot-downs of several Iraqi fighters. On January 23, more than 100 Allied planes blasted Iraqi positions with missiles and cluster bombs. In early February, Iraq launched missiles at French fighters, and missed. But a deadlier incident was coming, one on American soil, an incident that might have had Saddam's fingerprints on it.

The First World Trade Center Attack

February 26, 1993, was a cold day punctuated by blowing snow and gray urban slush in lower Manhattan. People in the twin 110-story World Trade Center towers were either riding elevators down to the street for their lunch hour, or were picking up food at one of the twin skyscrapers dozens of shops or restaurants. In the underground parking garage of Tower Number One, a one-ton Ford Econoline 350 van that had been rented from a Ryder rental agency in New Jersey was parked next to a support column. Inside the cargo compartment was 1,500 pounds of urea nitrate, a homemade explosive processed from fertilizer. The bags of urea nitrate sat on top of three large cylinders packed with compressed hydrogen gas.

Almost exactly at noon, two lengths of green explosive fuse leading into the bags had been lit. At 12:18 P.M., the van ignited, blowing a crater 150 feet across and five stories deep into the parking garage. Six people died, more than 1,000 were injured, and 50,000 people were evacuated from the mammoth skyscrapers. A few days later, as FBI agents interviewed the manager of the Ryder rental agency, a man named Mohammad Salameh called the agency and asked for his rental deposit back. The FBI arrested Salameh and four other men—Nidel Ayyad, Mahmud Abouhalima, and Ahmad Ajaj. In March 1994 all were found guilty of the bombing.

The standard explanation for the bombing has been that it was the work of nonstate-sponsored Islamic extremists living in the United States. But in subsequent investigations, a different sort of pattern emerges, centering around a man known only as *Ramzi Yousef*.

Who's Who

Ramzi Yousef was born Abdul Karim Rind in Pakistan in 1960. He grew up in Kuwait and established ties there with both the Hamas organization and Iraqi intelligence. He was convicted of plotting the 1993 World Trade Center bombing, as well as concocting a plan to blow up a dozen airliners simultaneously in 1995. He's currently serving a life sentence in the United States and has reportedly cooperated with American officials.

Yousef entered the United States in late 1992 on an Iraqi passport, claiming he was seeking political asylum. He associated with Salameh and others in New York, befriending the conspirators and helping design the bomb that was planned to ignite at precisely the moment the Gulf War cease-fire took effect two years earlier. The night after the explosion, Salameh drove Yousef to JFK Airport, where he left the country using a phony Kuwaiti passport. The other conspirators were left holding the bag.

Even though blind Egyptian cleric Omar Abdul Rahman, who was living in New York, was arrested and convicted as the plot's mastermind, and even though Yousef himself was finally found, tried, and convicted, suspicions linger that Yousef may have been working with Iraqi intelligence agencies. The evidence is hazy, but it centers around the Kuwaiti passport Yousef used to flee the country. It turns out the passport files in Kuwait City had been altered during Iraq's occupation, and that Yousef's vital statistics had been substituted in the files for those belonging to another man, a Kuwaiti named Abdul Basit. The real Basit seems to have disappeared.

Did Iraqi intelligence substitute other files like that, allowing its agents to travel the world using phony passports? Was Yousef an Iraqi agent? Was the first World Trade Center attack coordinated from Baghdad, using Islamic militants in the United States as pawns? That theory was favored by James Fox, the FBI agent in charge of probing the bombing until he was replaced in 1994. Even thought Yousef is in federal maximum security custody, the U.S. Justice Department refuses to divulge any of the information.

Heads Up!

"From all of the evidence available to it, the CIA is highly confident that the Iraqi government, at the highest levels, directed its intelligence service to assassinate former President Bush during his visit to Kuwait on April 14–16, 1993."

—U.S. government fact sheet presented to United Nations, June 27, 1993

The Plot Against Haji Bush

In mid April 1993, former Pres. George Bush made a three-day trip to Kuwait. It was his first visit there since the Gulf War, and he was greeted as a liberating hero affectionately nicknamed Haji Bush (Lord Bush). He was also almost killed.

The night of April 13, a Toyota Landcruiser packed with almost 200 pounds of explosives was smuggled across the Iraq-Kuwait border, enough punch to kill anyone within a distance of four football fields from the blast if it went off. U.S. and Kuwaiti intelligence received a tip that the plotters planned to ignite the device at Kuwait University, where Bush was scheduled to speak. Two of the men who were arrested—Ra'ad al-Asadi and Wali al-Ghazali—were Iraqis, and said they had been given orders by Iraqi intelligence in Basra to kill the former president.

Pres. Bill Clinton had defeated Bush in the November 1992 elections. The Clinton administration was almost exclusively domestically focused, with only a passing interest in international affairs. Washington announced there would be an "appropriate" response, but vowed to wait until more facts came out in the criminal trial underway in Kuwait City. After months of bickering inside the White House, the order was given to launch a volley of cruise missiles at Iraq.

On June 26, the destroyer USS *Peterson* and the cruiser USS *Chancellorsville* launched 23 cruise missiles toward Iraq's intelligence headquarters in the exclusive Baghdad district of Mansour. Twenty of the missiles landed in the targeted compound, but three missed and hit a residential neighborhood, killing eight people. The director of central intelligence at the time, James Woolsey, later claimed Saddam probably laughed off the attack, saying, "The only thing the Clinton administration did was launch a few cruise missiles at an empty building in the middle of the night. That probably made him laugh even harder."

The Kurd Disaster

By 1994, the CIA operations inside northern Iraq were going ahead despite mixed messages from the White House. Under the safety umbrella of the no-fly zone above the 36th Parallel, the CIA began working with a group called the *Iraqi National Congress*, whose goal was to topple Saddam.

In early 1994, the INC proposed a coordinated popular uprising against two cities in the north and against Basra in the south. They felt they could squeeze Saddam on two fronts, and had even received tacit promises of support from agents inside Iraqi army units. But Washington gave the plan the cold shoulder. The Clinton administration even forbade the INC from using any U.S. money to buy weapons. There were several problems at work simultaneously, and they would all eventually combine to doom the efforts in northern Iraq.

Desert Lore

The Iraqi National Congress (INC) was formed in consultation with the United States after the Gulf War. It attempted to unite various anti-Saddam elements, including Kurds, Shi'ites, and members of the Ba'ath Party who had defected. After the rout by Iraqi troops in northern Iraq, the INC established headquarters in London.

First, the INC had no way of knowing that a rival rebel group called the Iraqi National Accord (INA) had become the new darlings of Washington, mainly because the INA was funded by Saudi Arabia. This was to prove to be fatal, since the INA early on had been infiltrated by Saddam's agents. Second, the Clinton administration wasn't focused on or committed to solving the situation in Iraq. And third, one of the partners inside the INC—the Kurdish Democratic Party (KDP)—was so unsure of the American commitment that they were getting ready to cooperate with Saddam.

The INC launched the military operation anyway, and it proved to be successful, but limited. The INC achieved some military success, but was hamstrung by a lack of weapons, a lack of money from the United States, and the cost of caring for the thousands of Iraqi Army defectors and their families who crossed the battle lines rather than fight.

In July, American planes patrolling the northern no-fly zone accidentally shot down a pair of helicopters that were part of the anti-Saddam operation. Twenty-four people died, including 15 Americans, most of whom worked for various U.S. intelligence services. The operation's cover was almost blown, but the United States managed to keep most details quiet.

There was a stunning development in August 1995 when two of Saddam's sons-in-law defected to Jordan after apparently trying, and failing, to pull off a coup. One was a general, the other a colonel, and the public defection of both indicated Saddam was vulnerable at the highest levels. By early 1996, though, it became apparent to the two men that U.S. efforts to overthrow Saddam were disorganized and halfhearted. Both received "pardons" from the Iraqi government and returned to Baghdad in February. They were executed two days later.

Meanwhile, the CIA began funneling all of its help and expertise into the Saudi-funded INA opposition group. The rival INC tried to warn the CIA that the INA had been thoroughly infiltrated by Iraqi agents, and were ignored. In June 1996, Saddam's security forces swept down inside Iraq, arresting almost 300 members of the INA and Iraqi CIA agents. They seized CIA-supplied weapons, radio transmitters, and computers. The operation to stage a coup against Saddam was in a shambles.

Who's Who

Gen. Hussein Kamel Hassan and Col. Saddam Kamel Hassan were brothers, married to Saddam Hussein's two daughters. They defected to Jordan on August 8, 1995, and returned to Iraq on February 20, 1996, after being assured of pardons from Saddam. On February 23, they were killed, reportedly shot by members of Saddam's family.

But the Iraqi dictator was far from finished. He was sophisticated enough to know that internal Kurdish politics would bubble to the surface sooner or later, and also realized that the American efforts against him were, at best, slipshod. Sure enough, the Kurdish Democratic Party approached their old enemies, the Iraqis, with a deal—the KDP would cooperate with Saddam if he would use his troops to drive out the other Kurdish groups.

On August 31, 1996, three Iraqi armored divisions consisting of 40,000 troops and hundreds of tanks, rolled into northern Iraq. The no-fly zone north of the 36th Parallel wasn't a "no drive" zone, so Allied planes didn't strike when Saddam's forces blasted their way into the city of Irbil, routing the opposition and seizing the remnants of the CIA's Kurdish operation. The Clinton administration responded not by attacking in the north, but by firing cruise missiles at Iraqi air defense positions in the south.

Desert Fox

During 1997 and 1998, Saddam staged the mother of all cat-and-mouse games with the United States and the United Nations. Throughout 1997, the Iraqis had harassed U.N. weapons inspection teams, refusing them permission to visit certain sites, then relenting and letting them in, often after it appeared that materiel and equipment had been removed. In January, the U.N. offered a literal carrot to go along with the stick. The "oil for food" program was started, allowing Iraq to sell oil on the world market and deposit the proceeds in a U.N.-supervised account, then use to proceeds to buy medicine and food for Iraqis.

Saddam used the program to grow even richer, as he and his allies bought food and medicine on the open world market and then controlled its distribution inside Iraq, selling the goods at a markup of several hundred percent. While this was going on, weapons inspectors from the United Nations Special Commission (UNSCOM) kept finding and destroying Iraqi weapons stockpiles, but were also repeatedly thwarted in their attempts to visit many areas. Iraqi helicopters buzzed UNSCOM helicopters; UNSCOM inspectors were detained and harassed; UNSCOM teams were refused admittance to various facilities. Finally, in October 1997, Saddam expelled all U.S. members of the inspection teams, accusing them of being spies.

The U.N. withdrew the rest of its inspectors in protest, as critics maintained Saddam would use the absence of inspectors to hide even more evidence of his chemical and biological programs. The inspectors were allowed back in, but only if they stayed away from "presidential palaces and buildings". The U.N. kept passing resolutions, the United States kept expressing outrage, and the Iraqis kept up their chess game with inspectors.

By August 5, 1998, Iraq was confident enough in its strengthening position that it announced it was suspending all cooperation with UNSCOM inspectors until the oil embargo against Iraq was

> **Heads Up!**
>
> "The United States is not in the same position it was two years ago because its credibility has been eroded while Iraq is more able to break through the veils of deception than two years ago."
>
> —Saddam Hussein to his cabinet, December 8, 1997, as reported by Iraqi State Television

lifted. In September and again in November, the U.N. passed resolutions condemning Iraq's stance. The United States had been building up military forces in the area, and on November 14, Iraq agreed to let the inspectors back in, just as B-52 bombers had been launched. The bombers were recalled to their base on the Indian Ocean island of Diego Garcia.

Within two weeks, though, UNSCOM inspectors were again being obstructed, and by December 8, all U.N. personnel were pulled out of Iraq. On December 16, the United States and Great Britain launched Operation Desert Fox.

The bombing campaign was aimed at the suspected chemical, biological, and nuclear production facilities that UNSCOM had been denied access to. Desert Fox lasted three nights, with more precision missiles launched than during the entire air campaign of Desert Storm. More than 100 targets were hit, including Iraq's intelligence headquarters, missile production facilities, suspected chemical and biological production facilities, and Republican Guard units stationed in the Baghdad suburbs.

> **Desert Lore**
>
> On December 16, 1998, 26-year-old U.S. Navy Lt. Kendra Williams became the first female pilot in U.S. history to drop bombs and fire missiles in combat. Flying an F-18 off the USS *Enterprise*, Williams flew in the first wave of assaults against Iraq in Operation Desert Fox.

In the end, Desert Fox was inconclusive. President Clinton's impending impeachment vote for lying about his affair with Monica Lewinsky cost him important political support for moves against Iraq. Saddam Hussein continued work on various weapons projects, and Iraqi gunners and pilots kept occasionally firing on Allied plans patrolling both no-fly zones. Finally, in October 1999, a frustrated United Nations gave up on the UNSCOM weapons inspections. U.N. weapons inspectors have not been back to Iraq since late 1998.

Saddam and Osama?

In 329 B.C., Alexander the Great's Greek army approached a town called Arachoton in the eastern reaches of the Persian Empire. Alexander took the settlement, built a fort, and moved on, north toward the Hindu Kush and then east into India. The fort was called Alexander of Arachton, but in later years, the local Pashtun tribesmen shortened the name to just Alexander—Kandahar in the Pashto language. Some 2,300 years later, Kandahar, Afghanistan, became a center for the fundamentalist Taliban regime, and a headquarters for Osama bin Ladin and al-Queda.

In December 1998, just as Operation Desert Fox was getting underway, an Iraqi named Faruk Hejazi arrived in Kandahar for a meeting with Osama bin Ladin. Hejazi was a top official in the Iraqi intelligence apparatus, and according to DIA analysts, issued an invitation for bin Ladin to set up part of his terror training apparatus inside Iraq. The results of the meeting are sketchy, but many U.S. intelligence analysts believe bin Ladin accepted the offer because a training camp for fundamentalists had been set up at Salman Pak, the bioweapons research facility near Baghdad.

Apparently as a reward, Faruk Hejazi was appointed Iraq's ambassador to Turkey in August 1999. Under pressure from the United States, the Turks pressured Baghdad to recall Hejazi in November 2001.

The question of Saddam Hussein's involvement with Osama bin Ladin and possible complicity in the September 11 attacks is one that roiled Western intelligence agencies following the disaster. On one hand, many analysts argued, trying to forge cooperation between the secular Saddam and the fundamentalists was like trying to mix oil and water. Saddam had no interest in Allah or jihad, only in Saddam and his own power, they argued. Indeed, in the weeks following September 11, it seemed that any connection between bin Ladin and Saddam might lie in each appreciating the other's work against the United States.

But then the Hejazi meeting with bin Ladin came to light. And around the time of the attacks, an Iraqi defector offered information that seemed to confirm a closer relationship between the two. Gen. Abu Zeinab al-Qurairy was a top official in Iraq's Ba'ath party Mukhabarat intelligence service. He had helped organize terror training cells for years before he stumbled on a scheme by Saddam's eldest son, Uday, to bilk the Iraqi government by misappropriating military training money. Abu Zeinab, himself a torturer and terrorist trainer, was forced to flee for his life in July 2000. He ended up inside refugee camps in Turkey and finally, in August 2001, decided to contact the opposition Iraqi National Congress.

Abu Zeinab spoke to the INC, Western journalists, and American intelligence about the commando training efforts that had gone on for years inside the Salman Pak facility. He described a facility where the culture clash between the secular Iraqis and their fundamentalist trainees was sometimes comical, telling a British newspaper, "These guys would stop and insist on praying to Allah five times a day when we had training to do. The instructors wouldn't get home 'til late at night just because of all this praying."

But Abu Zeinab also described a training center where potential hijackers were taught to seize planes using small knives and where 5 percent of those who entered the camps were expected to die during exercises using live ammunition and explosives. Part of the training involved being released into a pen with angry attack dogs. The trainees had to kill the dogs by biting their necks and

Heads Up!

"Iraq presents a long-term strategic threat. Unfortunately, the U.S. is not very good at recognizing long-term strategic threats."
—Charles Duelfer, former UNSCOM weapons inspector, quoted in the *London Observer*, November 11, 2001

severing a major artery. Abu Zeinab concluded that the hijackings of September 11 bore all the tradecraft of Salman Pak graduates.

All of that evidence, however compelling, remains purely circumstantial. There is no evidence showing that any of the 19 September 11 hijackers attended the Salman Pak facility. Such evidence may exist, but no one has found it yet.

However, one piece of solid evidence has been supplied by the government of the Czech Republic, the same government that supplied chemical detection units to the coalition during the Gulf War. In November 2001, Czech Prime Minister Milos Zernan told U.S. Secretary of State Colin Powell that Mohammad Atta, one of the pilots who flew a 767 into the World Trace Center, had met in the Czech Republic with a top Iraqi intelligence official.

The official was Iraqi Col. Mohammad Khalil al-Ani, a top officer in the Mukhabarat's "special operations" unit, specializing in sabotage and terrorism. According to the Czechs, Mohammad Atta flew from the United States to Prague in April 1991 to meet with Col. an-Ani. Meantime, CIA officials have said that two of the other hijackers—Zeid Jarrah and Marwan al-Shehri—met with Iraqi intelligence operatives around the same time in the United Arab Emirates.

Hard evidence such as videotapes, documents, or personal accounts about the Saddam-Osama connection may never surface. But as this is written, it's becoming more and more apparent that the U.S. government is seriously considering taking on Saddam Hussein again as part of the war on terrorism. As we'll see in the next chapter, Saddam, terrorism, and Iraq are just part of the unfinished business left from Operation Desert Storm.

The Least You Need to Know

- Saddam emerged from the Gulf War as strong as ever, and managed to crush many of his enemies.

- American and British aircraft continued to strike at Iraq more than a decade after Desert Storm ended.

- CIA efforts to overthrow Saddam and 1998's Operation Desert Fox had minimal effect on the Baghdad regime.

- Some evidence began to emerge that Saddam might have had at least a peripheral role in the September 11, 2001, attacks.

25

Unfinished Business

In This Chapter

- The emergence of Gulf War Syndrome leads to charges of cover-ups about the exposure of Allied troops to chemical weapons
- Sanctions against Iraq punish the Iraqi population and make Saddam even richer
- Post–Gulf War politics cause the Allied coalition to fracture
- Saddam Hussein remains a thorn in the side of the United States

The euphoria of victory in the Gulf War was like a cocaine high—intense but short. In the cold, sobering light of the war on terrorism, it often seems that much of what the West thought at the time was delusional. There was a belief that Saddam Hussein would collapse, that the Arab coalition would hold together, that victory in the Gulf would pressure Israel and the Palestinians to achieve peace. None of that, of course, happened.

The emergence of Gulf War Syndrome led many veterans to feel as if they had been betrayed by their own governments. The suffering of everyday Iraqis under sanctions led to questions about whether the U.N.-sponsored measures were actually harming Saddam's regime. The simmering politics of the Middle East continued, regardless of 1991's high hopes. And a virulent anti-Western feeling swept across much of the Islamic world, leading to a war with terrorists that has both political and religious overtones.

The history of the Gulf War is, largely, a history of unfinished business. That's the focus of this final chapter.

Gulf War Syndrome

The first reports of illness among Gulf War veterans began to trickle into the media in the summer of 1991, mainly from units from Alabama, Mississippi, Georgia, and Texas. The symptoms were remarkably similar, including chronic fatigue, memory loss, sleeplessness, weight loss, and hair loss. Finally, in April 1992, the Pentagon commissioned a study 79 soldiers who had been deployed from the 123rd Army Reserve Command at Fort Benjamin Harrison in Indiana. The study concluded that "stress of homecoming" might be responsible for the symptoms.

The Machines
The chemical detection alarm used most often by Allied troops was the M21 Remote Sensing Chemical Agent Alarm (RSCAAL). The alarm can detect various nerve or chemical agents in a 60° arc at a maximum distance of a little over three miles.

As more veterans came forward with a variety of symptoms, the Pentagon was under siege from the media and veteran's groups, so that by October 1992, the U.S. Defense Department announced that vets suffering from Gulf War illnesses would be eligible for "incapacitation pay." But the U.S. government steadfastly denied that any of the illnesses were the result of exposure to any chemical, biological, or nerve agents, despite growing testimony from veterans about how *chemical detection alarms* went off in several sectors repeatedly during the Gulf War.

In September 1993, pressure became intense enough for the U.S. Senate Banking Committee to hold hearings chaired by Sen. Donald Reigle of Michigan. Reigle stated that he suspected that American troops had been exposed to at least low levels of some sort of chemical weapons during the war. Pentagon spokesmen denied it, but two months later, in November, admitted that chemical detection reports from Czech units were probably correct. The pentagon added, though, that it doubted the detections had anything to do with what was now known as Gulf War Syndrome. Later that same month, though, the Defense Department issued a statement casting doubt on whether any such syndrome existed.

Throughout 1994, Gulf War commanders, including Schwartzkopf, and current Pentagon officials, including Defense Secretary William Perry, denied having any information about any chemical contamination. In January 1995, a vets group in Georgia received copies of Gulf War chemical detection logs from the Pentagon. Several pages were missing. Then in June 1996, all hell broke loose when the Defense Department finally revealed that hundreds if not thousands of veterans might have been exposed to chemical and nerve gas toxins when the Kamisayah Ammunition Depot was blown up in March 1991.

In the years since the Gulf War, all sorts of theories have surfaced. Some, such as reports that a few vets might have passed on Gulf War Syndrome to family members or offspring due to exposure to biological agents, were intriguing. Others, such as theories that the Gulf War was a conspiracy by agents of the "New World Order" to reduce the earth's population, were merely paranoid. While the controversy continues, there are several things we do know as fact:

♦ The Pentagon denied for years, then admitted, that any chemical or biological agents detected in the Gulf might be related to Gulf War Syndrome.

♦ Saddam Hussein apparently ordered his troops not to use chemical weapons during the war.

♦ The Kamisayah Ammo Dump contained hundreds, if not thousands, of pounds of chemical and nerve agents that were blown up and sent airborne in March 1991.

♦ Studies from Texas indicate Gulf War veterans have an incidence of Lou Gehrig's Disease (Amyotrophic Lateral Sclerosis) at roughly twice the rate of vets who did not go to the Gulf.

♦ Research indicates that pyridostigmine bromide tablets (given to troops as an anti-nerve gas agent) could have a toxic chemical reaction when used with DEET and permethrin, two insect repellents commonly used by Gulf troops.

♦ A 1999 study found that many veterans complaining of Gulf War Syndrome had up to 25 percent lower levels than normal of the chemical N-Acetyl-Aspartate in their brains. Those low levels may indicate loss of brain cells in the basil ganglia and brain stem regions of the brain, possibly destroyed by chemical exposures.

♦ A 2001 study published in the *British Medical Journal* indicated a possible link between Gulf War Syndrome and multiple vaccinations given to troops to protect against possible chemical or biological agent exposure.

♦ The early 2002, the Pentagon ordered "further study" as to why the roughly 34,000 veterans initially exposed to parts of the fallout cloud from the Kamisayah Ammunition Depot had death rates roughly 10 times those for other exposed veterans.

But the controversy over Gulf War illnesses continues. Despite more than a decade of study, there is, as yet, no direct, undisputed link between possible chemical exposure in the Gulf War and the very real illnesses suffered by thousands of Gulf War veterans.

Suffer the Children

The United Nations initially slapped economic sanctions on Iraq on August 6, 1990, just a few days after the invasion of Kuwait. The idea was that the sanctions would pressure

Desert Lore

Sanctions against Iraq grew out of U.N. Resolution 661 in August 1990. Sanctions on food and medicine were supposed to have been lifted by the "oil for food" program started in 1995. But current sanctions prohibit any "dual use" technologies, that is, anything that might remotely be used by the Iraqi military. That means only directly consumable goods are not, technically, in violation of the sanctions.

Saddam's regime to reform. Since then, the U.N. has passed no fewer than 19 resolutions dealing with the Iraqi sanctions. The sanctions remain in place and Saddam remains in power, which was not how it was supposed to have worked.

Exact figures are hard to come by, but groups opposed to sanctions claim that the continuing embargo has caused the deaths of up to 5,000 Iraqi children every month. They arrive at this figure by looking at deaths due to diseases like dysentery and uncontrolled diarrhea, concluding that the deaths are the result of contaminated water. The dirty water, they say, results from Iraq not being able to buy pumps, pipes, and machinery to repair the water distribution and purification systems in the country.

As we've previously noted, the "oil-for-food" program allowed Iraq to sell a certain amount of oil and put the proceeds into a U.N.-supervised account to pay for food and medicine. Since the program started in 1995, conditions have generally improved throughout Iraq. But as always, Saddam has found a way to turn a liability into an asset.

Take, for example, medical equipment. Saddam's regime has purchased several sophisticated devices, including a "gamma knife," an extremely sophisticated device used for neurosurgery. Money spent on top-end medical equipment like this is obviously meant for Iraq's elite, meaning top armed forces officials and functionaries from the Ba'ath Party. The $6 million spent on the device might have been better spent on basic antibiotics and primary medical care for the Iraqi population.

Heads Up!

"We are losing five patients in the hospital (every day) especially in the premature unit and in the other general wards such as oncology. We are losing patients because of some small items. In the premature unit, we have a small valve to change their blood when they have severe jaundice. They haven't been available for months."

—Dr. Samir Kalander, director of Saddam Teaching Hospital for Children in Baghdad, quoted in Out There News.com, 1998

Since the regime controls distribution of food and medicine received through the oil-for-food program, it sells the goods to hospitals and markets at huge markups. The extra money has gone for several lavish projects, including a resort complex and artificial lake west of Baghdad for use by high-ranking government officials. The complex is said to have cost up to half a billion dollars to construct. From all the evidence, it seems that the sanctions, while having a very real and painful effect on the Iraqi people, have done little to weaken Saddam. To the contrary, they have actually made him richer.

The Fractured Coalition

The eighteenth-century English author Dr. Samuel Johnson presciently summed up the Gulf War coalition in his misogynistic quote about women delivering sermons: "Sir, a woman's preaching is like a dog walking on his hind legs. It is not done well, but you are surprised to find it done at all." The Desert Shield/Desert Storm coalition of U.S., European, and Arab allies may not have been done well, but it was a stunning diplomatic achievement to do it at all.

There was no way a coalition like that could last, despite the most optimistic hopes of 1991. The first sign of fracture came not from the Arabs, but the French, when the French defense minister resigned in January 1991 rather than approve the air war against Iraq. As soon as the shooting stopped, the Saudi government began pressuring the United States to remove as many troops and as much equipment as possible.

To the Syrians, the alliance with the West and Gulf Arab monarchies was a temporary marriage of convenience. For decades, radical Syria has campaigned against the conservative Arab oil states, and has sponsored and harbored various terror organizations. The Syrian Ba'ath Party's opposition to Saddam's version of Ba'athism—and Syria's suspicion of Iraq as a competitor—were the only reasons Syria was on board in the first place.

The "moderate" Islamic states—Turkey and Egypt—remain U.S allies because Turkey is in NATO and Egypt receives more U.S. aid than any country except Israel. The "conservative" Arab states—Saudi Arabia, Kuwait, the United Arab Emirates, Qutar, Bahrain— have kept their distance from the United States on many issues. But the one thing that unites all of the Islamic partners of the former Gulf War coalition, from radical Syria to moderate Egypt to conservative Saudi Arabia, is concern about the tide of radical Islamic fundamentalism that has swept much of the Muslim world since the Gulf War.

The Crescent Moon Rises

The Muslim world uses a lunar calendar that starts each month with the sighting of the crescent moon. The crescent moon symbol has, for centuries, stood for Islam in the same way the Star of David stands for Judaism and the cross stands for Christianity. From Turkey to Afghanistan, Indonesia to Nigeria, the crescent symbol is a powerful one in the Islamic world.

> **Desert Lore**
>
> The crescent moon symbolism in Islam is so important that there are two schools of philosophy about when the lunar month should begin. The first, *Ittehad ul-Matale* (Crescent Unity) says the sighting of a crescent moon anywhere on earth should start the lunar month at the same time planet-wide. The second, *Iktelaf ul-Matale* (Different Crescents) says since crescent moons are sighted at different times in different nations, each should be able to start the lunar month based on local observations.

Since 1991, the rising crescent has taken on new meaning as a wave of anti-Western Islamic fundamentalism has swept across much of the Muslim world. Up until 1950, there was only one active fundamentalist (or Islamic Renewal, to its supporters) movement in the Muslim world—the *Jamaate Islami* in Pakistan. But the last half of the twentieth century saw an increase in those movements, which is termed Renewalism, especially as Islamic countries gained independence from colonial powers. In 1979, Iran became an Islamic state. By 1989, with the defeat of the Soviets, Afghanistan was set to become one, too.

But about the time of the Gulf War, several things happened at once to accelerate the already rapid tide of anti-Western Islamic Renewalism:

- The United States was left as the only superpower. That meant American technology, entertainment, consumer goods, culture, and military might seemed omnipresent to Islamic radicals, threatening to swamp traditional Muslim values and societies.

- The Soviet Union collapsed. That turned several former Soviet republics with large Muslim populations into fertile ground for fundamentalist expansion, especially since it followed several decades of Soviet suppression of Islam. In addition, the Russians soon found themselves mired in a war with fundamentalist separatists in the Chechnya region.

- Some of those former republics, such as Uzbekistan and Tajikistan, established governments more or less based in Islamic law. Other regions, like Armenia and Georgia, saw an upsurge in Muslim insurgencies and guerrilla activity.

- The Sudan established an Islamic regime and increased its war effort against the Christian/animist southern Sudan. As we've seen, the Sudan gave Osama bin Ladin a base from which to operate.

- Yugoslavia disintegrated into a vicious war and genocide against the Muslim populations of Bosnia and Kosovo. This led to a rising tide of Islamic resentment.

- Elections in Algeria brought the Renewal movement to power. The military government there negated the election results, leading to a bloody insurgency by fundamentalist forces.

- In Africa, Renewalists gained allies in Nigeria after its 1999 return to civilian rule. Now, large swathes of Nigeria are governed by Islamic law. In Mali, only candidates who support Islamic law can run for office. In Tanzania, fundamentalists have repeatedly threatened to topple the government. And in Somalia, of course, Islamic law has been in effect since the ill-fated U.S. intervention of 1993.

- Pakistan has seen a rapid increase in strict Renewalist activity since 1991.

- Fundamentalists tried to topple the government of Tunisia in a 1991 coup.

- In June 1995, fundamentalists tried to assassinate Egyptian Pres. Hosni Mubarak during a visit to Ethiopia. Fundamentalist pressures on Egypt's government have continued to increase, including murders of foreign tourists.

- The southern Philippines has seen a drastic increase in kidnappings, bombings, and attacks on Christians by the fundamentalist *Abu Sayef* organization.

This is just a partial list, but it illustrates a vital point: Spurred by the Gulf War, Renewalist forces around the world have targeted pro-Western interests generally and pro-American interests specifically. Their driving forces have been both religious and political; religious, in that the fundamentalist upsurge is based on a strict form of Islam that originated with the Wahabi sect in Saudi Arabia, and political, in that the Renewalists oppose "corrupt" regimes in Muslim countries, U.S. global hegemony, and Israel.

Between the River and the Sea

The struggle between the Palestinians and Israelis over the land between the Jordan River and the Mediterranean Sea has continued to ignite radical Islamic hatred of the West. For some groups, like Hamas and Hezbollah, destroying Israel is the primary goal. For other players, like Saddam, the war in Israel and the Occupied Territories provides a convenient excuse for underwriting anti-American activity.

From the American point of view, the end of the Gulf War provided a unique opportunity to broker peace between Israel and the Palestinians. After all, with the Soviet Union collapsing, Yasser Arafat and the PLO seemed to have lost their primary financial sponsors. Arafat had backed the loser, Saddam, in the war. Israel, in turn, seemed marginalized for a change, since the United States had led the largest movement of men and materiel since Vietnam with no direct Israeli involvement. Both sides seemed susceptible to pressure, and the United States applied it, with Secretary of State James Baker making a half-dozen flights to the region before announcing that peace talks with Israel, the Palestinians, and neighboring Arab states would start October 30, 1991, in Madrid.

The talks coughed, sputtered, and continued off and on in Europe and Washington for more than a year. By December 1992, Israel had conditionally agreed to withdraw from part of the Golan Heights—seized from Syria in the 1967 war—when Palestinian extremists killed six Israeli soldiers. Hundreds of Palestinians were rounded up and expelled, but after months more of hard bargaining, there was a stunning breakthrough in mid 1993 when Israel agreed to limited autonomy for Palestinians in the West Bank and Gaza Strip. By September, the Clinton administration seemed to have achieved the impossible—Israel and the PLO would recognize each other after 45 years of bloodshed. By the summer of 1994, a new entity had been created on the world stage: the *Palestinian National Authority*.

Desert Lore

The Palestinian National Authority (known popularly as the Palestinian Authority, or PA) came into being on July 5, 1994. It's officially less than a government, but has all the powers and ministries one would find in a normal government. The PA is supposed to exercise self-governance over the West Bank and Gaza Strip until talks can be held to establish the full-fledged nation of Palestine.

Tentative treaties were also signed between Israel and Jordan, and Israel and Syria. But anyone who thought these would be the full fruits of the Gulf War was terribly mistaken.

The Arab world wasn't the only place where political disputes were settled by assassination. Throughout 1994 and 1995, the Israeli Labor Party, headed by Prime Minister *Yitzhak Rabin*, had pushed for Palestinian autonomy and the surrender of Israel's control over the West Bank and Gaza Strip—the so-called "land for peace" program. Hard-line Zionists within Israel called it a sellout.

In early November 1995, Rabin was gunned down by a radical university student after a Tel Aviv peace rally. During the following two years, the old pattern of terrorist strikes and Israeli retaliation continued. By the fiftieth anniversary of Israel's founding, in 1998, suicide bombers struck every few weeks. On the peace front, Israel finally withdrew from the West Bank city of Hebron, but also continued to extend Jewish settlements into West Bank areas.

Who's Who

Yitzhak Rabin was born in Jerusalem to Zionist settlers in 1922. He joined the Jewish underground, and fought against both the British and the Arabs around the time of Israel's creation. By the time of the 1967 Six Day War, Rabin was Israel's military chief of staff. He first became prime minister from 1974 until 1977. He was elected prime minister again and won the Nobel Peace Prize, along with Yasser Arafat and Shimon Peres, in 1994. He was assassinated on November 4, 1995.

President Clinton, barred by law from seeking a third term and worried that historians would focus on the Lewinsky sex scandal and the subsequent impeachment vote, jumped into the Israeli-Palestinian conflict as a mediator. In March 2000, Israel withdrew its final troops from Lebanon after almost 20 years. But hard-liners inside Israel began to oppose any more concessions.

Meanwhile, Yasser Arafat dug in his heels, demanding that the West Bank and Jerusalem be surrendered. Under pressure from a rising political and religious tide of anti-American and anti-Israeli feeling, Arafat's demand caused peace talks in August 2000 to collapse. By late September, hard-liners on both sides got what they wanted—violence against their enemies.

Ariel Sharon, Israeli military hero and rotund spokesman for the Israeli right wing, marched into Jerusalem with a phalanx of bodyguards on September 27, 2000. He visited the Western Wall, a holy site to Jews, which is located on the Temple Mount, holy to Muslims. It turned out to be a deadly bit of political theater. Arafat immediately met with leaders of the *Tanzim*—local Palestinian militia groups—and told them to prepare for a new round of armed confrontation.

The shooting started immediately. *Tanzim* cells ambushed Israeli patrols while teenagers took to the streets in an orgy of anti-Israeli violence. Israel responded with helicopter gunships and rockets. For the first time, Palestinian gunfire ripped through comfortable middle-class Jewish suburbs.

The war continued, through tentative peace negotiations and disappointments. The new administration of Pres. George W. Bush, contemptuous of the late-term Clinton negotiations, vowed to keep arm's length from Israel and the Palestinians, and let them hash out matters for themselves. Then came September 11.

Video flashed around the world during the Gulf War of Palestinians marching in support of Saddam Hussein had a negligible effect on world opinion one way or another. But TV pictures of Palestinians in the streets, celebrating the suicide attacks in New York and Washington on September 11, horrified and disgusted most Americans. In East Jerusalem, Palestinians honked car horns in and cheered as women handed out candies, a traditional Islamic gesture of celebration. Gunmen at Palestinian refugee camps in Lebanon and the West Bank fired shots in the air, and chanted "Death to America."

> **Heads Up!**
>
> "This is God's revenge for America's support of Israel."
>
> —Unidentified Palestinian gunman, Jenin refugee camp, West Bank, quoted in the London *Guardian*, September 12, 1991
>
> "We are completely shocked. It is unbelievable, unbelievable, unbelievable. It's touching our hearts. God help them. This crime is completely unacceptable."
>
> —Yasser Arafat, September 11, 2001

Within three months of the World Trade Center and Pentagon attacks, Palestinian extremists began their own campaign of suicide bombings inside Israel. It was like nothing the Jewish state had ever seen. Restaurants, hotels, shopping malls, supermarkets—all became targets as the Palestinians switched from attacking Israel's military to striking at its civilian population with cadres of young men and women carrying explosives strapped to their bodies.

By mid 2002, Israel moved its military in full force back into the West Bank and Gaza. To Islamic radicals, the ties between Israel and the United States seemed tighter than ever, and both of them seemed more tempting targets than ever. The last hope of the Gulf War—some sort of permanent peace between the Palestinians and Israel—was in tatters.

The End of the World As We Knew It

The twenty-first century, in a very real sense, began at 8:45 A.M. eastern standard time on September 11, 2001, when the first jet slammed into the World Trade Center. But the stage had been set a decade earlier, when the Gulf War, the collapse of Soviet communism, and the rise of anti-Western Islamic fundamentalism all intersected.

But what does that tell us about the world our children and grandchildren will face? What lessons are there to be learned once we connect the dots between Kuwait and the World Trade Center, between Saddam and bin Ladin, between American foreign policy and radical Islamic hatred of the West? There are lessons from the past that may help us chart the history of the future.

Terrorism

Traditionally, the philosophy of terrorism has been to attack targets to terrorize an enemy, and to force the enemy into an overreaction that will mobilize popular support for the terrorist's cause. Islamic terrorists targeting Israel, the United States, and their allies hope, eventually, to force the United States to withdraw its support for both Israel and moderate and conservative states throughout the Muslim world.

To do this, they aim to demoralize civilian populations with terror strikes. One suicide bomber can do as much damage as a strike by an F-16. With the proper weapons—nuclear, biological, or chemical—suicide terrorists could cause the kind of damage usually inflicted by entire invading armies. Cyberterrorism aimed at the world's financial systems could create chaos in the developed world.

Given the political climate and the ongoing Islamic Renewal, we can easily expect more terror attacks against "soft" civilian targets. One of the lessons of the Gulf War and its aftermath is that the best prevention is a robust intelligence capability. Will spies and infiltrators stop terror attacks? No, but they will prevent many of them.

The Islamic World

As we've seen, it's impossible to separate politics and religion when it comes to Islamic fundamentalism. The young adults being recruited as suicide bombers by the PLO, Hamas, Hezbollah, al-Queda, and other organizations were children during the Gulf War. They've been taught that the presence of American troops on sacred Saudi soil is the ultimate affront to Islam. They've also been taught that continuing American support for Israel and Arab monarchies means that the United States, and the West in general, are targets for Muslim rage.

There are more than 900 million Muslims around the world. Most of them are like most people everywhere. They have their own prejudices, beliefs, and habits, but the vast majority of them have no wish to declare jihad against anyone. But the Islamic world faces economic and social pressures that are leading more and more people to follow the lead of fundamentalist Islamic philosophers like *Sayyid Qutb*.

In Egypt, 55 percent of the population is under age 25. In Saudi Arabia, the figure is 60 percent. In North Africa and the Middle East, almost a third of the population lives on less than $2 a day. Illiteracy in many countries is rampant, up to 85 percent among women in Afghanistan. Islamic fundamentalism is providing a new meaning in life for young people throughout the Islamic world.

Who's Who
Sayyid Qutb was born in Egypt in 1906. He became a fundamentalist after living in the United States for three years, starting in 1948. Repelled by Western support for Israel and U.S. culture, he returned to Egypt and wrote influential commentaries saying the only way to achieve an Islamic revolution was through violence. He is credited with being the chief philosophical influence on many radicals in the Muslim world, including Osama bin Ladin. He was hanged by the Egyptian government in 1966.

Countries with heavily Muslim populations will continue to see a rise in extremism, fed by economics, population pressures, and the growing conviction among many everyday people that their situation is being imposed on them by forces beyond their control. Egypt has been fighting off a fundamentalist insurgency for decades. The weakened and corrupt Saudi monarchy faces a continuing threat. Renewalists from Algeria and Turkey to Indonesia and Pakistan continue to call for the overthrow of various governments and the establishment of "pure" Islamic states.

But this is not to say that extreme fundamentalism finds all of its followers among slum children. Far from it. Some of the most influential fundamentalists, from Sayyid Qutb to Osama bin Ladin, are from the middle and upper classes. Most of the September 11 hijackers had gone to college. As we've noted, Islam doesn't separate religion from politics, but in the case of educated Renewalists, politics often comes first. Osama bin Ladin's screeds following September 11 didn't complain about Western music, pornography, movies, or a generally "decadent" Western culture. Instead, they focused on U.S. foreign policy—American support for Israel, the presence of U.S. troops in Saudi Arabia, Washington's friendship with "corrupt" Islamic regimes.

Fundamentalists in the Muslim world often share a narrow, tribal view of the world with Christian and Jewish fundamentalists. They're opposed to globalization for the same reasons: fear that a tide of U.S. policy and culture based on the global economy will swamp and eventually drown their own religions and cultures. The Renewal movement itself, not just specific people or causes, will continue to be in violent opposition to the West for the foreseeable future.

Saddam Hussein

As this is being written, Saddam Hussein is still in power and is still a power broker. Whether or not the United States will go to war with him again and this time overthrow his regime could become a central question in the war on terrorism. Remember, at the end of the Gulf War, public pressure over the slaughter of Iraqis led to the ground war's termination. Fear of reaction from the coalition's Arab allies led to Saddam being left in power. But there was one other factor at work—the fear that overthrowing Saddam would cause Iraq to disintegrate and leave fundamentalist Iran as the major power in the Gulf. That's still the fear.

The evidence linking Saddam directly to the September 11 attacks is tentative at best. The evidence linking him to Osama bin Ladin is stronger, but still circumstantial. But his continued presence is a threat to American national security. Because of that, strategic planners have to weigh several options. Are they willing to sponsor an uprising against Saddam and risk Iraq splitting into (at least) two countries—the Kurdish north and the Shi'ite south—with the Shi'ites possibly aligned with Iran? Are they willing to launch air and ground strikes against Iraq? And are they willing to have every Arab ally desert the United States?

> **Desert Lore**
>
> A CIA assessment delivered to the U.S. Congress in February 2002 concluded that "it is likely" that Iraq has used the absence of U.N. weapons inspectors to rebuild its nuclear, chemical, and biological weapons programs. The report's chief concerns were the use of unmanned drone planes to deliver biological weapons, and Iraq's continued research on long-range missiles.

Once the options are weighed, a decision will have to be made whether to overthrow Saddam. If that does happen, we might expect some of the lessons from the Gulf War, its aftermath, and the war on terrorism so far to come into play. The Kurdish north and Shi'ite south of Iraq would probably become "no-drive" zones as well as no-fly areas. The United States would probably arm the Kurds and Shi'ites and direct them in attacks on

Saddam. U.S. military force will probably have less to do with the massed armor of the Gulf War than with the stealthy commando special forces teams of the war on terrorism.

Life from Now On

In President George Bush's words, the Gulf War and the collapse of communism were supposed to have ushered in "the new world order." They did, but not in the way anyone expected. Ethnic, nationalist, and religious rivalries erupted to replace the old superpower two-way contest. In times of uncertainty and change, mankind has always turned to religion for solace. But now, millions of people have twisted that around, instead turning to religion for justification for killing one's enemies.

The United States and the West are at war. We're not sure when it actually began—with the crusaders' sacking Jerusalem in 1099? With the founding of Israel in 1948? With stronger U.S. support for Israel after 1967? With the seizing of the U.S. embassy in Tehran in 1979?

We do know when it became apparent, though: September 11, 2001. And we don't know when it will end, or if we'll even know when it ends.

With whom are we at war? Certainly not with the world's 900 million or so Muslims, the vast majority of whom condemn suicide attacks and armed *jihad*. But we are at war with a particularly political form of radical Islam, an offshoot with roots in the fundamentalist teachings of the most extreme fringe of the Saudi Wahabi sect.

While it operates under the disguise of religion, it's actually a genocidal totalitarian movement not that different from Nazism or Stalinist Communism. Unless you are a Muslim of a particular type and belief, it preaches, you must be eliminated.

From the sewage-choked alleys of Palestinian refugee camps to the narrow-minded religious schools of Pakistan, that credo has found hundreds of thousands of willing followers among young people in the Islamic world. They feel their own governments ignore their needs, and that they are victims of forces they can't control except through violence. What we call terrorism they call armed struggle. The future of the war on terrorism can be seen in the eyes of millions of Muslim children around the world. And that's where the most important work is to be done.

The United States and the West will have to use all of the military, intelligence, law enforcement, and diplomatic muscle at their disposal to seek out and destroy a ruthless enemy. But they will also have to seek out and destroy the hatred that motivates the enemy, and that's the harder job. Unless an Osama bin Ladin cares enough to build schools and clinics and unless the hard-line Renewalists are willing to provide education, we can expect more of the same for the foreseeable future.

The Least You Need to Know

- ◆ The emergence of Gulf War illnesses led to revelations that the U.S. government hadn't told the entire truth about chemical exposure in the Gulf War.
- ◆ The Arab coalition forged during the Gulf War disintegrated.
- ◆ A tide of radical Islamic fundamentalism began to rise rapidly around the world after the Gulf War.
- ◆ The attacks on the United States launched a war against that form of fundamentalist terrorism.

Recommended Reading

al-Khalil, Samir. *Republic of Fear: The Inside Story of Saddam's Iraq*. New York: Pantheon Books, 1990.

Arnett, Peter. *Live from the Battlefield: From Vietnam to Baghdad, 35 Years in the World's War Zones*. New York: Simon & Schuster, 1994.

Atkinson, Rick. *Crusade: The Untold Story of the Persian Gulf War*. Boston: Houghton Mifflin, 1993.

Bergen, Peter. *Holy War, Inc.: Inside the Secret World of Osama bin Ladin*. New York: Free Press, 2001.

Blair, Arthur H. *At War in the Gulf: A Chronology*. College Station : Texas A&M University Press, 1992.

British Broadcasting Corporation World Service. *Gulf Crisis Chronology*. Detroit: Gale Research, 1992.

Campbell, David. *Politics Without Principle: Sovereignty, Ethics, and the Narratives of the Gulf War*. Boulder and London: Lynne Rienner Publishers, 1993.

Francona, Rick. *Ally to Adversary: An Eyewitness Account of Iraq's Fall from Grace*. Annapolis: Naval Institute Press, 1999.

Goodman, Sue A. *Persian Gulf War, 1990–1991: Desert Shield/Desert Storm*. Maxwell Air Force Base, Ala.: Air University Library, 1991.

Gordan, Michael, and Bernard Trainor. *The General's War: The Inside Story of the Conflict in the Gulf War*. Boston: Back Bay Books, 1996.

Grossman, Mark. *Encyclopedia of the Persian Gulf War.* Santa Barbara, Calif.: ABC-CLIO, 1995.

Hallion, Richard. *Storm over Iraq: Air Power and the Gulf War.* Washington, D.C.: Smithsonian Institution, 1992.

Hersh, Seymour. *Against All Enemies: Gulf War Syndrome, the War Between America's Ailing Veterans and their Government.* New York: Library of Contemporary Thought, 1998.

Holm, Jeanne. *Women in the Military: An Unfinished Revolution.* Rev ed. Novato, Calif.: Presidio Press, 1992.

Hutchison, Kevin Don. *Operation Desert Shield/Desert Storm: A Chronology and Fact Book.* Westport, Conn.: Greenwood Press, 1995.

Khadduri, Majid. *War in the Gulf, 1990–91: The Iraq-Kuwait Conflict and its Implications.* London: Oxford University Press, 1997.

Lacey, Robert. *The Kingdom: Arabia and the House of Sa'ud.* New York: Harcourt, Brace, Jovanovich, 1981.

Lewis, Bernard. *What Went Wrong?: Western Impact and Middle Eastern Response.* London: Oxford University Press, 2002.

MacArthur, John R. *Second Front: Censorship and Propaganda in the Gulf War.* New York: Hill and Wang, 1992.

Newell, Clayton R. *Historical Dictionary of the Persian Gulf War, 1990–1991.* Lanham, Md.: Scarecrow Press, 1998.

Powell, Colin, and Joseph Persico. *My American Journey.* New York: Random House, 1995.

Ryan, Chris. *The One That Got Away: My SAS Mission Behind Iraqi Lines.* London: Brassey's Inc., 1998.

Schwartz, Richard Alan. *Encyclopedia of the Persian Gulf War.* Jefferson, N.C.: McFarland & Co., 1998.

Schwartzkopf, H. Norman. *It Doesn't Take a Hero.* New York: Bantam Books, 1992.

U.S. Department of Defense. *Conduct of the Persian Gulf War: Final Report to Congress.* Washington, D.C.: Department of Defense, 1992.

U.S. News & World Report. *Triumph Without Victory: The Unreported History of the Persian Gulf War.* New York: Times Books, 1992.

Woodward, Bob. *The Commanders.* New York: Simon & Schuster, 1991.

On the Web

www.arabnews.com. Site of the Arab news, the largest English-language newspaper in the Arab world, based in Saudi Arabia.

http://Bushlibrary.tamu.edu. The George Bush Presidential Library contains a wealth of Gulf War–related documents at a site maintained by Texas A & M University.

www.chronicillnet.org. Contains information and links on Gulf War illnesses, as well as other chronic medical conditions. Links to medical and scientific journal articles.

www.cia.gov. The Central Intelligence Agency website, with links to country information and resources on Iraq, Kuwait, Saudi Arabia.

www.debkafile.com. Counterterrorism site maintained by former Israeli journalists and counterintelligence officers. Site provides the Israeli intelligence and military community's view of various terrorist and guerilla organizations.

www.desertstorm.com. Links to related Gulf War websites, including British and U.S. military, as well as veteran's and history sites. Maintained by a coalition of Gulf War veterans.

www.desert-storm.com. Website maintained by Gulf War veteran Scott O'Hara, with medical and military links, plus photos and first-person accounts.

http://fas.org/irp. Federation of American Scientist's Intelligence Resource program. This site provides links to various intelligence-gathering organizations around the world, and provides a constantly updated source of information for the latest on various terrorist and guerilla organizations.

http://fas.org/man. Federation of American Scientist's Military Analysis Network. This site links to complete descriptions of military weapons, units, and histories, as well as providing updated information about units of different nation's military operations.

www.globalsecurity.org. Excellent source of information on terrorism, counterterrorism, and international security. Site maintained by John Pike, former head of the Federation of American Scientists.

www.gulflink.osd.mil. Gulflink was set up to provide links on Gulf War illnesses. The site also includes a wealth of declassified intelligence and military documents and is maintained by the U.S. Department of Defense under an agreement reached with Gulf War veterans.

www.gulfwar.mod.uk. British site with links on Gulf War illnesses. Mainly focused on the British experience in Desert Storm.

www.gulfweb.org. U.S. site maintained by Gulf War veterans with links, chat site, and information pertinent to Gulf War illnesses and experiences.

http://historicaltextarchive.com. Links to first-person accounts of the Gulf War, as well as many other historical links. Site maintained in conjunction with Mississippi State University.

www.ict.org.il. International Policy Institute for Counter-Terrorism, Israel. This site gives the view of Israeli intelligence professionals about conflicts in the Middle East.

www.indict.org. This site makes the case for indicting Saddam Hussein for war crimes, and is maintained by opponents of Saddam Hussein who are members of the Iraqi National Congress opposition group.

www.iraq.net. Provides information on Iraq, including its government. Maintained by an anti-Saddam Hussein coalition.

www.islam101.com. This site, maintained by the nonprofit Sabr Foundation, is a basic guide to the beliefs and practices of Islam.

www.islamicity.org. Provides links to information about Islam. Maintained by Islamic organizations in California.

http://leb.net/IAC. The Iraq Action Network website, which is opposed to U.N. sanctions and is maintained by activists who oppose continued sanctions.

www.leyden.com/gulfwar. This is site of author Andrew Leyden with links and chronology of Gulf War.

www.military.com. Provides an overview of military strategy, equipment, and tactics, plus links. Maintained by Military Advantage, a marketing corporation aimed at military personnel.

www.muslimedia.com. A site updated biweekly with links to news and information from throughout the Muslim world. Maintained by the Institute of Contemporary Islamic Thought in London.

www.my-kuwait.com. This site provides an overall guide to Kuwait, maintained by a private Kuwaiti firm.

www.sacm.org. The website of the Saudi Arabian Cultural Mission, with official Saudi Arabian government information on the country and its people.

www.strategypage.com. This site provides information on military and intelligence affairs both in the United States and worldwide. Maintained by author and military analyst James Dunnigan.

www.terrorism.com. A site maintained by the Terrorism Research Center, a private think-tank in Washington, D.C. Links and information to analysis in the latest trends in terrorism and guerilla warfare.

www.terrorism.net. A guide to latest in counterterrorism, maintained by the Counter-Terrorism Professionals Network, a Canadian organization working with both government and private counter-terrorism specialists.

www.uruklink.net. This is the official website of the Iraqi News Agency, maintained by the government of Iraq.

Index

G

N

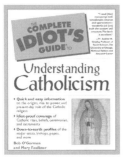

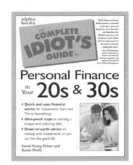

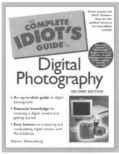
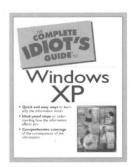